Social Relations and Spatial Structures

Social Relations and Spatial Structures

Edited by

Derek Gregory

Department of Geography, University of Cambridge

and

John Urry

Department of Sociology, University of Lancaster

St. Martin's Press   New York

Editorial matter and selection © Derek Gregory and John Urry
1985
Individual chapters © Philip Cooke, Anthony Giddens,
Derek Gregory, David Harvey, Doreen Massey, R. E. Pahl,
Allen Pred, Peter Saunders, Andrew Sayer, Edward W. Soja,
Nigel Thrift, John Urry, Richard Walker, Alan Warde 1985

St. Martin's Press, Inc., 175 Fifth Avenue, New York, NY 10010
Printed in Hong Kong
Published in the United Kingdom by Macmillan Education Ltd
First published in the United States of America in 1985

ISBN 0-312-73586-3
ISBN 0-312-73484-0 (pbk.)

Library of Congress Cataloging in Publication Data
Main entry under title:
Social relations and spatial structures
Bibliography: p.
Includes index.
1. Social interaction—Addresses, essays, lectures.
2. Anthropo-geography—Addresses, essays, lectures.
3. Personal space—Addresses, essays, lectures.
I. Gregory, Derek, 1951–   . II. Urry, John.
HM291.S588715 1985   302   85-2155
ISBN 0-312-73586-3
ISBN 0-312-73484-0 (pbk.)

Contents

List of Figures

Preface

We are very grateful to the contributors to this book, not only for the chapters they have produced but also for their other stimulating contributions to the various debates considered here. Although the volume is in no way a 'manifesto', it has been very much a collaborative project with all sorts of other arguments weaving in and out of its main themes and contributing to a sense of intellectual excitement at the contemporary cross-fertilisations between human geography and sociology.

Derek Gregory is particularly grateful to Michael Dear, Felix Driver, Tony Giddens, Peter Gould, Jack Langton, Chris Philo and Nigel Thrift for numerous discussions of many of the themes addressed in this volume, and John Urry is similarly grateful for discussions with members of the CSE Regionalism Group and the Lancaster Regionalism Group: especially Mike Savage, Dan Shapiro, Sylvia Walby and Alan Warde; and with other members of the Department of Sociology at Lancaster.

We are both indebted to Steve Kennedy for his encouragement and penetrating editorial criticism, to Elizabeth Black for copy-editing a difficult manuscript with both sensitivity and skill and to Christopher Philo for compiling the index.

DEREK GREGORY
JOHN URRY

Note: Notes and references are indicated by superscripts and are gathered together at the end of each chapter; all citations are listed in full in the bibliography at the back of the book.

List of Contributors

Philip Cooke is Lecturer in Town Planning at the University of Wales.
Anthony Giddens is Fellow of King's College and Professor of Sociology at the University of Cambridge.
Derek Gregory is Fellow of Sidney Sussex College and Lecturer in Geography at the University of Cambridge.
David Harvey is Professor of Geography at the Johns Hopkins University, Baltimore.
Doreen Massey is Professor of Geography at The Open University.
R.E. Pahl is Professor of Sociology at the University of Kent.
Allan Pred is Professor of Geography at the University of California, Berkeley.
Peter Saunders is Lecturer in Sociology and Social Administration at the University of Sussex.
Andrew Sayer is Lecturer in Geography at the University of Sussex.
Edward W. Soja is Professor of Urban and Regional Planning at the University of California, Los Angeles.
Nigel Thrift is Lecturer in Geography at St David's College, Lampeter.
John Urry is Professor of Sociology at the University of Lancaster.
Richard A. Walker is Associate Professor of Geography at the University of California, Berkeley.
Alan Warde is Lecturer in Sociology at the University of Lancaster.

1
Introduction

DEREK GREGORY AND JOHN URRY

Both human geography and sociology emerged in their modern forms in the nineteenth century and in the shadows of the natural sciences. This makes it possible to identify a number of connections – and even cross-fertilisations – between them; but in our view most of these have been stillborn. At the turn of the nineteenth and twentieth centuries, for example, there was a formative exchange between Paul Vidal de la Blache and Emile Durkheim, the one concerned to establish *la géographie humaine* as a (natural) science of independent integrity, and the other just as keen to bring it within the sphere of his own *morphologie sociale* and make it subservient to the grander designs of the new science of *sociologie*. The differences between the two, in terms of both institutional setting and intellectual framework, were sufficiently great to proscribe any simple mapping of the one into the other; but their common commitment to the moral-purposive character of collective social life and to what would now be called its 'contextuality' was, potentially, of the first importance. Similarly, the founding fathers of location theory, whose writings were selectively drawn upon in the middle of the twentieth century to reconstitute human geography as a 'spatial science', were by no means strangers to social theory. The apparently motionless rings of von Thünen's model of agricultural land-use scythed their way into a wider discussion of the social relations between landlords and labourers in early nineteenth-century Europe, in which the ties between the spatial margins of production and agricultural wages are conspicuously informed by Hegel's political philosophy. The isodapanes which circumscribed Alfred Weber's abstract model of industrial location were soon set spinning in his subsequent discussion of the dynamics of capitalist industrialisation in the late nineteenth and early twentieth centuries, and although this was only a skeletal account it nevertheless introduced an historically-sensitive political economy to what had been a timeless mechanical analogue; and these concerns were then spiralled through a much broader cultural sociology which had much in common with his brother Max's remarkable research programme, in the course of which Alfred roundly rejected the possibility of an autonomous, purely geometric (or even singularly economic) location theory. Finally, the ring-mosaics of urban land use identified by the Chicago School were not merely cages for the contemplation of a brute and invariant 'natural order', supposedly derived from Darwin, but also springs for the explication of a definite 'moral order', founded on public discourse and communication, and which derived in its essentials from Durkheim.

These interlacings of social theory and human geography – and the others which remain to be investigated – are, of course, much more complex than such a cursory review can indicate. But few of them were developed in any substantial sense, and some were even systematically repudiated. The 'social' was separated from the 'spatial' – a profoundly Kantian dualism – and in much the same way that Durkheim had tried to secure a niche for sociology by treating its object as the explanation of social structures by intrinsically social processes, so human geography came to be defined in equally exclusive notations: as the explanation of spatial structures by intrinsically spatial processes. Many of these 'spatial processes' were described in the terms of formal language systems, especially geometry and probability theory, and this further estranged human geography from the heterogeneous ordinary language systems deployed in social theory. Even so, for the most part both disciplines continued to share a naturalism, and to accept the precepts of positivism and of functionalism (which stood in the closest of associations to naturalism). The critique of these positions is, by now, extensive, and it is not our purpose to provide a summary of it in these pages. But we do want to signal one of its most important effects: for it represented, so to speak, a reading of the banns for a marriage between social theory and human geography – not a furtive liason but a public and protracted engagement – which was consummated, paradoxically, by a premature withdrawal from the analysis of spatial structure altogether. Space was seen as somehow epiphenomenal, as a 'codification' or a 'reflection' of human intentionality or social structure. This meant that any explanation of spatial organisation – in so far as one was called for at all – had to be sought within what remained a primarily aspatial or, as some commentators would prefer, 'compositional' social theory. The debates of most moment, therefore, came to pivot around whether social life ought to be conceived in terms of intentionality (the realms of interpretative sociology, constitutive phenomenology and hermeneutics, of 'idealist' and humanistic geography) or of structure (the realms of structural functionalism and structuralism, of systems theory and urban and regional political economy). At best, the problematic of spatial structuring was peripheral to these exchanges; at worst, it was flatly condemned as an irrelevant distraction.

But more recently the interpenetration of these polar positions within theories of 'structuration' has assumed a new prominence, and with it has come a return to the concrete which marks a major renaissance of the interconnections between social relations and spatial structures as a central focus for scientific inquiry. These intellectual realignments have been accentuated by a series of wider developments: the emergence of new spatial structures of combined and uneven development, particularly through the internationalisation of production and the restructuring of the spatial division of labour; the changing structuration and significance of social relations, and the formation of class and non-class social movements, many of which are urban- or regionally-based; transformations in the temporal and spatial organisation of everyday life, through profound revolutions in transport, communications and micro-electronics; and the heightened powers of states to maintain surveillance over distant and dispersed populations. As a result of these changes, spatial structure is now seen not merely as an arena in which social life unfolds, but rather as a medium through which social relations are produced and reproduced. It is in this sense, perhaps, that human geography and sociology can be said to confront a common (if scarcely classical) 'problem of order'.

These various developments have stimulated a series of major debates on the marchlands between human geography and sociology, and in this book we consider just four of them: the implications of a realist philosophy of science for these new analytical strategies; the general consequences of the incorporation of space into Marxian and non-Marxian social theory; the spatial structuring of classes and of other social forces; and the significance of time-geography and its extensions for a properly contextual social theory.

A concern with realism is a recurrent theme throughout the collection. In Chapter 2 **Doreen Massey** provides a thumbnail sketch of the evolution of modern human geography. She distinguishes those approaches in which generalisations about spatial patterns of events are the diagnostic criterion of scientific status from those which understand scientific inquiry as the identification of 'necessary' and 'contingent' relations within (social) structures constituted in both space and time. This distinction between events and structures is an ontological one; it means that science involves the description of those structures whose 'causal powers' contingently generate particular sets of events in specifiable space–time settings. The implications of these claims are pursued by **John Urry** in Chapter 3. There he examines the temporal and spatial structuring of social relations within the economy and 'civil society' of contemporary capitalism, and argues for a three-fold separation between (i) the distribution of events *in* time–space; (ii) the temporal–spatial structuring *of* particular social entities; and (iii) the changing temporal–spatial relations *between* different social entities. In Chapter 4, **Andrew Sayer** focusses on the second of these domains, and emphasises the importance of identifying necessary and contingent relations within social structures in order to establish 'the difference that space makes' to concrete research. If we are to determine the effects of the causal powers possessed by particular structures then, so Sayer argues, their particular space–time configurations and contextual settings must be disclosed. This in turn means that it is a mistake of an elementary category to separate 'space' and 'society' artificially and then recombine them in different ways. This Kantian dualism must be discarded once and for all.

But in Chapter 5 **Peter Saunders** insists that writers who advocate manoeuvres of this sort have characteristically failed to demonstrate the existence of distinct socio-spatial entities which could be the objects for some new socio-spatial science. In particular, he rejects four successive attempts to establish 'the city' as a distinctive object for an 'urban' sociology: those which treat the city as an ecological community, as a cultural form, as a system of resource allocation, and as a unit of collective consumption. In their place Saunders presses the case for what he calls a 'non-spatial' but not an 'aspatial' urban sociology – that is, one which is not preoccupied with a supposedly autonomous urban reality but which nevertheless remains sensitive to the wider settings of generic and localised social processes. Although Saunders professes 'dismay' at any attempt 'to establish a concern with space at the centre of sociological discourse', **Edward Soja** in Chapter 6 contends that there *is* an essential 'spatiality' to social life which is occluded in conventional theorisations. He urges the need to construct a new, materialist understanding of 'socially produced space' which he believes was prefigured in a series of interventions within the French Marxist tradition by Henri Lefebvre. In Soja's view there is now taking place a truly momentous convergence around many of Lefebvre's pivotal themes, a *rapprochement* which draws in and reworks both Marxian and non-Marxian social theory. The admission of space into such radically discrepant traditions has extraordinarily disturbing consequences, and in Chapter 7 **David Harvey** suggests that 'the issue of space and geography is a sadly neglected stepchild in *all* social theory because its incorporation has a numbing effect upon the central propositions of *any* social theory.' This clearly reaches back to Sayer's distinction between abstract and concrete research, and Harvey attempts to theorise the historical geography of capitalism by elucidating a necessary tension between fixity and motion within its space-economy. In identifying those forces which sustain and subvert the 'structured coherence' of production and consumption within and between 'regional spaces' therefore Harvey seeks to show not simply that the various crises of capitalism have their own geographies, but also that such spatial structures (or 'fixes') are intrinsic to the resolution of these crises and hence to the restructuring of the geopolitics of capitalism.

Harvey's essay provides a useful context for a number of those which follow. In Chapter 8 **Richard Walker** returns to the concept of ontological depth entailed by theoretical realism, and proposes that there are four 'layers' of structural determination involved in the excavation of social relations within capitalist societies: namely class, the division of labour, the junction of capital and labour within the workplace (the 'employment relation') and the junction of capital and labour in space and time (the spatial division of labour). Walker uses this schema to argue that Harvey's dialectic between fixity and motion is fundamental to any portrayal of class formation as a 'geographic process'. In his view, classes are constituted through the practical activities of people in production, which necessarily implicates them in (and constitutes them through) the social use of space. In Chapter 9 **Alan Warde** examines another 'geological' metaphor which promises to illuminate historico-geographical changes in the patterning of social relations. According to this thesis, which was originally advanced by Massey, successive cycles of accumulation deposit layers of 'industrial sediment' in geographical space, to produce a spatial division of labour which is bound into a continuous search for profit by highly mobile capital; it then follows that localities can be understood in terms of the ways in which these various layers 'congeal' to produce social structures differentiated over space and through time. Warde identifies several limits to this simple heuristic: the need to spell out rules of transformation between the logics of location in each layer, the need to specify rules of combination between various class residues which produce different political effects in different places, and the need to recognise local effects other than purely class effects. This then enables him to extend the original metaphor to include four mechanisms involved in the production of spatially differentiated political practices: class struggles over the labour process, the structuring of labour markets, the localisation of collective consumption and struggles over reproductive practices within 'civil society'. The notion of civil society also looms large in Chapter 10, where **Philip Cooke**, following in some part the work of Gramsci, argues that regional boundaries are largely coterminous with the contours of dominant class practices. For Cooke the comparative geography of class relations entails five fundamental components: the productive base, the labour process, the ownership of capital, and the specificities of social relations and of social institutions. Through a case study of South Wales Cooke is able to show that these differentiations are far from being uniquely economic in origin, and that political traditions were rooted in a rich and robust popular culture. In Chapter 11 **Ray Pahl** reinforces these conclusions through an investigation of various non-formal types of economic activity and their part in the production of a 'sense of place' within the Isle of Sheppey in Kent. He shows that the 'local political economy' encompasses much more than the labour process or the labour market, and although he accepts Massey's geological metaphor he also insists that an adequate 'social geomorphology' must include the household work strategies which are involved in spatially specific negotiations of the social division of labour, together with – crucially – the cultural practices and traditions which accrete around them. This emphasis on cultural diversity is clearly a corrective to approaches which relate the local textures of social life directly to the global recomposition of capital, and it is in this sense that Pahl endorses the concept of the 'personality' of place celebrated by Vidal de la Blache.

Concepts of place are increasingly prominent in modern theories of structuration, of course, and in his recent writings **Anthony Giddens** has drawn upon Hägerstrand's time-geography to show how the structuration of social systems is fundamentally constituted in space and time. In Chapter 12, however, he develops these notions beyond the sphere of Hägerstrand's particular formulations. Suggestive though Hägerstrand's ideas undoubtedly are, Giddens considers that they suffer from inadequate theorisations of both social agents and the organisation of settings of interaction. It is of the first importance, so he claims, to provide a much more rigorous scrutiny of the concept of place than can be found in classical time-geography. 'Place' cannot be used simply to designate 'a point in space', and Giddens introduces the term 'locale' to refer to the use of space to provide the settings of social interaction. The properties of these settings – in effect, the distribution of the conditions of action in space and time – are used by agents in the constitution of encounters across space and time. Furthermore, such settings are internally differentiated ('regionalised') and this plays a strategic role in the ordering and regulation of routinised social practices and hence in the production and reproduction of power relations. Giddens's critique of Hägerstrand dovetails with the commentary provided by **Derek Gregory** in Chapter 13. Gregory identifies several continuities between Hägerstrand's earlier spatial diffusion theory and his subsequent formalisation of time-geography, and argues that these limit the purchase of his problematic. But there are also important contrasts. Hägerstrand's diffusion theory contained no serious discussion of the structures of social relations and systems of social practices through which innovations filtered; it was bounded by an empiricism in which sequences of events (communications and adoptions) were connected through a simple spatial morphology. Time-geography, by contrast, signals a break with these analytical procedures: a recognition of time as something more than a mere metric, an awareness of interlocking constraints within which social life is spun out, and an acknowledgement of the salience of competition and conflict. These departures gesture towards a more rigorous, fully contextual structuration theory which can be made consonant with the protocols of theoretical realism. In Chapter 14 **Allan Pred** provides an exemplification of the integration of time-geography with structuration theory, in which (like Pahl) he invokes the spirit of Vidal de la Blache. 'Place' for Pred always represents a human product: it always involves a transformation of space inseparable from a transformation of society. The intersection of individual paths and institutional projects in space and time is embedded in the reproduction and transformation of structures of social relations, and this occurs simultaneously with the sedimentation of *genres de vie*, with the formation of individual biographies and with the transformation of 'outer nature'. Pred illustrates this theory of place as 'historically contingent process' through a case-study of enclosure in the Swedish province of Skåne in the eighteenth and nineteenth centuries. Although much of Hägerstrand's early work was concerned with information circulation, both Giddens and Gregory argue that he failed to fashion an adequate account of the *knowledgeability* of human subjects. In Chapter 15, however, **Nigel Thrift** treats the availability of knowledge as a vital component in the construction of a theory of 'situated social action' which again draws on both structuration theory and time-geography. Thrift describes the processes through which stocks of knowledge of various types are created and circulated through societies. This enables him to illuminate space–time differentials in the availability of knowledge and hence to see them as critical elements within the overall distribution of the conditions of action in space and time.

These chapters, then, are all related to the interface between human geography and social theory. They develop and elaborate some of the issues which have surfaced within journals like *Antipode*, the *International Journal of Urban and Regional Research*, *Progress in Human Geography* and *Society and Space*. But the contributors to these journals experience what Giddens would call a high degree of 'time-–space distanciation': the aim of this book is to minimise some of the academic space between human geography and social theory in order to establish a new agenda for theoretical and empirical work and so explore a new and challenging 'common ground'.

2
New Directions in Space

DOREEN MASSEY

Elements of the story so far

Those in the 'discipline' of geography have for long had a difficult relation to the notion of 'space' and 'the spatial'. There has been much head-scratching, much theorising, much changing of mind. Sometimes the notion has been clasped whole-heartedly as the only claimable distinguishing characteristic within the academic division of labour. Sometimes it has been spurned as necessarily fetishised. There have also, along with these switchbacks, been major shifts in the way in which 'space/the spatial' was itself to be conceived.

The 1960s and 1970s respectively provide instances of two extremes in this lurching relationship, and it is out of that history that emerges the first argument of this essay. The fundamental message is simple; that the radical critique of the 1970s – for very understandable reasons both intellectual and political – went far too far overboard in its rejection of the importance of the spatial organisation of things, of distance and perhaps above all, of geographical differentiation.

Go back a moment to the period before 1960; that bygone age when human geography, or at least a central part of it, was plainly about 'regions'. School and university courses were organised around sections of the world. There were courses on 'Africa', on 'Asia', on 'The Regions of the British Isles'. The focus was on place, on difference, on distinctiveness – on uniqueness. The concern was to understand how localities come to be as they are, how they get their particular character. Certainly, it was not always the most sophisticated theoretical work. There tended to be rather a lot of chapters which simply started with geology and ended up with politics. But what this focus *did* give to this section of the social sciences was an element of distinctiveness. First, it was concerned with putting things together, rather than tearing them apart; with trying to understand links, relationships, synthesis, rather than being concerned only with the dissection of analysis. It was, therefore, necessarily concerned with the unique. Second, this focus gave geography an object of its own, a bit of the world (quite literally) on which it could focus – the place, the region, the locality.

All this was overthrown in the 1960s. Along with other social sciences, geography too was hit by the 'positivist revolution' – in particular in its quantitative guise. The old regional geography was hidden away in embarrassment and the door closed firmly on it. It was explained away as part of our own Dark Ages, whence we had now emerged on to the High Plains of truly scientific endeavour. The story is familiar and we need not dwell on it. Such an enterprise, of course, went well with the wider characteristics of the period. This was the age of Wilsonism and of the 'white heat', of technological revolution, of the belief that you could save the world through the application of a neutral science and technology. So, with the urban problem beginning to nudge its way on to the political agenda, we built mathematical models of trip distribution, of modal split, and agonised over questions of the length of the journey to work. And, of course, all of that was common to many social sciences. Geography shared with them all the problems of that kind of an approach – the trivial notions of causality, the idea that a scientific 'law' was something that could be spotted simply through empirical regularity (so long as you had enough observations), the mathematics (or problems in the mathematics) leading the direction of enquiry rather than questions which arose from the real world processes themselves. But the new wave posed 'geographers' with a problem in addition to all these. For what exactly was being modelled? What kinds of laws and relationships were being sought? Laws about *what*, precisely? What had happened was that the convergence of method had left geography without an object. The insistence that only the general and the generalisable were scientific left geography shorn of one of its central concerns. The last thing in which one should be interested in this brave new world was the unique, the particular, the specific. Such stuff was to be disposed of by normalisation; it was a hindrance to the cause of science. Things were relatively easy for economics, for sociology, for politics – or so it seemed. However difficult it was to define, they had a section of the substantive world to study – the economy, the social, the political. Geography had no such segment of the world to claim for its own, no particular bit of social relations to section off and study. All it had – or all it appeared to have – was a dimension: space, distance.

So what happened was that geography set itself up as 'the science of the spatial'. There were spatial laws, spatial relationships, spatial processes. There was a notion that there were certain principles of spatial interaction which could be studied devoid of their social content. At a less highflown, but socially more significant, level, there was an obsession with the identification of spatial regularities and an urge to explain them by spatial factors. The explanation of geographical patterns, it was argued, lay within the spatial. There was no need to look further. As we have said, the inner city problem was coming to prominence at that time, and it provides a good case in point. For *there* was a clear spatial regularity. Geographers (and by no means only geographers), assuming that behind every spatial pattern lies a spatial cause, looked to the characteristics of the inner cities (in other words to the characteristics of the location itself) to explain their demise. This was probably the initial geographical version of blaming the victims for their own problems. What had happened in this combination of the rush for positivism and the need for an identity in the institutionalised academic division of labour was that geographers and geography had made some astonishing claims – that there was a world of the purely spatial, spatial laws devoid of substance or content, and spatial processes it was possible to wrench out of their social context.

The bulk of the 1970s and indeed until now, has been taken up with arguing that this is an untenable position, that there are no such things as purely spatial processes; there are only particular social processes operating over space. It was now argued that what was happening in the inner cities – the loss of industrial jobs – had more to do with industry than with the cities, that the cities were at the sharp end of what was to become a much more general process of de-industrialisation. It was also argued that the fact that they *were* at the sharp end had more to do with the character of their industry (that it was less competitive, more labour-intensive, with lower productivity) than with the cities' characteristics as locations. In other words, it was argued – to such an extent that it became a theme tune of the times – that the spatial is a social construct. It is a position which, in very general terms, still holds good.

But, in its turn, it also entailed some serious problems. First – and to talk only in terms of the academic division of labour – it meant that geography was deprived of its spatial role. It discovered, in other words, that the root causes of what it wanted to explain lay outside the discipline. Geographers either had to go off and learn another social science, or take up a position at the end of the transmission belt of the social sciences, dutifully mapping the outcomes of processes which it was the role of others to study. That problem of job demarcation in academe would not in itself have been important, had it not been also for its obverse. For conceptual work in many other social sciences continued to proceed blithely as though the world existed on the head of a pin, as though it were distanceless and spatially undifferentiated. The substance laws of the other social sciences, in other words, continued for the most part to be spatially blind. And what *that* meant, ironically, was that both spatial and substantive disciplines were now underestimating the importance of geography.

This was true in another way too. For along with this down-playing of the role of geography in general went a continued down-playing of the importance of the particularity, the individuality, of places. The focus of the radical critique of the 1970s was far less on the huge variety of outcomes we see in the world around us than in unravelling their common underlying cause. The argument on the whole was not just that spatial patterns are caused by social processes, but that they are caused by *common* social processes. This was an important argument to make, especially at that time. The inner cities were now beginning to vie with the regions as a political problem. And in such circumstances it was not inconvenient to government and policy-makers to let the two compete with each other. This story of divide and rule is now well known. And it was therefore of fundamental importance for those of us concerned with this problem to point out not only that you cannot just blame the victim, but that the victims were all going down to a common malady, that far from competing over *regional* policy it would be better to make common cause about *national* policies. So it *was* important and it is still important to stress what was general to those different geographical outcomes. But it was nonetheless done at some cost, and the cost once again was the down-playing of the importance of geography – in this case of geographical variations, of the uniqueness of outcomes.

My summary critique of the critique of the 1970s would be, then, that 'geography' was underestimated; it was underestimated as distance, and it was underestimated in terms of local variation and uniqueness. Space *is* a social construct – yes. But social relations are also constructed over space, and that makes a difference.

Industrial change and spatial change

Within studies of industrial location the big advance of the 1970s was to get production itself into the equation. Instead of the exclusive concentration on 'location factors' and on explaining one spatial pattern by another, it was argued that it was necessary to examine what was going on inside the factory or office, that 'location factors' were themselves the result of changes in production, and that in order to understand spatial change it was necessary to go behind 'spatial factors' and spatial pattern. The kind of substantive arguments around which this debate developed in Britain were the inner city problem (already discussed) and the evaluation of the impact of regional policy. Formally it led to a whole series of studies in which the dominant lines of causality were understood to run from causes of changes in production, through those changes themselves (changes in technology, reorganisations of the labour process, etc.) to an evaluation of the impact of those changes on the locational requirements of production, to the explanation of the (changes in) spatial pattern. There were, of course, variants. There was a strong line of argument that in many situations spatial considerations might be totally unimportant in the production of spatial outcomes. This might be true in cases where decisions were being made about closures, for example, or jobs were being lost through intensification of the labour process. In such circumstances spatial patterns of job loss (whether resulting from the operation of the market or from decisions within multilocational companies) might result entirely from internal characteristics of individual plants rather than from any more obviously spatial factors, such as the wider characteristics of the areas within which plants were located. But in very general terms the explanations tended to follow the stages indicated above. It was essentially a one-way, linear sequence. What was crucial to it (and what was new) was that spatial change was understood as being an outcome of production change.

It was, as I have said, an important point to make at the time, and it needed driving home, but it also now needs to be modified, for it is not the whole of the story – or rather, the story is not quite so simple. The sequence 'production change → spatial change' ignores the crucial impact of spatially-organised locational opportunities (or the lack of them) and of the use of distance and spatial separation themselves. Each of them can have an impact on what happens to production. The use by capital of locational change as part of a wider strategy for weakening workers' resistance is now well-known. It may also (perhaps more interestingly, though certainly more difficult to 'prove') work in the opposite direction – so that the spatial *im*mobilisation of certain elements of capital is part of what conditions the introduction of changes in the organisation of production. The accelerated development of sweated labour and homeworking in the clothing industry in the East End of London in the late 1960s was in part a product of the fact that this section of the industry (small family capital, short production runs, more connection to fashion outlets) was far less spatially mobile than that part of the industry under the control of large capital and concentrating on more mass-produced clothes. Both sections of the industry were under severe cost-pressures, mainly on labour-costs, but they solved their problems in entirely different ways. Big capital left the city, seeking out cheaper labour elsewhere. For the rest, such a strategy was impossible and a solution had to be found on site. For them new, cheaper and more vulnerable sources of labour were sought out by changes in the social organisation of production.

The examples could be multiplied. In our recent study of the brick industry it was clear that the fact that the London Brick Company was rooted to the spot by other factors (in particular, but not only, its reliance on Oxford clay) had an influence on its use of labour. Under pressure on wages it first imported immigrant labour (that is, labour moved, not the company) but finally had to resort to major changes in production. Unlike the large clothing companies it could not lower costs through its own spatial mobility, and that would seem to have hastened changes in production. It is not possible to move simply from production to location. Spatial organisation has its impact on production, too.[1]

Very much the same kind of argument can be made of the relation between the spatial organisation of production, on the one hand, and that of occupational and social structure, on the other. One significant development since the 1960s has been the concentration on the increasingly important elements of spatial differentiation of occupational structures within firms. In some cases this has gone along with the separation, within individual firms, of different stages of production (part-process spatial structures); in others it has been organised around 'product-cycle' hierarchies of plants; in yet others it has simply been a case of large numbers of branch plants each producing the same commodity.[2] In all these cases, however, lengthening managerial hierarchies were stretched out over space.

The fact that this was happening was recognised quite early. The work of Hymer and of Westaway was pre-eminent in pointing out the performance of different levels and kinds of managerial functions at different locations.[3] There was a hierarchy, social and spatial, from the strategic to the routine. There are two points to be made about this. First, what are really 'stretched out over space' are the relations of economic ownership and possession.[4] It is a hierarchy of particular places in these relations, related to the performance of particular functions. And those members of the managerial structure occupying different places within that hierarchy thereby have different places also in relation to the overall antagonism, within the relations of production, between capital and labour. Such differences are one element only in the determination of place in social structure. Roughly, the nearer to headquarters you are functionally, the higher your social status, and since the hierarchies have a spatial form, social and spatial differentiation are clearly related.

But second, it is the nature of this relationship (between social form – or in this case more accurately, *place* in the relations of economic ownership and possession within capitalist production – and spatial form) which is interesting. It is usually characterised, at least implicitly, as though a pre-existing managerial hierarchy is, in explanatory terms, subsequently allocated across space, as though the process is akin to dealing out between locations a pre-existing pack of cards. There is an implicit, perhaps unnoticed, assumption that the extended hierarchies of management and control were developed with the *aspatial* concentration of capital and *then* were distributed between plants as the large firms developed multi-locational patterns.

It did not, of course, happen like that. Becoming multi-locational was part and parcel of the growth of large firms; it was also part of the extension of the hierarchies of management and control. What is important to the argument here is that that very fact was one of the things which influenced the social divisions which developed within managerial hierarchies. The fact of multi-locationality itself will push towards the adoption of particular kinds of divisions in terms of the formal disaggregation of functions within the overall social relations of production. The hierarchy of managerial functions, and of managerial personnel, which stretches, say, from the headquarters in the metropolitan region, to a regional headquarters in a smaller city, to an outlying branch plant, is in part moulded in its form by the fact of spatial separation. So, too, is the hierarchy of social status and the detail of social structure. These are not just social divisions of labour distributed over space; the form of the social division is itself influenced by the *fact* that it is distributed over space.

It is also more than that. Spatial distribution and contrasting geographical contexts – spatial structure in a wider sense – will also mould the social divisions which exist. Certainly there is evidence for this in Britain today. At the lower end of management hierarchies, at the level of a lowly local branch–plant, management can be reduced to fairly routine administration and management can feel almost as much on the receiving end of, and in the dark about, decisions handed down from above as is the production workforce. That sense of differentiation, and potential antagonism, can be reinforced both by relative geographical isolation from other elements of 'their managerial class' and, when branch plants are in far-flung, production-only regions, by their very different social context. When managerial hierarchies within a country tend to take on fairly consistent interregional forms the social divisions which might anyway exist along them may be moulded and accentuated by the very fact of spatial division. The growing managerial strata in the UK would certainly merit further study along these lines.

Thus the fact that social processes take place over space and in a geographically-differentiated world affects their operation. Many of the most significant changes in social structure which have taken place in recent years in the UK could not really even be sensibly conceptualised outside a spatial geographically variegated form. From a point in the early 1960s where shortage of labour seemed for a moment to be a block on the hoped-for expansion of production, what has actually emerged is that the restructuring of British capital has taken place in a context of decelerating job-growth and subsequent decline. At the beginning of the period what was necessary was an expanded supply of labour. Later the requirement became much more simply cheaper labour. In both cases spatial expansion, geographical movement, was essential to capital's way out of its problems. In the first place the peripheral regions were needed as extensions to the supply of labour. Later their labour was used to undercut the strength of labour elsewhere. Since the 1960s, what new jobs have been created in the economy have, on the whole, gone elsewhere. In the early 1960s in economic terms labour in Britain was in a relatively strong position. It is no longer so, and not just because of the 'world' recession and the particularly spectacular collapse of employment in Britain. Spatial reorganisation has also been an important weapon in the changing balance of class forces.

That would have been true even had there been no recession, as industry expanded into new sources of labour, which in so many cases also meant new places, and that in turn functioned not only to expand, but to lower the price of labour below what it would otherwise have been.

Understanding the spatial organisation of society, then, is crucial. It is central to our understanding of the way in which social processes work out, possibly to our conceptualisation of some of those processes in the first place, and certainly to our ability to act on them politically.

The questions ahead

While this is easy to say – or seems so now as we forget the enthusiasm with which we denied spatiality in the 1970s! – it is not always so easy to see how to incorporate that understanding into analysis. Some things, perhaps, are clear enough. A re-recognition of the importance of spatial structure does not, for instance, imply that spatial structure in itself has determinate effects. Take for instance that well-known spatial form – small local labour markets with single dominant employers. It is a form frequently invoked in explanations of the state of labour relations within particular industries. But it is invoked, with equal equanimity, to 'explain' two very different results. For every time that it is invoked to explain 'paternalism' and labour quiescence (for instance in the textile-related industry of north-east Lancashire) it is also invoked as a part of the backcloth to militancy and solidarity (for instance in the colliery towns of the Welsh valleys). It is not, in other words, the spatial form in itself which has determinate effects. The social structures of which this *was* the spatial form were utterly different in the two locations – the kind of capital and the kind of labour were in complete contrast. It was these different social structures *in* these particular spatial forms which had such well-recognised outcomes.

I would argue then that one cannot formulate a world of spatial forms and spatial effects, in a manner reminiscent of the 1960s. But what of the obverse of that problem? Can we have social theories without spatial content or delimitation? Can we validly conjure with processes, structures, generative mechanisms or what have you, as though they occur on the head of a pin? In what sense is spatial form constitutive of social relations? If the spatial is not autonomous from the social, can the social be theorised autonomously from its spatial form, requirements and implications? What, in other words, is the effective import for research of this widening recognition of the significance of the spatial and the geographical?

A number of options appear to be available and to be being pursued. First, if we really mean that it is impossible to conceptualise social processes and structures outside their spatial form and spatial implications, then the latter must also be incorporated into our initial formulations and definitions, into our basic concepts – of capital, for instance, to point to the most obvious. That is no easy task. There are some clear possibilities – in the spatial implications of the self-expansion of capital, for instance. Yet so often the results seem either incredibly limited and banal (reinforcing the difficulties already being experienced in elaborating a wide and full range of generative mechanisms and causal properties) or we get involved in rather arbitrary series of multiple possibilities for how social processes will operate in a range of different and individually and formally-specified 'spatial contexts'. Neither seems on the face of it a very attractive possibility.

Yet necessary relations are not aspatial. How can 'necessary' relations be necessary if they depend, for example, on contiguity – unless that contiguity is specified? Inherent causal properties may depend on spatial form. What then happens to the argument that 'the spatial' is necessarily contingent? As a number of commentators have remarked, the whole realm of politics and culture, like the spatial, often also seems to be relegated to the arena of the contingent. The two seem to be closely related. But to accept that position would leave the range of possible necessary relations extremely limited, and limited primarily to the economic. Part of what is fundamentally at issue here is the reassessment of our definition of necessary relations within the social sciences.

It may indeed be argued that 'geography' only comes on to the scene at a later stage of analysis – that it is inherently contingent. The question then is what becomes of the injunction that social processes are constituted spatially? Williams has made a trenchant argument on the parallel relations between the social and the natural; that they are impossible to conceptualise separately and then 'put together'.[5] And what of Urry's important point that the operation of social laws over space may change the nature of those laws themselves?[6] Equating the geographical with the concrete seems to be a very minimalist position.

Research developments at the moment, however, seem to tend in the latter direction. This, I think, reflects in part the extreme difficulty and problematical nature of the first project. But it also reflects wider theoretical and political shifts. The unique is back on the agenda. The recognition and understanding of particularity is theoretically the mirror image of, and politically the equally-necessary obverse of, pointing to the generality and necessity of underlying mechanisms. And much of this particularity is spatially structured. In that sense the widening recognition of the importance of the geography of social structures, and of the fact that social structures are in the concrete world constituted geographically, is in tune with a widening and more general appreciation of specificity and of internal form. It is certainly important, both politically and theoretically, to developments within the social sciences. Even while some of the more fundamental theoretical questions remain unresolved (or, as they may, remain forever in dispute), it is vital that we accept, and continue to insist upon, the importance of space and spatial variations in *concrete* analysis.

Notes

1. Massey and Meegan (1982).
2. Massey (1984).
3. Hymer (1972); Westaway (1974).
4. Massey (1984).
5. Williams, S. (1981).
6. Urry (1981a).

3
Social Relations, Space and Time

JOHN URRY

Introduction

It is now becoming common to argue that one considerable deficiency of much of the contemporary social sciences is their neglect of time and space. Social analyses are held to be curiously negligent of the spatio-temporal location and structuring of the phenomena under investigation.[1] This is by obvious contrast with physical science where, for instance, Whitehead claimed that 'It is hardly more than a pardonable exaggeration to say that the determination of the meaning of nature reduces itself principally to the discussion of the character of time and the character of space.'[2] However, there are very considerable problems in seeing how space and time can be built into the examination of *social* relations. I will make a number of points of clarification to begin here.

First, most of the conventional distinctions between disciplines (especially those between economics, politics and sociology, on the one hand, and history and geography, on the other) make it difficult to relate time and space to this analysis of social relations. Specifically within sociology the distinction between social system or social structure *and* social change seems to restrict temporal analyses merely to the latter. Likewise the concept of 'society' constrains analysis within certain socio-spatial parameters and makes difficult the theorisation of structures and processes which do not conform to the concept of the individual 'society'. However, having said this, there are a number of examples of work within social science which do not demonstrate this obvious neglect of time and space. Examples within sociology include Goffman, in his distinction between front-stage and back-stage,[3] the symbolic interactionist analysis of the 'career',[4] and recent analyses of the collective action of different social classes.[5] It is noteworthy that in one of the most elaborate analyses of these issues,

Giddens concentrates in particular upon the temporal transformations involved in the development of capitalism, and in particular on the differences in the degree of time–space distanciation between capitalist and non-capitalist class-divided societies. It deals relatively little with the theorisation of space; in particular it tends to neglect the problem of explaining the causes and consequences of recent transformations in the spatial structuring of late capitalism.[6] Moreover, I shall try to show that this omission is particularly serious since it is space rather than time which is the distinctively significant dimension of contemporary capitalism, both in terms of the most salient processes and in terms of a more general social consciousness. As the historian of the *longue durée*, Braudel, argues 'All the social sciences must make room "for an increasingly geographical conception of mankind". This is what Vidal de la Blache was asking for as early as 1903.'[7]

Time, space and theoretical realism

There is a long-established philosophical debate as to whether space and time are to be viewed as in some sense absolute entities, possessing their own natures or particularities. For example, is space something which is causally productive; is it to be distinguished from matter since it possesses its own structure; or is it merely 'relative', a way of characterising the relations *between* the constituents of the physical world? The latter view was most famously articulated by Leibniz who argued that 'space is something merely relative' – it is 'an order of co-existences as time is an *order* of successions'.[8] According to this relational view the universe simply consists of pieces of matter, composed of various substances, and these pieces of matter exhibit spatial relationships between each other and between their own constitutive parts. Generally, relationists argue that if any statements do appear to assign properties to space it will be logically possible to reduce these properties to the relations *between* the objects concerned.[9]

The absolutist position has been maintained most famously by Descartes and Newton (and in a rather different way by Kant).[10] Here it is argued that space and time do designate particulars – that space, for example, possesses distinctive properties, in that it is continuous, quantitative, penetrable and immovably fixed. Absolutists have, however, disagreed about other properties which space may be said to possess, for example, whether there are three dimensions or four, whether space can be divided into intervals or is a continuum of infinitesimal points, and whether spatial relations are based on Euclidean geometrical principles or whether space is curved. Kant's absolutist position varied somewhat – and indeed his view that space is an *a priori* of knowledge has been seen as indicating that it is not a property of the things (*noumena*) themselves but is one category of the mind making knowledge possible.[11] However, Kant also argued that the analysis of enantiomorphs demonstrated the absolute character of space.[12] Enantiomorphs are a pair of objects which are related to each other as mirror images, as the right hand is to the left. Kant maintains that a purely relational description of a universe containing only one hand could not discriminate between it being either the left or the right hand. This is because the spatial relations between the parts of one hand are exactly the same as those between the corresponding parts of the other hand. Thus, if we thought that space were purely relative then there would be no way of distinguishing between a universe which contained only a left hand, from a universe that contained only a right. However, this is obviously incorrect since the hands *are* different and a left hand could not be fitted on to a right wrist (it would no longer be a 'hand'). Hence, there must be something about the relationship of each hand to something else which possess particular properties that means that a given hand *is* left or right. Kant maintains that it is the properties of space, absolute space, that determines this left- or right-handedness. Incidentally this argument has been extended to show that if we think that space is structured in non-Euclidean fashion, then it is not necessarily the case that hands are enantiomorphs since this depends upon exactly how space is structured.[13] A modern-day absolutist programme would thus have to concern itself with the analysis of varying topologies of space, with how space is *really* shaped.

   In the following pages I shall try to show that with respect to the social world neither of these positions – relationism or absolutism – can be sustained without qualification. I shall argue that this is because the social world (and by implication the physical world) is comprised of four-dimensional time–space entities; which bear complex and mutually modifying interrelations in time–space with each other; and these have the consequence of producing empirical distributions of social activities within time and space as a result of the partial and variable realisation of the respective causal powers of these entities. Regarding the social world in this realist manner does however require what one might loosely describe as a 'Copernican' revolution. This is because in our thinking, writing and experience of the social world it is common to believe that there is something epistemologically significant about the 'here and now' – that we are peculiarly constituted by and within the social relations which *currently* surround us. Furthermore, Smart argues that our particular notions of past, present and future are normally taken by us to apply objectively to the universe rather than being significant only at the level of human thought and utterances.[14] Indeed, the very tensing of our speech betrays an anthropocentricism, which is not given by the structuring of the universe in general, nor by the structuring of the social world in particular. The crucial point to note about both physical and social entities is that they endure, bodies extend in time as well as in space, and whether these exist in our past, our present or our future is simply contingent. Smart argues that we need a way of analysing such matters 'tenselessly' since past, present and future are not real properties of the entities involved. Likewise, I would argue that we also need a way of characterising such entities 'spacelessly' – that is, that notions of space should be conceptualised non-anthropocentrically.

What I am going to argue here is that the contemporary theoretical claim that there has to be a decentring of the 'subject' within the human sciences is inadequate without further analysis of the subject's temporal and spatial structuring. According to Foucault it is particularly in the post-1800 period that the human sciences (plus biology) came to focus upon the concepts of 'man' and 'history'.[15] But now, in the wake of structuralism, it is argued that 'man' need not, and indeed should not, be placed at the centre of the human sciences. In particular the 'linguistic turn' means that all kinds of social practice should be viewed as linguistic, as systems of meaning and signification.[16] It is these linguistic systems, especially their systematically arranged differences, which are held to be responsible for constituting the human subject as autonomous, self-conscious and self-willed. However, this decentring has not been sufficiently examined and it is necessary to specify further just how the individual subject is constructed in the 'here and now'. What are the processes which produce individuals as occupants and users of particular places, defined within a system of temporal and spatial differences? This means conceptualising time and space outside the limitations of the 'here and now', in particular, by analogy with that of language identifying the four-dimensional social entities which, through their interrelations, are responsible for producing individual subjects as occupants and users of particular places.

This is a rather unfamiliar project although, as I hope to show, much theoretical and empirical research does bear upon it, but often rather indirectly. The only recent work which directly addresses these issues is that of Giddens' *A Contemporary Critique of Historical Materialism*.[17] In this he argues that we should concentrate upon 'aspects and modalities of presence and absence in human social relations'.[18] These are notions which refer to both time and space. All social interactions, he says, are based on an intermingling of presence and absence. This intermingling expresses different modes in which structures are drawn upon to incorporate the long-term *durée* of institutions within contingent social acts. These structures convey time across time–space distances of indeterminate length. Thus societies can be compared as to the degree of 'time–space distanciation' which they embody – that is, the degree to which societies are 'stretched' across shorter or longer space of such distanciation. In non-capitalist societies authoritative resources are the prime carriers of such distanciation, while in capitalist societies it is allocative resources which are the prime carriers. In the latter case both time and space become commodified and separated from the substance of social activities with which they are fundamentally bound up in non-capitalist societies. There is 'time–space convergence' by which interaction expands over space and contracts over time; there is thus a profoundly heightened 'presence–availability' within contemporary capitalism. However, the main problem in Giddens' formulation is that he does not examine the *different* time–space constitution of the various causally powerful social entities which are involved. If he had done so he would have found it necessary to consider, first, the varying significance of temporal and spatial processes instead of their conflation through the employment of the notion of 'time–space' 'stretching' or 'distancing'. And second, he would have had to analyse the different levels at which spatial/temporal relations can be said to reside – relations which preclude a simple characterisation of time and space as either absolute or relational. I shall now try to confront the problem of time and space directly.

First, then, neither space nor time are substances in the sense that matter is made of various substances, the existence of each being independent of all other entities. Space and time only exist when there are entities in some sense *in* space and time. Hence, they do not exist without at least two existent objects, which occupy a relationship within time–space. This means incidentally that if there are at least two such objects then there is never nothing – there is, as Kant argued, space – that is, the space between these two objects. Thus space is a set of *relations* between entities and is not a substance. As a result, therefore, there is likely to be a category mistake involved if we talk of 'society' and 'space' as interacting. 'Society' is in some sense at least a substance (as well as sets of relations) while 'space' is not.[19] Likewise, we should avoid treating 'time' as itself productive – as producing effects as a simple consequence of its passage or of its 'flowing'.[20] There is no 'arrow of time' as though there were something concrete which could itself flow or fly or fall or pass us by.

Nevertheless, it does not follow that spatial and temporal relations can be unproblematically *reduced* to the relations within and between social entities.[21] However, to talk of entities and of their interrelations is to presuppose a particular conception of ontology and science. Here I would argue against what is generally known as an event-ontology, namely, that the natural or social world is to be viewed simply as sets of discrete, atomistic events (actions, interactions, personality characteristics, social institutions, and so on) which happen to be distributed in time and space. I would follow Harré and Madden in arguing in favour of a 'thing-ontology', that there are persistent and enduring structures, located within time–space, and that we do not have to give a special account of why such things persist.[22] They persist because of the causal powers which they possess and which are in part realised. However, I do not claim that a particular class of events can and should be explained in terms of a single such entity; in other words, it is incorrect to maintain that a given entity possesses of itself the causal power to produce a whole class of empirical events. This is because of the need to investigate the conditions under which such causal powers are in fact *realised*; and when we do that we find that such conditions will on occasions consist of other social entities and the at least partial realisation of their powers.[23] This fundamental interdependence of such entities thus means that the causal powers of some entities constitute the conditions necessary for the realisation of the powers of other entities. Hence, the empirical events generated (such as the spatial distribution of households or factories) are the product of highly complex *inter*-dependent processes. I take it that this is roughly what Marx was alluding to when he stated that 'The concrete concept is concrete because it is a synthesis of many definitions, thus representing the unity of diverse aspects.'[24] For Marx the concrete object is concrete not because it exists or is 'empirical', but because it is the effect of the specific conjuncture of many diverse forces or processes, of – in my terms – entities with specific causal powers. Furthermore, these processes are not to be simply listed, or added up, but rather are to be *synthesised*. Their combination qualitatively modifies each constitutive entity. How, then, does this discussion relate directly to the analysis of time and space?

First of all, as we have seen, empirical events are distributed *in time*–space. This is as true for the relatively routine features of everyday life, a weaving-dance through time–space, as it is for relatively distinct and unique social events.[25] Indeed the idea that individuals occupy 'paths' through time–space highlights the 'physical indivisibility and finite time resources of the individual' – hence there is, as Pred put it, an 'intimate, intricate interconnectedness of different biographics that is an essential part of the everyday process of social reproduction'.[26]

Second, any given entity implies particular spatial relations and a specific structuring of time. Thus, for example, civil society, where labour-power is substantially produced, is partly constituted of relatively separated households with a distinct 'friction of distance' between them.[27] The modern state, on the contrary, is highly centralised and contains spatially and temporally transformed means of surveillance.[28] Capitalist relations themselves involve the commodification of both time and space as capital is systematically restructured. Capitalist relations are now less dependent upon the immediate or potential presence of controllers of those relations. The need for spatial proximity, which derived from the time taken to convey information or decisions, has been transformed by the development of electronically transmitted information. The resulting functional and spatial splitting of offices from workplaces and of different workplaces from each other in terms of the different labour-forces and labour-processes employed, transforms the respective causal powers of different social classes which are themselves temporally/spatially structured.

Third, it is also necessary to consider the changing spatial–temporal relations *between* these different entities with their respective causal powers. There are varying relations existent between distinct entities which are specially interdependent over time. One example here would relate to the development of the state as in some sense the manager of everyday life – a development which decreases the 'space' (literally and metaphorically) between it and civil society. Another example concerns the changing profile of capitalist relations of production, which are, as I argue elsewhere, increasingly deep but increasingly concentrated within certain first world economies.[29] So although capitalist development involves the commodification of space, in that everyday life becomes progressively commodified, there is an increased distance between capitalist production *per se* and civil society within the emergent 'former industrial countries' of which the UK is the leading example. Capitalist production is progressively deepened yet is spatially concentrated. Many localities have become decapitalised and relatively separated and distant from direct capitalist relations of production *per se*.

Therefore it is necessary to investigate the changing temporal/ spatial relations between diverse determinate social entities, which are themselves temporally/spatially structured and which possess causal powers which may or may not be realised. Thus, empirical events in general, and the spatial patterning of such events in particular, are to be explained in terms of the complex, overlapping and temporally/spatially structured relations between such entities, which will involve the realisation/part realisation/blocking of the causal powers of such entities. Thus, time and space occupy complex and variable relations in the analysis: they characterise 'empirical events', the structuring of causally productive entities, and the interrelations between such entities.

There are a number of implications of this position.

1. It is incorrect to argue, as Althusser and others have done, that a given 'structure' is immanent in its effects (such as producing a particular spatial distribution). Althusser, for example, says:

   that the effects are not outside the structure, are not a preexisting object, element or space in which the structure arrives to *imprint its mark*: on the contrary, it implies that the structure is immanent in its effects ... that *the whole existence of the structure consists of its effects*.[30]

The theoretical realist position that I have outlined involves the rejection of this argument, which is little different from the notion of 'expressive causality' rightly criticised by Althusser. Theoretical realism necessarily involves the view that the 'structure' cannot, except paradigmatically, be expressed in its effects. Structures necessarily exist interdependently and it is a contingent matter as to the degree to which their respective causal powers are expressed within particular empirical events.

2. Althusser is correct, however, to argue that each structural level may involve different historical times. He argues that we should assign to each level a peculiar time, 'relatively autonomous and hence relatively independent . . . of the times of the other levels'.[31] But what Althusser ignores are two points already emphasised here: first, that each structural level not only enjoys a particular historical time but also a given geographical space and that there is no reason to suppose that there is any less relative autonomy spatially than temporally; and second, that it is necessary to investigate both the temporal and spatial interdependence *between* different levels or structures, not only those relations within each.

3. However, it is important to remember that neither temporal nor spatial relations of themselves produce particular effects. We have noted that time is not something that 'flows' and produces effects simply as a consequence of its passage.[32] Likewise we should avoid making a fetish of the spatial, either through making the category mistake of saying that one area (one 'space') exploits another area, or that a given social structure is determined *by* spatial relations. Apparently 'spatialist' explanations, such as Durkheim's argument that the division of labour increases as a consequence of heightened 'moral density', can be at best only suggestive of where a properly constituted explanation may lie.[33]

4. The view of the social world being sustained here – that it comprises a number of interdependent, mutually modifying, four-dimensional, space–time entities – means that we are confronted by a peculiarly complex 'open system', as Bhaskar puts it. He says:

> It is characteristic of open systems that two or more mechanisms, perhaps of radically different kinds, combine to produce effects; so that because we do not know *ex ante* which mechanisms will actually be at work (and perhaps have no knowledge of their mode of articulation) events are not deductively predictable. Most events in open systems must thus be regarded as 'conjunctures'.[34]

Two methodological points follow from this. First, as Sayer points out, what is involved is a form of retroductive inference à la Hanson.[35] That is to say, science involves the postulation of theories in order to explain empirical phenomena – these theories are built up 'in reverse', retroductively, and they are developed in order to make sense of a set of puzzling empirical phenomena. The elaboration of the theory is held to be worthwhile because if the theory were true, then this would explain the phenomena in question. Second, there are a number of independent grounds which have to be met in order for us to be relatively certain that this theory is at least partly correct – (i) other independent grounds for believing that the postulated entity or entities possess the particular causal powers; (ii) evidence for believing that within this conjuncture these powers are being realised, at least in part; (iii) the absence of grounds for thinking that these causal powers are no longer being realised because, for example, of their blockage by other entities; and (iv) some evidence that it is this entity or these interdependent entities and not other entities which are producing the phenomena in question.[36]

So far I have made some general comments upon the relations between time, space and social relations within a theoretical realist conception of science. In the next section I shall consider more precisely the changing relationship *between* time and space.

The significance of space

In John Berger's essay on portrait painting, he suggests that the satisfaction of portraiture needs to reside in the personal recognition and the confirmation of one's social position that it produced, but that in the latter part of the nineteenth and especially in the twentieth century, there was a dramatic decline in its importance. This stemmed partly from the growth of photography and from a declining belief in the value of the social positions that people occupied. But there is a further reason for its decline which suggests, according to Berger, that even if people were once more confident and assured in their social positions there could not be a rebirth of portrait painting. He argues this by drawing an analogy with the modern novel where there has been a change in the characteristic mode of narration. It is, he says, scarcely possible still to tell a straight story sequentially unfolding in time. This is because we are now too well aware of what may be traversing the story line laterally.

Instead of being aware of a point as an infinitely small part of a straight line, we are aware of it as an infinitely small part of an infinite number of lines, as the centre of a star of lines. Such awareness is the result of our constantly having to take into account the simultaneity and extension of events and possibilities.

The reasons for this include the enormous range of contemporary means of communication, the scale of modern systems of power, the indivisibility of the world (the 'global village') and the unevenness of economic development within overall patterns of world-wide exploitations. Berger thus suggests that it is space rather than time or history which is the significant dimension structuring personal experience in the contemporary world. Prophecy, he says, now involves a geographical rather than an historical dimension; we should now talk of people making not their own history but their own geography.[37]

What Berger is here suggesting is that the most important contemporary changes occurring in a wide range of causally powerful social entities are essentially spatial rather than simply temporal. In one sense, though, this is a partly arbitrary distinction to make since, as Earman points out, space is not a given entity like the earth – it is time–space that is given, and space must be sliced off from time–space in one of a number of different ways.[38] Bearing this in mind I will now clarify one difference between spatial 'slices' and temporal 'slices' which is of considerable importance.

Although I have argued that both temporal and spatial aspects of time–space have to be considered as comprising sets of relations, these relations are asymmetrical. In particular, relations within space must exhibit a constant sum, while relations within time are not so contrained: although two objects can occupy the same point in time (in different places) therefore they cannot occupy exactly the same point in space.[39] Hence, space is necessarily limited and there has to be competition and conflict over its organisation and control. Amongst other things, this means that if a causally powerful entity is to effect changes involving more than one object, but at the same point in time, then these effects will have to be produced at more than one point in space.

However, it is not appropriate simply to distinguish between time or the temporal and space or the spatial. Time necessarily involves direction so that once some time has elapsed it is impossible to return to the original point in time. Lucas argues that: 'Directionless time is not time at all ... A uniform direction of time is ... an essential condition of intersubjective experience'.[40] Hence, any finite movement through space must take time and hence the object concerned cannot move back to its temporal starting point. Although spatial change necessarily involves temporal changes, temporal change does not necessarily involve spatial change. Thus, we should distinguish between the 'temporal' and the 'spatial–temporal', rather than simply the temporal and the spatial.

Furthermore, it is the latter kind of change which will require more substantial powers to bring about, because such change must be affected at different points in space. Temporal changes occurring at the same or at closely related points in space require less powers to bring about and hence are more likely to be initially implemented in any social process. *Spatial*–temporal changes will be likely to follow when at least some of the possibilities of temporal change have been implemented. This somewhat provisional argument can be partly supported by considering the processes of capitalist accumulation within the sphere of production. There are three forms:

1. absolute surplus-value production which does not involve any spatial transformation – that is, increases in surplus-value are obtained through lengthening the working day or intensifying the work done;
2. relative surplus-value production where the spatial transformation involved occurs within the sphere of circulation – that is, involving movements of *commodities* including that of labour-power but not of productive capital;
3. relative surplus-value production where the spatial transformations involved occur within the sphere of *production* – that is, new technologies, a heightened division of labour, the employment of new machinery, etc., all involve spatial relocations of productive capital and the construction of highly diverse and spatially distinct circuits of capital.

Historically, there has been a movement from (1) to (2) to (3) although this has not occurred at the same rate nor to the same degree within each sector of production. At any point in time each sector will exhibit a distinct spatial division of labour. Furthermore, movement from (1) to (2) to (3) is not something that develops automatically but depends upon both the spatial–temporal limitations implied by the existing form of surplus-value production and the specific social struggles and forms of state action occurring within and with regard to that sector. In broad terms, I would suggest, accumulation since the Second World War has been characterised by the increasingly pronounced emphasis upon (3), upon capitalist restructuring based on spatial–temporal transformations at the level of production rather than circulation. However, it is incorrect to argue that capital will simply seek the most appropriate forms of capitalist restructuring, that *capital* will seek to move from (1) to (2) to (3). In this context Müller and Neusüss have provided an interesting discussion of the development of the Factory Acts within Britain.[41] These were important in preventing continued absolute surplus-value production based on extending the working day. Although these Acts stemmed from working-class resistance, in certain industrial sectors they had the effect of shifting the predominant form of surplus-value production from (1) to (2). Likewise the move from (2) to (3) has been partly produced by the struggles of labour, particularly within social democratic parties. There have been in Britain two especially distinctive developments – that of nationalisation and that of encouraging the centralisation of capital through the Industrial Reorganisation Corporation in the late 1960s. Both aided the move from (2) to (3).

Another way of expressing this heightened significance of *spatial-*temporal transformations is to point to the contemporary hypermobility of at least certain forms of capital,[42] and the contradiction between this and the existing practices within civil society. The latter revolve around and presuppose the constitution of individual subjects.[43] It is through their social experience, through their position within various discourses, that individuals come to act and to view themselves as autonomous, whole and independent subjects. There are moreover two crucially important interpellations of the subject, those of spatio–temporal location and of gender. The effect of the former is that individuals are constituted who are aware of their presence as subjects residing within a particular spatial location (street, town/countryside, region, nation) at a given period of time (born of a particular generation defined by its place in relation to others). As Webber says:

> The physical place becomes an extension of one's ego. The outer worlds of neighbourhood-based peer groups, neighbourhood-based family, and the *physical* neighbourhood place itself, seem to become internalized in inseparable aspects of one's inner perception of self . . . One's conception of himself (*sic*) and of his place in society is thus subtly merged with his conceptions of the spatially limited territory of limited social interaction.[44]

Such subjects are necessarily spatially distributed (especially into households) and spatially constrained. Households cannot occupy the same point in space and the movement of individual household members is constrained by intervening patterns of land use, ownership, and access.

This contrast between capital and civil society is particularly significant since it is within the latter that wage labour is produced and reproduced. Indeed it is important to note how Marx's analysis of capitalist production is seriously deficient because he did not concern himself with the process of *producing* wage-labour or labour-power.[45] The text *Capital* is concerned with analysing the production of capital, where labour-power is a mere presupposition of that process. Marx never completed the volume which would have involved analysing the *production* of the commodity, labour-power. This obviously involves a process not simply of consuming commodities produced within the sphere of capitalist production, but through human labour converting the articles for consumption into refreshed and energetic labour-power. This production of wage-labour is necessarily spatially located and constrained and attachment to 'place' is of particular significance. The key elements are those of spatio–temporal proximity, specificity and constraint. By contrast capital is progressively characterised by hypermobility, a functional rather than a spatial organisation of different circuits distributed throughout the world and taking advantage of diverse variations within the conditions of production of wage-labour. Hypermobile capital has no need for spatial proximity nor indeed for any particular spatial location. It can be characterised by the principle of 'spatial indifference'. Hence, there is a contrast between the production of capital (apparently social but in fact structured through private appropriation) and the production of wage-labour (that is, of individual subjects produced under conditions of relatively free, social but not socialised labour). Some commentators have assumed that the state is somehow able to overcome this contrast between capital and wage-labour, by constructing and reproducing the latter in forms appropriate to the former (in terms of size, skill, militancy, etc.) but I take this to be highly dubious.[46]

One way of analysing the consequences of this contrast between the production of capital and the production of wage-labour is via a regional analysis. Lipietz, for example, argues that a region is a concrete articulation of spatialities appropriate to different sets of social relations.[47] In particular we can identify a *dominated* region when it is specialised in branches organised *by* dominated modes or by archaic stages of the dominant mode. A region is *externally* dominated when small independent producers or small/medium sized local capitalists carry on an unequal exchange with capital within the dominant region. This unequal exchange is a block to autonomous regional development and will lower the costs of reproduction of labour-power. Indeed this prepares the basis for *integration-domination* as external capital takes control of local production and is able to enjoy a heightened rate of exploitation because of historically low costs of reproducing labour-power. By contrast with these dominated regions there are one or more central regions based on self-centred accumulation. There is a more or less self-sufficient regional market for both the producer- and consumer-goods that are generated.

However, Lipietz never justifies his employment of the concept 'region' and I have elsewhere argued against its contemporary applicability.[48] This is because the development of dramatic economies of labour-time through *spatial*–temporal transformations undermines the coherence of existing *regional* economies and has heightened the importance of the *locality*. This argument is not challenged by Lipietz's claims since what he says could as equally apply to localities as opposed to regions. Indeed he nowhere demonstrates that there are in fact coherent regional economies and his very useful analysis of the 'branch circuit'[49] shows the diversity of localities into which hypermobile capital may move. However, this requires some discussion of urban areas since it is within *them* that wage-labour is predominantly produced.

I will not discuss here the most elegant approach developed to explain the relationship between the economy and the urban form, namely central place theory,[50] because even if there was once some relationship between different levels of service function and city size, the spatial changes which I have been analysing have now undermined any such connection. With the development of large multi-plant enterprises in both the private and state sector, then the local plant (whether it is a chemicals factory, a university, or a computer firm) may well serve the whole national or international market and not just a region. Moreover, at the same time, there has been increasing concentration of research and managerial functions within central cities, and in London in the UK. So rather than there being an urban hierarchy, at least partly related to a *hierarchy* of functions, there has been the development of a *dual* economy. There is a large central mass (London in the UK) containing 80–90 per cent of the total office value, surrounded by a peripheral region – the rest of the

UK containing the remaining 10–20 per cent.[51] As Broadbent says in summary:

> The individual city appears less important because many processes which used to occur *within* the area, such as the different stages of production within a firm, or the circulation of funds from sales and profits back into investment in new building plant or equipment ... now go on *outside* the area through the centralized industrial/financial and state concentration of power in London.[52]

Thus *spatial*–temporal changes have transformed the distribution of urban areas. As the economic processes (size of firms, growth of multiplant private and state enterprises, etc.) have spatially transcended each individual city, so each area is increasingly reduced to the status of a *labour pool*. The important linkages within the city are those which pass through the household, through civil society, not through the private or public enterprises located within that area. The other linkages, involving the sale and purchase of commodities between enterprises, occur across the urban boundary. Cities are thus increasingly crucially significant sites for the production of wage-labour, they are sites within which pools of labour-power are systematically created and reproduced. The urban area, as Broadbent emphasises, is a system of *production*, a relatively closed system comprised of a large number of interdependent, relatively privatised households wherein wage-labour is produced. Cities are thus not so much an interlocking economy of producing and consuming enterprises but a *community of subjects* who produce and who consume in order to produce. Moreover, this production is necessarily local, it is principally produced for the *local* market, subject to the constraints of time imposed by the particular relations between households and workplaces. Cities are thus to be viewed as 'relatively independent labour pools',[53] each comprised of a large number of separately producing households, linked with each other and competing for urban space.

There is thus a substantial shift in the structuring of each urban locality. Previously such localities were integrated within the production and reproduction of capital. However, as each urban locality has been reduced to the status of a labour pool so they are now integrated not within the production process of capital but of wage-labour, within the spheres of civil society rather than of capitalist production *per se*. This has four important consequences: first, to heighten the dichotomisation between that capital which operates locally and which contributes in some sense to the reproduction of local wage-labour, and national/international capital whose circuits and inter-dependencies transcend the particular locality; second, to enlarge the possibilities of alliance between all those resident within a locality whether their class position is that of capital, labour or an inter-mediate class; third, to strengthen the potential influence of labour and intermediate classes at the local level, while lessening their in-fluence regionally and nationally;[54] and fourth, attempts to heighten the distinctiveness of each locality and especially to emphasise their respective merits as a pool of wage labour, given the particular structuring of the 'local civil society' – the over-availability of such locations, with relatively deskilled labour, has led Walker to talk of the 'lumpen geography' of capital.[55] The result of these transforma-tions in the connections at the local level between the relations of production and civil society means that localities are relatively un-structured by the former and much more subject to determination and change effected through the latter.

The analysis of space

I have so far talked generally of the relations between time, space and the social world. I have made relatively little reference as to how we might analyse such relations apart from noting the importance of the distinction between enduring entities and empirical events. Sayer has recently tried to discuss some of these issues – in the case of studies of industrial location – by distinguishing between external, contingent relations, on the one hand, and internal, necessary relations, on the other.[56] The former consist of those relations where the objects in question do not stand in any necessary relationship with each other, and when they can exist independently of each other and of the relationship between them. The latter, by contrast, consist of those relations which are necessary for the very objects to exist, so that they cannot exist without such relations. An example of the former would be the decision of a particular company to employ workers from one town rather than another; examples of the latter would be the rela-tions between capital and wage-labour, or landlord and tenant. Sayer points out that many relationships will in fact consist of some com-bination of the two forms of relations so that specific empirical events should not be viewed as simply resulting from *either* external and contingent *or* internal and necessary relations. For example, he says:

If there is one major lesson to be drawn from empirical research in economic geography, it is that areas are constituted by a diverse range of activities, some internally related, others externally related: they are 'conjunctures' whose content cannot be known 'in advance' on the basis of theoretical knowledge of necessary relations alone.[57]

In particular he criticises the generalisation of relatively specific and localised empirical developments into large-scale general laws of development. Such analyses are not based on the proper abstraction of the theoretical properties of given entities, but rather of collapsing the effects of several interacting entities into some supposedly general empirical trend. Sayer follows Massey who states that 'the social and economic structure of any given local area will be a complex result of the combination of that area's succession of roles within the series of wider, national and international, spatial divisions of labour'.[58]

However, there are two difficulties in Sayer's argument. First, he only discusses various forms of the spatial division of labour and does not consider what kind of 'internal relations' would characterise the 'state', 'civil society', 'social classes' and so on. He merely notes that the 'production' of labour-power can take a variety of forms.[59] Second, he does not consider what is in fact the most intractable problem here, namely, establishing the spatial/temporal relations *between* these interdependent entities, which are themselves spatially/temporally structured. These relations will not be either external and contingent, or internal and necessary. They will be structured, constraining, sometimes functional, and involving complex processes of mutual modification of the necessary causal powers of the entities involved.

As a way of illustrating these two points I will return to the relations between capitalist production and civil society.[60] They can be summarised in the following terms – (i) there are capitalist relations of production which are to be viewed as *necessary* or internal; (ii) there are particular agents who happen *contingently* to bear one function or the other; (iii) given that agents bear such functions then they are subject to *necessary* constraining laws; (iv) it is also *necessarily* the case that agents as bearers of such laws act as subjects possessing a consciousness or will; but (v) the particular practices of civil society within which such subjectivities are constituted and reproduced are to a degree *contingent* and depend in part upon collective organisation and struggle to extend or protect those practices.

It is also important to note that significant changes can occur among these five sets of relations. For example, in those industrial sectors where there has been development of the 'new international division of labour' then there has been a substantial increase of capitalist relations of production which are simultaneously necessary *and* contingent.[61] This is because the growth of a worldwide market for labour greatly expands the range of alternative localities within which the same necessary capitalist relations can be established and reproduced; it is then a relatively contingent matter as to exactly where those relations will in fact be found.

My discussion thus far has been very general; I will now try to make this more specific by considering: (i) some of the different forms of the spatial division of labour which result from particular patterns of capitalist restructuring in which decisions about spatial location are to be seen as subordinate to the necessities implied by accumulation;[62] and (ii) some of the different ways in which a given civil society is spatially structured – such structurings not being viewed as simple emanations of the mode of production, as Aglietta seems to claim for the 'mode of consumption'.[63]

Spatial divisions of labour

There appear to be six forms of the spatial division of labour which will characterise any particular industrial sector:

1. *regional specialisation* – up to the inter-war period many industrial sectors were characterised by a high degree of specialisation within particular regions (for example, cotton textiles and textile machinery within Lancashire; mining and shipbuilding within the northeast, woollen manufacture within West Yorkshire, and so on);
2. *regional dispersal* – other sectors are characterised by a high degree of dispersal with relatively little concentration in specific regions. Obviously 'consumer services' mostly take this form, as well as some 'producer services' and certain manufacturing industries such as food processing, shoe production, etc. Labour reductions in this case will take the form of 'intensification', that is, relatively uniform cutbacks spread throughout the different regions;
3. *functional separation* between management/research and development in the 'centre', skilled labour in old manufacturing centres, and unskilled labour in the 'periphery';
4. *functional separation* between management/research and development in the 'centre', and semi-skilled and unskilled labour in the

'periphery' (this example is found in the UK electrical engineering and electronics industry);[64]

5. *functional separation* between management/research and development and skilled labour in a 'central' economy, and unskilled labour in a 'peripheral' economy;[65]

6. *division* between one or more areas, which are characterised by investment, technical change and expansion, and other areas where unchanged and progressively less competitive production continues with resulting job loss. The former may involve the development of new products as well as new means of producing existing products.[66]

As we have already noted we should not analyse a given area purely as the product of a single form of the spatial division of labour. To do so, as Sayer points out, is to 'collapse all the historical results of several interacting "spatial divisions of labour" into a rather misleading term which suggests some simple unitary empirical trend'.[67] Rather any such area is 'economically' the overlapping and interdependent product of a number of these spatial divisions of labour and attendant forms of industrial restructuring.

The spatial structuring of civil society

Civil societies can be characterised in terms of a number of different dimensions, each of which contains implications for its spatial structuring. The following are the relevant dimensions:

1. the degree to which the existing *built environment* can be transformed. The given environment represents a literal freezing of the past being both capitalism's 'crowning glory' and its 'prison'.[68] The construction of a new 'built environment' (such as nineteenth-century towns, new towns, suburbanisation, etc.) permits a restructuring of civil society. The development of new 'created spaces' will allow novel civil societies to emerge which are freed from ties to particular 'localities'. A very good example of this was the development of suburbs in the USA after 1890 away from the 'facts of production' and involving the move towards the Arcadian ideal of ruralised living on the edge of the city.[69] This was an indication of class weakness on the part of the bourgeoisie who were unable to forge an alternative system for controlling industry and the working class apart from constructing a new 'created space' on the margins of the existing frozen past. At the same time,

however, suburbs have been actively developed because of their small scale, their social and political independence, and their ability to confer heightened status;[70]

2. the degree to which there is *integration* of the social relations of civil society into the wider capitalist economy; depending in particular on the distinctive mode of consumption characterising particular classes, nations or other social groupings. To take one example, there is variation in whether the domestic property market assumes a 'capitalistic' character. Agnew suggests in Britain that the 'home' is mainly regarded as a use-value and not as an investment with potential exchange-value.[71] This is in contrast with the USA where the high levels of geographical mobility, the pronouncements of state agencies, the emphasis within popular culture, and the lack of regional land-use planning laws, all reinforce the notion that the home (the cell-form of civil society) is a capitalist commodity to be acquired and disposed of in a manner broadly similar to any other commodity. Agnew summarises:

> In the contemporary United States historical circumstances have kept the population more closely wedded to the classic capitalist order. In other societies, which we often conventionally designate as 'capitalist', there is less correspondence between the capitalist model and the reality which people face in their everyday lives.[72]

3. the degree to which more generally the social relations within civil society are based on the 'local community' rather than on either commodity relations or on the state. Where this is the case then this involves sets of social relationships which are multiplex (neighbours who are workmates who are leisure-time companions, etc.) where 'everyone knows everyone else' and where these sets are organised into a locally structured and delimited system.[73] The consequence of such a community structuring of the local civil society is to produce *communion* so that one's neighbourhood has an emotional meaning derived from the people who live there and from the mutually supporting ties of trust, friendship and reciprocity within that local civil society, even if this is a 'mutuality of the oppressed'.[74] Market transactions within such a place-bound community are indelibly suffused by considerations of long-term reciprocity and community. Interactions occur within a given physical setting, and one's living space is necessarily personalised,

particularised and non-directly commodifiable. Such a community-based civil society, stated here in its ideal–typical form, is based upon mutuality and reciprocity, locally derived criteria of power and status (such as patriarchy) and non-maximising economic behaviour. It provides a considerable insulation from commodity relations of a capitalist economy and from the 'capitalist production of a mode of consumption'.[75]

4. the degree to which there is a *heterogeneity* of class experiences based upon the distinctive characteristics of particular communities, places of work or kinship relations. This issue is explored later in Cooke's analysis of radical regions. Cox however argues that mass education and the mass media have both undermined such class heterogeneity; Seabrook argues that there is increased homogenisation across classes. 'The consciousness of many young people ... has been fashioned, not by work, not by place, not by kinship, but by a homogeneous culture of shops, images and *réclame*. A freely chosen sameness?"[76]

5. the degree of *spatial concentration* of different social classes or other social forces. In Italy, for example, Paci points out that the working-class concentration in the North is higher than in more or less any other area in Europe, and this is of some relevance in explaining why Italy has one of the strongest Communist parties in the West.[77] Also, however, one important development especially in Britain in the past decade or so has been the shift of both employment and of the population out of the former heavily industrialised urban connurbations.[78] The movement of population has been permitted by the growth of widespread private transport and by the development of cities as labour pools, as particular, localised civil societies. As a consequence, individual households of at least the 'central' working class are able to choose where their labour-power is to be reproduced. One important dimension within civil society has been a return to 'nature', to get closer to the 'natural'; and this is in part reflected in the urbanisation of the rural.[79]

6. the degree to which either local or national civil societies are *vertically* organised; that is, when diverse social groupings and voluntary and informal associations are specific to particular classes and there is relatively little independent organisations.[80] By contrast, civil society can be said to be horizontally organised when there are a large number of social groupings and other social practices which are non-class-specific and which generate relative-

ly autonomous forms of organisation and representation.
7. the degree to which local civil societies are *long-established* with
   inter-generationally reproduced and sedimented patterns of life
   and cultural forms. This will obviously be undermined by a range
   of factors, including certain forms of economic restructuring as
   already described, and by the possibly related transformations of
   civil society through rapid in- or out-migration.[81]

There are two other crucial considerations here which I have not
considered: first, the spatial structurings of other social entities,
especially the state;[82] and second, the analysis of how the complex
spatial/temporal interdependence between these diverse entities with
varying causal powers in fact produce specific sets of empirical
events.[83] Many of the other chapters relate to these issues and I will
not consider them further except with regard to one issue, namely, the
conditions under which 'collective organisations' may develop out of
social classes or out of other social groupings. It is obvious that the
formation of such organisations is an absolutely crucial issue with
regard to the realisation of the causal powers of such classes or
groupings. But it is also an issue which relates very directly to the
complex interrelations between capitalist relations of production and
civil society.

The reason for the last claim stems from the classic analysis of such
issues by Olson.[84] He maintains that it is not in fact correct to argue
that the absence of the kind of class conflicts that Marx expected
shows that Marx overestimated the strength of the rational choices
that workers will make. On the contrary, says Olson, it is precisely
because workers do act in terms of rational self-interest that class
actions and organisations are not more marked. This is because the
achievement of 'socialism' is a public good whose benefits accrue to
all workers whether or not they participate in the class struggle that
produced it. Class actions are thus a specific manifestation of the
general logic of collective action. Such action is very difficult to
produce and especially to sustain since the gains to be derived from it
are in the nature of public rather than private benefits. How do these
restrictions on the collective actions of social classes relate to the
issues already discussed?

Marx seems to have believed that individual selfishness and calculation were the principal human characteristics generated by
capitalist production, and that as the production became more and
more widespread so rational self-interest and utilitarian calculation
would also become more common. But this makes it *increasingly*

difficult to organise classes to overthrow capitalist relations of production, a fact which Marx generally overlooks. However, Marx's analysis and that of Olson concentrate upon the relations of production as the relevant entity. It is also necessary to consider the structuring of civil society and the interrelations between the two. Marx himself devoted relatively little attention to such considerations, maintaining that since it was in workers' long-term interests to organise on a class basis in order to overthrow capitalist relations of production, this is indeed what they would ultimately do. However, we now know that this is simply not the case. A further crucial step in the analysis is to consider whether a given civil society is structured in such a way that there are already established or potential bases for collective action which can in a sense dissipate the individual self-interest generated within the capitalist economy. Such collective bases are particularly important because, as Offe and Wiesenthal point out, the only way in which the organisations of labour can be systematically sustained is in fact through the existence of some kind of 'collective identity' which deflates the standards by which the costs of membership are assessed and where the lack of immediate success is seen as being of relatively minor significance.[85] Establishing and maintaining such identities depends upon the particular temporal and spatial structurings of civil society. Such structurings are crucial in providing some non-collective benefits from collective organisation which may thereby be contingently and precariously sustained.

I will now set out somewhat formally some conditions under which *class* may be the basis for collective action as opposed to either no such action or mobilisation in terms of some other organised grouping.[86] Thus the actions of individual agents are more likely to take a class character the more:

1. the spatially separated experiences of groups of individual agents can be interpreted as the experiences of a whole class – this depends upon particular 'local civil societies' being both class-divided and perceived as structured by class rather than by other significant social entities;
2. that there is a high rate of participation and of organised action within a range of spatially specific yet overlapping collectivities.[87] Potential collective agents are thus involved in a face-to-face contact within dense, mutiplex relations where there is a high certainty of the participation of others;[88]
3. that other collectivities within civil societies are organised in forms consistent with that of class rather than being in conflict with it –

this depends upon the organisation of popular-democratic politics locally and nationally;[89]

4. other kinds of gains and benefit which could be attained through non-class actions (such as higher incomes, lower prices, better conditions of work, etc.) are perceived to be, and are, unavailable – this will be more likely to result where social inequalities are, and are believed to be, produced by antagonistically structured *national* classes;

5. large numbers of individual agents located within different spatial locations conclude that class actions *can* be successful.

Conclusion

I have thus made some suggestions as to how we should conceptualise social relations once we understand that such relations are both temporally and spatially structured in a number of different ways. I have argued that the social world is comprised of space–time entities having causal powers which may or may not be realised depending on the patterns of spatial/temporal interdependence between such entities. In particular, I have suggested how 'capitalist relations of production' and 'civil society' are spatially structured. I have not considered the spatial structurings of other social entities; especially the state. Nor have I provided more than a cursory analysis of the significance of the temporal and spatial interdependencies between the different entities in relationship to the conditions for collection action. Nevertheless I would argue that the kinds of issue considered here represent important advances on the typical anthropocentricism of epistemological studies and the analysis of an unreconstructed 'here and now'.

Notes

I am grateful for the comments of Derek Gregory, Mike Savage, Don Shapiro and Alan Warde on earlier drafts of this chapter.

1. Within British sociology see Giddens (1981b) and Urry (1981c) as well as some of the literature relating to the 1982 British Sociological Association Conference on 'Core and Periphery'; and see the chapters by Saunders and Sayer in this volume.

2. Whitehead (1930) p. 33.
3. See Giddens (1979) p. 207, for a brief discussion of Goffman (1959) as well as Giddens in Chapter 12 of this volume.
4. See the discussion in Layder (1981) p. 70.
5. These are well-illustrated in some of the essays in Cronin and Schneer (1982) and Calhoun (1982).
6. On non-capitalist/capitalist societies, see especially Chapters 4 and 5 in Giddens (1981b) as well as Gross (1982) and Harvey in Chapter 7 of this volume. The analysis of spatial restructuring is found only on pp. 198–202 in Giddens (1981b). His concentration upon time rather than space is well indicated by the fact that the main writer discussed under 'The Time–Space Constitution of Social Systems' is Heidegger. In his *Being and Time* (1962), a phenomenological description of the transcendental self, the meaning of human existence is based on man's temporality, especially on an orientation to the future.
7. Braudel (1980) p. 52.
8. Quoted in Körner (1955) p. 33.
9. See Leibniz (1898) and Hinkfuss (1975).
10. A very clear defence of an absolutist position is to be found in Nerlich (1976). On Kant, see Garnett (1939) and Körner (1955).
11. See Nerlich (1976) pp. 6–7; and Kant (1961) pp. 65–101.
12. This is to be found in Kant (1968); see the discussion in Nerlich (1976) ch. 2.
13. This is amplified in Nerlich (1976).
14. See Smart (1963) pp. 132–5.
15. See Foucault (1970).
16. This is most clearly argued in Coward and Ellis (1977).
17. See Giddens (1981b) and the critique by Gross (1982).
18. Giddens (1981b) p. 38.
19. For a discussion of the thesis of 'spatial separation' in relationship to a positivist conception of science, see Sack (1974). Also see Williams, S. (1981).
20. See Jacques (1982) p. 33. Incidentally, I am not going to discuss here the relationship between time and space *per se* nor their measurement. Since Hinkfuss, for example, shows that it is possible to believe in absolute distances without therefore being committed to a fully-fledged absolutism, the connections between the two are not necessarily particularly strong (Hinkfuss, 1975, p. 59).
21. See Hinkfuss (1975) *passim*, on reductionism.
22. See Harré and Madden (1975); Bhaskar (1975); Bhaskar (1979) as well as Harré (1971) especially p. 248. And see Braudel (1980) for his objections to an 'event-ontology'.
23. This is further developed in Keat and Urry (1982) Postscript; and see Urry (1983b).
24. Marx (1973) p. 101. Also see Sayer (1979) on some of these methodological points.
25. Pred (1977) p. 208.
26. Pred (1981a) p. 10.
27. See Urry (1982) for further analysis.

46   *Social Relations, Space and Time*

28. See Giddens (1981b) ch. 7.
29. See Urry (1981c) for further elaboration of this argument.
30. Althusser and Balibar (1970) pp. 188–9.
31. Althusser and Balibar (1970) p. 99.
32. Smart (1963) ch. 7.
33. See Durkheim (1964) p. 260.
34. Bhaskar (1975) p. 119.
35. See Sayer (1979b) pp. 115–7; and see Hanson (1969).
36. See Bhaskar (1975) p. 182, and Keat and Urry (1982) Postscript.
37. See Berger (1971) pp. 35–41. Some of these issues are also considered in his work (with J. Mohr) on migrant workers in Europe (1975). See also the discussion in Soja and Hadjimichalis (1979).
38. Earman, pp. 288–92 (1970).
39. See Harré (1971) p. 241; although see Hinkfuss (1975) pp. 68–9.
40. Lucas (1973) pp. 40 and 42 and see Jacques (1982) pp. 28ff.
41. See Müller and Neusüss (1970); and my discussion in Urry (1981b) ch. 6.
42. Aspects of this are well brought-out in some of the papers edited by Carney, Hudson and Lewis (1980) especially pp. 29ff.
43. See my discussion of this in Urry (1981b) pp. 72ff.
44. Webber (1964) p. 63; and see Cox (1981b) as well as Joyce (1980) p. 94, who talks of the 'communal basis of deference, and the undoubted significance of the territorial, the local, and the immediate'. He suggests that the ecology of the factory town and of employer paternalism 'powerfully retarded the growth of impersonality, calculation, and class segregation ... Later nineteenth century industrial society developed in such a way as to make localism and territory more rather than less significant'.
45. This is very well demonstrated in Lebowitz (1980); and see my brief discussion of this in Urry (1982).
46. See Aumeeruddy, Lautier and Tortajada (1978) and my discussion in Urry (1981a) ch. 8.
47. See Lipietz (1980).
48. See Urry (1981b, c) pp. 466–8, as well as Massey (1978a).
49. Lipietz (1980b,) pp. 67–71.
50. For an introductory account see Carter (1981).
51. See Broadbent (1977) p. 108.
52. Broadbent (1977) p. 110. Walker (1978) p. 30, points out that in the USA there are no apparently 'autonomous' cities or regions – all cities thus function in this manner. Some further discussion of this can be found in Pahl (Chapter 11 of this volume).
53. Broadbent (1977) p. 115.
54. See Cawson and Saunders (1983) for a partly similar argument.
55. See Walker (1978) p. 32 and my brief elaboration in Urry (1981c) as well as longer discussion and justification in Cooke (1983a).
56. See Sayer (1982); and Williams, S. (1981) more generally on realism and space.
57. Sayer (1982) p. 79.
58. Massey (1978) p. 116; Sayer (1982) p. 80. See also their Chapters 2 and 4 in this volume.

59. See Sayer (1982) p. 80.
60. Also see Urry (1981a) and (1982).
61. See Fröbel, Heinrichs and Kreye (1980).
62. See Massey (1978a); Massey (1981); Massey and Meegan (1982); Walker and Storper (1981) from whom these are largely derived, at least implicitly.
63. See Aglietta (1979) ch. 3.
64. See Massey (1981).
65. See Fröbel, Heinrichs and Kreye (1980) on the new international division of labour especially in the German textiles and garments industries. For a trenchant critique, see Jacobson, Wickham and Wickham (1979).
66. See Murgatroyd and Urry (1983) on the effects of the development of new products, such as cheap carpets and plastic floor coverings, on the existing linoleum industry in the UK.
67. Sayer (1982) p. 80.
68. See Harvey (1975) p. 13, and Walker (1981) pp. 405–6; more generally see Harvey (1973) on his claim that if there is over-accumulation of productive capital then capital will move into the 'property circuit'.
69. See Walker (1981) especially pp. 396ff; and see Cox (1981).
70. See Ashton (1978) pp. 75–9.
71. See Agnew (1981) pp. 472–5; more generally see Blackburn, Green and Liff (1982).
72. Agnew (1981) p. 475.
73. See Bell and Newby (1976); Cox (1981b) pp. 435ff; and Roberts (1971) amongst countless sources.
74. R. Williams (1973) p. 104.
75. Seabrook (1978) pp. 80 and 95 present an interesting discussion of the recent collapse of working class 'community' through the development of 'commodity' relations. On the nineteenth century, see Joyce (1980) especially chs. 3 and 4. More generally, see Aglietta (1979).
76. Seabrook (1978) pp. 174–5; and see Cox (1981b) p. 435.
77. Paci (1981a) p. 211.
78. On employment, see Fothergill and Gudgin (1982); on population see OPCS Monitor (1982).
79. See Newby (1979) ch. 6.
80. See Abercrombie and Urry (1983) ch. 8.
81. See Cooke (Chapter 10 of this volume) and Paci (1981b) on the restructuring of the existing north Italian labour force through 'unnecessarily high' in-migration in the 1960s; and see Seabrook (1978) p. 51.
82. Some useful provisional comments can be found in Duncan and Goodwin (1982).
83. See the essays in Anderson, Duncan and Hudson (1983) for some examples of appropriate analyses.
84. See Olson (1985) especially pp. 105–10.
85. See Offe and Wiesenthal (1979).
86. See Calhoun (1982) p. 221. Elster suggests that collective action is more likely and more successful – (i) the more that actors *perceive* that there is some kind of contradiction characterising the society within which they are implicated; (ii) the lower the 'communicational distance' (a function

of geographical distance plus transport technology) between the members; (iii) the less the rate of *turnover* in group membership; and (iv) the greater the degree to which such contradictions are *irreversible*. See Elster (1978) pp. 134–50.

87. See Stark (1980).
88. See Calhoun (1982) p. 231. More generally he argues:

> This new working class was typically reformist because it could seek a variety of ends within capitalist society. In contrast, the very existence of the older, more traditional communities of artisans and other workers was threatened by capitalism ... Their communities, families, and sense of who, exactly, they were all came under attack. The newer working class derived this sort of fundamental sense of identity from capitalist society, and struggled over more transient, malleable, and optional goals.

89. See the discussion of this in Hall (1980).

4
The Difference that Space Makes

ANDREW SAYER

In what sense does space make a difference? How important is it and how should space and its supposed effects be understood? Can there be a general theory of space and society? What are the implications of space for social theory and practice? I shall try to answer these questions by using concepts from realist philosophy. I shall argue that despite the considerable growth of interest in space, the difference it makes and its possible implications for social theory are still widely misunderstood, largely because of a failure to distinguish abstract from concrete research. Yet even when clarified, space still presents both social research and actual practice with considerable difficulties, and these are discussed in the final section.

Before beginning the analysis of space it is necessary to say a few words about the realist philosophy on which the arguments are based.[1] First, I assume a distinction between abstract and concrete research. Abstractions involve concepts designed to refer to particular *one-sided* aspects of objects. Normally, our objects of study are many-sided or 'concrete'; to be understood, the many constitutive elements isolated by abstractions need to be synthesised.[2] In this sense, 'abstract' certainly does not mean 'vague' and it is assumed that abstractions can refer to real objects no less than concrete concepts, that is, abstract need not mean 'lacking reference to a real object'. However, as we shall see, there are at least some widely-used abstractions which do not have actual objects. Everyday thought uses both abstract and concrete concepts but these are usually unexamined and tend to characterise complex and concrete wholes such as 'cities' as simple unities.

Second, realism pays considerable attention to the nature of relations. One important distinction is that between necessary and contingent relations. In the former the nature of the relata depends on the relation; in the latter it is independent of the relation. For example, necessarily related objects like husband and wife can only exist as such through their relation: one cannot exist without the other. There are also necessary conditions for the existence and reproduction of objects and relations; the institution of marriage is a necessary condition for the occurrence of weddings. On the other hand patriarchy can exist independently of capitalist social relations and hence their relation is said to be contingent, although some particular forms of either may become interdependent. When necessity in the world is discovered, we can make strong theoretical claims about it, by using abstractions to isolate necessity from the web of contingencies in which it usually exists. Where relations or conditions are contingent (that is, neither necessary nor impossible) abstract theory must remain agnostic about their form on any particular occasion or at least make claims about what might happen in them conditional upon an assumption about their existence. For example, it is contingent where industrial capital is located and it can involve itself in the production of an enormous variety of commodities, but if it happens (contingently) to be involved in producing a fixed resource such as coal (conditional statement) then obviously its location is constrained.

A third aspect of the realist approach adopted here concerns causation. Objects are understood to possess causal powers and liabilities to do or suffer certain things by virtue of their structure and composition, but whether these powers or liabilities are activated depends on contingently related conditions. For example, labour power is a causal power necessarily possessed by people by virtue of their physical and mental structure, but whether and with what effects this power is exercised depends on contingently-related conditions such as the availability of employment. It follows from the previous point that abstract theory can recognise the powers or liabilities as necessary properties of their objects but can only remain agnostic or make conditional statements about what actually happens in concrete circumstances. To explain the latter, concrete research is needed which discovers the actual (contingent) conditions in which the causal mechanisms of interest are located.

These concepts are essential for understanding the difference that space makes.

The difference that space makes

It seems obvious enough that space makes a difference. We have only to reflect upon the most mundane of our activities to recognise its effect: that things must be in the right place if we are to use them or be affected by them is commonsense. Yet, geographers apart, few social scientists have paid any attention to space and the difference is supposedly makes. Recent work on space by human geographers has reached the conclusion that space can only be understood in terms of the objects and processes that constitute it, with the implication that the study of space must be rooted in social theory. In the case of Marxist theory, there have been re-readings or plunderings of Marx's works in search of insights about space.[3] These have generated the inaccurate impression that Marx had a great deal to say about space. In fact, as Saunders has observed, neither Marx, Durkheim nor Weber paid more than passing attention to space.[4] I want to argue that while space makes a difference, these and other social theorists have been largely justified in giving it so little attention in their abstract theoretical work, although the position with regard to concrete research is quite different. This may seem a surprising combination of ideas, at least until we look more closely at the meaning of 'space'.

Much has been written on this in geography and although a virtual consensus about concepts of space has emerged it will be argued that it is not yet a satisfactory one.[5] The clarification of its meaning is a metaphysical problem. Like many such problems, it involves a term which is both thoroughly familiar and apparently unproblematic, and yet mysterious: explications of the term are necessary to distinguish legitimate from confused uses, but they will inevitably produce a possibly infuriating mixture of insights and leaden banalities. Whatever the popular hostility to this kind of discussion, the real prisoners of metaphysics are those who think they do not need it!

The usual discussions that have taken place in geography distinguish between an absolute concept in which space is empty and a relative concept in which space only exists where it is constituted by matter. The absolute view is implicit in commonsense, but is incoherent because 'what is empty is nothing, and what is nothing cannot be',[6] and because nothingness is implied to be capable of having an effect – as when we speak of the 'friction of distance' or the 'effect of space'. Terms such as these are really shorthand for frictions between particular substances which constitute space, and as we know from natural science, the coefficient of friction varies from substance to substance.[7]

However, what is often overlooked by advocates of the relative concept is that while space is constituted by objects it is not reducible to them. Following Harré,[8] the subtleties of the relative concept can

be explained by considering the spatial relations between the following sets of letters

A   B   C

P   Q   R

The spatial relations of B to A and C, and Q to P and R are exactly
equivalent: swapping B with Q would not change this spatial relation
of 'between-ness', though depending on what kind of things the
letters represent, the moves might trigger off or block certain causal
mechanisms possessed by those objects. *In other words, although
space can only exist in and through objects, it is independent of the
particular* **types** *of object present.* It is this point on which most of the
rest of the arguments of the paper depend. And it is this independence
of spatial relations from the type of objects composing it that gives the
absolute concept of space a certain plausibility in commonsense
thinking. (We must not only criticise inadequate concepts but also
show why they are held.)

Now in already speaking of 'spatial relations' I am abstracting
form from content. This is obviously not an abstraction which can be
objectified: 'space-as-such', 'form' or 'spatial relations' are literally
contentless abstractions. Matter *always* necessarily has spatial exten-
tion and spatial relations only exist through objects, of whatever
kind. To the best of our knowledge, empty space or spaceless matter
are physical impossibilities. Despite this, as Sack notes, we repeatedly
abstract form from content or more commonly, content from form.[9]

Since the idea of understanding what happens in the world in
abstraction from its content is manifestly absurd, there can be no
independent 'science of space' as some geographers used to believe.
The spatial relation of between-ness cannot, of itself, be said to have
any effects or make any difference. Yet *depending on the nature of the
constituents*, their spatial relations may make a crucial difference, as
for example in the case of one spatial relation with the walls of a
prison. So *space makes a difference, but only in terms of the particular
causal powers and liabilities constituting it.* Conversely, what kind of
effects are produced by causal mechanisms depends *inter alia* on the
form of the conditions in which they are situated.

However, it is common to separate space and substance and speak
of the effects or uses of space – as if it were a thing existing independently of objects. This is partly a problem of the deceptive structure of
our language which uses separate spatial and temporal and process
categories to refer to what are actually inseparable aspects. Given this

redundancy in our language, we frequently refer to the whole by reference to just one of the three internally-related aspects. Although this practice is common enough and rarely causes any problems in everyday life it can lead to confusion in providing theoretical explanations. Consider examples such as: 'multinationals have used space to their advantage' or 'space can provide a barrier to accumulation'. Are these dangerously misleading forms of expression or a harmless shorthand which avoids clumsy language such as 'the particular temporal and spatial distribution of relevant processes can provide a barrier to accumulation'? Strictly speaking it is possible and indeed necessary to interpret such statements in terms of the particular kinds of process consitituting the spatially (and temporarily) extended systems. Because 'space', 'time' and 'process' are contentless abstractions, it is easy to be misled into obscuring the specific causes of the effects they are supposed to explain.

The multinational learns how to exploit not space but the variety of different kinds of material and social environments at different times and places: raw materials here, affluent markets there, cheap labour here, managerial labour there, and so on. Even when it is pointed out that these must be accessible to the firm, that is, 'be in the right place', the spatial relation involved, expressed as a distance, is really a surrogate for the energy and time expended in travelling or exchanging information between places by a specific mode of transport and across a 'space' consitituted by particular kinds of matter – oceans, roads, or whatever. Our descriptions of the world would indeed be clumsy if we refused ever to use 'space' and cognate terms as surrogates for its constituents. As long as we remember that they are surrogates such usages need not cause any problems.

Now in geography, critiques of absolute space have become so common that the accusation of spatial fetishism – of attributing to 'pure space' what is due to its constituents – no longer arouses any interest. Nevertheless, in the work of the accusers one often finds references to the effects of space as if it were a thing, as in 'the political economy of space'. Is this a case of the pot calling the kettle black or only an apparent fetishism of space? To answer this we must turn to the converse of the problem: if we cannot abstract space from its content and hope to say anything about the world, can we abstract content from form and hence have an aspatial science?

The answer depends on the kind of research involved – in particular whether it is abstract or concrete. It will be recalled that abstract research is concerned with structures (sets of internally or necessarily related objects or practices) and with the causal powers and liabilities necessarily possessed by objects in virtue of their nature. As it is contingent whether and how these are exercised (since it is affected by contingent conditions) concrete empirical research is needed to determine the actual *effects* of the causal powers.

Abstract social theory need only consider space insofar as *necessary* properties of objects are involved, and this does not amount to very much. It must acknowledge that all matter has spatial extension and hence that processes do not take place on the head of a pin and that no two objects can occupy the same (relative) place at the same time. So, for example, in an abstract discussion of rent we can note that even if people do not need land for its soil or minerals, they need it as room for their spatially-extended activities and that perhaps also they need it to be accessible to certain other objects if they are to do certain things. Things then might be taken as necessary conditions and therefore as material for abstract theory. From this many seem to have concluded that social theory can and should be spatial.

But note just how little this says about actual spatial forms. To observe that capital must be accessible to property-less workers says very little about the actual spatial form of labour markets, which of course is not surprising, given the contingent nature of this form. Even where objects necessarily have certain spatial forms – as in the linearity of many types of communication medium – this still leaves room for enormous contingent variety, and the spatial form of the conditions in which such objects exist, for example, settlement patterns, is also contingent. Hence, while it is important for abstract theory to be aware of the existence of space, the claims that can be made about it are inevitably rather indifferent ones, such as Anthony Giddens' 'distanciation' and 'time–space edges'.[10] That the coalescence and integration of communities and economies which were formerly independent produces an increased 'distanciation' of actors and institutions from one another is an important feature of capitalist societies, as we shall see later. But the actual nature of the difference that this makes can again only be specified further by empirical research on concrete instances. In other words, concepts such as 'distanciation' have a useful theoretical or meta-theoretical role but they do not and should not be expected to say much about concrete spatial forms.

Even where social theory deals with objects whose spatial form has been deliberately arranged so as to take advantage of certain properties of the objects, for example, new towns, the variety of possible concrete forms is still considerable. As with any manipulation of nature, this involves exploiting contingency so that certain effects are realised. Abstract social science cannot ignore the fact that the possibilities and problems of reproducing and transforming social forms depends on the integration of their elements in space–time and several theorists have drawn attention to this in their abstract work. Here I am including the many – perhaps all – types of communication or symbolic interaction which rely on symbols and contexts having a particular spatio-temporal form for their meaning to be successfully communicated. Yet again, apart from some particularly ritualised activities, such as certain religious or art forms, there is usually a degree of flexibility in the spatio-temporal context within which the communication can still be successfully interpreted as intended. However, the conduct of successful communicative interation is not a mechanical process. Even the most routine social actions are conducted in space–time in the face of numerous contingent factors and their successful completion is a skilled achievement which is always at risk from contingent events.[11]

Now some social theories attempt to go beyond the analysis of structures and their causal powers to the postulation, and in some cases, calculation of their possible effects. This is often the aim of approaches using formal, predictive modelling. To do this assumptions have to be made about the state of the contingent relations holding between objects which affect the results of the activation of causal mechanisms. The most formal way of doing this is by assuming some sort of 'closed system', that is a system in which (i) the objects of interest do not undergo qualitative change (for example, technological change in economic systems) and (ii) the relations between objects and their conditions are constant.[12] Under such circumstances, mechanisms will produce regularities in events. In natural science, closed systems often either exist spontaneously or are created in experiments. The contingencies of spatial form are rendered constant except where they concern spatial relations between objects which do not causally interact. For example, an experiment on the mechanics of levers or the periodicity of a pendulum must carefully control for the spatial extension of the relevant objects, but it makes no difference (gravitational variations excepted) whether it is conducted in London or Tokyo. This characteristic is encapsulated in what Harré terms the 'principle of spatial indifference'[13] and presumably an equivalent principle of 'temporal indifference' could be coined. (Note: there is no contradiction between the former principle and the idea that space makes a difference, for the principle concerns the position of mechanisms with respect to conditions with which they do not happen to interact. If there is a major spatial variation in a condition which *does* affect the outcome of the experiment – for example, a strong anomaly in the earth's gravitational field in the pendulum experiment – then space will make a difference in the sense outlined above. Otherwise, the position of the experiment within some arbitrary system of co-ordinates is irrelevant.) Social systems are open because of the capacity of people to change their own nature and their environment; hence closed system experiments are impossible. Theorists therefore have to rely upon 'thought-experiments' using models whose assumptions ensure that the hypothetical system is closed, for example, equilibrium assumptions in economic and isotropic plains in geography.

In many cases the models are both spaceless and timeless. Insofar as they therefore deny *necessary* features of behaviour, they can only be of interest as fictions. The difference that spatial form makes can be assessed using models only by assuming that certain (contingent) spatial relations have a particular configuration – for example, the uniform distribution of purchasing power in Löschian models of the space economy.[14] Such models provide striking demonstrations of the difference that space can make; for example, the aspatial perfect competition model becomes a model of spatial monopolies. To make such models dynamic one must again incorporate assumptions about the form of sequences of contingently related events, such as a particular rate of growth. Estimating the difference that space and time make in such thought-experiments therefore requires prior assumptions about the space–time patterns of causal powers.[15] In other words, the modeller has to determine in advance precisely those circumstances which are contingent and relevant to the processes of interest.

A less formal and more approximate way of speculating on possible effects of mechanisms in concrete systems as they are mediated by spatial form, involves imagining a number of possible configurations and making conditional statements about results. For example, it could be hypothesised that in a competitive capitalist system, firms which are located in regions having cheaper than average labour power will be able to delay automation longer than those in regions with scarce and expensive labour power. David Harvey's book, *The Limits to Capital*,[16] contains many such conditional statements. Given the difficulty of anticipating the range of possible concrete configurations of social systems such theorising often underestimates the range of possible outcomes. However, it is certainly useful to consult this kind of work before conducting empirical research.

A further characteristic of social systems which limits the effectiveness of abstract theory in anticipating the difference that space makes might be termed 'polyvalency'.[17] People, as self-interpreting beings able to monitor their situations and learn from them, have an exceptionally wide and volatile range of causal liabilities. As our understanding of the world changes we become susceptible to new influences. As pendulums learn nothing from what we do to them, their behaviour stands in a fixed relation to particular conditions; the difference that spatial form makes is constant and the principle of spatial indifference holds. But people can come to be influenced by their contexts (which always have particular spatial forms) in *new* ways, so that the difference that space makes is never entirely constant and the principle of spatial indifference has less scope. This does not mean that all is chaos or that there is no hope of understanding the changing effects of form, for unlike the movement of pendulums, actions can be done for reasons whose meaning can be understood: social scientists have an internal access to their objects of study which is not available to their counterparts in natural science. Nevertheless, as we shall see, polyvalency is enormously important in accounting for the difficulties experienced by concrete social research.

Misconceptions of space

Let us now look a little further at some of the misconceptions of space common among theorists – often Marxists – who claim to be using a concept of relative space. As might be expected from the foregoing argument, these are often associated with misunderstandings of the roles of abstract and concrete research.

Perhaps the most common error is the implicit assumption that because space only exists where it is constituted by objects, it is wholly reducible to them. Thus, Castells, for example, sprinkled his book, *The Urban Question*, with references to 'space' and 'urban space' but these turned out to concern the constituent elements of urbanism, classified and analysed in abstraction from the spatial forms which they constituted, so in fact despite appearances, very little was actually said about space.[18] In view of our earlier comments on abstract theory this might be expected but Castells also seemed to assume mistakenly that abstract theory could pre-empt or capture the specificities of concrete systems without empirical research, in the manner of what I have termed elsewhere 'pseudo-concrete research'.[19]

Some theorists, such as Lefebvre, appear to place considerable explanatory weight on space, arguing that urbanism and space modify the relations of production and are indispensable for understanding capitalist society.[20] An uncharitable interpretation of this view is that it is guilty of spatial fetishism. More charitably, it could be taken as emphasising the importance of the concrete, which always has a particular spatial form, as against the abstract. While the latter is essential for understanding the former, it can say very little about the difference that space makes, precisely because it abstracts from the contingencies of form. However, contemporary urbanism defies definition in terms of spatial form. In *everyday* usages, terms like 'city' and 'town' are unproblematic and convey clear spatial images of built-up areas, and hence the form is intrinsic to the definition: in other words, it is analytic. Yet theoretical analyses of capitalist urbanisation have shown that there is no material basis for this definition; the relations and activities found in such areas are not unique to them and so what seems analytic and necessary in everyday thought is shown to be synthetic and contingent by theory.[21] While form does make a difference to the working of social processes, according to Saunders, it was not considered by Durkheim, Weber or Marx to be a fundamental one which affected the basic structures and mechanisms isolated by abstract theory; capitalist relations of production, for example, could be reproduced in a vast variety of spatial forms. Not surprisingly, the study of contemporary urbanism now finds itself without an object that can be identified with everyday uses of urban terminology, and Saunders' agenda for 'urban sociology' makes no pretence at a connection with spatial concepts of the urban.[22]

Another type of error, common among self-styled 'dialecticians' is contained in the following argument:

1. Space – particularly in the sense of territory – is not just something existing outside and prior to society, but something produced *by* society.
2. The spatial is therefore social.

Spot the *non-sequitur*! This is usually coupled with the slide from the recognition of the constituents of space to the reduction of space to those constituents, only this time the constituents are further reduced to just those which are socially produced, arbitrarily ignoring its non-social constituents. The spatial is *partly* constituted by the social, but it is reducible neither to natural nor social constituents. Certainly spatial structures may have 'roots in production and class relations' as Soja puts it, but there are plenty of other possible constituents – natural and social – of space.[23] (Note that the fact that natural phenomena are only intelligible to us through social media has nothing to do with the question of their production, which is independent of social phenomena.)

The reduction of space to its constituents can be a fertile source of confusion. Let us take two examples. The first is from Castells' *The Urban Question*:

> Space is a material product, in relation with other material elements [1] – among others, men, [sic] who themselves enter into particular social relations, which give to space (and to other elements of the combination) a form, a function, a social significa-tion. It is not, therefore, a mere occasion for the deployment of social structure, but a concrete expression of each historical ensem-ble in which a society is specified. It is a question, then of establish-ing, in the same way as for any other real object [2], the structural and conjunctural laws that govern its existence and transforma-tion, and the specificity of its articulation with the other elements of a historical reality [3]. This means that there is no theory of space that is not an integral part of a general social theory, even an implicit one [4].[24]

Let us examine this difficult passage more closely. To use the term 'space' is to use a contentless abstraction, and hence this description of space as a material product [1] or a real object [2] is confusing especially where as in [1] and [3] it is treated as equivalent to elements such as 'men'. There are *no* structural laws 'that govern . . . [the] . . . existence and transformation' of *space as such*, only the elements that constitute space. The last sentence of the quotation [4] can be taken in two ways: either that a general social theory should be able to specify, in advance, the form (including the spatial form) of concrete systems; or merely that in referring to objects which have spatial extension, any general social theory is implicitly spatial. Only the latter interpretation is tenable; as already noted, actual concrete forms cannot be anticipated purely by reference to the implicit spatial dimension of abstract theory but must be discovered through empirical investigation.

The second example of sloppy statements typified by much of the literature on space is from Lefebvre:

> Space is not a scientific object removed from ideology and politics; it has always been political and strategic . . . Space is political and ideological. It is a product literally filled with ideologies.[25]

Note how space appears to mean 'territory', and once this is one-sidedly reduced to its political and ideological significance, we begin to forget space in the sense of form or configuration altogether, and the difference between this kind of analysis and unashamedly aspatial theory diminishes.

As Sack has shown, we continually separate and recombine space and substance in our thinking, but errors are often introduced through an unsuccessful recombination. For example, it is popular to discuss relations between developed and underdeveloped regions in terms of 'centre and periphery'. Developed and underdeveloped regions must have *some* spatial form but it does not have to be one of centre and periphery, even loosely interpreted. Once we start to think of the former in terms of the latter *contingent* spatial forms and hence use them as surrogates for economic relations, some of which may be necessary, confusion and error enter, for it becomes difficult to see that the spatially peripheral is not necessarily functionally peripheral, nor the spatially central, functionally central. Space and process in this case cannot be successfully recombined at this level.

Crude separations and recombinations of space and substance are even more common in everyday thinking as when people from the North of England characterise the South-east as middle class and refuse to believe that a town like Tunbridge Wells could have any working-class people. The appropriate spatial unit for conceptualising class is people, not towns or regions.

In the preceding sections I have argued that the spatial specificity of abstract theory differs markedly from that of research on concrete systems and that insofar as space makes a difference to the latter, concrete research must take spatial form into account even if it is not directly interested in it. While I have been concerned to illustrate some common errors in the treatment of space I do not want to underestimate the genuine difficulties of conducting concrete (and hence spatial) research even where such errors are avoided. Too often philosophical critiques give the impression that all difficulties will evaporate as soon as certain errors are removed; in my view philosophy should help to explain why some difficulties persist.

Problems of dealing with space

One source of difficulty in concrete research arises from the fact that it is often simply not *feasible* to achieve a perfect recombination of space and substance. Consider the example of research on labour markets. We cannot expect to make much sense of the pattern of events in such systems if we abstract from the spatial relations between job-seekers and job-vacancies, and aggregate up all the local area statistics into a national total as if there were a single, homogeneous, national market, located on the head of a pin. In a system as open as this (in the sense defined earlier) there are likely to be few intelligible links between aggregate quantitative relations and actual causal interactions; hence the usual mismatches between numbers of vacancies and unemployed. However, it would hardly be feasible to take into account spatial form as it concerns each pair of job-seekers and relevant vacancies. The usual compromise solution is to break down the national data into fairly discrete labour market areas, but this is only an approximate way of handling the effect of the spatial form of the phenomena of interest. Given that social systems are so heterogenous and open, it is small wonder that enduring empirical regularities are not found, despite the hopes of positivist approaches.

Empirical studies which abstract from space can hardly be called concrete because they conceal the actual forms of combination of system elements. To those habituated to this kind of research, spatial variations are little more than deviations from the norm and only of interest as such; some even treat the deviations as somehow 'less real' than the norm. Yet it is of course the norm or average which is the statistical fiction; the individual voter, for example, however unusual, is certainly no less real than the average voter.

But if there is a problem of explanation for single, concrete, open social systems such as labour markets, the problem is all the greater in studies which attempt to synthesise the concrete effects of the interaction of many systems, such as the history of the industrial revolution, or the nature of regional change. Researchers in such fields are faced with a choice of relying upon aggregates and averages which describe the whole system but occlude causality by ignoring spatial form or conducting studies which allow concrete analysis and causal explanation of limited parts of the subject but which leave substantial areas uncovered. In practice, through the method termed by some historians 'colligation', they tend to try to combine elements of both with abstract theory: on the one hand the broad generalisations which are descriptively comprehensive but explanatorily weak; on the other the local or sectoral case studies are explanatorily more comprehensive but limited in their coverage, it being rarely possible to do or find more than a few of them. So for example, accounts of the industrial revolution in Britain typically combine system-wide descriptive generalisations about demographic and economic change while references to case studies show how particular class structures and economic mechanisms produced specific concrete effects under specific conditions in various parts of the system. This is not simply a choice between scales of study or degree of detail; it concerns whether or not we take into account form and hence do concrete research. Even where the research is focussed on a particular spatial unit such as a country, we have to switch repeatedly between a number of different spatial scales, each of which is appropriate to or congruent with a particular object, be it the empire, a region or a factory. Inevitably, reading such studies invariably leaves us with queries about whether the examples and particular local concrete studies were 'representative' of the whole, and whether any inferences about individuals or parts of the system can be drawn from the aggregate descriptive generalisations without falling foul of the ecological fallacy. These are genuine practical problems of social research and they derive not from the immaturity of social science but from the nature of its object; and when we consider the latter, the expectations of those who believe we should emulate experiemental natural science seem all the more absurd.[26]

The tendency to separate space and substance, only to fail to recombine them adequately, is also, as Sack points out, a common source of *practical* problems, particularly for organisations which attempt to co-ordinate activities at different times and places. For example, the British government abstracts from space in most of its expenditures, but then has to allocate other expenditures to particular places, most obviously in its regional policy. Yet the spatial effects of supposedly non-spatial policies, such as those concerning nationalised industries and defence spending, can contradict and outweigh those which come under the 'spatial' heading of regional expenditure.

But again, as Sack notes, the policies of regionally-based organisations such as the Welsh Development Agency 'are no more or less
spatial than those of other jurisdictions. They are simply local'.[27]
Moreover, 'aiding the regions' invariably means aiding just some of
the interests in the regions, particularly those of capital, rather than
the mythical entity of 'the region'.[28] Similarly with area-based
policies such as Educational Priority Areas: having allocated most
expenditure to education without regard for location, the government then went to the opposite extreme of designating certain *areas*
(not particular schools) for special attention. These were an excellent
example of an inadequate recombination of space and substance
because the areas internalised some quite privileged schools and
pupils and in centring on spatial concentrations of educational deprivation only managed to pick up a minority of the national total, as
educationally-deprived children were widely dispersed across the
country.

These are genuine organisational problems, and solutions are not
easy to prescribe, still less to implement. A possible, though difficult
remedy suggested in the Labour Party's *Alternative Regional Strategy*
is to consider the spatial implications of *all* expenditures, and not just
those which happen to fall under the jurisdictions of a subset of
localities, such as Development Areas.[29]

A further case requiring careful integration of space and substance
is the design of democratic political structures, which can scarcely
expect to conform to the tidy hierarchies – whether controlled from
above or below – of abstract political theory. Given the interdependencies between interests and activities operating at vastly different
scales (for example, the interests of capital, the nation state, consumers and workers) more democratic forms of economic and
political organisation are bound to be more rather than less complex
than those we have now.[30]

One of the most difficult subjects in social science and one where
space makes a difference is the study of consciousness and culture in
society. If our consciousness is shaped by the particular unique
material circumstances in which we live then it should vary spatially
with these conditions. But matters are not as simple as this for we can
only interpret our surroundings through an available language and
range of concepts. To a certain extent these are *common* to a range of
different groups at different times and places, indeed the whole
function of communication is to span such differences, for without

differences in experience to share, communication is redundant. So the determination of consciousness is not purely local. This problem is central to cultural analysis, but given the limited range of groups who tend to be chosen for study, the prevalence of stereotypes and the tendency to generalise about 'working-class culture' on the basis of very small numbers of local studies I wonder if it is taken seriously enough.

There is a further problem here concerning the differences between lay-persons' consciousness and that of social theorists. The former is shaped by the particular concrete circumstances or locales in which individuals live, but the understanding they have is nevertheless not generally a concrete one, for concrete objects tend to be taken superficially, as simple; in other words the content of lay understanding does not correspond to its determinants. In real life we live in conjunctures whose boundaries are arbitrary; they haphazardly cut across structures and causal relations, and unless we devote considerable energy to their understanding, we only disentangle such conjunctures sufficiently for us to cope with everyday tasks. As theorists however, we seek to understand the world by making rational abstractions which isolate unified objects, structures or groups, and we try to conduct concrete research by starting from such abstractions. Now as we have seen, abstract theory largely abstracts from spatial form and so our consciousness as theorists is less parochial (at least in some respects!) than that of the lay-person. However, it is an occupational hazard of social science that we forget this difference and project our own way of interpreting the world onto those we study and underestimate local variations. The result is that, as in the recent British election, we are repeatedly surprised by the actual content of political (or other) consciousness.

Note that I am *not* saying that the theorist's understanding is abstract and that of the lay-person concrete. The theorist can use abstractions to understand the concrete. The lay-person could be said to use abstractions in conceptualising complex objects in a simple, one-sided fashion, but these are rarely examined abstractions as hence are frequently chaotic. Although they refer to objects which are concrete, they rarely understand them concretely. So while the lay-person's consciousness is probably more influenced by local circumstances, theorists have more conceptual resources for understanding those circumstances, provided they take into account the difference that form makes.

Conclusion

The recent interest in space and social theory should not allow us to overlook the questions of how social theory has managed to pay space scant attention without too much trouble and how those theorists who have been preoccupied with space have not been able to say very much about it. However, in the sphere of concrete studies, both the difficulty of such research and its poor record in developing explanations owes a great deal to the failure to consider spatial form.

Notes

1. Sayer (1981).
2. This interpretation of the concrete is derived from Marx's oft-quoted statement 'The concrete concept is concrete because it is a synthesis of many determinations, thus representing the unity of diverse aspects', in the *Grundrisse*: Marx (1973) p. 101.
3. e.g. Harvey (1982) is in part such a re-reading.
4. Saunders (1981).
5. Perhaps the best of this literature are Blaut (1961) and Sack (1980) pp. 55–78, although the latter is marred by a failure to present a consistent use of realistic philisophy.
6. Blaut (1961).
7. Sack (1973).
8. Harré (1971); Sack (1980).
9. Sack (1980).
10. Giddens (1981b).
11. See Bourdieu (1977).
12. Bhaskar (1975).
13. Harré (1970).
14. Lösch (1954).
15. Cf. Sack's discussions of non-congruent or contiguous laws in Sack (1980) pp. 66ff.
16. Harvey (1982).
17. Sayer (1984).
18. Castells (1977).
19. Sayer (1979).
20. Lefebvre (1976a).
21. See Sayer (1984).
22. Saunders (1981).
23. Soja (1980).
24. Castells (1977) p. 115. I do not know what Castells means by 'conjunctural laws'.
25. Lefebvre (1976b).

26. Sayer (1984).
27. Sack (1980) p. 18.
28. Pickvance (1981).
29. Labour Party Parliamentary Spokesmans Working Group (1980).
30. Cf. Williams (1979); (1982).

5
Space, the City and Urban Sociology

PETER SAUNDERS

All social activity is situated in time and space. As a number of writers have recently suggested,[1] this means not simply that all human activity occurs in particular places at particular times – an assertion described by Giddens as 'banal and uninstructive'[2] – but that where and when such activity occurs is important in explaining and understanding it.

It is important to remember that the significance of time and space in the explanation of social phenomena has long been recognised in social science. Political geographers, for example, have for many years been interested in analysing the importance of place in influencing voting behaviour and have shown that manual workers living in predominantly middle-class areas tend to be more conservative in their voting than those who live in working-class areas. Work by sociologists on class imagery has similarly demonstrated the significance of the local environment in sustaining deferential, proletarianised or privatised images of society. More recently, research on the 'local state' has pointed to the way in which different local histories have given rise to different local political cultures which can help to explain why local authorities in some areas adopt radical programmes (for example, as in the so-called 'Socialist Republic of South Yorkshire') while those in other areas do not. Clearly time and space have not been ignored by social science.[3]

Despite this, there has begun to emerge in recent years a new orthodoxy which holds that sociologists 'have paid insufficient attention to spatial variations in social phenomena',[4] and even that time and space should be 'incorporated into the centre of social theory'.[5] In this view it is not enough simply to take account of variations in spatial and temporal context through historical and comparative analyses of social phenomena. Rather, it is argued that a concern with variations in time and space lies at the very heart of the sociological enterprise.

This argument has the further implication that, if sociology is to be centrally concerned with the spatial dimension of human activity, then its core substantive concern will be on spatially-defined units of social organisation. Put another way, if space is central to social theory, then the study of different socio-spatial arrangements – villages, towns, cities – would appear to be fundamental to social analysis. This is an implication which Giddens at least is happy to follow, for he argues that the city constitutes the core object of concern for sociology and that urban sociology lies at the very heart of the discipline:

> The city cannot be regarded as merely incidental to social theory but belongs at its very core. Similarly, 'urban sociology' is more than just one branch of sociology among others – it stands at the heart of some of the most fundamental problems of general sociological interest.[6]

Not unnaturally, many 'urban' sociologists, 'urban' geographers and other academics with a specialist 'urban' interest have begun to seize upon this straw offered by Giddens. This is because after years of crippling uncertainty about whether there is anything specific about 'urban' studies and anything of any sociological importance about cities, they are now informed by one of our generation's leading social theorists that urban sociology and its object of study – the city – lie at the heart of what the social sciences are all about! Little wonder, then, that on the conference circuit, volume one of Giddens's *A Contemporary Critique of Historical Materialism* seems to be replacing Castells's *The Urban Question* as the book which every paper needs to cite.

It has often been said that it is a sad sign of the immaturity of sociology and related disciplines that it is so easily swayed by fickle academic fads and fashions. At least since the breakdown of the functionalist hegemony of the 1950s, sociology has lurched from one orthodoxy to another – phenomenological sociology, critical theory, structuralist Marxism, humanist Marxism, and so on – without ever dwelling long enough with any one of these approaches to develop a systematic theoretical and empirical research programme.[7] The same may be said of that specific area of the social sciences relating to 'urban studies'. Here, in the space of just fifteen years or so, the orthodox intellectual position has swung violently away from a view of space and the city as important, to a dismissal of such work as 'ideological' and now, in the work of Giddens and others, a reassertion, not simply of the importance of the city and spatial forms, but of their centrality to social science.

Perhaps, before joyously leaping on to this latest bandwagon which is about to start to roll, we should pause and take stock. In particular, we need to ask whether the arguments now being advanced by Giddens and others actually meet, overcome and go beyond the objections which have been raised over the past ten years or so to the project of urban sociology as the study of the city and spatial forms. It is my assertion that they do not. Indeed, I believe that Giddens's work itself serves rather to reinforce than to undermine the argument that in the contemporary period, a sociology constituted around the study of specific spatial forms such as the city cannot be sustained.

The problem: a sub-discipline in search of an object of study

Urban sociology has existed as an institutionalised sub-discipline within western academic sociology, with its own professorial chairs, specialist journals and foci of debate and argument, for the best part of the twentieth century. For most of this period, it has been assumed or asserted that urban sociology has been constituted by its distinctive object of study – the city – just as other areas of the discipline have delineated their specific concerns as, for example, the family (sociology of the family), the firm (industrial sociology), the state (political sociology), and so on. However, it has also been generally recognised that these other areas of the discipline are founded, not simply on the identification of a particular empirical object of study (families, firms, nation-states), but more especially on the study of specific aspects of social relations which are situated within these 'objects' (for example, relations between wives and husbands or parents and children within the family; relations between workers and management within the firm; relations between parties, pressure groups and civil service within the nation-state; and so on). Having identified as its object of study the city, the task for urban sociology has therefore been in addition to specify the peculiar sets of social relations or social processes which are situated within cities.

As I have suggested in much greater detail elsewhere,[8] there have been four main attempts over the past seventy years to identify a particular type of social relationship or social process as distinctive to social life in cities. All four attempts have failed, although all four have bequeathed some interesting and useful legacies in the process. The fact that they have failed suggests that the attempt to relate particular social processes to particular spatial forms, and thereby to establish a rationale for an 'urban' sociology concerned with the study of cities, may be futile. This futility stems from the fact that the city has ceased to represent a significant social unit of organisation in advanced industrial societies. Just as a sociology of the tribe is likely to appear oddly anachronistic in modern industrial societies where tribes have long since been transcended as units of social organisation, so too does a sociology of the city.

The first attempt: the city as an ecological community

The first, and perhaps still most systematic,[9] attempt to develop a sociological theory of the city was that by Robert Park and his associates at the University of Chicago between the wars. For Park,[10] urban analysis was to take as its object of enquiry the 'ecological community' which, in contrast to 'society', was characterised by an unconscious process through which human beings were engaged in a 'biotic' struggle for existence resulting in a functional adaptation between themselves and their environment. Human ecology was in this way constituted as the study of a basic process (competition) and its unintended effects (functional adaptation).

From the outset, however, there was in Park's work an uneasy tension between his concern with biotic competition as a process and his concern with the city as an object. This tension was manifested in a marked ambiguity about whether human ecology was a new and separate discipline within the social sciences with its own theoretical concerns with competition and adaptation, or whether it was simply a branch of sociology distinguished by its empirical interest in cities.[11] The problem, in short, was whether human ecology was to be defined in terms of its interest in a process (biotic struggle) or an object (the city) for it was clear from very early on that the two were not complementary.

The fundamental tension between these two themes emerged as work in the ecological tradition progressed. If human ecology was to be understood as a theory of the city and was thus to be defined in terms of the city as an object of enquiry, then there seemed no justification for its exclusive theoretical focus on processes of biotic competition. Indeed, as Alihan showed in her influential critique published in 1938, it was both undesirable and impossible to study the city without analysing cultural as well as biotic processes, 'society' as well as 'community'.[12] If, on the other hand, human ecology was to be understood as a theory of adaptation and was thus to be defined in terms of a general process, then there was no evident reason why its application should be confined to the study of cities since biotic struggles were presumably occurring in all aspects of human affairs. In short, the theoretical focus of human ecology was not specifically urban in the sense of city-based, and the inevitable result was that the twin and discrete concerns of the human ecologists eventually fell apart. Those who remained committed to studying the city continued to produce community study monographs, but these now lacked any coherent theoretical framework or rationale, while those who retained the theoretical focus on adaptation were obliged to drop the Chicago school's characteristic concern with the city and instead developed and applied Park's theoretical insights to the functionalist analysis of how various types of social groups and organisations adapted to their external environments. By the outbreak of the Second World War, the first attempt to establish a theory of the city had collapsed.

The second attempt: the city as a cultural form

It has long been recognised in sociology that the size and complexity of social aggregates affects the forms of social organisation which develop within them. As Simmel argued early this century:

It will immediately be conceded on the basis of everyday experiences that a group upon realising a certain size must develop forms and organs which serve its maintenance and promotion but which a smaller group does not need. On the other hand, it will also be admitted that smaller groups have qualities, including types of interaction among their members, which inevitably disappear when the groups grow larger.[13]

Given that cities, however else we may define them, are clearly large and complex (socially differentiated) human aggregates, it is not surprising that 'urban' theorists have attempted to identify specific patterns of interaction which are associated with cities and explicable in terms of their size and heterogeneity. Simmel himself sought to identify a distinct 'metropolitan personality type', while thirty years later, Louis Wirth argued that to the extent that ways of life in cities were anonymous, superficial, transitory and segmental, this could be explained as the product of the size, density and heterogeneity of their settlement.[14]

The problem with both these formulations, however, is that they confuse the sociological effects of size with effects which are better explained with reference to the cultural impact of capitalist social relations. The confusion is obvious in Simmel's essay where he explains the 'metropolitan personality' as a product both of the effect of settlement size (a characteristic specific to cities) and of an advanced division of labour and money economy (a characteristic of capitalist society as a whole). The same confusion is also evident in Wirth's work for, as Gans has shown, the ways of life which Wirth identified in the city are better explained in terms of the social class and life cycle stage of those who live there than as the outcome of large, dense and heterogeneous settlement.[15]

None of this is to deny that factors such as size and complexity do have some effect on patterns of social relationships; life in large settlements, for example, is in general more anonymous than life in small ones, and people packed together in dense settlements (as in tower block flats, for example) may well respond to physical proximity through maintenance of social distance. But this leaves us a long way from identifying a distinct 'urban way of life', still less from explaining it solely in terms of peculiarly 'urban' variables. Investigation of the sociological effects of number is, as Simmel's work showed, a potentially fruitful and fascinating area, but it is not a sociology of the city.

The third attempt: the city as a system of resource allocation

A third approach to specifying distinct urban processes developed in Britain in the mid-1960s through work, principally by John Rex and Ray Pahl,[16] which sought to show that the city was the course of distinct patterns of inequality and distinct patterns of social conflict arising over and above inequalities and conflict generated through the world of work. The specific task of urban sociology was to study and explain the ways in which inequalities in the city arose out of the actions of 'urban managers' (that is, individuals such as estate agents, local authority bureaucrats, social workers and so on who controlled access to strategic 'urban' resources such as housing) and how these inequalities were in turn the subject of 'urban class struggles' (in particular 'housing class struggles' between different groups in the city who enjoyed different degrees of access to scarce and desirable housing resources).

The first problem encountered by this reformulation of the concerns of urban sociology concerned the supposed autonomy of urban managers, for it soon became clear that, far from constituting the 'independent variables' in any analysis of unequal resource allocation, as Pahl had first suggested, such managers were in fact tightly constrained in their distributive actions both by the operation of a capitalist market economy and by the policies and directives imposed upon them by central government. Pahl's response to this was to amend his earlier argument by suggesting that urban managers (whom he now identified as public sector gatekeepers operating at local level) should be seen, not as the independent, but rather as the intervening or mediating variables of urban analysis. By so arguing, however, Pahl effectively displaced the independent variables of his urban sociology beyond the confines of the city; urban inequalities were to be explained primarily in terms of the operations of private capital and the national state and were only mediated by the actions of local managers. It is hardly surprising, therefore, that in his later work, Pahl virtually abandoned his concern with urban managers in favour of a consideration of the relation between the central state and the private sector (which he saw in terms of a theory of corporatism).

A second and in many ways parallel problem with this whole approach concerned the use of the concept of 'housing classes'. This concept has been widely criticised, partly because the groups which come into conflict over housing are not themselves 'housing' classes but are rather particular social groups such as black people or one-parent families (that is, it is misleading to talk of a *housing* class conflict when the conflict is drawn on lines of ethnicity, gender, etc.), partly because such groups cannot in any case be theorised in 'class' terms, even within a Weberian perspective such as that adopted by Rex (that is, it is misleading to talk of a housing *class* conflict) and partly because housing may not in fact represent an issue of conflict between these groups (for example, in his later work with Sally Tomlinson in Handsworth,[17] Rex found that black people in the inner city had no strong desire for a suburban house in a predominantly white area, in which case it is misleading to talk of a housing class *conflict* between groups who aspire to different kinds of housing).

Clearly, what Rex is discussing in his work is not housing classes but racial and ethnic conflict, not 'urban' inequality but racially-based inequalities. This becomes clear in his work on Handsworth where he talks of the development of a 'black underclass' which is systematically disadvantaged in respect of schooling and employment. While this is a crucial issue for sociology, it is clearly not a specifically 'urban' question, for although most black people live in big cities in Britain, problems of racial exclusion in jobs and education are not to be explained in terms of peculiarly 'urban' variables. As with Pahl's work on urban managers, therefore, Rex's work on housing classes necessarily involves an analysis of economic and political factors in society as a whole, and neither concept provides us with a theoretical rationale for a sociology of the city.

The fourth attempt: the city as a unit of collective consumption

While the question of the specificity of the urban had been posed implicitly by earlier writers outside the Marxist tradition, Castells, writing in the 1970s, was probably the first to address it explicitly while at the same time attempting to reformulate the urban question in theoretical terms.[18] Although his critique of earlier approaches as 'ideological' was in many ways unsatisfactory given its reliance on an Althusserian epistemology which has subsequently been the subject of much criticism (not least by Castells himself[19]), Castells's work was significant in urban sociology for its attempt to specify the 'urban question' in relation to an analysis of the capitalist mode of production.

Castells's project was to identify a specific function within the capitalist mode of production (CMP) which was located within cities. Starting with a theory of the CMP as comprising three inter-related 'levels', he showed that neither the ideological/cultural (for example, urbanism as a way of life) nor the political (for example, urban managerialism) levels were contained within cities, while at the economic level, production was similarly non-spatially specific. Consumption, however, was in his view a process which could be specified in terms of urban spatial units, and he concluded that urban sociology was thus concerned with the analysis of the social organisation of consumption and its function in reproducing labour-power:

> The 'urban' seems to me to connote directly the processes relating to labour-power other than in its direct application to the produc-

tion process... The urban units thus seem to be to the process of reproduction what the companies are to the production process.[20]

Castells did not, of course, deny that processes other than consumption also take place within an urban context, for all levels and elements of the CMP are present within the urban system. Rather, he argued that the only process which was specific to the urban system was that of consumption (reproduction of labour-power), and that 'urban' problems, 'urban' crises, 'urban' politics and so on were thus to be understood through an analysis of consumption processes within the CMP.

Of all the criticisms which have been made against Castells's formulation, two are pertinent for our present concerns. The first is that the identification of consumption with the spatial unit of the city is arbitrary and unconvincing since processes of consumption, no less than processes of production, of politics or of ideology, are not territorially bounded. As Mingione observes 'The consumption process itself is not definable in a purely territorial context, it does not correspond to any "urban question" but is rather an important part of the general social question'.[21]

The second is that any attempt to theorise the city in terms of its functions within the CMP cannot ignore the question of production, for as Lefebvre, Harvey and others have argued, capital investment in the 'urban system' may represent a crucial 'circuit' within overall investment flows, while the physical infrastructure of the city may provide an effective subsidy to the production costs of private capital.[22]

What these two lines of criticism indicate is that, like human ecology, the Marxist urban sociology of the 1970s was effectively set upon two irreconcilable stools. On the one hand Castells, like Park, was concerned with a particular process in society (for Castells, consumption/reproduction; for Park, competition/adaptation). On the other, he was also, again like Park, concerned to retain an empirical focus on the city even though this necessarily entailed much wider processes (for Castells, production as well as consumption; for Park, the cultural as well as the biotic).

Just as human ecology eventually split between those who retained the theoretical focus but abandoned the city as their specific object of enquiry and those who retained the city but lost the theoretical rationale for studying it, so too does Marxist urban sociology seem destined to split in much the same way. On the one hand, we are likely to see the development of a 'sociology of consumption' divorced from the specific question of the city or space (of which, more later); on the other, Marxists will presumably continue to analyse cities and their role in the process of capital accumulation, even though they lack any coherent theoretical framework for understanding 'urbanism' as a specific process within capitalism.

Urbanism, capitalism and the nation-state

It is my contention (hardly original but nevertheless crucial) that with the development of capitalism, the city has ceased to be a sociologically significant unit in Western societies. This means that any future attempts to develop a sociology of the city in the contemporary period are likely to suffer exactly the same problem as that confronted by the four approaches discussed above: that is, an inability to identify any specific social process which is peculiar to, or explicable in terms of, the city as a spatially-bounded unit.

This does not mean, however, that the city is irrelevant to social theory. Far from it, for it is notable that the so-called 'founding fathers' of modern sociology all included an analysis of cities as an important component of their overall theories. When we consider their work, we find that, despite deep theoretical, methodological and political divisions between them, writers such as Weber, Durkheim and Marx and Engels tend to focus on common themes in their analysis of cities. Three particular themes emerge: the role of cities in the transition from feudalism to industrial-capitalism in Western Europe, the modern city as an expression of industrial-capitalism society, and the city as a secondary or contingent factor in influencing social change. What we do not find in their work, however, is any attempt to theorise the city in the context of developed industrial-capitalist societies, for all these writers are agreed that in the contemporary period, the city is not a significant economic, political or social unit of analysis.

The city in the transition to industrial-capitalism

Marx, Weber and Durkheim all saw the city as of immense sociological importance at one particular period in history; namely, in the transition from feudal to industrial-capitalist society in Western Europe.

For Marx, this was because the antithesis between town and country was at this time, and at this time only, the phenomenal expression of the deeper and more basic class division between the rising industrial bourgeoisie and the declining landed feudal nobility. The town-country division was thus the manifest form of the underlying contradiction between two competing modes of production; a capitalist mode which became established in the new industrial towns away from the feudal restrictions of rural serfdom and the medieval guilds, and a declining feudal mode based mainly on agriculture.

Unlike the period of Antiquity, when cities such as Rome were simply administrative centres for a predominantly agricultural society based on a slave mode of production, and unlike the contemporary capitalist period, where capitalist social relations have pervaded both town and countryside alike, Marx therefore saw the city in the late feudal period as an 'historical subject' for the first and only time.[23]

Weber likewise focused his attention on Western cities in the medieval period. His theoretical concern was with different types of human association and particularly with the origins of calculative rationality in social relationships. He argued that in the ancient world, the basis of human association was the family or the clan irrespective of whether the place of residence of particular family units was in town or countryside. In the medieval period, however, the traditionalism of clan or family authority was eroded by the growth of city guilds and corporations in which individuals were constituted as citizens with rights and duties legally defined through membership of the city as the unit of legal and political organisations.[24]

The occidental city in the medieval period was thus the basic unit of social organisation legally, politically and economically, and the break which it represented with traditional bonds represented the necessary condition of the later development of economic rationality and political democracy in the West. Today, however, the city as the basic unit of social organisation has been replaced by the nation-state, for the city is no longer the locus of autonomous markets, autonomous law, autonomous military organisation and so on. Like Marx, therefore, Weber suggests that it is only in the medieval period that the city constituted a sociologically and historically significant entity.

Durkheim's analysis is similar. His concern is with the changing source of social cohesion over time consequent upon the development of a complex division of labour in society. In the Middle Ages, social organisation grounded in interdependence fostered by the division of labour was contiguous with the spatial boundaries of the corporate city – that is, territorial boundaries were at one and the same time social and economic boundaries. But as the division of labour developed, so it extended across territory (and ultimately across nations) with the result that city boundaries became less and less significant for social life:

> As advances are made in history, the organisation which has territorial groups as its base (village or city, district, province, etc.) steadily becomes effaced ... These geographical divisions are for the most part artificial and no longer awaken in us profound sentiments. Our activity is extended quite beyond these groups which are too narrow for it and, moreover, a good deal of what happens there leaves us indifferent.[25]

Like Weber, then, Durkheim sees the basis of social organisation and solidarity today as nothing less than the nation-state (indeed, at one point he likens the nation-state to 'one big city'). The implication of this is that, in advanced capitalist societies, an attempt to develop a sociology of the city will inevitably broaden out into a sociology of the society as a whole.

The city as a social microcosm

When these classical theorists did discuss the modern city (and Weber, generally, did not) they often did so in order to illustrate processes operating within society as a whole. Engels's essays on the condition of the English working class and on the housing question, for example, both draw on evidence of urban squalor and misery in order to document the consequences for working people of an unremitting process of capital accumulation.[26] What is clear in both these essays is that the explanation for these phenomena is not to be sought in an analysis of urbanisation *per se*, but rather in an analysis of processes unleashed by the development of a capitalist mode of production in society.

Similarly, Durkheim notes that crime rates, suicide rates and other indicators of social pathology tend to be highest in cities, but insists that this is not to be explained in terms of a theory of urbanism. Rather, such phenomena are the products of an abnormal form of the division of labour in society as a whole (in the modern period, an anomic form). It is society which is anomic, and the indicators of anomie are simply revealed most clearly in those areas (cities) where social life is most intense and concentrated. Problems which become manifest in urban areas are not 'urban' problems, nor do they have 'urban' solutions (a point to which I shall return).

The city as a contingent factor in social change

Although neither Marx nor Durkheim saw the contemporary city as of central theoretical significance, they both recognised that concentration of population may facilitate or strengthen the development of certain processes whose origins lie elsewhere. Marx and Engels, for example, argued that the concentration of the industrial proletariat in cities may facilitate the emergence of a radical class consciousness whose cause nevertheless lies in the growing contradiction between the forces and relations of production in society – urbanisation does not engender class consciousness but it may function as a condition for its full development.[27] In similar vein, Durkheim sees urbanisation as an important condition of the development of organic bonds of social solidarity given its significance in eroding the moral bind of the collective conscience in traditional societies. Migration to the cities weakens the traditional authority of sacred ties and thus enables (but does not cause) the transition from mechanical to organic solidarity to take place.

Two main conclusions follow from all this. The first is that we need to modify Giddens's assertion that a concern with the city lies at the very core of social theory. The second is that any explanation of contemporary social phenomena must nevertheless remain alert to the possible implications of spatial organisation as a factor inhibiting or facilitating the development of certain processes in society as a whole. Summarising these two themes, we may say that the first points to the development of a 'non-spatial' sociology while the second points to the inadequacy of an 'aspatial' sociology.

By a 'non-spatial' sociology I mean that there can be no social theory of the city in contemporary industrial capitalist societies. This is the clear lesson to be drawn both from the work of the 'classical' social theorists and from the failure of all attempts over the past sevety years to develop a specifically urban social theory. Giddens's

assertion of the centrality of the city to social theory is thus misleading, for while the city is indeed a crucial and central concern of those
aspects of social theory which relate to pre-capitalist (and possibly
non-capitalist) societies and processes of change and conflict within
them, this is certainly not the case for the sociology of advanced
capitalist societies.

In fact, Giddens appears to recognise precisely this himself, for
shortly after arguing for the centrality of the city to sociological
theory, he writes:

> The development of capitalism has not led to the consolidation of
> the institutions of the city, but rather to *its eradication as a distinct
> social form*.[28]

It seems clear from this that his earlier emphasis on the crucial
theoretical significance of the city can only refer to pre-capitalist (or
what he terms 'class-divided' as opposed to 'class') societies, for a
social form which has been 'eradicated' under capitalism can hardly
remain central to its analysis.

Giddens's argument concerning the role of the city in pre-capitalist
societies is in many ways reminiscent of that of Weber. For Weber,
the city was an autonomous political, legal and military unit, while
for Giddens it was a 'crucible of power' or a 'power-container'
through which the absolutist state exerted social domination by
virtue of the concentration of authoritative resources (that is, information which was necessary for surveillance). And just as Weber saw
that in the modern period, the city has been replaced by the nation-
state as the territorial unit which claims a monopoly over the
legitimate use of force, so too Giddens recognises that, with the
advent of capitalism from the late eighteenth century onwards, the
city gave way to the nation-state as the crucial 'power-container' in
society:

> The absolutist state was part of a class-divided society in which . . .
> the city–countryside relation was the foundation of the social
> order. My argument, in essence, is that the nation-state replaces the
> city as the 'power-container' shaping the development of the
> capitalist societies as the old city–countryside symbiosis becomes
> dissolved. The precision with which the boundaries of the nation-
> state are drawn is the modern analogue to the circumscribing of the
> city by its walls.[29]

Indeed, as he notes elsewhere,[30] the territorial boundaries of the nation-state are today of such overriding significance that sociological analysis frequently equates 'nation-state' with 'society'. As Weber (and Durkheim) so clearly recognised, and as a long line of 'urban' social theorists from Robert Park onwards apparently failed to appreciate, the smallest discrete spatial unit which can be taken as the basis for sociological analysis in contemporary capitalist societies is that defined by the territorial boundaries of the nation-state. There can, therefore, be no specifically spatial sociology, no sociology of the city, no specialist branch of the discipline defined in terms of a peculiar focus on sub-national spatial units.

This does not mean, however, that space is unimportant for sociological explanation, for as we saw above in respect of the work of Durkheim on anomie and Marx and Engels on class-consciousness, certain social phenomena, generated out of tendencies in society as a whole (such as an abnormal division of labour or a growing contradiction between forces and relations of production) may only become manifest in particular areas such as cities (because of the greater intensity of social life, or the increased possibilities for mass organisation, which cities represent). While this does nothing to undermine my previous argument for a 'non-spatial' sociology (since these phenomena are not specifically 'urban') it does point to the need to avoid an 'aspatial' sociology – that is, a mode of sociological analysis which takes no account of space as a potentially inhibiting or facilitating factor in the development of various social processes. A non-spatial sociology need not be aspatial.

It is such a distinction between non-spatial and aspatial social analysis which appears to inform Urry's argument about the sociological significance of time and space:

[It] is impossible and incorrect to develop a general science of the spatial. The latter cannot be separated from the social in such a manner that a general set of distinct laws can be devised. This is because space *per se* has no *general* effects ... it only has effect because the social objects in question possess particular characteristics, namely, different causal powers. Such powers may or may not manifest themselves in empirical events – whether they do or not depends upon the relationship in time – space established with other objects.[31]

While I would not wish to endorse entirely the realist epistemology which lies at the heart of this argument, Urry's basic theme – that certain capacities for action will only be released or triggered off in certain temporal or spatial contexts – is an important one. The point may usefully be illustrated with reference to the riots which occurred in many British cities in the summer of 1981.

These riots, which involved both white and black youth but which tended to break out mainly in areas of high black concentration (for example, Brixton and Southall in London or Toxteth in Liverpool) can probably only be explained in terms of a variety of sociological factors.[32] Unemployment rates among young people – especially young West Indians – certainly constituted one factor, but we would also need to take into account police practices over a number of years which were (or were experienced by many as) racist, provocative political activities by Fascist and white supremacist movements such as the National Front, mobilisation by left fringe parties such as the SWP, and so on.

Nor, of course, could any analysis of these events afford to ignore the fact that most riots occurred in inner city areas (and, for that matter, that they occurred during the summer time). However, it would clearly be a mistake to try to find the causes of the riots in either the spatial (in this case, high-density decaying inner-city areas) or the temporal (long, warm summer evenings) dimensions, for their explanation lies in the development of certain tendencies in British society as a whole. As we saw earlier in the discussion of Rex's work on 'housing classes', conflicts which take place in cities are generated by factors which are not specifically 'urban' in origin. Racism in British society, for example, is a product of a long history of imperialist expansion, government action and inaction, scientific and pseudo-scientific speculation, and so on, none of which is 'urban'. Similarly, unemployment is the product of an international recession, dramatic restructuring in British industry, government monetarist policies, etc., and again, none of these are 'urban' factors. The spatial dimension of the riots cannot be overlooked, but it was clearly only a secondary factor acting to facilitate them in some areas (for example, where disadvantaged and frustrated sections of the population were concentrated and were able to come together as a mass, albeit disorganised, force on the streets) and to inhibit them in others (for example, areas where such people were dispersed).

It also follows from this argument that interventions by governments or other agencies which seek to bring about social change through specifically 'urban' policies are fundamentally flawed, for if the 'causes' of problems which become manifest in cities lie outside the cities themselves, then it follows that their 'solutions' (if, indeed, there are any) lie there too. Three points may be made about such interventions.

First, it is by no means clear that the 'social problems' which governments have set out to 'treat' through a long succession of 'urban policies' are spatially concentrated in the way in which it has often been assumed. In his conclusion to a recently-published collection of papers on the British conurbations, for example, Cameron suggests:

We have shown that the very strong spatial bias in much recent thinking about the deprived may have been overdone. The evidence relating to employment, for example, tends to show that ... for any given type of workers, the level of unemployment in inner areas is not higher than in other parts of the conurbation. The evidence on poverty does not suggest that it is highly spatially concentrated but instead strongly focused on the old and spread throughout many parts of the conurbations ... All of this might push us in the direction of solutions which attack deprivation in terms of support for particular types of client group wherever they are located.[33]

Second, even if it could be demonstrated that certain 'problems' – family breakdown, unemployment, crime or whatever – were spatially concentrated in, say, inner-city areas, 'urban' programmes would still make no sense in terms of providing a solution when such problems are generated in society (the nation-state) rather than in cities. As Engels was well aware, even an apparently 'urban' phenomenon such as slum housing cannot be overcome at the city level:

The breeding places of disease, the infamous holes and cellars in which the capitalist mode of production confines our workers night after night, are not abolished; they are merely shifted elsewhere! The same economic necessity which produced them in the first place produces them in the next place also![34]

Whether we also agree with Engels that the only solution to such problems lies in the transcendence of capitalism is a matter for debate, but where we must surely concur is in his diagnosis that 'urban' problems can only have 'societal' solutions.

This brings us on to the third point. We have seen that although the spatial unit of the city is not a sociological unit in capitalist industrial societies, spatial factors may nevertheless inhibit or facilitate the development of processes originating in society as a whole. It follows from this that governments may be able to adopt spatially-specific programmes which, while not solving the problems to which they are addressed, nevertheless influence *where* those problems manifest themselves. British regional policy since the war provides one example, for the battery of regional incentives and penalties which have been adopted by central government and local authorities has not solved the problem of unemployment and under-investment but has had some effect in shifting it around from one area to another. Similarly, the introduction of urban 'enterprise zones', development corporations, 'freeports' and so on may well have some effect in stimulating private enterprise in the designated areas, but this is likely to be at the expense of adjacent areas which cannot offer the same advantages to existing businesses. Spatially-specific policies and programmes may therefore have some effect in determining where problems arise, but they have had precious little effect in preventing such problems from occurring or recurring elsewhere. Such policies may be justified on grounds of spatial equity, but they cannot be justified on grounds of social effectivity.

Conclusions: the legacy of urban sociology

We saw in the first section of this chapter that although all four attempts this century to establish a theoretical foundation for a sociology of the city have failed, each attempt has left a fruitful legacy in the form of particular questions and issues which remain pertinent once they are divorced from a concern with territorial arrangements.

From human ecology we have been left a theoretical concern with the problem of how human groups manage to adapt to their physical environment. This is an important and legitimate question for sociologists to pose, and in the post-war years it has been taken up and incorporated within mainstream functionalist sociology. Talcott Parsons, for example, has identified adaptation as one of the four 'functional prerequisities' of social organisation.[35]

From the 'cultural' tradition of writers such as Simmel and Wirth we have been left two distinctive concerns. The first is the question of the sociological significance of number. The second is a concern with the impact of capitalism and/or industrialism on the quality of social relationships. The concern with number has now been assimilated into social psychology while the qualitative question of social relationships in the modern world forms part of a long and continuing tradition of social thought relating to the problem of alienation.[36]

The work in the 1960s on the city as a system of resource allocation has left us with a number of themes, many of which have been further pursued in other branches of sociology. Rex's concern with ethnic inequalities and conflicts has, for example, been subsumed within the sociology of race relations, just as Pahl's interest in the development of corporatism is today reflected in the political sociology literature on the state and its relation to civil society. Some of the themes explored in this tradition have not, however, been taken up or developed elsewhere. One of these is the relationship between the national and local.[37] Another is the concern with the specific patterns of inequality and conflict which arise outside the workplace in the 'community' or in the process of consumption.

The question of consumption also emerges as the most important legacy from the 'neo-Marxist' urban sociology of the 1970s. Castells in particular is significant for having directed our attention to the new patterns of social and political cleavage which arise out of the social organisation of consumption in advanced capitalist societies.

What, then, can valuably be salvaged from the shipwreck of contemporary urban sociology? While many of the legacies of earlier traditions are best subsumed under other approaches, some do remain distinctive. Indeed, some of these themes, once rescued from the tangled wreckage of a concern with space or cities, may (à la Giddens) be said to lie at the heart of contemporary social theory.

The most important of these themes is the concern with the process of consumption which characterises the work of both Pahl and Castells. As feminist critics of radical sociology have often pointed out, sociological theories, concepts and empirical concerns are still firmly rooted in the sphere of production. Our theories relate to changing 'modes of production', our concepts refer to 'social classes' which are constituted through relations of production. To the extent that the social organisation of consumption is studied at all, it tends to be through a 'reduction' to these production-based theories and concepts: women are located in the class system via the productive activity of their husbands, community movements are located within a class theory of politics by emphasising their relation to the labour movement, and so on. What is lacking in such work is the crucial recognition of the need to analyse inequalities of consumption, the politics of consumption and so on on their own terms. This is precisely what urban sociology has started to do over the past twenty years.

The theoretical vacuum left by the collapse of urban sociology as the study of cities may therefore be filled by the development of urban sociology's distinctive concern with questions of consumption. This is not to suggest, of course, that processes of consumption can be analysed in isolation from the question of production, but it is to assert that the social organisation of consumption is today a crucially important yet vastly neglected area of study for social science. As I have argued elsewhere,[38] the social and political cleavages which have arisen round consumption of resources like housing, health care, transport and education are today as important as, if not more important than, the class divisions which arise out of the social organisation of production. Indeed, we cannot begin to understand the apparent popularity of Thatcherism, the crisis of the British welfare state, the growing intensity of conflict between centre and locality or a host of other contemporary phenomena until we explicitly develop a 'sociology of consumption' with its own distinctive theories and concerns.

This is not the place to develop such theories or outline such concerns – I have attempted to do this elsewhere.[39] Nor need we dwell for too long on the semantic question of whether a sociology of consumption, drawing as it does on some of the core concerns of urban sociology over the past twenty years, may still be termed 'urban sociology' even though it has lost any specific concern with the city or the social organisation of space. For the sake of continuity, I would refer to it as a 'non-spatial urban sociology', but such a label is unimportant and is merely a matter of convention and convenience. What is important, by contrast, is that the crucial theoretical concerns of recent urban sociology should be freed from the anachronistic, restrictive and ultimately futile preoccupation with spatial forms which has hitherto always reappeared to choke new theoretical initiatives whenever they have appeared. It is for this reason that I view with dismay the possibility of a new orthodoxy emerging which seeks to establish a concern with space at the centre of sociological discourse.

Notes

1. Notably Giddens (1979) ch. 6; Sayer (1979b); and Urry (1981c).
2. Giddens (1979) p. 202.
3. An example of the work in political geography on the effect of location on voting behaviour is Foladare (1968). See also Pelling (1967). For a discussion of working-class imagery, see Lockwood (1966). On the 'local state', see Duncan and Goodwin (1982).
4. Urry (1981c) p. 454.
5. Giddens (1979) p. 292.
6. Giddens (1981b) p. 140.
7. On research programmes in science, see Lakatos (1974). He argues that all research programmes encounter anomalies but that these do not warrant the abandonment of the 'positive heuristic' which defines them unless and until an alternative and superior programme is developed.
8. Saunders (1981). The four attempts to develop a social theory of the city are discussed in chapters 2 to 6.
9. This view is expressed by Reissman (1964) p. 93. This was before two of the four approaches discussed here had been developed. Nevertheless, it is arguably still the case that human ecology was the closest that urban sociology has come to developing a coherent theoretical and empirical research programme.
10. Probably the single most concise statement of Park's approach can be found in Park (1952) ch. 12. This piece was originally published in 1936 after twenty years of empirical and theoretical developments.
11. One of Park's best-known students believed that it was the former: 'Human ecology, as Park conceived it, was not a branch of sociology but rather a perspective, a method and a body of knowledge essential for the scientific study of social life and hence, like social psychology, a general discipline basic to all the social sciences' (Wirth, 1945, p. 484).
12. 'The concept "community" is approached in a way that denies its social attributes. In its very definition it is an abstraction of the asocial aspect of human behaviour. Yet the ecologists find themselves compelled in many ways to take account of the social factors which in reality are intrinsically related to and bound up with the asocial community' (Alihan, 1938, p. 48).
13. cited in Wolff (1950) p. 87.
14. See especially Simmel (1950) and Wirth (1938). It should perhaps be noted that in Wirth's view ways of life in cities were not necessarily 'anonymous, superficial, transitory and segmental'. This famous phrase should be understood, not as a description of city life, but as an ideal typical characterisation of urban social relations. To suggest, as many critics have done, that evidence of *gemeinschaftlich* relationships in cities refutes Wirth's theory is to misunderstand his argument, for his concern was with explaining those relationships which did approximate to the ideal type.
15. As Gans concludes 'If ways of life do not coincide with settlement types, and if these ways are functions of class and life cycle stage rather than of

the ecological attributes of the settlement, a sociological definition of the city cannot be formulated' (1968, p. 114). See also Pahl (1968) who concludes that 'Any attempt to tie particular patterns of social relationships to specific geographical milieux is a singularly fruitless exercise' (p. 293).
16. See especially Rex (1968); Rex and Moore (1967); Pahl (1975), ch. 7, 10 and 13.
17. Rex and Tomlinson (1979).
18. See in particular Castells (1976a) (1976b) and (1977).
19. Notably in the 'Afterword' to *The Urban Question* and in the introductory essay in Castells (1978).
20. Castells (1977), pp. 236–7.
21. Mingione (1981) p. 67.
22. Lefebvre (1970); Harvey (1978).
23. The term comes from Lefebvre (1972). Probably the most significant work by Marx and Engels on all this is *The German Ideology* (1970).
24. 'Here, in new civic creations, burghers joined the citizenry as single persons. The oath of citizenship was taken by the individual. Personal membership, not that of the kin group or tribe, in the local association of the city supplied the guarantee of the individual's personal legal position as burgher' (Weber, 1958, p. 102).
25. Durkheim (1964) pp. 27–8.
26. Engels (1969a) and (1969b).
27. 'Without the great cities and their forcing influence upon the popular intelligence, the working class would be far less advanced than it is' (Engels, 1969a, p. 152).
28. Giddens (1981b) p. 148, emphasis added.
29. ibid, p. 12.
30. Giddens (1979) p. 224.
31. Urry (1981c) p. 458.
32. See Rex (1982).
33. Cameron (1980) p. 318–9. Townsend's exhaustive poverty survey similarly revealed a wide geographical dispersion of poverty in Britain – see Townsend (1979) ch. 15.
34. Engels (1969b) p. 352.
35. The other three being goal-definition, integration and latency – see Parsons, Bales and Shils (1953). At the level of the social system, Parsons sees adaptation as the function of the economic sub-system, but Hawley has suggested that ecological processes may subsume economic ones (Hawley, 1950, ch. 4) in which case Parsonian systems theory could easily be amended to accommodate ecological theory in respect of the adaptive function.
36. Alienation, that is, in the broad sense of that term. Note that Simmel uses 'alienation' as a key theme in his work on the effects of a money economy and an advanced division of labour.
37. This theme emerges out of Pahl's reformulation of the urban managerialism thesis in which managers are seen as mediating, not only between the market and the state sectors, but also between the central government and the local population. This concern with the relation between the

centre and periphery, the national and the local, was already present in Pahl's earlier work, however – notably in Pahl (1968) – and in other influential urban sociological writings during the 1960s such as Stacey (1969). It is a theme which has resurfaced in academic debates in the 1980s by virtue of the clashes between central government and radical local authorities.

38. Saunders (1982).
39. In addition to the above, see Saunders (1981), ch. 8; Saunders (1983); and Cawson and Saunders (1983).

6
The Spatiality of Social Life: Towards a Transformative Retheorisation

EDWARD W. SOJA

Tenacious layers of mystification have recently begun to be peeled away from our understanding of the spatiality of social life, from the ways in which we account for and act upon the socially-produced geographical configurations and spatial relations which give material form and expression to society. This process of critical reinterpretation is revealing what has been obscured in both social and spatial theory and in day-to-day practice: that *spatiality situates social life* in an active arena where purposeful human agency jostles problematically with tendential social determinations to shape everyday activity, particularise social change, and etch into place the course of time and the making of history.

To be alive is to participate in the social production of space, to shape and be shaped by a constantly evolving spatiality which constitutes and concretises social action and relationship. This has always been true, but has remained largely outside our conscious awareness, relatively untheorised and buried under multiple illusions which have constrained the development of an appropriately materialist interpretation of spatiality and spatial *praxis*. Now more than ever before, however, the essential and encompassing spatiality of social life is being progressively revealed and provocatively repositioned at the very heart of social theory and political consciousness.

Expressions of this transformative materialist interpretation of spatiality punctuate the recent theoretical literature more densely than at any other time. Moreover, there has been a significant expansion in the scale and scope of interpretation beyond the long-established boundaries that have traditionally confined and limited the debate on the theorisation of space to particular disciplinary or philosophical approaches. The contemporary reinterpretation of spatiality engages and extends deeply into much broader realms of social theory, philosophical argument, and practical application – into areas of inquiry, discourse and social practice where it has in the past received only perfunctory and peripheral attention.

Although broader in its origins and impact, this new theorisation of spatiality has been most systematically asserted and explored within the framework of a rejuvenated critical social theory which draws heavily, either directly or through a vigorous reconstructive critique, upon a Marxist tradition and adaptations of historical materialist analysis. This is not surprising, for in so many ways the materialist interpretation of spatiality, in its demystification and politicisation of the *production of space*, is integrally linked with an historical materialism broadly aimed at demystifying and politicising the *making of history*. In the reinterpretation of space and time, spatiality and history, that is so prominent a feature of contemporary critical social theory, there is the basis for a distinctly historical *and* geographical materialism, a more complete and balanced formulation of the materialist dialectic to encompass both human history and human geography as social products, sources of political consciousness and arenas of situated social struggle.

There is more, however, to the emerging materialist interpretation of spatiality than a conformative and facile addition to conventional Marxism. The balanced conjuncture of spatiality and history in the constitution of material social life, and the formation of an accordingly historico-geographical materialism, exposes contumaceous realms of theoretical and political discourse which resist easy incorporation into established paradigmatic traditions. Demanded instead is an extensive and flexible rethinking of both theory and practice, a reconstruction which will continue to draw upon the achievements of Marx but which must also be more directly attuned to the specificity of contemporary capitalist (and socialist) spatiality and temporality.

Framing these observations is a belief that a momentous change is occurring in the formulation of social theory that compares with the transformative developments of the latter half of the nineteenth century, the period in which both Marxism and the classical social sciences took distinct shape. The last three decades of the past century were marked by decelerated economic growth, deepening crisis, and far-reaching attempts to restructure social, economic, and political conditions to recapture the expansive boom that followed the European revolutions of 1848. As social life changed, so too did its theorisation. The last three decades of this century appear likely to repeat a similar process of crisis and restructuring in both theory and practice, and the demystification and politicisation of the spatiality of social life are pivotal to these contemporary changes.

In this chapter I propose to elaborate further upon and defend these introductory assertions. I begin with a brief presentation of the fundamental premises which have come to define and direct what I have termed the materialist interpretation of spatiality. Spatiality is portrayed as a social product and an integral part of the material constitution and structuration of social life. Above all else, this means that spatiality cannot be appropriately understood and theorised apart from society and social relationships and, conversely, that social theory must contain a central and encompassing spatial dimension. At first thought this assertion seems so obvious and straightforward, yet it bursts with implications and indicative insights which have remained either ignored or persistently misunderstood throughout the history of social and spatial theory. I then provide a critical analysis of the alternative interpretative frameworks which have blocked the development of an appropriately materialist interpretation of the spatiality of social life. In the final section, I attempt to chronicle (and chorograph) the emergence of a new theorisation of spatiality from its formative origins within French Marxism (and especially in the works of Henri Lefebvre) through its rather ambivalent extension in anglophonic Marxist geography, to its convergent presentation within a more broadly-based critical social theory and philosophy. There will be little or no empirical application or illustration; nor will I attempt a detailed examination of the many more specific theoretical ramifications arising from the reinterpretation of spatiality currently taking place.[1] These are necessary and conducive to a more convincing argument, but they must await another time and place.

The social production of space and the spatial construction of society

The generative source for the materialist interpretation of spatiality is the recognition that spatiality is socially produced and, like society itself, exists in both substantial forms (concrete spatialities) and as a set of relations between individuals and groups.[2] Spatiality, as socially produced space, must thus be distinguished from the physical space of material nature and the mental space of cognition and representation, each of which is used and incorporated into the social construction of spatiality but cannot be conceptualised as its equivalent.

Within certain limits (which are frequently forgotten), physical nature and human cognition can be theorised independently with regard to their particular spatial dimensions or attributes. The classical debates over 'absolute' and 'relative' qualities of physical space exemplify the former, while such questions as whether we construct mental maps which are geometrically Euclidean, Minkowskian, Riemannian, or otherwise, illustrate the latter. This possibility of independent theorisation, however, does not mean rigid separation or unassailable autonomy, for the three spaces interconnect and overlap. Furthermore, not only are the spaces of nature and cognition used and incorporated into the social production of spatiality, they are significantly transformed in the process. This social incorporation and transformation sets the primary limitation upon the independent theorisation of physical and mental space, for each is to a significant degree socially produced and must therefore be theorised and understood as part of the spatiality of social life.

Conversely, the social production of spatiality cannot be completely separated from physical and cognitive space. Natural and biological processes affect society, and social life is never entirely free from the physical friction of distance. The impress of this 'first nature', however, is not naively and independently given. It is always socially mediated and recast as part of the 'second nature' that arises from the organised and cumulative application of human labour and human knowledge. The space of physical nature is thus *appropriated* in the social production of spatiality – it is literally made social.[3]

Two major conclusions can be drawn from these observations. First, the social production of spatiality encompasses and incorporates the social production of nature, the transformation of physical space in the creation of a second nature which concretely manifests its essentially social origins. Following from this, it can be argued that the results of an independent theorisation of physical space cannot be directly applied to a materialist interpretation of spatiality. To do so would obscure the social origins of spatiality and its *social transformability* in the causal logic of unalloyed naturalism and physical mechanics.

A parallel argument can be made with respect to cognitive space. The 'presentation' of concrete spatiality is always wrapped in the complex and diverse 'representations' of human perception and cognition, without any necessity of direct and determined correspondence between the two. Nevertheless, the social production of spatiality appropriates and recasts the representations of mental space by concretising them as part of social life, part of second nature. The production of ideas (and ideologies) is thus an important component of the production of spatiality, but this relationship is rooted in social origins. To interpret spatiality from the purview of socially independent processes of ideation is consequently also inappropriate and misleading, for it buries these social origins (and potential social transformations) under a distorting screen of idealism and psychologism.

Tied to this interpretation of the connections between physical, cognitive, and social space is a key assumption about the dynamics of spatiality and hence about the relations between (social) space and time: spatiality is simultaneously the product of a transformation process and transformable itself. As a social product, spatiality can be continuously reinforced or reproduced over time, presenting an appearance of stability and persistence. But it can also be substantially restructured and radically reconstituted, invoking again its origins and grounding in social practice and the labour process. The production of space is thus not simply a mechanical extrusion of a frozen matrix which acts passively to contain society. Spatiality and temporality, human geography and human history, intersect in a complex social process which creates a constantly evolving historical sequence of spatialities, a spatio-temporal structuration of social life which gives form not only to the grand movements of societal development but also to the recursive practices of day-to-day activity.

The production of space (and the making of history) can thus be described as both the *medium* and the *outcome* of social action and relationship. This duality of spatio-temporal structuration connects social and spatial structures in such a way that the former appears in its concretised form in the latter – that is, spatial structures and relations are the material form of social structures and relations. The realisation that *social life is materially constituted in its spatiality* is the theoretical keystone for the contemporary materialist interpretation of spatiality.

This provocative extrapolation of social and spatial structure was anticipated by Henri Lefebvre in *La Production de l'Espace*, where he argued:

> The social relations of production have a social existence only insofar as they exist spatially; they project themselves into a space,

they inscribe themselves in a space while producing it. Otherwise, they remain in 'pure' abstraction, that is in representations and consequently in ideology... verbalism, verbiage, words.[4]

It is in this sense that spatiality *is* society, not as its definitional or logical equivalent, but as its concretisation, its formative *constitution*. Spatiality and temporality as manifest social products are central to the construction of all social interaction and must therefore also be central to the formulation of social theory, not merely adjuncts or dimensionalities. As Thrift emphasises:

This does not just mean that social theory must be historically and geographically specific. More importantly, social theory must be about the time–space constitution of social structure *right from the start*.[5]

A similar interpretation of the constitution and structuration of social relations in space–time, of spatiality and temporality as both medium and outcome, is posited by Nicos Poulantzas in his analysis of the spatial and temporal 'matrices' of capitalism:

This primal material framework is the mould of social atomization and splintering, and it is embodied in the practices of the labour process itself. At one and the same time presupposition of the relations of production and embodiment of the labour process, this framework consists in the organization of a continuous, homogeneous, cracked and fragmented space–time such as lies at the basis of Taylorism: a cross-ruled, segmented and cellular space in which each fragment (individual) has its place, and in which each emplacement, while corresponding to a fragment (individual), must present itself as homogeneous and uniform; and a linear, serial, repetitive and cumulative time, in which the various moments are integrated with one another, and which is itself oriented toward a finished product – namely, the space–time materialized *par excellence* in the production line.[6]

Spatial and temporal matrices are thus described as simultaneously *presuppositions* and *embodiments* of the relations of production. This refers not to a mechanical causality in which pre-existing relations give rise at some subsequent stage to these matrices. Instead, spatial and temporal matrices are a 'logical priority' (what Marx termed

Voraussetzung) and appear 'at the same time' as their presupposition. The terminology may differ but the fundamental argument parallels Lefebvre's: socially-produced space and time are the concrete manifestations, the material references, of social structure and relations, and as such must be placed at the initiating service of social theory.

A concomitant interpretation has been taking shape within the writings of the so-called 'structuration school',[7] where Giddens in particular argues that:

> social theory *must acknowledge, as it has not done previously, time–space intersections as essentially involved in all social existence*... Social activity is always constituted in three intersecting moments of difference: temporally, paradigmatically (invoking structure which is present only in its instantiation) and spatially. All social practices are *situated* activities in each of these senses.[8]

A key postulate in Giddens' theory of structuration is the 'duality of structure', a notion which Giddens uses explicitly as a means of assuring the pertinence of creative human agency in contraposition to the enduring impress of structural determination:

> Structure is both the medium and outcome of the practices which constitute social systems. The concept of duality of structure connects the *production* of social interaction, as always and everywhere a contingent accomplishment of knowledgeable social actors, to the *reproduction* of social systems across time–space.[9]

Like Lefebvre and Poulantzas, Giddens brings his conceptualisation of spatiality and temporality to the analysis of the specificity of capitalist society, especially with respect to the generation of power, the quotidian processes of social reproduction, and the growing influence of the State.

The view of spatiality/geography and temporality/history which can be derived from these three leading socio-political theorists contains much more than the banal assertion that everything takes place *in* space and time. It also differs significantly from the commonly adopted conceptualisation of space as the reflective mirror or embracing container of social life. While the former obscures the specificity of the connections between spatiality and society, the latter breaks the connections by externalising spatiality into a receptacle or backdrop. As a result, both these illusive simplifications divert attention away from the problematic complexity of the social production of space and time and the space–time constitution of social systems. This problematic nature of spatiality – by which I mean its openness to contradiction, conflict and transformation – is an essential part of its contemporary retheorisation. Whether seen as the formation of a spatial matrix or as spatial structuration, the social production of space is not a smooth and automatic process in which social structure is stamped out, without resistance or constraint, onto the landscape. From its origins the development of industrial capitalism, for example, was rooted in a conflict-filled and socially-transforming construction of a specifically capitalist spatiality: in the destruction of feudal property relations and the turbulent creation of a proletariat 'freed' from its former means of subsistence; in the related uprootings associated with the spreading enclosure and commodification of rural land; in the expansive geographical concentration of labour power and industrial production in urban centres (and the attendant if incomplete destruction of earlier forms of urbanisation); in the induced separation of workplace and residence and the equally induced patterning of urban land-uses and the built environment. In this transformation of feudal spatiality into a capitalist spatial matrix; Poulantzas argues:

> The direct producers are freed from the soil only to become trapped in a grid – one that includes not only the modern factory, but also the modern family, school, army, the prison system, the city and national territory.[10]

The production of capitalist spatiality, however, is no once-and-for-all event. It must be reinforced and restructured when necessary; that is, spatiality must be socially *reproduced*, and this reproduction process presents a continuing source of struggle, conflict and contradiction. The conjunction of social and spatial reproduction has become another key nexus for the contemporary retheorisation of spatiality, connecting these questions to debates on the theory of the State, politics and the generation of power; the urban process and regionalism; historical periodicity and crisis in the capitalist accumulation process; geographically uneven development; and the internationalisation of capitalism as a world system. Each of these arenas of materialist theory is being rethought and reconceptualised around an underlying spatial problematic of social reproduction. The conjunction of social and spatial reproduction follows logically from the preceding arguments. If spatiality can be interpreted as both outcome-embodiment and medium-presupposition of social relations and social structure, as their manifest material reference, then spatiality is both product *and producer*. Stated somewhat differently, social life is both space-forming and *space-contingent*, a double relationship which I earlier described as shaping a 'socio-spatial dialectic'.[11] This double relationship demands a restatement of Marx's acutely perceived social principle:

> Men make their own history, but they do not make it just as they please; they do not make it under circumstances chosen by themselves, but under circumstances directly encountered, given and transmitted from the past.[12]

What is being 'made' is both history and geography, a summative process of social production and reproduction that is constrained by circumstances 'directly encountered' in the already constituted spatiality of social life, itself an historical and social product:

> Concrete socio-economic space appears both as the articulation of analysed spaces, as a product, a reflection of the articulation of social relationships, and at the same time, as far as already existing space is concerned, as an objective constraint imposed upon the redeployment of these social relationships. We shall say that society recreates its space on the basis of a concrete space, always already provided, established in the past.[13]

The spatial contingency of social reproduction is thus embedded into the making of history and the production of space.

To summarise, we can say that the materialist interpretation of spatiality builds upon the following series of linked premises:

1. Spatiality is a substantiated social product, part of a 'second nature' which incorporates as it socialises and transforms both physical and cognitive space.
2. As a social product, spatiality is simultaneously the medium and outcome, presupposition and embodiment, of social action and relationship.
3. This spatio-temporal structuration of social life (and of the labour process) defines how social action and relationship are materially constituted, made concrete.

4. The constitution/concretisation process is problematic, filled with contradiction, conflict, and struggle (amidst much which is recursive and routinised).
5. Conflict and contradiction arise primarily from the duality of produced space as both outcome-embodiment-product and medium-presupposition-producer.
6. Concrete spatiality is thus a competitive arena for both social production and reproduction, for social practices aimed either at maintenance and reinforcement of existing spatiality or at significant restructuring and possible transformation.
7. The temporality of social life, from the routines and events of day-to-day activity to the longer-run making of history, is rooted in spatial contingency in much the same way that the spatiality of social life is rooted in temporal/historical contingency.
8. The materialist interpretation of history and the materialist interpretation of spatiality are inseparably intertwined and theoretically concomitant, with no inherent prioritisation of one over the other.

Materiality and illusion in the theorisation of spatiality

Taken together, the interlocking premises just outlined define a conceptualisation of spatiality that is only now taking shape. They still have to be teased out of the current literature since, for the most part, they have remained implicit rather than directly expressed and developed separately rather than together, and as premises, of course, they are the starting-points for a rigorous materialist interpretation of spatiality and not conclusions or unchallengeable assertions. Nonetheless, contained within them is an approach to spatiality (and to social theory) which differs significantly from previous conventions. This is an interpretive approach which has been almost invisible in the historical development of social and spatial theory, seemingly buried from view by the hegemony of alternative theoretical and philosophical perspectives. Just as the contemporary retheorisation of spatiality revolves around the demystification and politicisation of the social production of space, so too must it reveal the mystifying and depoliticising imprint conveyed by the production and prevalence of these alternative perspectives.

I think it possible to show that a certain myopia has persistently distorted spatial theorisation for centuries by creating an *illusion of opaqueness*, a short-sighted interpretation of spatiality which has focussed on immediate surface appearances without being able to see beyond them. Spatiality is accordingly interpreted as a collection of things, as substantive appearances which may ultimately be linked to social causation but which are explainable primarily as things-in-themselves. This essentially empiricist interpretation of spatiality reflects the 'substantive-attributive structure' that has dominated scientific thought since the philosophy of the Enlightenment, a powerful heritage to which spatial and social theorists have repeatedly appealed for both insight and legitimacy.[14]

From this perspective, spatiality is comprehended and theorised as objective appearances grasped through some combination of sensory-based perception (a purview developed by Hume and Locke and later revised in Comtean and other less sceptical forms of positivism), Cartesian mathematical-geometric abstraction (extended to manifold non-Euclidean variations) and the mechanical materialism of a Newtonian 'social physics'. In all these approaches, spatiality tends to be reduced to physical objects and forms, and naturalised back to a 'first' nature to become susceptible to prevailing 'scientific' explanation in the form of orderly, reproduceable description and the systematic discovery of empirical regularities. Social space is thus interpreted as if it were physical space.

Such an approach has proved productive in the accumulation of accurate information about geographical appearances, the traditional objective of the discipline of geography. It becomes illusive, however, when geographical appearances are substituted for explanation of the social production of space and the spatial organisation of society; or when they are posited as the epistomological basis for such understanding and explanation. And yet this is precisely what has happened in the development of theoretical geography and most forms of conventional spatial analysis, so much of which has revolved around either the systematic description and categorisation of geographical facts or the less theoretically 'innocent' permutative correlation and locational covariation of phenomenal forms. Even when a narrow empiricism or positivism is explicitly eschewed, the 'spatial organisation of society' is made to appear natural, mechanical, or organic, a product of the ordering discipline of distance decay and of the relativity of location. Within this optic, theories are constructed which mask social conflict and recognise social practice, if at all, as little more than the aggregate expression of individual 'preferences' which are typically assumed to be (naturally?

mechanically? organically?) given. This pattern has dominated the theorisation of urban morphology; the distributional arrangement of workplaces, residences and human settlements; the spatial diffusion of information and the incidence of human migrations; the location of transportation routes and the siting of industry; and aggregate areal variations in economic development.

The vision of these theorisations can thus properly be described as myopic: what they fail to see are the conflictful social origins of spatiality and its problematic production and reproduction. Instead, spatiality is uprooted from its social structuration and presented as a series of flat, mappable facts, pure form. It is worthwhile recalling Lefebvre's trenchant critique of this distorting objectification of spatiality:

> If space has an air of neutrality and indifference with regard to its contents and thus seems to be 'purely' formal, the epitome of rational abstraction, it is precisely because it has already been the focus of past processes whose traces are not always evident on the landscape. Space has been shaped and moulded from historical and natural elements, but this has been a political process. Space is political and ideological. It is a product literally filled with ideology.[15]

It is not surprising that the development and persistence of this illusion of opaqueness, with its rational abstraction, naturalisation, and universalisation of space, its submergence of social conflict and attendant separation of social and spatial theorisation, has been increasingly interpreted as an integral part of the evolution of capitalism itself. As one critic observed, 'Time and space assume . . . that character of absolute timelessness and universality which must mark the exchange abstraction as a whole and each of its features.'[16] Time and space, like the commodity form, the competitive market, and the structure of social classes, are represented as a natural relation between things, explainable objectively in terms of the physical properties and attributes of these things. Like spatiality itself, this myopic reification in theory construction is filled with politics and ideology.

The same is true of the second source of illusion, which evolves in a complex interaction with the first, often as its attempted philosophical negation.[17] Whereas the empiricist myopia cannot see the social production of spatiality behind the opaqueness of objective appearances, a hypermetropic *illusion of transparency* sees right

through the concrete spatiality of social life by projecting its production into purposeful idealism and immaterialised reflexive thought.
Seeing is blurred not because the focal point is too far in front of the
retina, but because it lies too far behind. The production of spatiality
is represented as cognition and mental design, and an illusory
ideational subjectivity substituted for an equally illusory sensory
objectivism. Spatiality is reduced to a mental construct, a way of
thinking, an ideational process in which the image takes epistemological priority over the tangible substance or the generative
process. Social space folds into mental space, into representations of
spatiality rather than its material social reality.

The philosophical parentage of this Platonic theorisation is typically traced back at least to Liebniz' assertion of the relativism of space,
its existence as an idea rather than a thing. The primary legitimising
source, however, is Kant, whose system of categorical antinomies
assigned an explicit and sustaining place to geography and spatial
analysis, a place which has been carefully preserved in a continuing
neo-Kantian interpretation of spatiality. The hallmarks of the Kantian legacy of transcendental idealism pervade what is variously
called phenomenological, existential, idealist, and humanistic
geography, but extend into many other forms of geographical
analysis as well. Spatiality, with occasional nods to its actual physical
appearances and social origins, is considered primarily as a mental
ordering of phenomena which is either intuitive and given or alternatively relativised into various and variable 'ways of thinking'. Ideas
about space are emplaced within categorical structures of cognition
in such generalised forms as 'human nature', culture, science, 'the
spirit', or a collective social consciousness.

Just such a Kantian chorography characterises Sack's recent major
work, *Conceptions of Space in Social Thought*.[18] Although it
propounds a realist approach and explores far beyond the limits of
spatial subjectivity, Sack's analysis of the 'elemental structures' of
modes of thought is virtually divorced from the influence of 'socio-
material conditions', a subject which Sack assigns for future research.[19] He packages the conceptualisation of spatiality into a
typical Kantian categorical dualism, between the 'sophisticated-
-fragmented' spatial meaning of the arts, sciences, and contemporary
industrial society; and the 'unsophisticated–fused' conceptualisation
of the primitive and the child, of myth and magic. In many ways, this
spatial dualism parallels and can be mapped into such equally
Procrustean dualisms of social theory as *Gemeinschaft* and *Gesells-*

chaft, mechanical and organic solidarity, or the primitive and the modern.

Again, there are useful insights to be drawn from such approaches, but they have also served to maintain and reinforce fundamental illusions about the social production of space, especially insofar as the ideation of spatiality becomes substituted for its problematic and politically-charged social production and reproduction. Mental space may have some intrinsic qualities, but if spatial fusion-fragmentation defines one of the elemental structures of social thought, it too must be grounded in the material conditions of social life, for it does not appear out of thin air.[20] Conceptions of space do not necessarily arise from material spatiality in some simple, deterministic fashion. Neither are they only the complex reflection of material conditions, for they also reflect back to shape the social production of space. What is illusive, rather, is the assumption that the spatial organisation of society can be seen and understood as a projection of modes of thought hypothetically (or otherwise) independent of socio-material conditions, social space interpreted as if it were mental space.

The illusion of transparency is typically compounded by a tacit acceptance of an intellectual division of labour (indelibly Kantian) which separates spatiality from history and both from social theory and material life. Space and time for Kant were subjective forms of perception, substanceless and transcendental schemata. In his peculiar combination of Newtonian and Liebnizian theories, Kant saw space and time as a way of thinking and not, in themselves, something objective or real.[21] Geographical understanding, as chorological science, accordingly arises from the schematic description and subjective representation of the *results* of material forces, objects and phenomena existing in space and is distinct from an understanding of the *development* of phenomena, which is the preserve of history (chronological science). The interpretation of this conceptualisation has helped to sustain a remarkably long-lasting set of conventions which have rigidly compartmentalised geographical, historical and social analysis and theory-building.

Throughout its history, for example, the institutionalised discipline of geography has repeatedly sought philosophical legitimacy in its distinctive (if not unique) perspective, often using this sustaining legitimisation as a means of confining geographical analysis to pure description of phenomenal forms regardless of their causal origins. In both the chorological tradition of regional description and the allegedly more 'nomothetic' explanations of quantitative–theoretical geography, the analysis of spatiality tended to remain static, fragmented and introspectively separatist in the sense of being only tangentially linked to developments within the broader realms of social theory, historiography and philosophy. The latter were occasionally tapped, but remained largely out-of-bounds as 'not geography', their insights not 'indigenous'.[22]

On the other side of this dividing wall and from at least the last decades of the nineteenth century, spatiality was systematically expunged from the increasingly separate social sciences. This 'suppression of space in social theory', as Giddens calls it, can be traced in large part to the determination of social theorists to remove any suggestion of 'geographical determinism' in their works. As Giddens notes:

> The importation of the term 'ecology' into the social sciences has done little to help matters, since this tends both to encourage the confusion of the spatial with other characteristics of the physical world that might influence social life, and to reinforce the tendency to treat spatial characteristics as in the 'environment' of social activity, *rather than as integral to its occurrence.*[23]

A similar suppression of spatiality took place within Marxism. Space presented itself to Marx primarily as a physical context, the sum of the places of production, the territory of different markets, a crude friction of distance to be 'annihilated' by increasingly unfettered capital.[24] Even the town–countryside relation, so intrinsic to capitalist spatiality and geographically uneven development, was treated primarily as a pure and direct reflection of the social division of labour, an incidental externality (albeit an organisational schema around which, Marx claimed, the history of all class societies could be written). It can be argued that Marx recognised the opaqueness of spatiality, that it can hide under its objective appearances the fundamental social relations of production; and that he also approached, if not so directly, the basic problematic embedded in the social production of space, namely, that the interplay between social and spatial relations results not only in spatiality being shaped by social relations but also in a certain spatial contingency of social relations themselves. But this spatial contingency, especially with its inherited connotations of environmentalism, was reduced primarily to a form of fetishisation and false consciousness and never received from Marx an effective interpretation.[25]

It is worthwhile remembering the particular achievement of the materialist interpretation of history set forward by Marx, for it helps to explain why Marxism evolved without a corresponding materialist interpretation of spatiality. Instead, spatiality remained until recently under a Marxian illusion of transparency which reduced it to ideation and hence *only* to ideology, and an explanation of this requires some attention to the relation between Marx and Hegel.

In grounding the Hegelian dialectic in material life, Marx not only responded to Hegelian idealism, denying the spiritual navigation and determination of history, but also rejected its particularised form, the territorial state, as history's principal spiritual vehicle. Standing the Hegelian dialectic 'on its feet' thus represented both a denial of idealism *and* a specific rejection of territorial or spatial fetishism, in which history and historical determination centered in an innately given spatial consciousness (whether focused on the State, cultural nationalism, regionalism, or localism). Marx thus attempted to re-establish the primacy of revolutionary time over revolutionary spatiality by asserting class consciousness and class conflict, stripped of all mystification, as its driving force. Despite his sensitive analyses of the spatiality of capitalism, therefore, time became the primary 'variable container' for Marx, and history the resultant product of the appropriation of nature through human labour and de-territorialised struggle. The outcome was an historical materialism which, from the very beginning, built in significant inhibitions against what was perceived as a divisive and diversionary emphasis on the spatiality of history (and, it should be added, a relative theoretical weakness with regard to the role of the State, territoriality, and nationalism in capitalist development). These inhibitions became codified and conventionalised in the subsequent evolution of Marxism (the early works of Lukács spring particularly to mind) and shaped a tradition of treating spatial contingency primarily in terms of ideology and false consciousness. As Poulantzas observed, then:

> For its part, Marxist research has up to now... considered that transformations of space and time essentially concern ways of thinking: it assigns a marginal role to such changes on the grounds that they belong to the ideological–cultural domain – to the manner in which societies or classes *represent* space and time. In reality, however, transformations of the spatio-temporal matrices refer to the materiality of the social division of labour, of the structure of the State, and of the practices and techniques of capitalist econ-

omic, political and ideological power; they are the *real substratum* of mythical, religious, philosophical or 'experiential' representations of space–time.[26]

The retheorisation of spatiality: precedence, ambivalence, convergence

The development of a materialist interpretation of spatiality has moved through three phases which can be described as periods of precedence, ambivalence and convergence. The formative roots of the contemporary reinterpretation are found most clearly and assertively in a conceptualisation of space which develops initially within French Marxism, primarily through the contributions of Henri Lefebvre and his associates.[27] Perhaps nowhere else is spatiality placed so explicitly on the theoretical and political agenda as it is in France, an historical–geographical event which demands more substantial analysis than I can give it here.

Some of the ideas and arguments associated with this prototypically French conceptualisation influenced a parallel development during the 1970s within what can be loosely labelled Marxist geography, as characteristically anglophonic as the former was francophonic. From the beginning, however, Marxist geography was equivocal about the importance of spatiality, alternatively asserting its central significance while backing away from too forceful a spatialisation of conventionally accepted historical materialist analysis. In the heated conceptual battleground that was created few ventured into explicit theorisation.

More recently, however, this ambivalence has been cut through in a growing theoretical convergence around a comprehensive materialist interpretation of spatiality which builds upon the accomplishments of both Marxist geography and the French spatial tradition, but adds to them some new theoretical frameworks, practical applications and philosophical emphases. Also added have been new participants to the debate on the theorisation of spatiality, which has suddenly broadened to involve a much wider constituency of social theorists, philosophers and practitioners than ever before. Let me trace through these three phases in greater detail.

Precedence: spatiality in the French Marxist tradition

Marxism in France was a relative latecomer in comparison with Britain, Germany, and the United States. This has been attributed largely to the powerful inheritance of earlier French socialist thought, which continued to offer an attractive indigenous political alternative.[28] When French Marxism did expand under the immiserating conditions of global economic crisis in the 1920s and 1930s, it was shaped by some special spatio-temporal circumstances. For example, it built upon a heritage of political and social theory which, from Fourier and Proudhon to the anarchist geographers Kropotkin and Reclus, contained a sensitive and persistent emphasis on the politics of spatiality and territorially-based communalism. It also grew with less of the anti-spatial encumbrance that had already become established within the more 'advanced' Marxisms of other Western industrial countries, via what I have described earlier as the double inversion of Hegel. Although it is difficult to prove such an argument definitively, there seems to be a convincing basis for claiming that French Marxism, from the onset, was more inclined towards incorporating an explicit spatial perspective and theorisation than Marxisms elsewhere.

From the late 1920s to at least the early 1950s, Lefebvre probably had more influence in shaping the course and character of French Marxist theory and philosophy than any other individual. Together with his associate Norbert Guterman he published the first French translation of key sections of Marx's 1844 economic and philosophical manuscripts and, in a series of anthologies accompanied by extensive editorial notes and discussion, introduced to a French audience many other key works by Marx and Engels as well as Lenin's *Philosophical Notebooks*. The latter was Lenin's critical appreciation of Hegel and contributed to the major Hegelian revival which marked the early expansion of Marxism in France.

In his own elaboration of the Hegel–Marx relation, Lefebvre sought to combine a strand of 'objective idealism' within the materialist dialectic, to encourage attention to contradictions in thought and consciousness as well as to the bases of contradictions in concrete reality and history. *La Conscience Mystifiée*, the title of one of his earlier original works, became an insistent theme not only for Lefebvre but for many other French Marxist writers.[29] Lefebvre explicitly accepted Marx's argument about the primacy of material life in the production of consciousness – that being produced consciousness rather than the reverse – but refused to relegate thought and consciousness to a determined aftergloss or automatic ideation.

In a pattern which would characterise his work for over fifty years, Lefebvre thus took a stance against dogmatic reductionism in the interpretation of Marx, pushing instead in his reformulated

Hegelianism for an open Marxism able to grow and adapt without predetermined truncation. By forcefully maintaining the openness of Marxist thought and avoiding any premature narrowing of the materialist dialectic, Lefebvre was to become the most influential early critic of Stalinist economism, through his widely circulated and translated text, *Le Matérialism Dialectique*, originally published in 1939.[30] Later, both existentialism and structuralism received the sting of Lefebvre's pen, via biting critiques of the early Sartre and the ascendant Althusser, both similarly aimed against the dangers of reductionism.[31]

There have been many who have refused to see Marx's 'inversion' of Hegel as a rigid stricture against all forms of idealism and subjectivity entering the materialist dialectic other than as reflected and predetermined superstructure. Lefebvre, like these other commentators, saw the negation of idealism as an invitation to a reformulated dialectic which could combine the relational contradictions of both thought and being, consciousness and material life, superstructure and economic base. But perhaps more than anyone else, Lefebvre also followed a similar dialectical logic with regard to his critiques of existentialism/phenomenology and structuralism, rejecting any attempt at Procrustean reductionism yet seeing in these major twentieth-century philosophical movements a creative opportunity to improve and strengthen Marxist analysis. Over the past thirty years, Lefebvre has drawn selectively from each of these perspectives in his insistent attempt to combine simultaneously both subjectivity and objectivity in materialist analysis and praxis.

The comprehensiveness, adaptability and contextual roots of Lefebvre's Marxism are essential to any explanation of his eventual 'turn' towards a materialist interpretation of spatiality. Against those writers who are evidently puzzled by this manoeuvre,[32] it can be argued that Lefebvre's assertion of the central significance of the social production of space to the survival of capitalism and his attempt to redirect historical materialism towards a spatial problematic was a direct and logical extension of the same open and creatively adaptive approach to Marxism that had always characterised his writings. It thus did not represent a 'break' from his earlier work, but a continuation, a perceptive expansion rather than a perverse narrowing of materialist analysis. In time, it may yet prove to be his most important and lasting contribution to the development of Marxism and to critical social theory more generally.

Lefebvre's theorisation of space cannot be summarised very easily, for it is embedded in an extraordinarily large number of published works which touch upon virtually every aspect of social theory and philosophy. When probed for its origins, Lefebvre himself points to the influence of his Occitanian birthplace and his frequent returns home to observe the massive changes taking place in rural land and life.[33] His more explicit theorisation, however, evolved through a series of what he called 'approximations' of a central thesis, the first being his emphasis on *la vie quotidienne*, everyday life in the modern world (itself an extension of his arguments in *La Conscience Mystifiée*).[34] By the time his projected trilogy on this subject was completed, he had recast his work around other themes, which included urbanism and the 'urban revolution', and the 'repetitive vs. the differential'.[35] The central thesis became more clearly articulated in *La Survie du Capitalism* (1973; English translation, 1976) and especially *La Production de l'Espace* (1974). It can be most succinctly summarised in the notion that social space is where the reproduction of the relations of production is located:

> Capitalism has found itself able to attenuate (if not resolve) its internal contradictions for a century, and consequently, in the hundred years since the writing of *Capital*, it has succeeded in achieving 'growth'. We cannot calculate at what price, but we know the means: *by occupying space, by producing a space.*[36]

> *We are not speaking of a science of space, but of a knowledge (a theory) of the production of space ... This dialectised, conflictive space is where the reproduction of the relations of production is achieved. It is this space that produces reproduction, by introducing into it its multiple contradictions.*[37]

For Lefebvre, then, the survival of capitalism – its continued reproduction – has been built upon the creation of an increasingly embracing and socially mystified capitalist spatiality. He explores this mystification using the same categories that I set out earlier: illusions of opaqueness and transparency.[38] And he introduces an analysis of the essential features of this capitalist spatiality to which he returns again and again in his subsequent writings.

Capitalist spatiality is characterised by its distinctive combination of *homogeneity*, *fragmentation*, and *hierarchisation* – a description directly echoed in Poulantzas' observation cited earlier.[39] So structured, capitalist spatiality increasingly penetrates and shapes everyday life while simultaneously expanding to a global scale, organising social life into multiple layers of domination and subordination, cores and peripheries. In a four-volume work, *De L'Etat*,[40] Lefebvre develops this argument further, to say that this production of capitalist spatiality has only been possible through the aegis of the capitalist State, and he concludes that this has led to what can appropriately be called *le mode de production étatique*.

Whether or not there now exists a 'state mode of production', the main thrust of Lefebvre's theorisation of spatiality is challenging and politically resonant. Spatiality is not only a product but also a producer and reproducer of the relations of production and dominant, an instrument of both allocative and authoritative power. Class struggle, as well as other social struggles are thus increasingly contained and defined in their spatiality and trapped in its 'grid'. Social struggle must then become consciously and politically spatial struggle to regain control over the social production of space.

The materialist interpretation of spatiality presented by Lefebvre is aimed at revealing the societal contradictions – in both consciousness and in material life – that are embedded in the social production of space and its persistently effective mystification. His argument is pushed to a summative, historical conclusion:

> The dialectic is back on the agenda. But it is no longer Marx's dialectic, just as Marx's was no longer Hegel's . . . The dialectic today no longer clings to historicity and historical time, or to a temporal mechanism such as 'thesis–antithesis–synthesis' . . . To recognise space, to recognise what 'takes place' there and what it is used for, is to resume the dialectic; analysis will reveal the contradictions of space.[41]

Ambivalence: spatiality in Marxist geography

Concurrent with the consolidation of Lefebvre's work around the interlinkage between the production of space, the reproduction of the relations of production, and the growing empowerment of the State, there developed in North America and Britain an increasing involvement with Marxism within the field of geography (paralleling a similar development in the other social sciences). French geography was not as significantly affected by Lefebvre's work as was French urban sociology, which became preoccupied with spatial issues and themes to a degree far greater than its counterparts elsewhere. When

Lefebvre's ideas did filter into anglophonic Marxist geography, it was primarily through the intermediary and often distorting screen of imported French Marxist urban sociology.

Especially important was the English translation of *La Question Urbaine*, written by Manuel Castells, himself a student of Lefebvre.[42] Castells's biting critique of Lefebvre's 'urbanistic ideology' was based on the latter's earlier 'approximations' which revolved around his notions of everyday life and the 'urban revolution'. Although Castells's urban sociology drew heavily from Lefebvre, therefore, it rebounded against what Castells perceived as an excessively urbanistic determination of politics and class struggle – hence the Engels-like recasting of the urban into a 'question' as opposed to the source of a revolutionary impetus. Only in the Afterword to the English edition of *La Question Urbaine* did Castells note the 'new important work' produced by Lefebvre in the early 1970s.[43]

David Harvey, in *Social Justice and the City*, unquestionably the most influential work in the early development of Marxist geography, referred sympathetically to both Castells (in his original French writings) and to Lefebvre (again primarily in French).[44] But Harvey ultimately adopted Castells's critique, and Harvey's interpretation of Lefebvre remained virtually the only major discussion of Lefebvre's work within Marxist geography through the 1970s. *La Production de l'Espace*, as well as his later writings on the State, were almost entirely ignored.

Marxist geography grew somewhat incohesively, compartmentalised around separate geographical scales (urban, regional, international) and without a comprehensive and integrative materialist theorisation of spatiality.[45] It also grew within a tradition which was persistently aspatial if not actively anti-spatial, especially in comparison with its French counterparts. As a result, the deliberate attempt to examine the spatial implications and dimensions of historical materialism and to redirect geographical analysis along Marxist lines met almost immediately with marked resistance not only from non-Marxist geographers, as might be expected, but also from other Marxists. The latter, often geographers themselves, saw in much of the new Marxist geography a theoretically and politically unacceptable diversion from the centrality of class analysis, class consciousness, and class struggle: one which too often overstepped the bounds of conventionally accepted historical materialism by asserting too powerful and determinative a role for space and spatiality.

Throughout the 1970s, it appeared that an explicitly materialist interpretation of spatiality would remain lost in an ambivalent dance-step which moved forward only to glide back again, a space versus class *gavotte* choreographed to avoid the long-established dangers of diversionary and bourgeois spatialism. So seemingly equivocal and inconclusive was this dance that it provoked observers (as well as some participants) to conclude that spatiality could fit into Marxism only as an ancillary detail, a perfunctory reflection of more fundamental social relations of production and spatially abstracted 'laws of motion'. Geographers could look back over the decade and feel compelled to explain 'why geography cannot be Marxist',[46] or to note that spatial structure was being prematurely abandoned in radical geographical analysis.[47] Larger theoretical and philosophical arguments about the essential spatiality of social life, such as those raised by Lefebvre, were either glanced over or squeezed into a rigid categorical interpretation which led too easily to their facile dismissal, especially through an imposed compulsion to determine inherent priority. Thus, in a debate which presumed space and class to be separate and possibly antagonistic orders, there seemed little choice. Class must be recognised as dominant and determinative, space as reflective and subordinate. So too with any perceived opposition between social versus spatial relations of production and historical versus geographical materialism. Attempts to break with this categorical imposition, to balance and combine these perceived dualities, tended to be seen as a dithering dialectics ineluctably impelled to spatial determinism.[48]

Missing from the debates was a convincing and cohesive argument that spatiality is inseparable from society, is its real material substratum, the medium and outcome of social action and relationship – the fundamental premiss for a materialist interpretation of spatiality. Marxist geography nevertheless edged closer and closer to this transformative retheorisation, implicitly if not explicitly advancing an interpretation of capitalist spatiality which increasingly echoed Lefebvre's prefigurative conceptualisation. The broader theoretical conclusions remained unstated, but in their analyses of the urbanisation process, class conflict over the built environment, industrial restructuring and the changing territorial division of labour, geographically uneven development and regional crisis, Marxist geographers together with urban and regional political economists began effectively to demystify and politicise the social production of space and explore the problematic spatial contingency of capitalist development.[49] Behind much of this work was the stated intention to make geographical analysis more Marxist. But it also served the obverse aim, by imbuing historical materialism with a salient and elaborated spatial perspective, often where no direct precedent could be found in the writings of Marx.

The most important specific accomplishment of Marxist geography was its attachment of a spatial problematic to the generation of capitalist crisis and related attempts to restructure the capitalist accumulation process. Through this attachment, spatiality, class struggle, and the dynamics of capitalist development became increasingly intertwined in a formulation which could only tenuously be traced back to Marx. Perhaps the best encapsulation of this spatial problematic was presented by Harvey:

> Capital represents itself in the form of a physical landscape created in its own image, created as use values to enhance the progressive accumulation of capital. The geographical landscape which results is the crowning glory of past capitalist development. But at the same time it expresses the power of dead labour over living labour and as such it imprisons and inhibits the accumulation process within a set of specific physical constraints ... Capitalist development has therefore to negotiate a knife-edge path between preserving the exchange values of past capital investments in the built environment and destroying the value of these investments in order to open up fresh room for accumulation. Under capitalism, there is then a perpetual struggle in which capital builds a physical landscape appropriate to its own condition at a particular moment in time, only to have to destroy it, usually in the course of crises, at a subsequent point in time.[50]

This 'perpetual struggle' between what Lipietz called 'inherited space' and 'projected space'[51] illuminates the historical and social origins of spatial contingency and infuses capitalism with an inherent spatial problematic. It also provides a conceptual purview from which to interpret the increasing role of the capitalist State, the nature of geographically uneven development, and the entire conflictful sequence of spatialities that has marked the historical experience of capitalist societies. Although focussed on the logic of capital, it also implies a programme for labour and spatially-conscious class struggle, a conceptualisation of social action which is imbricated in the spatiality of social life. And it is no mere coincidence that this conceptualisation has been explicitly recognised and consciously examined during a period of deepening crisis in the world capitalist economy.

More recently, Harvey has expanded his interpretation of the spatiality of capitalist crisis in a theorisation of what he calls the 'spatial fix'.[52] Although he traces the origins of this theorisation back to Marx and Hegel (and to von Thünen as well), the interpretation he presents is much less a recapitulation of past notions than the systematic assertion of the contemporary achievement of Marxist geography and its growing convergence around a materialist interpretation of spatiality. In this way, he does indeed reveal the 'limits' to *Capital*.

Convergence: spatial praxis and critical social theory

Under the current conditions of global economic crisis and accompanying attempts at restructuring capital and labour to establish the bases for renewed expansion, the production and restructuration of space has become consciously politicised as never before: in the demands for a new international (territorial) order in response to the changing geographical division of labour created by accelerated capital mobility and the internationalisation of production; in regional and national struggles triggered by the same forces and intensified by competition for reduced fiscal resources; in the mobilisation of local communities and urban neighbourhoods in response to the spatial restructuring of urban-metropolitan areas; in radical environmental movements aimed at regaining control over the production of nature and the weaponry that could destroy it; in the efforts of women to redirect the architectonics of a built environment which imposes and sustains male domination. A powerful mystification of spatiality still persists, but the 'spatial fix' that is currently taking place has been more politically visible than any other that has preceded it.

The retheorisation of spatiality is being built upon this increasing demystification and politicisation of spatiality in social practice. Its fundamental premiss is that spatiality is the real manifestation of social relations rather than their incidental reflection or mirror, that social space is where the reproduction of society is located and where it must accordingly be acted upon and progressively transformed. The alleged categorical opposition of space and class is being replaced by a transformative notion of spatial *praxis*: the active and informed attempt by spatially-conscious social actors to reconstitute the embracing spatiality of social life.

Castells evokes this notion of spatial praxis as follows:

> It has been a custom in the recent literature of urban studies to use the formula according to which space is the expression of society. Although such a perspective is a healthy reaction against the technological determinism and the short-sighted emphasis too frequently predominant in the space-related disciplines, it is clearly an insufficient formulation of the problem . . . Space is not a 'reflection of society', it *is* society . . . one of its fundamental material dimensions . . . Therefore, spatial forms, at least on our planet, will be produced, as all other objects are, by human action. They will express and perform the interests of the dominant class according to a given mode of production and to a specific mode of development. They will express and implement the power relationships of the state in an historically defined society. They will be realised and shaped by the process of gender domination and by state-enforced family life. At the same time, spatial forms will be earmarked by the resistance from exploited classes, from oppressed subjects, and from dominated women. And the work of such a contradictory historical process on the space will be accomplished on an already inherited spatial form, the product of former history and the support of new interests, projects, protests and dreams. Finally, from time to time, social movements will arise to challenge the meaning of spatial structure and therefore to attempt new functions and new forms.[53]

In his influential work, *Ideology, Science and Human Geography*, Derek Gregory pointed to a similar reinterpretation of space and class:

> The analysis of spatial structure is not derivative and secondary to the analysis of social structure . . . rather, each requires the other. Spatial structure is not, therefore, merely the arena within which class conflicts express themselves but also the domain within which – and in part through which – class relations are *constituted*.[54]

Elsewhere, Gregory extends this argument, urging that in the effort to achieve 'an adequate understanding of situated social practice', a cycle must be completed. It began with the striking realisation that social reproduction is a key 'moment' in the formation of spatial structure, a discovery which turned geographers toward class analysis and materialist social theory. To it, however, must be added its theoretical complement, the equally striking recognition that the formation of spatial structure, the production of spatiality, is a critical 'moment' in social reproduction.[55] This completion of the cycle calls for a concomitant reorientation of class analysis and materialist social theory around an explicit and formative spatial problematic, a recognition of the spatial as well as historical contingency of social life.

Here then is another affirmative elicitation of the central theoretical project which threads through the contemporary convergence around a materialist interpretation of spatiality. At its core is a theory of social action activated by spatiality, by what I have defined as spatial praxis. This praxis-orientation in turn has drawn together three major groups of theoreticians who have hitherto had relatively little contact with one another. The first consists of those who are continuing to build upon, clarify, and extend the conceptualisation of spatiality which originated within French Marxism and is now being carried forward not only by Lefebvre (who remains active and productive) but by many others who are directly or indirectly influenced by him. The second involves the further development of anglophonic geography toward a critical theory of capitalist spatiality, periodicity and crisis, based in analyses of empirical conditions and events. The third includes the 'structuration school' of critical social theorists and proponents of an associated critical philosophy of theoretical realism.

Illustrative of the work of the first group is Poulantzas' *State, Power, Socialism*, the last major work published before his death. In it, Poulantzas shifted from his relatively spaceless analyses of politics and the State to focus upon the institutional materiality embodied in the spatial and temporal matrices of capitalism. For Poulantzas, social formations are defined as the 'actual sites' for the existence and reproduction of modes of production. At these sites under capitalism, the State in its various forms acts through its increasing authoritative and allocative powers, 'creating and making reality' in the form of spatial and temporal matrices.[56] Here again there is a two-way relationship. These matrices (which he encapsulates in the terms 'territory' and 'tradition') organise and structure the frameworks through which the State exercises its power. Law in its formal and abstract character, for example, is bound up with 'space–time as the material frame of reference of the labour process'.[57] It serves to 'consecrate' fragmentation (individualisation) and to legitimate the peculiar fabric of increasingly homogenised social time and space created in territory and tradition. Concurrently, however, the State increasingly reserves social space and time for itself, intervening in the creation of these matrices by tending to monopolise the instruments and procedures which organise them – that is, the very networks of power and domination that these matrices define. The State thus shapes and is simultaneously shaped by the material frameworks of spatiality and historicity.

In his specific depiction of the spatial matrix of capitalism, Poulantzas restates Lefebvre's description of homogenisation, fragmentation and hierarchisation, and repeats his own argument about spatiality as the presupposition and embodiment of relations of production:

> Separation and division in order to unify; parcelling out in order to structure; atomization in order to encompass; segmentation in order to totalize; closure in order to homogenize; and individualization in order to obliterate differences and otherness. The roots of totalitarianism are inscribed in the spatial matrix concretized by the modern nation–State – a matrix that is already present in its relations of production and in the capitalist division of labour.[58]

This direct connection between spatiality, social reproduction, politics, power and the State is the core of Lefebvre's theorisation. It runs through the work of Lipietz, Castells, and many others currently writing within a broadly defined French Marxist tradition. It also outlines the key themes which are shaping the contemporary materialist interpretation of spatiality in Marxist geography and structurationist social theory as well, a further manifestation of the theoretical covergence currently taking place.

The interplay of spatiality, politics and the role of the State is now central to Marxist geography and linked segments of urban and regional planning, political economy and sociology. This has helped to erode the former conceptual divisions between the urban, regional, and international scales by focussing all three upon the same general processes and problematic. Illustrative of this comprehensive materialist interpretation of spatiality has been the increasing

clarification and systematic elaboration of a theory of geographically
uneven development, for so long a source of confusion and controversy within (and without) Marxism. Geographically uneven development is an essential condition of capitalist spatiality, an inherent
feature of the concretisation of relations of production and the
division of labour that defines spatiality itself. It too can be described
as both medium and outcome, formative product and contingent
producer and reproducer of social action and relationship. It is
characteristically patterned into cores and peripheries defined not by
absolute location but by the aggregate properties of localised production systems and the resultant geographical relationships between
these systems (such as the geographical transfer of value in its various
forms).[59]

Just as capitalism develops unevenly over time and can be
periodised into distinct sequences, phases or other temporal patterning, so too has capitalism developed unevenly over space in similarly
identifiable configurations and patternings of spatiality. These
specific patternings are not incidental extrusions but changeable
products of social struggle, part of the succession of spatialities
punctuating the course of capitalist development. As such they are
embroiled in politics and power relations and reinforce the link
between spatiality and the role of the State. Lipietz specifies this link
with regard to geographically uneven development at the regional
level:

> Faced with the uneven development of socio-economic regions, the
> State must take care to avoid sparking off the political and social
> struggles which would arise from too abrupt a dissolution or
> integration of archaic modes of production. This is what it does in a
> general fashion when it inhibits the process of articulation (protec-
> tionism) or when it intervenes promptly to remove social con-
> sequences (permanent displacement allowances). But as soon as
> internal and international evolution make it necessary, capitalist
> development assigns to the state the role of controlling and en-
> couraging the establishment of a new inter-regional division of
> labour. This 'projected space' comes into more or less violent
> conflict with 'inherited space'. State intervention must therefore
> take the form of organising the substitution of projected space for
> present space.[60]

As he notes, the capitalist market alone is unable to accomplish this
spatial restructuring.

Geographically uneven development is thus not only being linked with politics and the State but also with the generation of capitalist crisis and associated restructuring efforts. This combination points to another theme which exemplifies the current research and theoretical directions of Marxist geography and related approaches: an analysis of time–space structuration defined as *periodisation–spatialisation*. With increasing clarity, the mechanisms and processes underlying the historical sequence of spatialities which mark the development of capitalism are being rigorously examined, revealing the embracing macro-rhythms of social life.

To complete this picture of theoretical convergence, it is necessary to add another significant set of participants. Although not aimed explicitly at propounding a materialist interpretation of spatiality, their work has provided major theoretical and philosophical insights for its systematic and effective advancement. Three general features characterise the contributions of this group of critical social theorists and philosophers. First, their aim has been to reconstruct social theory around, to use Gregory's words, 'an adequate understanding of situated social practice', around a philosophy of praxis.[61] Second, this search for a philosophy of praxis has been built upon a far-ranging critique of the persistent dualisms which have dichotomised conventional social theory: determinism–voluntarism, structure–agency, objectivism–subjectivism, compositional versus contextual approaches. Third, their reconstructive critiques have led them to some form of dialectical synthesis which maintains the real tensions and inter-contingencies of the old oppositions but denies their recalcitrant dichotomisation and grounds their resolution in constrained but knowledgeable human agency and social action.

The tight interpretive cycle which leads from theoretical objective to reconstructive critique to dialectical synthesis back again to the theoretical objective has had major repercussions on contemporary social theory, especially with regard to historical materialism. Significantly, the interpretative cycle has become anchored in a reconceptualisation of time and space which situates social practice (and thus social theory as well) in the time–space constitution and structuration of social life, to use the terms closely associated with Giddens' recent writings. It has been this particular reconceptualisation that reverberates throughout the contemporary retheorisation of spatiality, drawing into it to a degree unmatched in the history of geographic thought over the past century the leading edge of critical social theory.

Given his reputation as one of the foremost interpreters of social

theory currently writing in English, Giddens' turn toward a materialist interpretation of spatiality has had a particularly powerful impact.
In *Central Problems in Social Theory* and *A Contemporary Critique of
Historical Materialism,* Giddens recomposes the evolving theory of
structuration contained in his earlier work to focus attention upon
the *situation* of social life, its embeddedness in time–space relations,
in the fundamental temporality and spatiality of being. Although
Giddens is more comfortable and emphatic about temporality and
history than about spatiality and geography, there is an insistent logic
of epistemological balance between time and space in his theoretical
formulations and his recent writings are more explicitly and atypical-
ly spatial than those of perhaps any other major anglophonic social
theorist. This has not only drawn geographers, especially those with a
materialist theoretical perspective, to the works of Giddens; it has
increasingly involved Giddens himself with the current debates
surrounding the materialist interpretation of spatiality.

Giddens' critical social theory has been built upon the creative
conjuncture of two theoretical discourses which have developed
through the twentieth century in competitive and discordant opposition: interpretive sociology or hermeneutics on the one hand, structuralism on the other. The critical synthesis contained in the theory of
structuration revolves around the contingent interplay of agency and
structure, the experiential subjectivity, competence, and practical
consciousness of the knowledgeable human agent and the constraining and coercive tendencies arising from the enduring structural
determinations of social life. Agency and structure, intentionality and
determination, conjoin in the social practices which structurate and
'give form' to social life, from the routine to the epochal. Giddens
goes further, however, to situate social practice in the time–space
constitution of social systems, an epistemological assertion of major
importance:

> Most forms of social theory have failed to take seriously enough
> *not only the temporality of social conduct but also its spatial
> attributes.* At first sight, nothing seems more banal and uninstruc-
> tive than to assert that social activity occurs in time and in space.
> But neither time nor space have been incorporated into the centre
> of social theory, they are ordinarily treated more as 'environments'
> in which social conduct is enacted . . . rather than [as] integral to its
> occurrence.[62]

In many ways, Giddens' approach to social theory parallels the
approach to 'geographical explanation' taken by Gregory.[63]

Through a similar deconstructive critique of the distorting prisms of positivism, functionalism, and idealism, and a similarly sympathetic reconstructive critique of hermeneutics and (largely Marxist) structuralist analysis, Gregory selectively combined 'reflexive' and 'structural' theorisation to argue for a necessarily 'committed', praxis-oriented explanation of spatiality.

Less direct and visible, however, are some striking comparisons between Giddens' interpretation of spatiality and Lefebvre's project. Both, for example, vigorously resist the submergence of subjectivity in a categorical and reductionist structuralism which presents the human agent as a cultural dope, merely a bearer of structures. Yet each incorporates salient elements of a more open structuralism in their recognition of the tendential constraints imposed upon human agency and practical consciousness by the social structuration of material life. From the individualised routines of day-to-day activities to the longer *durée* of the rise, expansion and survival of capitalism, human society is seen as constituted through both agency and structure and concretised in socially-produced time and space. In Giddens' description of 'time–space distanciation' and the generation of power, the commodification of time and space in capitalist development, the production of everyday life and the theory of urbanism, the rise of nationalism as a manifestation of the capitalist State and its increasing influence, and the development of capitalism as a world system, he so frequently echoes the major arguments of Lefebvre that – as an unintended consequence – he has become a major channel for the importation of what are in effect Lefebvrean ideas into contemporary social theory.[64]

As these various strands of the materialist interpretation of spatiality become increasingly intertwined, they are simultaneously being tied into more general debates on the philosophy of social science, especially with regard to the development of the philosophical perspective alternatively called 'transcendental' or 'theoretical' realism. The full implications of this growing connection between philosophical realism and the retheorisation of spatiality, as with the connections between both and the structurationist school, are not yet clearly established, but the logic behind their now more than tentative engagement can be easily explained. The realist philosophy of social science seems almost ready-made to sustain and rationalise the theoretical directions taken by the contemporary materialist interpretation of spatiality. For this emerging form of realism revolves around a particular interpretation of the relation between appearances and essences, and echoes Marx's astute comment that 'all science would be superfluous if the outward appearances and essences of things directly coincided'. Realist science is a means of conceptual discovery based on the movement, at any given level of analysis, from manifest phenomena to knowledge of the structures and mechanisms which generate them. These structures and mechanisms (as well as their 'causal powers') are just as real and comprehensible as the manifest phenomena themselves. In this sense, the new realism contrasts with the positivism of conventional spatial science by rejecting a scientific ontology which is limited to the observable and by proffering an epistemological emphasis on causal laws which express *tendencies* of occurrence versus the empirical conjunction of events. Empirical analysis is thus given an alternative explanatory methodology rooted in these tendencies and causal powers, and their nondeterministic effect within an external domain of objects. My earlier comments on empiricist myopia in the theorisation of spatiality obtain a broader interpretation for Keat and Urry:

> Any social theory based on a positivist conception of science will be substantively inadequate, since it will misdirect and limit the scope of theoretical and empirical work, and often in ways that have distinct ideological consequences.[65]

Theoretical realism is also opposed to an idealism which is also to be found in conventional conceptions of spatial structure and for which the apparent externality of the objects of scientific knowledge is illusory and transparent, misleadingly objectified away from essentially ideational causality. Here, too, however, reflexive thought and knowledgeable human agency – the touchstones of hermeneutics – are not denied but instead embedded in historically and geographically specific social forms. What is rejected is a sociological individualism (behaviourism, psychologism) which fails to *situate* thought and knowledge in particular conjunctures of time and space, akin to the hypermetropia I have described in association with the illusion of transparency in the theorisation of spatiality.

In its attempt to avoid the limitations and distortions of positivism and idealism, its affirmation of a redefined synthesis of structuralism and hermenuetics, its situation of social theory and social practice in the conjunctural effects of time and space, its adaptation of an essentially Marxist notion of praxis while simultaneously subjecting Marxism to vigorous reconstructive critique and 'modernisation: in all these, the new theoretical realism directly adjoins with and helps to reinforce the connections between the structurationist school and the contemporary transformative retheorisation of spatiality.

Looking back: a brief epilogue

In this chapter I have only skimmed the surface of a still evolving materialist interpretation of spatiality. I have almost surely attributed more unity of thought than is warranted by the explicit intentions and written statements of the contributors I have drawn together, and more formative influence to certain individuals than to perhaps others equally deserving. I also recognise that what has been described as a momentous and convergent movement may be seen by those familiar with the same literature as only fitful and irregular development in many different, and possibly irreconcilable, directions.

And yet that there *is* an extraordinary convergence of thought taking place in contemporary social theory seems beyond challenge. That it involves a theorisation of space and space–time that differs significantly from prevailing traditions in both Marxist and non-Marxist social science seems equally clear. How central and transformative this retheorisation of spatiality will be, however, remains to be seen. To conclude, I can only return to where I started and reassert, with additional confidence, the introductory remarks with which this essay began, not as an affirmation of accomplished 'truth' but as an invitation to further critical inquiry and spatially-informed social practice.

Notes

1. I refer here, in particular, to current work on the theory of the state, the spatiality of capitalist crisis, and geographically uneven development. For example, see Carney, Hudson, and Lewis (1980) especially the essay by Lipietz; Harvey (1982); and Soja (1981).
2. I have deliberately chosen the term *spatiality* to refer specifically to socially-produced space, the created forms and relations of a broadly-defined human geography. All *space* is not socially produced, but all spatiality (as it is used here) is. It should be noted that this definition allows for arguments and analysis which confer causal influence to particular spatial configurations and spatial relations (as in the interrelation of core and peripheral regions or the effect of a specific built environment, behaviourally-defined territories, or particular locational patterns). This spatial contingency of social life, however, arises not from

an independently established determination but from the social origins of spatiality, its socially created structure and composition. To speak, for example, of regions affecting (exploiting, politically dominating, influencing the production process in) other regions does not necessarily abrogate the ultimate basis of the relationship in people, human beings. It also must be recognised that such spatial contingency can be changed; and it can be made to disappear at very high levels of abstraction, for it is 'conjunctural', meaning that it must be examined empirically in particular times and places.

3. See N. Smith (1982) for an interesting and, I think, compatible discussion of the 'production of nature'.

4. Lefebvre (1974) p. 152, translated from the French. No published English translation of this book exists, although it is crucial to an understanding of Lefebvre's analysis of space.

5. Thrift (1983) p. 31.

6. Poulantzas (1978) pp. 64–5.

7. Giddens (1979, 1981b); see also Thrift (1983) and Soja (1983).

8. Giddens (1979) p. 54.

9. Giddens (1981b) p. 27. There are differences in this notion of duality and my earlier description of spatio-temporal structuration as medium and outcome. However, if structure is 'present only in its instantiation' and this instantiation occurs only in temporal and spatial specification, then it seems appropriate to infer that structuration is inherently spatio-temporal and can be so qualified.

10. Poulantzas (1978) p. 105. The details of this entrapment are richly described in the works of Foucault.

11. Soja (1980).

12. From *The Eighteenth Brumaire of Louis Bonaparte*, in Marx and Engels (1970b) p. 96.

13. Lipietz (1980) p. 61.

14. See Zeleny (1980). Also related here are the critiques of positivism contained in Keat and Urry (1982); Bhaskar (1975) and (1979); and with regard to geographical analysis, Gregory (1978b).

15. Lefebvre (1976) p. 31.

16. Sohn-Rethel (1978) quoted in N. Smith, 1982, p. 145.

17. The historical 'see-saw' between the dominant naturalist current of positivism and its 'anti-naturalist hermeneutical foil' is vividly described in Bhaskar (1979).

18. Sack (1980).

19. Ibid, p. 198. 'In the future we must systematically consider the socio-material context and its relationship to the conceptions of space. (These matters were only touched upon in the book.)'.

20. For a very different interpretation of the contrasts between 'fused' and 'fragmented' conceptualisations of space, see Lefebvre (1980) especially his discussion of spatial fragmentation and 'L'Espace et Mode de Production'. To illustrate, he writes 'In social space, which is both the material and non-material support of social relations, fragmentation is an instrument of political power' (p. 154). See also the earlier references to Poulantzas on capitalist spatiality.

21. Whether Kant's theory of space was based on absolute or relational theories, Newtonian or Liebnizian, is still a controversial question. Buroker (1981, p. 127) sums up her excellent treatment of this issue thus: 'I have argued that the transcendental analysis of space as a subjective form of sensibility is Newtonian insofar as Kant maintains the independence of space from spatial objects, but Liebnizian in the underlying theory of relations. By contrast, the metaphysics of motion is pure Liebniz.'

22. I am tempted to add to the ocular analogy another source of illusion to describe this eclectic geographical particularism, a astigmatic vision of spatiality in which the many specific lines of sight never focus at all.

23. Giddens (1979) p. 202; emphasis added. A detailed history of the expungement of spatiality in social theory and social science has yet to be written. The expungement was not total, however, for there continued to be several key points of contact – such as the *Annales* School of history and the Chicago School of urban ecology.

24. Lefebvre (1974, 1980).

25. Arguments about the spatial contingency of social relations, that social relations can be affected, modified, even transformed by the spatiality that makes them concrete, are still perhaps the most difficult part of the materialist interpretation of spatiality for Marxian scholars to accept. The lingering fear of spatial fetishism and geographical determinism often obscures the fundamental nature of spatial contingency – that it exists as a social product itself, it is not independently imposed, and is never immutable. It is also complex, problematic, and conjuncturally based (see note 2). We have only begun to explore its causal power after having blocked it from view for so many years.

26. Poulantzas (1978) p. 98.

27. Other figures can be mentioned, such as the urban sociologist Raymond Ledrut (1977) and such major social philosophers as Merleau-Ponty, Bachelard, and even Sartre. Lefebvre, however, stands out among them as the key contributor.

28. See Kelly (1982) and Poster (1975).

29. Lefebvre and Guterman (1936). The main argument of this work was that all forms of consciousness, individual and collective, are manipulated under capitalism to hide the fundamental mechanisms of surplus-value extraction. That this meant that the working class itself was also not aware of the means of its own exploitation caused widespread political controversy within the Communist Party at the time the book was published.

30. See Lefebvre (1968c) for the English translation.

31. Lefebvre (1946) and (1971) and Poster (1975).

32. The most recent analyses of French Marxism written in English (Kelly, 1982 and Hirsch, 1981) do not even mention Lefebvre's writings on urbanism and space, while Poster (1975) only briefly and with puzzlement discusses Lefebvre's 'new praxis' of urbanism in conjunction with the events of May 1969, in France – which began in Nanterre, where Lefebvre was teaching.

33. See Lefebvre (1975) ch. 9, for his response to the question of how he

developed his interest in space.
34. Lefebvre (1946a, 1961, 1968a).
35. Lefebvre (1968b, 1970, 1971a, 1971b, 1972).
36. Lefebvre (1976) p. 21.
37. Ibid, pp. 18–19.
38. Lefebvre (1974) especially pp. 46–53.
39. For a more recent and detailed explanation of this triple structuring, see Lefebvre (1980).
40. Lefebvre (1976–8).
41. Lefebvre (12976) pp. 14 and 17.
42. Castells (1977) (original French edn, 1971).
43. See Soja (1980) and Martins (1983). Saunders (1981) presents one of the best treatments of Lefebvre's work (and Castells's critique of it) in the recent urban sociology literature. However, it too concentrates primarily on Lefebvre's more urban-centred conceptualisation of the spatial problematic and contains no reference to the key work that marked Lefebvre's shift away from his urban 'approximation', *La Production de L'Espace*, published in 1974.
44. Harvey (1973).
45. It was assumed, for the most part, that this comprehensive theorisation of spatiality was immanent in Marx's writing and only needed assiduous exhumation.
46. Eyles (1981); for a French example, see Claval (1977).
47. Gregory (1982a).
48. See, for example, Eliot Hurst (1980) and Smith (1979).
49. Harvey (1973, 1978, 1982); Massey (1978a) and (1981); Massey and Meegan (1979) and (1982); Walker and Storper (1981); Carney, Hudson, and Lewis (1980).
50. Harvey (1978) p. 124.
51. Lipietz (1980).
52. Harvey (1981) and (1982) and this volume.
53. Castells (1983) p. 4.
54. Gregory (1978b) p. 120.
55. Gregory (1982a).
56. Poulantzas (1978) pp. 25 and 30.
57. Ibid, p. 80.
58. Ibid, p. 107.
59. See Hadjimichalis (1980).
60. Lipietz (1980a) p. 74.
61. The emphasis on praxis is the key link to Marx's writings, which are sympathetically but selectively drawn upon by virtually all the contemporary proponents of critical social theory and philosophy.
62. Giddens (1979) p. 202.
63. Gregory (1978b).
64. There are only a few references to Lefebvre in Giddens' writings and these are to the few books which have been translated into English. Giddens clearly does not accept Lefebvre's arguments on the pre-eminence of spatiality (as against 'temporal mechanisms') in contemporary capitalism nor does he conclude from his analysis of the capitalist state

that there has emerged a *système étatique*, equivalent to a new 'state mode of production', as Lefebvre, at his most polemical, has asserted. But in many other ways, Giddens' theory of structuration incorporates an interpretation of the production of space that is very much like Lefebvre's, translated into the conceptual vocabulary of English critical social theory.

65. Keat and Urry (1982) p. 237.

7
The Geopolitics of Capitalism

DAVID HARVEY

I wish to consider the geopolitical consequences of living under a capitalist mode of production. I shall construct my argument theoretically, but its historical relevance will, I hope, be self-evident enough to encourage debate and, perhaps, political action on a matter of deep and compelling urgency.

I The core features of a capitalist mode of production

The phrase 'mode of production' is controversial, but for the purpose of my argument I can put a relatively simple interpretation upon it. We can, I think, all reasonably agree that the reproduction of daily life depends upon the production of commodities produced through a system of circulation of capital that has profit-seeking as its direct and socially accepted goal. The circulation of capital can be viewed as a continuous process in which money is used to buy commodities (labour power and means of production such as raw materials, machinery, energy inputs, etc.) for the purpose of combining them in production to make a fresh commodity that can be sold for the initial money outlay plus a profit. Schematically, this can be represented as a system of circulation of the following sort:

$$M - C \begin{cases} LP \\ \ldots P \ldots C' - M + \Delta m, \text{ etc.} \\ MP \end{cases}$$

The theory that follows is based on an analysis of such a circulation process. I shall also assume an atomistic form of competitive market society in which many economic agents engage in this form of circulation. Deviations from this assumption, except under conditions later to be specified, in no way affect the logic of my argument. I do not mean to imply, however, that everything that happens under capitalism can be reduced to some direct or even indirect manifestation of the circulation of capital. Some commodities are produced and traded without appeal to profit incentives and there are innumerable transactions between economic agents which exist outside the circulation of capital. But I do insist that the survival of capitalism is predicated on the continuing vitality of this form of circulation. If it breaks down because, for example, profits can no longer be had, then the reproduction of daily life as we now know it would dissolve into chaos. Furthermore, I shall also insist that a constant source of preoccupation under capitalism is the creation of social and physical infrastructures that support the circulation of capital. This, again, does not mean that I interpret all such phenomena as tightly functional for the circulation of capital. But legal, financial, educational, and state administrative systems, together with built environments, transportation, and urban systems, to mention but a few of the key arrangements I have in mind, have to be ranged broadly in support of the circulation of capital if daily life is to be reproduced effectively.

A deep, rigorous analysis of the circulation of capital reveals a number of core features. This was, of course, the analytic task that Marx set himself in *Capital* and I shall follow the line of thinking he constructed. Since I have explored, analysed, and to some degree extended Marx's results at length elsewhere,[1] I feel free to summarise without detailed proofs and justifications. At the risk of gross oversimplification I will reduce the core features of the circulation of capital to the ten points I need to ground my argument.

1. The continuity of the circulation of capital is predicated upon a continuous expansion of the value of commodities produced. This is so because the value of commodities produced at the end of the sequence (C') is greater than the value of commodities absorbed in production (C). It is this increase in value that is captured in the money form of profit (Δm). A 'healthy' capitalist economy is, therefore, one with a positive growth rate. The closer we get to a stationary state (let alone actual decline), the more unhealthy the economy is judged to be. This translates into an ideology of growth ('growth is good') no matter what the environmental, human, or geopolitical consequences.

2. Growth is accomplished through the application of living labour in production. To be sure, individual capitalists may gain profits

from buying cheap and selling dear, but in so doing their gain is another's loss. Redistributions of social power through unequal exchange may be important to the rise and subsequent reorganisations of capitalism (for example, the initial concentration of wealth through merchant trading and the subsequent centralisation of capital in giant corporations). But redistribution is no adequate basis for the continuous circulation of capital. A healthy capitalist economy is one in which all capitalists earn positive profits. And this requires that real value be added in production. Living labour (as opposed to the 'dead labour' embodied and paid for in other commodities) is, then, the exclusive source of real value added in production.

3. Profit has its origin in the exploitation of living labour in production. 'Exploitation' can here be stripped of its more emotive connotations. It denotes a moral condition in which living labour is treated as a reified 'factor' of production and a technical condition in which it is possible for labour to create more in production than it gets through the exchange of its labour power as a commodity. It does not follow that the labourer receives as little as possible. Situations arise in which the labourer gets more at the same time as the gap between what labour gets and what it creates in production also increases. Put another way, a rising material standard of living for the labourer is not necessarily incompatible with a rising rate of exploitation.

4. The circulation of capital, it follows, is predicated on a class relation. 'Class' is also a loaded term. But I can here give it a restricted and very simple meaning. The circulation of capital entails the buying and selling of labour power as a commodity. The separation between buyers and sellers opens up a class relation between them. Those who buy rights to labour power in order to gain a profit (capitalists) and those who sell rights to labour power in order to live (labourers) exist on opposite sides of this buyer–seller divide. The division of class roles that this implies is not exhaustive of all possible or even important class relations under capitalism. Nor is the buying and selling of labour power exclusively restricted to the domain of capital circulation. But without the capital–labour relation expressed through the buying and selling of labour power, there could be no exploitation, no profit and no circulation of capital. Since all the latter are fundamental to commodity production and social reproduction, so the class relation between capital and labour is

arguably the most fundamental social relation within the complex weave of bourgeois society.

5. This class relation implies opposition, antagonism, and struggle. Two related issues are at stake. How much do capitalists have to pay to procure the rights to labour power and what, exactly, do those rights comprise? Struggles over the wage rate and over conditions of labouring (the length of the working day, the intensity of work, control over the labour process, the perpetuation of skills, etc.) are consequently endemic to the circulation of capital. There are, of course, innumerable other sources of tension, conflict, and struggle, not all of which can be reduced directly or indirectly to a manifestation of the capital–labour antagonism. But class struggle between capital and labour is so fundamental that it does indeed infect all other aspects of bourgeois life.

6. Of necessity, the capitalist mode of production is technologically dynamic. The impulsion to fashion perpetual revolutions in the social productivity of labour lies, initially, in the twin forces of inter-capitalist competition and class struggle. Technological and organisational changes give individual capitalists advantages over their rivals and help secure profit in the market. They provide a weapon (not always used with unmitigated success) to control the intensity of work and to diminish the power of workers in production through the replacement of monopolisable skills. They also enable capitalists to exert leverage over the supply of labour power (and consequently the wage rate) through the creation of technologically-induced unemployment. Changes in one sphere necessitate parallel changes in another and create massive reverberations throughout the whole fabric of bourgeois society (particularly in the military sphere). Technological dynamism then appears self-perpetuating. Small wonder that the ideology of progress and its inevitability becomes deeply rooted in bourgeois life and culture.

7. Technological and organisational change usually requires investment of capital and labour power. This simple truth conceals powerful implications. Some means must be found to produce and reproduce surpluses of capital and labour to fuel the technological dynamism so necessary to the survival of capitalism.

8. The circulation of capital is unstable. It embodies powerful and disruptive contradictions that render it chronically crisis-prone. The theory of crisis formation under capitalism is complex and

controversial in its details. But consideration of the preceding seven points reveals a central contradiction. The system has to expand through the application of living labour in production whereas the main path of technological change is to supplant living labour, the real agent of expansion, from production. Growth and technological progress, both necessary features of the circulation of capital, are antagonistic to each other. The underlying antagonism periodically erupts as full-fledged crises of accumulation, total disruptions of the circulation process of capital.

9. The crisis is typically manifest as a condition in which the surpluses of both capital and labour which capitalism needs to survive can no longer be absorbed. I call this a state of *overaccumulation*. Surplus capital and surplus labour power exist side by side with apparently no way to bring the two together to accomplish socially useful tasks. The irrationality that lurks at the heart of a supposedly rational mode of production comes to the surface for all to see. This is the kind of irrationality, with massive unused productive capacity and high unemployment, into which most Western economies have sunk these past few years.

10. Surpluses that cannot be absorbed are devalued, sometimes even physically destroyed. Capital can be devalued as money (through inflation or default on debts), as commodities (unsold inventories, sales below cost price, physical wastage), or as productive capacity (idle or underutilised physical plant). The real income of labourers, their standard of living, security, and even life chances (life expectancy, infant mortality, etc.) are seriously diminished, particularly for those thrown into the ranks of the unemployed. The physical and social infrastructures that serve as crucial supports to the circulation of capital and the reproduction of labour power, may also be neglected. Crises of devaluation send deep shock waves throughout all aspects of capitalist society. They often spawn acute social and political tensions. And out of the associated ferment new political forms and ideologies can spring.

I hold that crises are inevitable under capitalism no matter what measures are taken to mitigate them. The tension between growth and technological progress is just too powerful to be contained within the confines of the circulation of capital. It is, however, open to human ingenuity and political action to alter both the timing, spatial extent, and form of manifestation of the crisis. We shall, in what follows, examine some of these possibilities. It is also open to human ingenuity and political action to convert crises into catalytic though traumatic moments in human progress, rather than letting them dissolve into barbarism, testimony to the frailty and futility of all enlightened human aspirations. To seize the moment of crisis as the opportunity for creative revolutionary change, however, requires deep understanding of how crises form and unfold.

II Surpluses of capital and labour power – the pivot of capitalist development

The historical geography of capitalism can best be viewed from the standpoint of the triple imperatives of production, mobilisation and absorption of surpluses of capital and labour power. Without the prior creation and mobilisation of such surpluses, the circulation of capital could not even begin nor expansion be sustained. On the other hand, the continuous production of potential capital surpluses in the form of profit, coupled with revolutions in technology that throw people out of work, just as perpetually pose the problem of how to absorb such surpluses without devaluation. The probability of crisis perpetually brews within this tension between the need to produce and the need to absorb surpluses of capital and labour power.

Original accumulation, according to Marx, rested upon the violent expropriation of the means of production that put capital surpluses in the hands of the few while the many were forced to become wage labourers in order to live. The migration of surplus labour power from the country to the city, the urban concentration of wealth by merchants (looting the world through unfair exchange) and usurers (undermining landed property and converting it into money wealth) together with the extraction of a surplus product from the countryside for the benefit of the city, facilitated both the social and geographical concentration of the surpluses. The important point, however, is to recognise that capital and labour power surpluses can be generated *outside* the circulation of capital and mobilised through diverse processes of primitive accumulation and geographical concentration.

The necessary surpluses can also be produced *within* the circulation process of capital. Profit can be converted into capital. Indeed, a necessary condition for the realisation of profit in the present is a conversion of a part of past profit into fresh capital investment. Only in this way can the necessary expansion upon which the survival of capitalism depends be sustained.² The production of labour power surpluses poses a deeper problem. Unemployment can be created by technological change but the maintenance of a constant pool of surplus labourers by such a mechanism means that the crises sparked by the tension between technological change and growth would be frequent and deep.

Primitive accumulation, the mobilisation of 'latent' reserves (women and children, workers from non-capitalist sectors) and population growth provide alternative sources of surplus labour power. Within a purely capitalist society it appears that a positive rate of population growth is the securest long-term foundation for relatively trouble-free accumulation, although in the short run the massive movement of, say, women into the workforce can also suffice.³ But here we encounter a problem because the reproduction of labour power is not under the direct control of the capitalist. The latter may pay a social wage sufficient to reproduce and expand the labour force, improve its qualities even. They may create all kinds of social means to try and influence workers to have or not to have children. But the workers' response cannot be guaranteed. Labour power is not, therefore, a commodity like any other. How the dynamics of accumulation mesh with population growth cannot be predicted in advance and the whole relation of the circulation of capital to the reproduction of labour power remains a thorny, perhaps unresolvable problem.

Capital and labour power surpluses, however produced, have to be absorbed. Under normal conditions we might expect the capitalist penchant for accumulation to take care of matters, albeit with strong cyclical rhythms and occasionally uncomfortable discontinuities. There are two general circumstances where this is not the case and both merit discussion. First, strong disproportionalities in the ratio of capital to labour power surpluses can leave one or the other devalued. Second, during crises produced surpluses of both capital and labour power cannot be absorbed and both are then devalued.

The processes whereby surpluses of capital and labour power are produced do not guarantee that they can be assembled in time and space in exactly the right proportions to be absorbed into a given process of circulation of capital. To some degree, the technologies embedded within the circulation of capital can adjust to accommodate such differences, though often at the cost of radical restructuring. Free geographical mobility of unevenly distributed surpluses can also help. Nevertheless, situations arise and even persist, in which surpluses of one sort cannot be absorbed because surpluses of another sort are not present in the requisite quantities and qualities.

Either capital or labour power are devalued, but not both. To the degree that the dominant power relation favours capital, so the most likely persistent condition will be that of capital shortage and labour power surpluses with all the attendant social devastation that attaches to the devaluation of labour power.

The condition that interests me most, however, is that in which unemployed surpluses of capital and labour power exist side by side. This is the condition of crises into which capitalism is periodically and inevitably plunged because its technological dynamic undermines its capacity to sustain growth. Both capital and labour power are then devalued. Is there no way to avoid such an unmitigated social, economic and perhaps even political disaster? To pose that question is in effect to ask: are there ways to absorb the surpluses productively through opening up new conduits and paths for the circulation of capital? In what follows I shall argue that spatial and temporal displacements offer ample opportunities to absorb the surpluses with, however, dramatic consequences for the dynamics of accumulation. I shall then go on to show that neither stratagem offers a permanent resolution to the inner contradictions of capitalism but that resort to either (or both) fundamentally alters the way in which crises are expressed.

III   Temporal displacement through long-term investments

The circulation of capital has to be completed within a certain time span. This I call the 'socially necessary turnover time', the average time taken to turn over a given quantity of capital at the average rate of profit under normal conditions of production and circulation. Individual capitalists who turn over their capital faster than the social average earn excess profits. Those who fail to make the average suffer relative devaluation of their capitals. Competition then generates pressures to accelerate turnover times through technological and organisational change. Any aggregate acceleration releases surpluses of both capital and labour power. By the same token, abnormal conditions of devaluation are usually signalled by a general slowdown (we speak of a 'sluggish' economy, with unsold inventories piling up, and the like).

But some capital necessarily circulates at a much slower pace, such as fixed capital (machinery, physical plant and infrastructures) and within the consumption fund (consumer durables, housing, etc.). The production of science and technology, and the provision of social infrastructures of education, health care, social services, judiciary, state administration, law enforcement and military protection, define areas in which the gestation time of projects is typically long and the return of benefits (if any) spread out over many years. Investments of this sort depend upon the prior creation of surpluses of both capital and labour power relative to current consumption needs. We now encounter the happy circumstance that such surpluses are continuously being generated within the circulation process of capital. What better way to absorb them than to shift them into long-term projects in the formation of physical and social infrastructures? Indeed, investment in science and technology and in the habituation of workers (through education or repression) to more intensive work rhythms, as well as in new machinery, transport and communications systems, information systems, new distribution capacities and the like, can all help to promote faster aggregate turnover times. A part of the circulation of capital slows down in order to promote accelerating turnover times for the remainder.

The possibility exists here for a dynamic equilibrium in which surpluses are absorbed in the creation of physical and social infrastructures that facilitate the creation of even more surpluses. Such a 'spiral' form, I believe, largely accounts for those phases of capitalist development where internal growth appears self-sustaining. It will also almost certainly be marked by massive transformations in employment structures because increasing productivity in basic production is accomplished by increasing absorption of surpluses in the production and maintenance of social and physical infrastructures.

But at some point the spiral encounters barriers that cannot be overcome. It is then typically interrupted by a crisis in which the labour power and capital deployed everywhere are subject to devaluation. I now have to show how and why such interruptions are unavoidable. To do this I must first explain how surpluses are actually shifted from current production and consumption into long-term investments in physical and social infrastructures.

Consider, first, the reallocation of labour power. There are serious frictional problems because redundant shoemakers cannot instantaneously become scientists and it would be a very talented road-mender indeed who could switch easily into teaching as conditions dictate. Labour power is not qualitatively homogeneous and surpluses of one sort cannot usually be instantaneously absorbed elsewhere. The transformation of employment and occupational structures is inevitably slow and this itself can check the persistence of any spiral form of development. The reallocation of surplus capital likewise poses problems. The surplus can exist as money, commodities or productive capacity. If it exists as particular use values (shoes and shirts) or productive capacity (lathes and lasts) it cannot be converted directly into a railroad or a new educational service. It must first be converted into money. This presents the first barrier to be overcome because overaccumulation defines a state in which the smooth conversion of capital from one form to another, and into money in particular, has become impossible. Credit can surmount this barrier but it does not do so unambiguously. Why would that credit not be used to create even more surpluses of the same sort? Why would it be attracted into long-term investment when every capitalist is deeply conscious of the need to conform to the dictates of socially-necessary turnover time? Here is the second barrier to be overcome. The answer to it is as old as capitalism itself. It lies in the creation of 'fictitious capital' – bonds, mortgages, stocks and shares, government debt, etc.[4] What fictitious capital does is to convert a long-drawn-out circulation process (the capital embedded in a railroad, for example) into an annualised rate of return. It does this by facilitating the daily buying and selling of rights and claims to a share in the product of future labour. The rate is sometimes fixed (bonds) or variable according to what labour actually produces year by year (shares). But it is measured in terms exactly comparable to the rate of profit over socially-necessary turnover time in current production.

Through the use of credit and fictitious capital, surplus capital can flow from one sphere to another. When, for example, the annualised yield on some fictitious capital (railroad shares, government debt, etc.) exceeds the rate of profit in current production, then there is an incentive for capital to switch from present to future uses. The switch is unlikely to be smooth, however, because of the 'lumpiness' of many of the investments involved (railroads, hospitals, etc.) and the different working periods required to make a project operational. Furthermore, the nature of many of the investments – public uses and the difficulty of charging directly for their use – often precludes action on the part of individual capitalists, so that new special organisational forms (joint stock companies, state and quasi-public enterprises) have to be created if railroads, ports, universities, scientific and educational centres, etc. are to be created. Capital markets must also be well organised if clear market signals as to differentials in the annualised rate of return are to be defined. And, finally, the fictitious qualities of investments tied to the product of labour stretched out long into the future introduces strong elements of risk, uncertainty, human judgement and anticipation.

In this intricate world where myriad investors make decisions as to how best to deploy their capital within a financial system where commodity futures trade side by side with government and corporate debt, property mortgages, stocks and shares, etc., dynamic equilibrium between short- and long-term circulation processes could be achieved through the purest fluke. There lurk within this world all manner of traps and pitfalls, so many opportunities for errors of judgement to compound into configurations of savage disequilibrium. Credit plus fictitious capital may be the magic potion to make all capitals instantaneously convertible, but plainly it is a volatile mix, capable of almost instantaneous combustion in the fires of crisis formation. Yet we cannot here define the *necessity* for crises, only so many possibilities that could still, in principle at least, be kept in check through compensating oscillations. The necessity for crisis must be otherwise established.

Consider, then, dynamic equilibrium at its smoothest and simplest. The credit equivalent of surplus use values (commodities and productive capacity) is added to surplus money capital arising out of current production and invested as fictitious capital in long-term projects. Surplus labour power then finds employment. The extra demand for wage goods and means of production matches the surplus use values in current production. Inventories shrink and capacity utilisation rises. Prices and profits recover, reinvestment in current production resumes and further surpluses of both capital and labour power are generated to be absorbed once more through fictitious capital formation and further investment in long-term projects. Such a process can plainly continue *ad infinitum* provided there is no limit to the volume of fictitious capital formation.

Fictitious capital, however, is a claim on future labour. If its value is to be realised then future labour must be deployed in such a way as to ensure a rate of return on the initial investment. What happens, in effect, is that present problems are absorbed through contracting future obligations. To the degree that the problem is absorbed rather than eliminated, dynamic equilibrium means continuous temporal displacement through accelerating fictitious capital formation. The volume of indebtedness increases and future labour is increasingly imprisoned within a framework of contractual obligations (Figure

7.1). At some point the debts must be paid. Exactly when depends upon the turnover time of the capital deployed in particular physical and social infrastructures. But accelerating fictitious capital formation – the true heart of the spiral of development – means that more and more living labour in current production has to be given over to working off past obligations.

FIGURE 7.1 *Indebtedness in advanced capitalism, 1946–80*

Two possibilities for crisis formation then arise. Under the first, overaccumulated capital stored in physical and social infrastructures is realised through an active growth in current production (facilitated in part through improved infrastructures). But then overaccumulated capital flows back from storage to combine with excess capital in current production to create ever-greater pools of surplus capital. The capacity for further fictitious capital formation is blocked either by labour or resource constraints or by the circulation of capital in the existing infrastructures which cannot be disturbed before their life is out without devaluation. A general crisis ensues with surpluses everywhere subject to devaluation. Under the second, the capital stored in physical and social infrastructures is not realised and is devalued. The crisis now appears to be provoked through the lag of productivity (and perhaps through shortages of both capital and labour) in current production relative to the volume of debts contracted. Devaluation then focusses on the debts. These can be devalued socially through monetisation (inflation) or individually through default on privately contracted obligations.

In the long run, crises cannot be avoided. But how long is the long run? By stretching out the tendency to overaccumulate far into the future, crises can perhaps be staved off for many years. But the longer the crises are staved off, the greater the quantity of fictitious capital, the more the overaccumulation problem itself accumulates in pent-up form, and the deeper the ultimate crisis. But 'ultimate' has no strict date. Even in the midst of crisis, debts can be restructured and stretched out to avoid the full impact here and now.

The form of crisis can also change. For example, the absorption of surpluses of capital and labour power in bouts of speculative railroad and urban building, so typical of the nineteenth century, produced periodic crises of overaccumulation of such assets. The timing of the crises was largely dictated by the typical turnover times of such projects. The fictitious capital (railroad stocks and shares, builders' debts) was devalued, debts written off, enterprises bankrupted and labour laid off. Though increasingly intolerable from the standpoint of both capital and labour, this system had the virtue of leaving the use-value of the asset behind while cleaning out overaccumulated capital vigorously and unambiguously. By contrast, the massive absorption of surpluses through state action (highway construction, health care, education) so characteristic of the period since 1945, together with state support for private indebtedness, has more recently put the accent on state-backed debt. The construction cycle has all but disappeared and traditional restraints to fictitious capital formation have been removed through state action that effectively underwrote an extended economic boom that lasted a whole generation. The state could monetise the debt away by printing money. But this produced inflation – a form of crisis that builds slowly and spreads devaluation across the whole of society. The trouble, of course, is that any attack upon inflation reveals the chronic debt problem and any attack upon that reveals that productivity has not kept pace with accelerating debt formation (how could it?). The end result is the conversion of an inflationary crisis into a more conventional deflation in which devaluation has to be administered by the state.

While it is not my intention to clothe this theoretical argument in historical verisimilitude, I do not believe it would be hard to do so. The post-war boom, for example, was in part fuelled through accelerated fictitious capital formation and increased indebtedness backed by state power. The effect has been to create such a pent-up force for devaluation that it is hard to see how capitalism can work its way out of it. We now see capital and labour power being devalued in production, investment and maintenance of social and physical infrastructures neglected and part of the debt written off (usually through restructuring and stretching out, as has been done with New York City, Mexico, Brazil, Poland, etc.). And state policy is caught between the Scylla of accelerating inflation and the Charybdis of savage devaluation. The prospect looms that we may be paying for the 1945–69 boom through stagnation and depression until the end of the century. We cannot, however, push such an argument much further without exploring the spatial dimension.

IV Theorising the historical geography of capitalism

The question now to be resolved is whether the interior dilemmas of capitalism can be resolved through geographical expansion or restructuring. Is there, in short, a 'spatial fix' to the internal contradictions of capitalism? The export of surpluses of labour power and capital, after all, appears an easy enough way to avoid devaluation. All kinds of possibilities exist here to stave off crises, sustain accumulation, and modify class struggle through geographical shifts and restructurings. But the end result, I shall conclude, is that crises become more global in scope at the same time as geopolitical conflicts become part and parcel of the processes of crisis formation and resolution.

The path to this conclusion is strewn with all number of difficulties. The issue of space and geography is a sadly neglected stepchild in *all* social theory in part, I suspect, because its incorporation has a numbing effect upon the central propositions of *any* corpus of social theory. Microeconomists working with a theory of perfect competition encounter spatial monopolies, macroeconomists find as many economies as there are central banks and a peculiar flux of exchange relations between them, and Marxists looking to class relations find neighbourhoods, communities, regions and nations. Marx, Marshall, Weber, and Durkheim all have this in common: they prioritise time and history over space and geography and, where they treat of the latter at all, tend to view them unproblematically as the stable context or site for historical action. Changing space relations and geogra-

phical structures are accommodated by *ad hoc* adjustments, externally imposed redefinitions of regions and territories within and between
which the perpetual flow of the social process takes place. The way in
which the space-relations and the geographical configurations are
produced in the first place passes, for the most part, unremarked,
ignored.

There is something extremely unsatisfactory about all this. To
begin with, the suspicion lurks and many a theory of imperialism
asserts that the survival of capitalism into the twentieth century has
been assured only through the transformation of space-relations and
the rise of distinctive geographical structures (such as core and periphery, First and Third Worlds). The 'innovation waves' that others,
impressed by Schumpeter, see as so fundamental to the absorption of
surpluses of capital and labour power over time have often had
everything to do with the transformation of space – railroads and
steamships, the automotive industry, aerospace and telecommunications. The multinational corporation, with its capacity to move
capital and technology rapidly from place to place, to tap different
resources, labour markets, consumer markets and profit opportunities, while organising its own territorial division of labour, derives
much of its power from its capacity to command space and use
geographical differentials in a way that the family firm could not. In
any case, the implications of the dramatic transformations wrought
in the geography of production, consumption and exchange throughout the history of capitalism are in themselves, surely, worthy of
study.

Direct confrontation of that task might help heal divisive and
wounding schisms within the Marxian tradition. Marx himself boldly
sketched a theory of capitalist history powered by the exploitation of
one class by another. Lenin, on the other hand, spawned a different
tradition in which the exploitation of people in one place by those in
another (the periphery by the centre, the Third World by the First)
takes centre stage. The two rhetorics of exploitation coexist uneasily
and the relation between them remains obscure. The theoretical
foundation of Marxism–Leninism is thereby rendered ambiguous,
sparking savage debates over the right to national self-determination,
the national question, the prospects for socialism in one country, the
universalism of class struggle, and the like.

To be sure, I caricature to some degree the thought of both Marx
and Lenin to highlight a fundamental problem. Marx frequently
admits of the significance of space and place in his writings. The

opposition of town and country, the significance of the territorial division of labour, the concentration of productive forces in urban agglomerations, geographical differentials in the value of labour power and even in the operation of the law of value, the importance of reducing spatial barriers through innovations in transport and communications, are all present in his works.[5] And historically he has to admit that the transition to capitalism (and the prospects for socialism) differs from place to place even within Western Europe (to say nothing of Russia and Asia). The politics of the Irish question also forced him to confront regional and cultural divergence as fundamental to waging class struggle. But none of this is really integrated into theoretical formulations that are powerful with respect to time but weak with respect to space. Geographical variation is excluded as an 'unnecessary complication'. His political vision and his theory are, I conclude, undermined by his failure to build a systematic and distinctively geographical and spatial dimension into his thought.

At first sight this is the gap that Lenin appears to fill. Overtly he roots his arguments deep in Marx, but his study of the origins of capitalism in Russia and the fact of inter-imperialist rivalries culminating in the First World War led him directly to introduce geographical and spatial dimensions into his arguments. But the modifications, it turns out, are *ad hoc* adjustments that say no more than that capitalism undergoes its own specific course of development depending upon conditions in this or that territory and that the fundamental dynamic of capitalism forces the major capitalist powers into geopolitical struggles and confrontations. To convert the Marxian insights into a geopolitical framework, Lenin introduced the concept of the state which, to this day, remains *the* fundamental concept whereby territoriality is expressed. But in so doing Lenin largely begged the question as to how or why the circulation of capital and the deployment of labour power should be national rather than global in their orientation and why the interests of either capitalists or labourers should or even could be expressed as national interests. Lenin gave geographical expression to the dynamics of capitalism at the expense of reopening the historical question of the relation between civil society and the state.

I do not accept the idea that space-relations and geographical structure can be reduced to a theory of the state, or that a prior theorisation of the rise of the capitalist state is necessary to reconstruct the historical geography of capitalism. Our task is, rather, to construct a general theory of space-relations and geographical development under capitalism that can, among other things, explain the significance and evolution of state functions (local, regional, national, and supra-national), uneven geographical development, interregional inequalities, imperialism, the progress and forms of urbanisation and the like. Only in this way can we understand how territorial configurations and class alliances are shaped and reshaped, how territories lose or gain in economic, political, and military power, what the external limits are to internal state autonomy (including the trasition to socialism), or how state power, once constituted, can itself become a barrier to the unencumbered accumulation of capital, or a strategic centre from which class struggle or inter-imperialist struggles can be waged.

The historical geography of capitalism has to be the object of our theorising, historico-geographical materialism the method of enquiry. Bravely said, but hard to do. To begin with, we encounter an incredible variety of physical and biotic environments across the surface of the earth, many of which have been substantially modified by centuries of human action. The diversity of that action has produced a variegated geographical landscape in which cultural and socio-structural differentiations have taken deep root. Such particularistic geographical differentiation may be encompassed but by no means totally crushed under the homogenising heel of the circulation of capital. Viewed abstractly, space also possesses more complex and particularistic properties than time. It is possible to reverse field and move in many different directions in space whereas time simply passes and is irreversible. The metric for space is also less easily standardised. Time or cost of movement over space do not necessarily match each other and both yield different metrics to simple physical distance. Compared with this, the chronometer and the calendar are wondrously simple. Geographical space is always the realm of the concrete and the particular. Is it possible to construct a theory of the concrete and the particular in the context of the universal and abstract determinations of Marx's theory of capitalist accumulation? This is the fundamental question to be resolved.

V The production of spatial organisation

Marx was not necessarily wrong to prioritise time over space. The aim and objective of those engaged in the circulation of capital must be, after all, to command surplus labour *time* and convert it into profit within the *socially-necessary turnover time*. From the standpoint of the circulation of capital therefore, space appears in the first instance as a mere inconvenience, a barrier to be overcome. Capitalism, Marx concludes with remarkable insight, is necessarily characterised by a perpetual striving to overcome all spatial barriers and 'annihilate space with time'.[6] But it transpires that these objectives can be achieved only through the production of fixed and immobile spatial configurations (transport systems, etc.). In the second instance, therefore, we encounter the contradiction: spatial organisation is necessary to overcome space. The task of spatial theory in the context of capitalism is to construct dynamic representations of how that contradiction is expressed through historical–geographical transformations.

The starting-point for such a theory must lie at the interface between transport and communications possibilities on the one hand and locational decisions on the other. Marx, for example, argued strongly for the idea that the capacity to overcome spatial barriers and annihilate space with time through investment and innovation in transport and communications systems belongs to the productive forces of capitalism. I note in passing that G. A. Cohen lists space but not the capacity to overcome space in his otherwise definitive list of productive forces.[7] The impulsion to revolutionise productive forces is as strong in this field as in any other. The history of capitalism has therefore been marked by dramatic reductions in the cost or time of movement together with improvements in continuity of flow. Space relations are thereby continuously subject to transformation. Other forms of technological change can achieve the same objective but by a different route. There are abundant contemporary examples of changes that liberate production from dependence upon localised labour skills, raw materials, intermediate products, energy sources and the like. By increasing the range of possible substitutions within a given production process, capitalists can increasingly free themselves from particular geographical constraints.

But since technologically-defined spatial constraints of some sort always exist, the question remains: what happens within their confines? Obviously, capital and labour power must be brought together at a particular point in space for production to proceed. The factory is such an assembly point while the industrial form of urbanisation can be seen as a specific capitalist response to the need to minimise the cost and time of movement under conditions of inter-industry linkage, a social division of labour, and the need for access to both labour supplies and final consumer markets. Individual capitalists, by virtue of their particular locational decisions, shape the geography of production into distinctive spatial configurations.

The upshot of all such processes is a tendency towards what I will call a *structured coherence* to production and consumption within a given space. This structured coherence, as Aydalot notes, embraces the forms and technologies of production (patterns of resource use inter-industry linkages, forms of organisation, size of firm), the technologies, quantities, and qualities of consumption (the standard and style of living of both labour and the bourgeoisie) patterns of labour demand and supply (hierarchies of labour skills and social reproduction processes to ensure the supply of same) and of physical and social infrastructures (on which more anon).[8] The territory within which this structured coherence prevails is loosely defined as that space within which capital can circulate without the limits of profit within socially-necessary turnover time being exceeded by the cost and time of movement. An alternative definition would be that space within which a relatively coherent labour market prevails (the space within which labour power can be substituted on a daily basis – the commuter range defined by cost and time of daily labour movement – is a very important spatial disaggregation principle under capitalism). The territorial coherence becomes even more marked when formally represented by the state. Policies regulating the labour process, labour organising, standards of living of labour (welfare policies, etc.), appropriate regulation and remuneration of capital and the like, apply across the whole territory. The coherence is reinforced informally, though no less powerfully, through the persistence or creation of national, regional or local cultures and consciousness (including traditions of class struggle) that give deeper psychic meaning to territorial perspectives.

There are processes at work, therefore, that define *regional spaces* within which production and consumption, supply and demand (for commodities and labour power), production and realisation, class struggle and accumulation, culture and life style, hang together as some kind of structured coherence within a totality of productive forces and social relations.

But there are processes at work that undermine this coherence. They are contained in the core features of capitalism identified in Section I. First, accumulation and expansion, together with the need to produce and absorb labour power and capital surpluses, build pressures within a region that spill outwards (for example, capital export) or pull inwards (for example, immigration). Second, revolutions in technology that liberate both production and consumption from spatial constraints, together with improved capacity to overcome spatial barriers and annihilate space with time, render the boundaries of a region highly porous and unstable. Territorial specialisation and interregional linkages grow with increased facility of spatial integration. Third, class struggle within a territory may force capitalists or labourers to look elsewhere for conditions more conducive to their respective survival. Fourth, revolutions in capitalist forms of organisation (the rise of finance capital, multinational corporations, branch plant manufacturing, etc.) permit greater command over progressively larger spaces by associated capitalists.

Such forces tend to undermine any structured coherence within a territory. They may emphasise the international rather than the locally-integrated division of labour and make interregional interdependence more significant that a regionally defined coherence. They may render state territorial boundaries inappropriate and force their modification. They may even undermine the power of the local or nation-state through the production of a fiscal crisis that demands its remedy in a state-backed attack upon standards of living of labour, upon traditional hierarchies within the labour force, upon the power of local capitalists *vis-à-vis* the multinationals. Regional consciousness and culture may likewise be undermined, transformed into pale shadows of their former selves.

The persistence of any kind of structured regional coherence, in the face of such powerful forces, appears surprising. It is due in part to the peculiar infrastructural requirements to improve the spatial mobilities of capital and labour power. Since improvements of this sort are correctly judged as eminent threats to regional coherence, we evidently have a paradox on our hands that deserves further explication.

Consider, first, the mobility of capital. This, I have shown elsewhere,[9] must first be disaggregated into the mobility of capital of different sorts. The cost and time of money movement in these days of sophisticated credit systems and telecommunications is phenomenally low. Here more than anywhere else we can see the state of perfection achieved under capitalism in annihilating space with time. The cost and time taken to move commodities has also fallen over the past century and a half to the point where transport costs no longer play an important role in the location decisions of all but a handful of industries. The geographical mobility of production capacity, on the other hand, faces tougher constraints. The more an industry depends upon fixed and immobile capital equipment of relatively long life, the less easily it can move without devaluation. These differential capacities for geographical mobility of capital in different states within the overall circulation process of capital introduces all kinds of tensions *within* that circulation process in space.

I will lay these aside for the moment in order to get to the fundamental point. Each form of the geographical mobility of capital requires fixed and secure spatial infrastructures if it is to function effectively. The incredible power to move money around the world, so characteristic of the contemporary era, demands not only a well-organised telecommunications system but – as a minimum – secure backing of the credit system by state, financial, and legal institutions. The territoriality of money and the significance of state power to guarantee the quality of money within its territory come into their own. The capacity to move commodities likewise depends upon the construction of a sophisticated, efficient, and stable transport system backed by a whole set of social and physical infrastructures (from legal services to warehouses) to facilitate and secure exchange. Production for its part, uses not only the fixed and immobile capital directly employed by it, but also depends upon a whole matrix of physical and social services (from sewers to scientists) that must be available *in situ*. Producers, it then follows, can improve their capacity to move to the degree that agents other than themselves (primarily the state) become responsible for greater and greater portions of the fixed and immobile infrastructural costs. The enhanced mobility of production capital over the past two decades has derived exactly from such stratagems.

Consider, now, the geographical mobility of labour power. All kinds of cross-currents of complexity prevail here which nevertheless bring us to a similar basic result. From the standpoint of the capitalist development process as a whole, the free geographical mobility of labour power and its easy adaptation to the shifting circulation of capital in space appears a necessary condition. On the other hand, individual capitalists plainly prefer a stable, reliable workforce and captive labour supplies (with adequate labour power surpluses to ensure capitalist control over both the labour process and wage rates). To this end they may actively support basic social reproduction processes (education, religion, health care, social services, even welfare) geared to the production and preservation of labour power of a certain quantity and quality within a given territory. They may support state actions that constrain the free mobility of labour power.

The labourers, for their part, face a similar dilemma. If they cannot escape from the wages system altogether they will presumably move in order to improve their real wages, work conditions, etc. The irony here is that the capitalist development process relies on exactly such behaviour to co-ordinate the demand and supply of labour power in space. But on the other hand, workers can also improve their lot if they stay in place, collectively organise, and fight for a better life. To this end they may build their own social and physical infrastructures (or co-opt those promoted by the bourgeoisie), struggle to control the state apparatus and thereby enhance their power to improve their lives. And to the extent they succeed, they too may support measures that constrain the free geographical mobility of labour power (immigration in particular). The tension between free geographical mobility and organised reproduction processes within a confined territory exists for both capitalists and labourers alike. And how that tension is resolved for either depends crucially on the state of class struggle between them. Capital flight (and the consequent undermining of territorial coherence and state power) is as typical a response to working-class victories within a territory as is individual worker mobility to escape the more vicious forms of capitalist exploitation. Again, I will lay these tensions aside for the moment in order to get to my immediate point: none of this can occur oblivious of the immobile social and physical infrastructures necessary to ensure the reproduction of labour power of a certain quantity and quality.

We can now draw a fundamental conclusion. The ability of both capital and labour power to move at short order and low cost from place to place depends upon the creation of fixed, secure, and largely immobile social and physical infrastructures. The ability to overcome space is predicated on the production of space. But the required infrastructures absorb capital and labour power in their production and maintenance (see Section III). We here approach the heart of the paradox. A portion of the total capital and labour power has to be immobilised in space, frozen in place, in order to facilitate greater liberty of movement for the remainder. But the argument now can be brought full circle because the viability of the capital and labour committed to the production and maintenance of such infrastructures can be assured only if the remaining capital circulates down spatial paths and over a time-span consistent with the geographical pattern and duration of such commitments. If this condition is not met – for example, if insufficient traffic is generated to make the railroad profitable, or expansion of production does not follow on massive investment in education – then the capital and labour com-

mitted are subject to devaluation. Geographical shifts in the circulation of capital and the deployment of labour power can have an
equally devastating, though geographically specific impact upon
physical and social infrastructures as the temporal disruptions described in Section III.

Let me now summarise the argument. The structured regional
coherence towards which the circulation of capital and the inter-
change of labour power tends under technologically-determined
spatial constraints itself tends to be undermined by powerful forces of
accumulation and overaccumulation, technological change and class
struggle. The power to undermine depends, however, upon the
geographical mobilities of both capital and labour power and these
depend, in turn, upon the creation of fixed and immobile infrastructures whose relative permanence in the landscape of capitalism reinforces the structured regional coherence being undermined. But then
the viability of the infrastructures is in turn put at risk through the
very action of the geographical mobilities they facilitate.

The result can only be a chronic instability to regional and spatial
configurations, a tension within the geography of accumulation between fixity and motion, between the rising power to overcome space
and the immobile spatial structures required for such a purpose. This
instability, I wish to stress, is something that no amount of state
interventionism can cure (indeed, it has the habit of generating all
manner of unintended consequences out of seemingly rational state
policies). Capitalist development must negotiate a knife-edge between preserving the values of past commitments made at a particular
place and time, or devaluing them to open up fresh room for
accumulation. Capitalism perpetually strives, therefore, to create a
social and physical landscape in its own image and requisite to its own
needs at a particular point in time, only just as certainly to undermine,
disrupt and even destroy that landscape at a later point in time. The
inner contradictions of capitalism are expressed through the restless
formation and re-formation of geographical landscapes. This is the
tune to which the historical geography of capitalism must dance
without cease.

VI The formation of regional class alliances and the instability thereof

All economic agents (individuals, organisations, institutions) make
decisions on the circulation of their capital or the deployment of their

labour power in a context marked by a deep tension between cutting and running to wherever the rate of remuneration is highest, or staying put, sticking with past commitments and recouping values already embodied. How this tension between fixity and motion is worked out is fundamental to our theory. This is the conceptual bridge that allows us, if properly constructed, to integrate Marx's history with Lenin's geography of capitalist dynamics.

What I will try to show is that regional class alliances, loosely bounded within a territory and usually (though not exclusively or uniquely) organised through the state, are a necessary and inevitable response to the need to defend values already embodied and a structured regional coherence already achieved. The alliance can also actively promote conditions favourable to further accumulation within its region. But I shall also show that such alliances are bound to be unstable. They cannot contain the fundamental forces making for crises while they internalise potentially explosive class and factional divisions. Their boundaries are also highly porous and subject to modification.

Different factions of capital and labour have different stakes within a territory depending upon the nature of the assets they control and the privileges they command. Some are more easily drawn into a regional class alliance than are others. Land and property owners, developers and builders, those who hold the mortgage debt, and state functionaries have most to gain. Those sectors of production which cannot easily move (by virtue of the fixed capital they employ or other spatial constraints) will tend to support an alliance and be tempted or forced to buy local labour peace and skills through compromises over wages and work conditions. Factions of labour that have through struggle or out of scarcity managed to create islands of privilege within a sea of exploitation will also just as surely rally to the cause of the alliance to preserve their gains. If a local compromise between capital and labour is helpful to both accumulation and the standard of living of labour (which it can be for a time), then most factions of the bourgeoisie and the working classes may support it. Nor, I want to stress, is the alliance purely defensive in posture. Experience shows that an efficiently organised regional economy (that structured coherence to which we have already referred) replete with adequate social and physical infrastructures, can be beneficial to most. Community and regional boosterism becomes very much part of the game as all elements within the alliance seek to capture and contain the benefits to be had from channelling flows of capital and labour power through the territory under their control. The struggle for community, regional or national solidarity as the ideology behind the alliance, may support, reconstitute or in some cases (as I believe can be shown for the United States) actively create local and regional cultures and traditions. The conclusion is inescapable: if regional structures and class alliances did not already exist, then the processes at work under capitalism would necessarily create them.

I advance this proposition independently of any appeal to the concept of the state. I do so because I want to stress that the drive towards state formation and dissolution under capitalism has to be understood in the context of forces making for the formation and dissolution of regional class alliances. The state is different, however, from other agents in a variety of respects. First, territory and the integrity of territory is the objective of its personnel to a degree uncharacteristic of other agents. Second, by virtue of its authority, it can give firmer shape and cohesion to regional class alliances through the institutions of law, governance, political participation and negotiation, repression and military might. Third, it can impose relatively firm boundaries on otherwise porous and unstable geographical edges. Finally, by virtue of its powers to tax and to control fiscal and monetary policy, it can actively promote and sustain that structured regional coherence to production and consumption to which capitalism in any case tends and undertake infrastructural investments that individual capitalists could not tackle. It can also become a central agent for the promotion of nationalist ideology. For all these reasons the state becomes the key to the expression of the tendency to form regional class alliances and adds its own specific rationale to this fundamental underlying process.

The upshot is a regional class alliance that typically builds upon the apparatus of state power, engages in community boosterism and strives for community or national solidarity as the means to promote and defend an amalgam of various class and factional interests within a territory. Spatial competition between localities, cities, regions and nations takes on new meaning as each regional alliance seeks to capture and contain benefits in competition with others. Global processes of class struggle appear to dissolve before our eyes into a variety of interterritorial conflicts. Lenin is vindicated.

But the stability of any regional class alliance is undermined by exactly the processes that Marx described so well. Accumulation and overaccumulation, class struggle and technological change disrupt and transform regional alliances in much the same way that they affect all fixed spatial configurations (see Section V). Even the most solid partners in a regional alliance may be tempted to move even at the best of times and at the worst of times individual behaviour becomes very unpredictable. Competition forces all economic agents to be on the alert for the main chance to make a geographical move that gives them an advantage over their rivals. The instability in part results simply because individuals do not have the luxury of knowing exactly what their rivals will do. Similar problems arise in the realms of class struggle. While capital and labour may move into an alliance on some issues (barriers to cheap imports, for example) and compromise on others (collective bargaining procedures, for example) the antagonism between them can never totally disappear. And when class struggle sharpens, the alliance becomes more and more fragile. Factions of capital may be tempted to flee the region altogether or strike back at the power of labour by threats to move or threats to open the floodgates to cheap imports or low-wage immigrant labour. Such threats can antagonise other factions of capital who cannot so easily escape local commitments. Financiers, producers, merchants, landlords, etc. do not necessarily see eye to eye. And labour, which once adopted conciliatory policies to consolidate its position within the class alliance, may be tempted to resuscitate more revolutionary demands. The conditions for breakdown and disintegration of the regional alliance are ever present. The dynamic of capitalism in the end tends to break apart the very alliances it initially promotes. The stresses become particularly fierce under conditions of crisis. It then seems that the only way to keep the alliance intact is to seek an external resolution to the region's problems.

VII The search for a 'spatial fix'

We now return to the initial question, suitably modified to take account of the general geographical conditions under which accumulation occurs. In the face of an 'inner dialectic' that tends towards disequilibrium, can a regional alliance maintain its cohesion and stave off overaccumulation and devaluation through geographical expension and restructuring? Can the surpluses of capital and labour power be disposed of and remunerated by entering into external relations with other regions?

An expansion of foreign trade does little or nothing to resolve the problem. Surplus commodities are traded away and their equivalent in value shortly received back in the form of other commodities. This does nothing to relieve a condition of general surplus. If, however, the trade is credit financed (or the country concerned is prepared to run a negative trade balance *ad infinitum*) then matters look rather differently.

A region can lend surplus money capital to another and thereby finance the purchase of its own surplus commodities thus ensuring full employment of both its productive capacity and labour power. This combination of temporal and spatial displacement can work well, often for extended periods of time, until the debts fall due. The only way they can be paid is by expanding commodity imports that can only exacerbate the overaccumulation problem at home. Either that, or the debts cannot be paid and the money lent is lost.

Surplus labour power can be sent abroad to found colonies. There are two problems with this solution. First, if labour can freely move to an unalienated existence on some frontier, the capitalist control over internal labour supply breaks down and an important condition for the perpetuation of capitalism is undermined. Second, the export of excess labour power does nothing for the surplus capital left behind unless the latter is absorbed through a rising demand from the colonies. But then the colony must may for the goods it buys through commodity production. And that means more surplus commodities and capital in the long run.

The export of capital unaccompanied by labour power or the reverse flow of labour power without capital can have a half-hearted and temporary palliative effect on the tendency towards overaccumulation. The benefit arises because the rapid expansion of labour supply forms, as we saw in Section II, a more secure basis for relatively trouble-free accumulation than would be the case under conditions of slow population growth. Processes of primitive accumulation outside the region are here mobilised as means to manage and control the supply of labour power in relation to the available capital within the region. The drive to create labour surpluses within the region by processes internal to the circulation of capital is thereby diminished. The effect is 'half-hearted' from the standpoint of most labourers, though for the privileged groups within a regional alliance the effects may be positive because relatively full employment can be maintained at home. The latter may support controlled guest worker programmes and external neo-colonialism as a matter of immediate self-interest. But in the long run, the higher rates of exploitation and expansion produce more and more capital. So important though the processes of primitive accumulation on the exterior are, they provide no permanent solution to the problem even if there were no limit to the population available or to the resistance encountered.

If, however, the excess capital and labour power are both put to creating new productive capacity in new areas, then the surpluses stand to be absorbed for much longer periods. Investment in basic infrastructures, as we have seen in Section III, is long-term while the continuous expansion of a whole new regional capitalist economy creates a continuous and rising demand for the surpluses of capital and labour power produced at home. The only problem with this solution is that the new regional economy tends to achieve its own internal structured coherence, to fashion its own regional class alliance to promote and protect its interests, and is itself bound to become expansionary, technologically dynamic, beset by class struggle and inherently unstable. It, too, begins to produce surpluses of capital and labour power that become increasingly difficult to absorb. It, too, in the long run is forced to look to its own 'spatial fix'. In so doing it inevitably finds itself in competition with the home country on the world market and, if it wins, it can force devaluation onto the home economy through international competition. To take an obvious example, in the nineteenth century, massive quantities of surplus capital and labour power from Britain were syphoned off to the United States, but in the end it was the United States that defeated Britain on the world market.

To avoid such an eventuality, the home country may impose dependent forms of development on the new region. The subservient economy then produces only what the home country wants and in the quantities it needs. The free development of a new regional capitalism is kept in check and whatever regional class alliance arises is kept firmly under the control of the home country. But the dependent territory cannot then expand fast enough to absorb the surpluses being generated at home. The export of capital quickly subsides into a mere trading relation that can do nothing to relieve the underlying problems of overaccumulation. Thus India, under British domination from the start, mounted no competitive challenge to British industry but by the same token it was far less significant as a field for the absorption of surpluses than, for example, the United States. The same principle was at work after the Second World War. Surpluses from the United States found a far more accommodating home in Western Europe and Japan than they did in the Third World, but it was the former that mounted the major competitive challenge to the United States in world markets.

There is, evidently, a 'catch–22' of the following sort: if the new region is to absorb the surpluses then it must be allowed to develop freely into a full-fledged capitalist economy that is bound in the end to produce its own surpluses and so enter into international competition with the home base. If the new region develops in a constrained and dependent way, then the rate of expansion is not fast enough to absorb the burgeoning surpluses in the home economy. Devaluation occurs: unless, of course, new growth regions can be opened up. The effect, however, as both Marx and Lenin long ago observed, is to spread the contradictions of capitalism over ever wider spheres and give them even greater latitude of operation.

But, *nota bene*, capitalism can open up considerable breathing-space for its own survival through pursuit of the 'spatial fix' – particularly when combined with temporal displacements of the sort described in Section III. It is rather as if, having sought to annihilate space with time, capitalism buys time for itself out of the space it conquers. So although we can continue to assert that crises cannot, in the long run, be avoided, we have to countenance the possibility that the long run might be very long. Yet the long run must also be punctuated by what I have elsewhere called intense 'switching crises',[10] cataclysmic moments that reshape the whole geography of capital accumulation, break down rigid spatial structures and regional class alliances, even undermine the power of state formations and reconstitute them all in a new geographic configuration that can better accommodate the powerful expansionary, conflictual and technological dynamic of a restless, shifting, capital flow. But the question perpetually hovers: what happens when, for whatever reason, the 'spatial fix' is stymied and the debts incurred by temporal displacement fall due?

Marx's exclusion of any spatial fix permits him to concentrate attention on the fundamental processes of crisis formation. The theory of overaccumulation–devaluation reveals the intense destructive power that lurks beneath capitalism's façade of technological progress and market rationality. In the course of a crisis vast quantities of capital are devalued and destroyed, the labourers and their labour power suffer a like fate, and capitalists cannibalise and liquidate each other in that 'war of all against all' that is the ultimate hallmark of a capitalist mode of production.

What Marx nowhere anticipates but Lenin emphasises, is the conversion of this process into economic, political and military struggles between nation states. We have now constructed a more general proposition. In the face of the inexorable processes of crisis formation, the search for a spatial fix converts the threat of devaluation into a struggle between unstable regional alliances over who is to bear the brunt of the crisis. Faced with the prospect of splintering into a thousand warring pieces, a regional alliance may consolidate itself and turn its destructive tendencies towards the outside. The export of unemployment, inflation and idle productive capacity become the stakes in an ugly game. Trade wars, dumping, tariffs and quotas, restrictions on capital flow and foreign exchange, interest-rate wars, immigration policies, colonial conquest, the subjugation and domination of tributary economies, the forced reorganisation of the territorial division of labour within economic (even corporate) empires and, finally, the physical destruction and forced devaluation achieved through military confrontation and war, can all be caught up as part and parcel of the processes of crisis formation and resolution. The search for a 'spatial fix' takes a viciously competitive and perhaps even violent turn.

VIII The geopolitics of capitalism

1980 ushered in a difficult and dangerous decade in the historical geography of capitalism. By 1983 unemployment had soared above 10 per cent in most industrial nations (with the notable exception of Japan) and unutilised productive capacity and unsold inventories had risen to unprecedented levels. The inflationary surge of the late 1960s and the stagflation of the 1970s in retrospect appear as but preludes to a classic crisis of devaluation of both capital and labour power under conditions of rampant overaccumulation.

The interregional and international divison of labour is now in course of rationalisation and reconstruction through a mixture of strong processes of technological change and geographical mobility of capital. Previous patterns of regional coherence are thrown into disarray and traditional regional class alliances either disintegrate or forcibly consolidate in an effort to project devaluation onto the exterior. The new geographical differentials in productivity that have opened up generate in turn dramatic transformations in global and regional trade patterns and money flows, creating conditions of chronic national and international monetary instability. The geographical uncertainties force time horizons to shorten, thus exacerbating an already serious debt problem (private and public, local, national and international) accumulated out of many years of rapid and in retrospect excessive fictitious capital formation. The capacity to absorb surpluses of capital and labour power through temporal and geographical displacement, at least under the general conditions laid down in the immediate post-war period, appears to have run out. The only solution consistent with those conditions is for the deficit-ridden to bail out the bankrupt and the bankrupt to pay off the deficits.

Short of such an unreal expectation, we can expect only a rising tide of devaluation that disrupts regional class alliances and sours relations between them. Protectionist responses of all sorts (not just at the national level and by no means confined to tariffs and other conventional devices) abound. Aggressive moves are made to export devaluation to other regions. The US steel industry in alliance with trades unions, to take a recent example, forces restrictions on cheaper imports from Europe and Japan which in turn restrict imports from Brazil and South Korea. But then US steel yields to temptation and decides to import cheaper British slab steel, provoking charges from its competitors and union alike that it is undermining national interest and exporting jobs for narrow commercial gain.

By myriad processes of this sort, regional and international shifts in economic and political power occur, shifts which the policies of particular governments appear powerless to prevent by normal means. Indeed, both national and international policies lose whatever coherence they may once have had. Plans to improve the competitiveness of industry within a regional alliance entail accelerating technological changes that remove living labour from production at home while exporting unemployment abroad. Policies designed to export devaluation to the Third World, not only spark riots in Sao Paulo and Santiago, but put at risk the vast debt owed by those countries. That debt, which in a classic case of combined geographical and temporal displacement rose from just over $20 billion to almost $200 billion for the three largest borrowers (Brazil, Mexico and Argentina) between 1972 and 1983, now appears largely uncollectable. The top ten US banks that hold nearly $40 billion of it face financial ruin in the event of a default. Has the Federal Reserve any choice under such circumstances except to loosen the money supply in the United States, bail out the banks, and reignite domestic and international forces of inflation? And in any case, the only way the debt can be paid is by expanding imports from the Third World which means, at a time of general devaluation, importing unemployment into the United States. If the deficit-ridden bail out the bankrupt, how can the bankrupt pay off the deficits without deepening the problems of the deficit-ridden?

Geopolitical realignments and conflicts appear inevitable under such conditions. Even NATO, the geopolitical centrepiece of post-war capitalism, is threatened by internal economic rivalries and disaffection. The Pentagon may seek to enhance NATO's solidarity but the Federal Reserve just as surely undermines it by monetary policies judged appropriate to control inflation but which also force unacceptable levels of devaluation upon Western Europe. Policies directed overtly at the Soviet bloc by the United States affect adversely those countries, such as West Germany, which sought outlets for surplus capital in East–West trade (squabbles over credit to the Soviet Union, the gas pipeline, and the Polish debt are recent cases in point). Some governments in Western Europe seek another round of the spatial fix by the export of unchecked capitalist growth to the Third World (as proposed in the Brandt Report). They envisage a geopolitical realignment of Western Europe with more dynamic regions in the Third World and in so doing run up against the United States which still, for example, so interprets the Monroe Doctrine as to mean the right to neo-colonial domination (in the name of anti-Sovietism and anti-communism) throughout much of Latin America. The Japanese, perceived correctly as the main competitive threat to the commercial hegemony of the United States and Western Europe, have constructed a special kind of capitalist economy that is highly dynamic and expansionary but also inflexible downwards, with little capacity to absorb the devaluation of either capital or labour power. The Japanese look fearfully to consolidate their hold on Third World markets while levelling off their inroads into the industrialised world. Meanwhile, the United States finally forgets Pearl Harbour and in a bid to reduce its own defence burden and budget deficit urges rearmament on Japan where militarism is in any case quietly resurgent.

The seemingly solid presuppositions upon which the post-war boom was built have just melted into air. Gone is the strong and stable dollar as the pivot of the international monetary system (Bretton Woods). Gone, too, are the open spaces for surplus capital through the reconstruction of war-devastated economies (the Marshall Plan) and the commitment to expand world trade by elimination of barriers to commodity exchange (GATT) and capital flow. Heightened international and interregional competition and accelerating technological change undermine the expansionary dynamic and put the whole global economy into a tailspin. The 'disintegration of the west' as Mary Kaldor so graphically depicts it, proceeds apace.[11] Can the disintegration be arrested, depression, revolution, war (or some combination of the three) be averted?

Under such conditions we can but look back nervously at the economic and diplomatic history of the 1930s, that tortured prelude to a global inter-capitalist war that did more to transform the historical geography of the world than any other sequence of events in history. Can that happen again? And, if so, how and why? Pure analogies may never satisfy, but they can provoke serious analysis and reflection. First, we should note how rapidly geopolitical and economic alignments shifted in the face of economic chaos. While there were many tell-tale signs of fragility in the 1920s (hyperinflation in Germany, grumbling unemployment in Britain, speculative bombast in the United States) the main geopolitical cleavage in the world was certainly that between the Soviet Union and the capitalist powers. But by 1933, the capitalist world had split asunder into so many hostile camps, the British sheltering behind Commonwealth Preference, the Japanese within a 'co-prosperity sphere' forcibly appropriated, and the Germans about to embark upon a policy of *Lebensraum* through political, economic and ultimately military domination. Only the United States vainly sought (in its own self-interest) to sustain an 'open door' policy in a world where alliances of regional class alliances (with strong working-class support for the most part) progressively sealed themselves off, politically and militarily, within closed trading empires. But if the strong expansionary dynamic culminating in overaccumulation prevails as inexorably as we have here depicted it, then the regional class alliance faces a dismal choice of depression and (perhaps) revolution at home or military confrontation abroad (the ultimate form of 'the spatial fix').

Second, in spite of all the high drama of 'New Deal' politics in the United States or *autobahn* construction in Fascist Germany, there is very little evidence that such inner transformations of civil society in any way actually resolved the internal contradictions of capitalism. Unemployment was rising strongly in the United States on the eve of its entry into the war and there had been little or no revival of world trade or of reinvestment over and above that directly created by government expenditures by 1939. Then, as now, the need for fiscal responsibility stymied the best-laid plans to absorb the surpluses of capital and labour power. It was in fact the Second World War that brought full employment and reinvestment, but it did so under conditions where vast amounts of capital stood to be physically destroyed and many idle workers consumed as cannon fodder. And it was precisely the geographical unevenness of that destruction that opened up new spaces in the post-war period for the absorption of surplus US capital under the aegis of that benevolent 'spatial fix' known as the Marshall Plan.

Third, the inner transformations wrought in the 1930s paled into insignificance when compared with the dramatic institutional and geopolitical reconstruction wrought out of the ashes of the Second World War. At the insistence of the United States (by then the hegemonic world power) the 'open door' prevailed, buttressed by an array of supranational institutions (such as the World Bank and the International Monetary Fund) under the *de facto* control of the United States and an international monetary agreement that effectively made the United States the world's banker. The dissolution of closed trading empires (the British were forced to dismantle Commonwealth preference in return for Lend-lease during the war) and decolonisation spawned numerous independent but economically powerless new states throughout the Third World (in much the same way that new states had been carved out of Europe after the First World War). Everything was ordered to prevent the emergence of rival power blocs within the capitalist world and to facilitate the internationalisation of (mainly US) capital under conditions of fairly restricted geographical mobility of labour power. Co-optation and repression, at home and abroad, to keep the free world free for the circulation of capital, became the dominant political theme. To this end, new geopolitical alliances were forged and new foundations laid for the cohesion of regional class alliances within an internationalist framework. And, of course, the Soviet threat and anti-communism became the central ideological tool to ensure the solidarity of potentially competitive regional class alliances. To the degree that this ideology needed a material base, the geopolitical confrontation of the Soviet Union and the communist bloc became central to the survival of capitalism irrespective of Soviet policies or action.

This is the relatively stable geopolitical framework within which the post-war boom took place. And it is also the framework threatened by the very success of that dynamic. Overaccumulation and devaluation, as we began by noting, are everywhere in evidence and the internal cohesion of the capitalist world as a whole, as well as

The Geopolitics of Capitalism

of regional class alliances within it, threaten to dissolve into a chaos of competing and warring forces. Is there, *can* there be, some way to prevent such disintegration and all its untold associated horrors?

IX Requiem for a conclusion

The theoretical argument I have here set out is, I hold, as fundamental to the elucidation of our present plight as it is to the interpretation of the historical geography of capitalism. If I am correct, and I hasten to add that I hope I am grossly in error and that history or others will quickly prove me so to be, then the perpetuation of capitalism in the twentieth century has been purchased at the cost of the death, havoc and destruction wreaked in two world wars. But each war has been waged with ever more sophisticated weapons of destruction. The bourgeois era has certainly witnessed a growth in destructive force that more than matches the growth of productive force so essential to the survival of capitalism. That the latter should also require the use of that destructive force appears insane. Yet the ideologists of capitalism shed no tears but, like Schumpeter, sing paeans of praise to what they term the 'creative destruction' through which capitalists so dramatically transform the world. But our present plight must surely give us pause. As temporal and geographical solutions to the inner dialectic of overaccumulation run out, the crisis tendencies of capitalism once more run amok, inter-imperialist rivalries sharpen and the threat of autarky within closed trading empires looms. The struggle to export devaluation within a disintegrating world order comes to the fore and belligerence dominates the tone of political discourse. With this comes the renewed threat of global war, this time waged with weapons of such immense and insane destructive power that not even the fittest stand to survive. The message which Marx long ago jotted down in that notebook that became the *Grundrisse* impresses upon us more urgently than ever:

> The violent destruction of capital not by relations external to it, but rather as a condition of its self-preservation, is the most striking form in which advice is given it to be gone and to give room to a higher state of social production.[12]

Capitalism did not invent war any more than it invented writing, knowledge, science or art. Not all wars, even in the contemporary era, can be truly regarded as capitalist wars. And war will not necessarily disappear from the human scene with the demise of capitalism. But what our theory strongly urges is that we see the replacement of the capitalist mode of production, that expansionary and technologically dynamic process of circulation that we began by examining, as a necessary condition for human survival. And that is a task beyond the prerogative of any single class or community. It is, I submit, a task that should be the immediate focus of every atom of our collective attention.

Notes

1. Harvey (1982).
2. Harvey (1982) ch. 3.
3. Harvey (1982) ch. 6.
4. Harvey (1982) ch. 9 and 10.
5. Harvey (1975); (1982).
6. Marx (1973) p. 539.
7. Marx (1973) pp. 533–4; Cohen, 1978.
8. Aydalot (1976).
9. Harvey (1982) ch. 12.
10. Harvey (1978); (1982) ch. 13.
11. Kaldor (1978).
12. Marx (1973) pp. 749–50.

8
Class, Division of Labour and Employment in Space

RICHARD A. WALKER

Class is arguably the single most crucial axis on which human life turns in the modern world, yet is at the same time one of the most difficult of social facts to grasp. Marx provided a powerful conception, rooted in the mode of production, with which to understand the class character of capitalist societies. This theory remains subject to doubt, however, because of persistent failure of vision in the face of a social reality that does not conform to tidy conceptual systems. Space is another fundamental dimension of human life, yet the geographic element in the social sciences has atrophied for want of a way in which spatial relations might comfortably be integrated into social theory. Fortunately, the recent revival of philosophical discourse in the social sciences, which seeks to conjoin 'theoretical realism' with so-called 'structuration theory', has rekindled the spirit of inquiry once known as dialectical materialism, while contributing much in the way of clarity and systematic development of basic tenets. This mode of thought offers a way out of the dead-ends to which class analysis and geography have come, although the refined tools of philosophy need to be fitted into the powerful machine of Marx's theory of capitalism in order for the analytic work to proceed.

Class analysis has been persistently stymied by four problems in social theory which can be fruitfully addressed by a dialectical materialist, or Marxist 'structurationist' approach. The first is that posed as the question of structure and agency, which is addressed in section I.

The second problem confronting class analysis is the stratification of the social world. Social systems consist of several layers of nested

Richard A. Walker 165

and overlapping sub-systems with their own irreducible structures. The interplay of structure and agency is not a simple dualism between structural mechanism and contingent forces; real events are always the result of multiple 'determinations' or causes. While these can be ranked in importance, the study of other levels cannot be entirely left until after the problem of class has been solved, because these mediating systems help to create the problem in the first place. The principal conundrum of class analysis along these lines has been the conflation of class with division of labour. Therefore, in sections II, III and IV I attempt to sort out the differences between these two fundamental categories of social analysis.

The third problem to be confronted is the lodging of class in the mode of production. The social construction of class takes place in relation to the unfolding dynamics of social production and capital accumulation, which means that class analysis cannot be restricted to the realm of sociology. It goes hand in hand with the difficult work of building a framework for understanding the capitalist economy on the foundations laid down by Marx. I take up this issue in the discussion of class and division of labour, and continue it in the more detailed inquiry into the employment relation, in section V.

Fourth, the theory of class repeatedly bumps into the hard reality of space. The abstract, aspatial character of most Marxist conceptions of class has left a glaring hole which has been filled by classless theories of exploitation between centre and periphery, and the like. In section VI the geographic element is addressed as a necessary part of the meshing of class and division of labour in the workplace. It is argued that class in a structured and stratified capitalist world incorporates an irreducible spatial dimension.

Along the way I wish to counter two errors in the geographic study of classes. One is the fallacy of sequential ordering, or treating the use of space (location) as a problem to be addressed by pre-existing classes. This is the normal mode of analysis of industrial and social geography. It lacks any understanding of structuration, or of the incorporation of space into the process of class formation itself. The second error is of more recent vintage, and comes hard on the 'rediscovery' of space by many radical social scientists. This is the fallacy of decomposition, which regards the introduction of space as necessarily undermining classes as coherent social entities. This view lacks sufficient appreciation of the complexity and agency involved in class formation.

I The structuring of class

The 'problem' of class begins with the inability to see classes revealed in a self-evident way through empirical scrutiny of the everyday social world. There have been various attempts by Marxist theorists to wrestle with the unhappy correspondence of class theory to apparent reality, and I shall indicate these in summary fashion. The first is to treat class as a strictly empirical category. Classes then appear as boxes into which individuals may be sorted on the basis of their measurable characteristics. This empiricist fallacy, which goes back at least to Kautsky, usually leads to reading nonconforming groups out of the class structure of capitalism altogether, herding them into sizeable middle classes (new petty bourgeoisie, new class, etc) which come to ingest so much of the populace as to render the bourgeoisie and proletariat mere shadows of their Marxian selves.[1]

One answer to this dilemma is to push all the problems of nonconformity between theory and reality into the realm of consciousness. That is, objectively the proletariat includes the vast mass of people, but they do not all know it or act on it. This is Lukács' dualism of class-in-itself and class-for-itself (conscious of itself).[2] E. P. Thompson's influential break with tradition was to make a virtue of adversity, and to focus on the everyday, subjective experience of people as the heart of the process of class formation, rather than an afterthought.[3] History, ambiguity and struggle were thus reinserted into what had become an academic debate. Life was breathed into the history of classes and class struggle. But Thompson's grasp on the dialectics of agency and structure has subsequently been shown to be slippery, and the ties between the subjective, creative aspects of experience and their objective base in economic relations frequently becomes so attenuated in this approach as to bear little resemblance to Marx's analysis.[4] Agency overwhelms structure and the problem of empiricism remains. History stays a great flood with many eddies but no central currents. Przeworski's effort to grasp the dialectics of structure and agency for class analysis has admirably recaptured the spirit of Thompson, but remains subject to the same limitations: the economic relations virtually disappear from the discussion.[5]

Recently there have been several attempts to restore the 'objective' character of Marxist class analysis while recognising certain complexities of correspondence between class categories and empirical positions. Poulantzas introduces structural theory into the study of class, but he does so in such a rigid structural–functionalist manner that he remains fixated on class position and class boundaries, allowing no real room for the interplay of structure and agency. In the end, he joins the ranks of empiricist critics of Marxian theory by reading virtually everyone out of the working class.[6] Wright's solution, by contrast, is to introduce the concept of contradictory class locations, whereby people are allowed to straddle class boundaries for objective, economic reasons.[7] This tackles the problem of ambiguous class position head-on, and is a point well taken. But Wright, too, fails to take the idea of structuration to heart, and in the end has merely inserted boxes between boxes at the empirical level.[8]

All these treatments of class suffer from a lack of philosophical vision, which hamstrings all subsequent theorisation. It is therefore necessary to set out four basic elements of a dialectical materialist view of class which I take to be compatible with modern structuration theory.[9]

Class is first of all a structural category. It is part of the essential 'mechanism' of the capitalist mode of production. That mechanism exists, independent of individual will, because of the aggregate social relations in which people are enmeshed. The mechanism of class can only be witnessed through its effects, as refracted through the innumerable contingent causes of human history. It has no one-to-one empirical manifestation because social development is an open system, not a closed experimental situation. Such an appeal to underlying structure cannot, however, be used to beg certain questions about non-conforming categories, contradictory locations, mixed modes of production or even the place of additional classes in the capitalist scheme of things. What it does, rather, is to break the discussion out of the empiricist straitjacket in which it is usually confined. Class is felt as lines of force, then, not as the bars of a cage that define existence.

Second, class operates in a stratified social world in which many sub-systems come into being with their own substructures; hence there are multiple determinations or forces at work, not one structure encountering a series of random contingencies. These structured sub-systems are far more various than the Althusserian triad of economy–polity–ideology implies. Some are formal institutions, while others are much harder to delineate; some are fundamental, while others are of less importance. Part of the work of social analysis is carving away the nested layers of a stratified reality, determining the coherence of different sub-systems and the strength of their structures as effective causes, and assigning weights to these causal forces in the overall scheme of things. Living societies are woven from many colours and patterns which give the overall fabric its distinctive character.

Third, class formation is also a creative process; classes are the product of human agency. This is not a matter of people learning fixed class roles, but of their coming to understand in a practical way the class-based rules of the game. These rules are both limiting and enabling. While structural reproduction depends heavily on strong patterns of thought and action, or what Bourdieu calls 'the habitus', it also allows room for creativity and change in a way that puts to shame the finest formal games.[10] In that sense, structure is enabling. It follows that agency cannot merely be grafted onto structure; it is not a counterpoint of 'free will' to 'determination', but the way most creative activity of groups and individuals is bound up with unseen structuring conditions. Structural forces may operate behind people's backs, but they nevertheless depend upon human agency. Without the creative exercise of individual and group initiative, the structure of class would not be reproduced and capital would never accumulate. Class power is not a sort of potential energy which agents put into effect more or less completely depending on their resourcefulness. It must be exercised in the pursuit of practical interests in order to maintain the conditions from which it flows, for example, a capitalist must control the workers sufficiently that his/her capital investment is realised profitably or s/he will not be in a position of power over them in the future.

Finally, the preceding points lead to a fourth: class formation is an historical process and class structure is subject to change. As human creativity harnessed to capital introduces new ways of doing things, old forms of life, organisation, thought, etc. are transformed. New forms arise which bear the stamp both of the past and the functional pressures and limits of the present order. Class relations must be repeatedly formed and reformed under changing circumstances, through a whole host of intersecting levels of institutions, group agents and individual life paths. The problems of power, exploitation, ideological hegemony and the rest must be fought out again and again on a shifting terrain. Furthermore, a dialectical conception of class must allow room for the innovative and the non-functional – even the substantially unexpected, contradictory and dysfunctional. Agency wrestles with structural logic, stratified sub-systems collide and interpenetrate, and the past confronts future possibilities. None the less, lest all this seem a return to relativism and historicism, capital does still accumulate, the working class rears its head with the spread of capitalist relations of production around the world, and the social scientist can, after all, slice through the uncertainty to reveal something of the shape of underlying mechanisms at work: although capturing the essentials of social history is perhaps harder work and less precise business than generations of optimistic scientific socialists and positivist social scientists have been willing to acknowledge.

It is not surprising, then, that people have found class to be an elusive phenomenon. But we can understand something of both the dilemma and the opportunity opened up by a structuration approach once we begin to enrich class analysis through the inclusion of the division of labour, employment and location of workplaces as intersecting 'levels' of capitalism.

II Class power and production

We must start by saying something about the substance of class as a particular kind of structuring relation. At the most abstract, or metahistorical, level, class is a relation of power between groups of people. If we cast the net this wide, however, we come up not with Marx's conception of class, but that of Dahrendorf.[11] We shall leave concerns with domination in human life in all its dimensions to Foucault and his followers; class in the Marxist sense requires an object of power, and an end other than domination in itself.[12] The Marxist definition of class rests on the relations of production, or the social conditions under which the human labour of transforming nature to support the populace is undertaken. Central to these relations are the way in which surplus labour (surplus output) is extracted from the direct producers (exploitation/distribution), the form of possession of the means of production (property rights) and the degree of domination over production (control of the labour process). Modes of production, such as capitalism, are taken to be particular constellations of these factors, in relation to a set of forces of production. This much is common knowledge and common ground among Marxists. But here the trouble begins.

It is obvious that at such a level of generality the concept of class is only a guideline for thought which cannot bear the weight of much historical specificity. It tells us where to look, not what we shall see. Class is too slippery a phenomenon to be captured by a handful of historically frozen categories. One needs, therefore, constantly to go back and forth between the abstract and the concrete, the better to clarify and enrich both.

A common mistake here is to confuse generalisation and abstraction.[13] The level of abstraction at which the concept of class, derived from the study of capitalism, is generalisable to other modes of production is not the same question as the essence of class under capitalism – or rather, at what level of abstraction we can begin to say anything very meaningful about capitalist societies and their histories using class as a tool of analysis. Marx may have begun his probing of class with the classic triad – extraction of surplus, ownership of means of production, and control of the labour process – but he did not end there. For class is an historical construct.

Let me illustrate. In the period immediately preceding the rise of industrial capitalism in England or the United States, there was a class of merchant capitalists defined, in part, by their control over the means of commerce and control of commercial money, but who did not control production or the means thereof. At the same time a class of small masters existed which owned its own tools and directed the work of apprentices. (Wright is quite wrong to assert, against John Roemer, that there cannot be a relation of class exploitation without the exercise of class power over the labour of the direct producers: that is precisely the *modus operandi* of the nexus between petty commodity production and merchant capital. He is quite right, on the other hand, to call Roemer's model of economic exploitation without *any* exercise of class power a fiction.)[14] The separation of the peasants from the land and the artisans from their tools, and the creation of an army of wage labour – a process in which, observes Marx, 'lies a world's history' – added a new element to the pre-capitalist system, but did not immediately revolutionise it nor usher in a whole new class system. Wage labour coexisted for a long time with petty commodity production, as day labour on docks or building roads. As Przeworski argues, the formation of classes under capitalism depends as much on the way in which wage-workers are absorbed into the new economy as the fact of their divorce from the means of production.[15] Thus, to say that class is defined by wage labour is not enough.

Perhaps, then, the crucial moment was the real subsumption (control) of labour by the rising class of industrial capitalists. This corresponds to the stage of manufacture (small workshops with a developed detail division of labour but little machinery) in which small capitalists mastered production and hired wage labour, but did not displace the class of merchants on whom they were dependent. The critical step may then be the displacement of merchant capitalists at the stage of widespread development of the factory system and credit money, and the achievement of financial and commercial independence by industrialists; this point was reached roughly by the time of the Civil War in the US. It is the state of things that corresponds to Wright's tripartite definition of class: control of the labour process (variable capital), control of the means of production (physical capital) and control of investment (money capital).[16] But one cannot freeze the matter there. It ignores, for example, the problem of the degree of control which capitalists have over the labour process, which was rather low in many factories employing skilled labour in relatively unmechanised processes, as in the steel industry of the late nineteenth and early twentieth century. As one solution to this analytic problem raised by this independence, Braverman introduces the phase of 'monopoly capitalism' which sees the destruction of such pockets of traditional skilled labour.[17] On another front, just as the industrial capitalists were freeing themselves of merchants, a whole new world of finance and financiers emerged to complicate the class structure. Does control over industrial capital also mean control over the credit and banking system? Arguably it meant just the opposite in the heyday of J. P. Morgan. And what of the modern corporation that arose from Morgan's manoeuvrings? That introduced a whole new question of the control of corporate management.

Without taking positions on these issues of capitalist control, it is easy to see the dilemma. It is impossible to say at which point the real capitalist class stood up. In short, one cannot settle on a tidy definition of class that stops history in its tracks.

Nor can the number of dimensions of class be easily delimited. Again Wright is illustrative. He is determined to reduce class to a classic triad, but that triad changes as he recognises additional dimensions of class. In one article he begins with the labour process and chooses for his three elements control of one's own labour, control of the tools and control over the labour of others. In a later text he realises this is inadequate because it leaves out control over investment, so the triad becomes control over money capital, physical capital and variable capital (labour).[18] The dilemma is that the list could easily be extended to other aspects of the production, circulation and organisation of capital, such as control of the product of labour (commodity capital), control of credit (fictitious capital) or control of business organisations (corporate capital). Marx's method was to spiral up and out from a 'bare bones' definition of class, not just adding elements to the analysis, but recasting the initial categories as they are seen from new angles. In other words, Marx's analysis of the dimensions of class is part of his entire study of the dimensions of capital.[19] (The 'secret' of the mysterious unfinished chapter of *Capital* on class is that there are unlikely to be any surprises there to anyone who had read the rest of the book.)

As Marx shows, once industrial capital stood up on its own feet, it began to revolutionise economy and society in ways that soon left the issue of enclosures or the hand-loom weavers, that is, the mere fact of wage-labour, far behind. New areas of economic importance such as the engineering and sales functions have been opened up which have become the cutting-edge of class change and as much a part of the 'essence' of class as the formal condition of working for wages, which has lost some of its force in class formation today. This does not in any way reduce the historical significance of classic proletarianisation, but wage-work now establishes capitalist class relations only in the weak sense. Class is a relation of power which must continually be maintained, extended and recreated in the face of changing conditions. It is therefore inextricably entwined with the development of capital(ism) as a system of production, circulation and exploitation. Carchedi, despite other problems with his analysis, is thus right to insist on lodging the definition of class within a framework of the evolution of capitalism.[20]

In short, not only does the course of class struggle, or the everyday clash of people in a class-structured context, 'determine' the strength of the class relation and the clarity of class formation, but that struggle must be placed on the shifting ground of an unfolding economy, or system of production as a whole. The latter cannot be adequately treated, nor the problem of class formation tackled, however, without delving into another fundamental level of political economy – the division of labour.

III The division of labour

The division of labour refers to the organisation of work in society, or the allocation of social labour. It has generally atrophied as a category of social science, including Marxist thought. On one side it has been replaced by the term 'function', which is disconnected from labour and production and associated with post-war functionalist sociology.[21] On the other side it has been reduced to bare technology, as in the phrase' the technical division of labour'. Wright makes use of both terms as counterpoints to his concept of class, for example.[22]

The distinction between division of labour and technology, or the forces of production, is especially difficult. Technology has at least four meanings. The first refers to the practical mastery of nature (knowledge); the second to the techniques of production, or the physical steps/processes to be followed in order to create a desired end-product; the third to the means of production and their capabilities; and the fourth to the overall capabilities of social labour given all the above.[23] None of these is the same as the organisation (or division) or labour to carry out the many particular technical projects of production. This is part of the social relations of production.

The distinction is not as clear as this would indicate, however. On the one hand, the division of labour as individual work tasks, systems of tasks and divisions among work units has a strong technological basis. On the other hand, technology is infused with social relations, not only in the practical choice of techniques in place, but in the very form of some tools and machinery, and even in the paths down which technical knowledge travels. Finally, the organisation of work is a kind of technology itself: organising capabilities as mastery of human interaction, organisational schemes as techniques of labour alloca- tion, and organisations as means of production. But the technical base, the practical mastery of both nature and our own nature, never determines the way people actually do things.

Under capitalism there are at least two fundamental considerations other than technology involved in the organisation of work: econ- omic calculation by competing capitals and class (control of labour). But the division of labour is not a simple product of these three forces, nor of any others. It has an integrity as a distinct level of social ordering in itself. That level becomes, in turn, a structuring force on the rest of social life, distinct from the social relations of class.

Marx distinguishes the *detail* from the *social* division of labour[24] and we need to amplify this simple dualism. For the term 'division of labour' causes no small confusion: the word 'division' emphasises the differentation of projects among work groups *and* tasks among in- dividuals. But the connections between projects and tasks are equally important to the way labour is allocated in social production. We can say, therefore, that the detail division of labour refers to distinctions of task (occupation) within a given project, or work unit, whereas the social division of labour refers to distinctions between projects.

The practical meaning of the detail division of labour poses no great problem. It should not, however, be equated simply with task specialisation, because very few workers actually perform a single, technically given task; the key to successful work organisation is how to combine and allocate many tasks to a smaller number of workers.

The social division of labour is harder to pin down, since it is a vague and broadly inclusive concept in Marx. It develops along with the appearance of new commodities, new methods of production, new means of circulation and new forms of organisation. The following distinctions need to be made, at the very least:

1. among branches of commodity production, or what are normally called 'industries';
2. among stages in the whole production cycle of a commodity, including both (i) the immediate process of production, that is, sequential stages of processing or component-assembly systems; and (ii) the extended process of production, including product research and development before regular production and maintenance and repair services after product delivery/installation;
3. between production and exchange (commodity circulation), and, in the sphere of exchange, among branches of activity such as wholesaling, retailing, advertising and transport;
4. between the circulation of commodities and the circulation of money and money–capital (including credit money and fictitious capital), that is, the various branches of banking, insurance, etc.;
5. among organisational units of capital, that is, corporations and other types of firms. This division overlaps the others.

The line between the social and detail divisions of labour is a fluid one. Production systems normally consist of several technically discrete sequential or simultaneous processes, which may be combined or separated in various ways, with varying degrees of impact on economics, labour control and other considerations. Although the association of tasks or work groups in close proximity is often physically necessary for carrying out the collective project, one cannot assume that work tasks carried out side by side always have strong technical connections. For example, Marglin argues that the earliest factories of the industrial revolution gathered workers under one roof chiefly in order to extract more effort (absolute surplus value), not because it was technically necessary or economically efficient.[25] But notice that as soon as one engages the difference between the detail and the social division of labour, space enters into the discussion as a matter of course. The spatial division between discrete workplaces is usually the most practical basis for distinguishing between the two. It does not follow, however, that division of labour is merely an empirical concept, to be contrasted with the 'structural' force of class.[26] One has to extract the underlying structure of work organisation and production systems from the cacophonous reality of corporations, factories, departments and jobs – and the spatial division of labour.

Both the detail and social division of labour are cross-cut by a vertical, or hierarchical, division of labour. This introduces further confusion, which is compounded by the intersection with such concepts as management and corporate hierarchy. Within the detail division of labour, for instance, one finds various levels of managers, or directors, of the immediate labour process. It is not satisfactory to treat such distinctions only in terms of 'authority structures', or systems of class control, separate from the detail division of labour, as Giddens does.[27] The organisation of all large labour processes requires direction, independent of the class character of society. It also requires various kinds of labour skills, with more or less command over the techniques of production and different levels of social status. The confusion arises because under capitalism administration and command of techniques readily become the province of capital, infused with a heavy dose of class relations.[28] The vertical element in the social division of labour, not only within firms but between what appear to be higher and lower functions of capital, is even tougher to handle. Regardless of capitalist class relations, command over large organisations, research and marketing activities, or the circulation of money implies very different levels of command over social production as a whole. This hierarchical differentiation is compounded by distinctions of skill and scarcity of certain kinds of labour.

Thus relations fraught with power differentials emerge from the division of labour and the practical carrying out of social production. That is, the division of labour provides a material axis around which people develop capabilities, knowledge, associations – and power. These power relations are independent from those of class, in the first instance, although they may easily become overlapped or even absorbed into the nexus of class power. All discussions of class trip over this tangle of social relations. Critics of Marx have asked repeatedly how ownership and exploitation can be the only sources and objects of power. The answer is they cannot. The problem, then, is to mesh the division of labour and class without eliminating the distinctive character of either.

IV Class and the division of labour

Class and division of labour are perennially conflated; either class becomes a dimension of the division of labour or vice versa. There are several ways not to consummate a marriage of the categories.

The first kind of error is to make class a dimension of the division of labour. This has several variants. One sees class as a product of the forces of production and the inherent command function in all social production. While class may historically grow out of differences in the division of labour, both take on lives of their own at a certain point. A second variant speaks of occupational classes, which trivialises class power by attributing it to any and all differences thrown up in social production.[29] A third assigns different class positions to producers and non-producers of surplus value.[30] A fourth distinguishes exchange classes from production classes.[31] The last two fail to grasp the unity of production and circulation under industrial capitalism (which is not to say that under a different mode of production, such as the nexus between petty commodity production and merchant capital classes might not be defined, with care, along the line between production and circulation).

A second kind of error inserts division of labour into a prior framework of class. One variant subjects each class (capitalists, workers, etc.) to an internal division of labour that does not alter predetermined class boundaries.[32] Another variant, Wright's contradictory class locations, allows the blurring of class lines. The intermediate position of managers and professionals is based on their control over the work of others or of themselves, respectively. Wright fails to recognise that these characteristics rest, in fact, on their position in the division of labour, either as organisational workers or skilled technicians; instead, he tries to shoehorn all these features into class relations.[33] A third variant, also due to Wright, is to relegate division of labour to the position of 'function' while preserving for class the notion of 'structure' – as if class did not have a function (for example, exploitation) or division of labour a structure.[34] In other words, Wright lacks a notion of multiple structured levels/systems which must be meshed in order to comprehend the complexity of the social order.

Much of the confusion surrounding the debate over class can be sorted out once division of labour is allowed its rightful degree of independence as a level of social structuration. This is the heart of the dilemma faced by Wright and Carchedi, the two most sophisticated advocates of the Marxist theory of class in recent times. They have tried to give some subtlety and multidimensionality to the concept of class relations, but have, in the process, mixed in elements of the division of labour. It is essential not to collapse division of labour into class and to recognise the causal efficacy of both. But the two also do not exist as separate systems to be brought into juxtaposition once the wheels of industry begin to turn; this is the sort of billiard-ball structuralism one finds too often in Poulantzas and other Althusserians.[35] Class and division of labour are simultaneous features of capitalist production, its social relations and social practices: interactive and mutually modifying, yet independently structured. Both revolve around the axis of capital: its production, distribution, circulation and accumulation. As a first pass, we may say that class is the capital–labour relation approached from the value side, or the way in which one group lives off the labour of another, while division of labour is the same relation approached from the use–value side, or the physical/practical aspects of production and circulation needed to extract surplus value. (This distinction is not strictly true, since the division of labour enters into the value system in the form of the allocation of labour to different sectors; but I find it a useful first approximation.)

Class may occupy a more fundamental place in a world of stratified determinations, but division of labour is not merely a modifier in the grammar of class. The two evolve in tandem. In the industrial revolution capital and the capitalists seized upon the existing division of labour and profoundly altered it through the destruction of household units, gathering workers into workshops and factories, rationalising the detail division of labour, etc. Over the last century and a half this process of change in the division of labour has continued. Some of the change has been the result of the direct exercise of class power, some an indirect result of the economic system which class power helped to install. The idea that technology/technique is permeated with class relations in its line of development, even in physical products themselves, is by now well established. It is even more true that the organisation of labour (division of labour), as only a semi-technical system, is steeped in class.

The converse, however, is also true – but less widely acknowledged. As the division of labour has been expanded, elaborated, subdivided and reorganised, it has given rise to new dimensions of human acticity – new jobs, new processes, new knowledge, new workplaces, new companies, etc. – and, consequently, new sources of power. These become, in turn, sites and tools of class struggle. Capital must try to secure to itself a prevailing position *vis-à-vis* most important components of the economy if it is to operate effectively. Capitalist class power, like capital, must be extended in order to be reproduced.

It begs the question to assert that class is superior to division of labour or that class power is fully encompassed by control over labour, physical means of production and money. Carchedi has gone the farthest in recognising the advancing front and multidimensionality of class power, by grappling with what he calls the 'functions' of 'global capital' and 'collective labour'.[36] Unfortunately, he, too appears to put class on ice at a certain point. The modern credit system, for example, is of fundamental importance to the operation of capital, giving rise to new groups of financiers, new kinds of monetary instruments and new institutions, such as the Federal Reserve Bank, which must be incorporated into the capitalist class and its practices. Because the relationship to pre-existing capital and capitalists is so clear in this case, the transition happens rather automatically. But the situation is different with, say, the modern medical complex, professional sports or the engineering profession, which have been brought within the constellation of capital more or less imperfectly.

Precisely because the question of class integration is still partly or largely open for many people and positions in the division of labour, the various issues raised by the 'service sector' and the 'professional--managerial class' are a lively subject of debate.[37] If we try to jam them into a rigid set of predetermined class boxes, they do not fit. We would do much better, as Wright suggests, to recognise the ambiguities and contradictions of many positions in relation to class, while stressing the ongoing fact of class power in society. But even this is not enough. A changing division of labour cannot be fully encompassed, in Wright's fashion, by judicious combinations of existing dimensions of class. The dimensions must themselves be extended in theory as they are in practice to deal with new problems of reproducing power and accumulating capital. Since both are imperfect and fraught with difficulties, and change is persistent under capitalism, class formation is necessarily partial, class structuring incomplete. The openness of history must be faced straight on. But it cannot be faced without a powerful conception of the division of labour. Without the inevitable tensions between division of labour and class, the difficulties of class analysis appear to rest entirely with the overburdened and inadequate category of class, and the vindication of Marx's approach to history is impossible.

We can now isolate one fundamental site of the construction of lived experience and the formation of class: the encounter between capital and labour in the workplaces thrown up by the evolving capitalist division of labour. We will find that even if one goes where class relations ought to be the simplest and most readily apparent, one must deal with the problem of structural levels, human agency and the need to analyse capitalism as it evolves in its full complexity, as part of settling the question of class.

V Where labour and capital meet: the employment relation[38]

In every workplace of the capitalist economy labour and capital come together in order to carry out a concrete work project. Each workplace thus combines the detail division of labour and class in one project in the social division of labour. This intersection of classes in production is necessary for the reproduction of both capital and labour, that is, for the creation of surplus value and for securing the means of existence, respectively.[39] Work and the division of labour necessary to carry it out does more than secure the exchange and exploitation of labour (-power), however; the concrete activity of work is an essential part of the experience and formation of class.[40] The junction of capital and labour in the workplace is thus more than the sum of division of labour and class; it generates a certain life of its own – 'relative autonomy' – as a structured sub-system in its own right. We therefore require a new category to deal with it; the employment relation.

The employment relation is structured by the following elements:

First, every workplace has a production process with a definite 'performance structure' that is strongly determined by the practical, technical problems of the project. While it is essential to recognise the technical component of work organisation, I do not want to introduce it as a strictly exogenous variable, lacking a social and historical base. The ends of capitalist production are, of course, strongly wrapped up in the character of that system and the needs it engenders; but so are the means. On the one hand, projects do not call forth technologies from an ideal scientific matching of human labour to natural systems. What we do depends on what we can do, which depends on the state of scientific-engineering knowledge, of practical shopfloor knowledge and skills of the workers, and of the technical capabilities of existing materials and machines, all of which develop over time through practical problem-solving in production as much as by abstract leaps of scientific insight.[41] On the other hand, there is usually some range of technologies available to reach the same end (or roughly comparable ends) from which to choose. Exchange (price) and worker control conditions (see below) have a considerable impact on choice of technique in the short run and the long-run technical development path as well.

Second, the workplace has a structure of capitalist (management) control and worker resistance, which, while based in class relations, is also strongly embedded in the technical nature of the project. That is, the individual tasks to be performed require a certain kind of worker skill, discipline, autonomy, creativity, etc., and the intersection of tasks demands certain kinds of social interaction among workers. These conditions provide a basis for worker resistance. Against this management establishes various kinds of control systems in order to elicit performance, suppress militancy and maintain its prerogatives over the organisation of the labour process.[42] Capital never rules the kingdom of production absolutely because of the necessary element of worker knowledge and creative involvement in all work.[43] It must therefore balance the desire for control and intensification of labour against the requirement for worker co-operation and sources of worker resistance arising from the nature of the project (and elsewhere). The 'control structure' of production always contains this contradiction.

Third, the employment relation has an economic exchange component, or 'reward structure', deriving from the need to hire labour (power) on the open market. The labour exchange includes, besides the formal wage, such things as benefits, worktime, work environment, and rate of advancement; but its core is the distribution of surplus value between labour and capital. On the one hand, the reward system is strongly limited by capital's ability to pay, based on the economic conditions of the industry and firm: robustness of markets, input costs, degree of competition, competence of management, etc.

On the other hand, reward demands of the labourforce depend on historical/regional standards of living, scarcity of labour (-power), degree of militancy and organisation, etc. In between these two poles lie the contradictory considerations of production, with the reward system serving as both inducement to perform and a form of labour control.

Finally, there is the way in which the three preceding structuring elements are actually put together through the active 'war of position' between managers and workers. This is not a strictly rational ends–means calculation carried out at the level of 'discursive consciousness', or insight into the structures themselves.[44] It is, rather, based on practical knowledge of the immediate situation, its social rules and payoffs. Individual behaviour is socialised into the peculiar social order of every workplace. Certain social 'games' with a life of their own come into being which, while grounded both in the job to be done (division of labour) and in class relations, also mask the latter and often interfere with the former. Burawoy refers to the social order of the workplace as 'relations *in* production'.[45]

This view of the employment relation differs markedly from other extant theories in economics and sociology: the neo-classical view in which the labour exchange is reduced to a direct reward for performance; the radical labour process view in which the labour exchange and performance (technology) follow chiefly from considerations of labour control; the labour market segmentation view in which the labour exchange (labour markets) is organised principally for economic exploitation (based on ability to pay and the principle of divide and conquer); or the industrial sociology view in which resistance (alienation) and control (authority systems) flow from technology and the division of labour without reference to class power or economic exploitation. The approach set out here seems to be borne out empirically by a study of four industries which found a statistically extraordinarily high independence of the three variables, performance, control and reward, and distinctive combinations of the three in each industry.[46]

While giving the employment relation the attention it deserves as a determinant force of social ordering and class formation, I do not want to exaggerate the degree of freedom to be accorded it. Despite the potential variability across industries which this multivariate and open view of employment allows for, there are none the less constant forces across all capitalist workplaces and limits to the whims of the actors involved. Employment is still a structured relation with definite limits and pressures inherent in the reproduction of capital.[47] That is, employment is structured by the prior relations of class, technology and economics of the market (competition, product uses, etc.) in which the workplace is situated.

Together with Storper, I place particular emphasis on labour-process technology as a force cutting across the myriad individual product lines and workplaces to give them a broader ordering, for example, batch process versus assembly line. Elsewhere we have distinguished six important labour process types, from small batch assembly to continuous flow processing.[48] The particulars are immaterial here; the essential point is that the technical basis of the division of labour exerts a powerful structuring force on the employment relation and hence on the social order of the workplace, that particularly critical site of class encounter and class formation.

Up to this point, I have treated employment in a rather static fashion, which is clearly inadequate to our task of elucidating class formation as a dynamic historical process. We must, then, develop the time–space dimension of employment, or what has traditionally come under the heading of 'industrial location'. That hidebound field can be given a new twist in the process.

VI   Employment in space and time: the spatial division of labour

Labour and capital must come together in time and space. Employment not only takes place *in* space; the participants *use* space as a strategic variable in the creation, destruction and re-creation of viable employment relations over time. This is the key to understanding the spatial division of labour.[49] It is also vital to the process of class formation; labour and capital exist only in and through their encounter in space and time.

Employment becomes a spatial problem – that is, a spatial division of labour arises – because of three inescapable facts of production and reproduction at this stage of history.

First, capitalists must invest in fixed and immobile capital (plant and equipment) in order to produce, and they must secure a flow of circulating capital (materials and labour) at the point of production, as well as putting their own output into circulation (marketing). This is the standard fare of traditional location theory: markets and transportation to and from a fixed place of production. Because industrial workplaces differ in their specific production processes, their input and output linkages and labour demands will be different.[50]

Second, workers require a certain fixity for their reproduction. This refers both to fixed capital in the consumption fund, such as houses, schools and parks, and the time necessary for secure social relations to develop, in the sense of habituated practices. Without these, life ordinarily becomes both materially and socially impoverished. The element of fixity in the formation of working-class communities itself introduces a degree of social divergence among labour forces. People do not randomly mix across space. These differences are compounded by diverse roots in pre-capitalist social formations and the industrial histories of particular communities.[51] The sphere of consumption and labour personnel reproduction thus cannot be treated as if it were wholly unrelated to work, as is so often done.[52]

Finally, the employment relation requires some time and stability for a workable social order of the workplace to arise. Conversely employers must recreate the relations of class by repeatedly reconquering the workplace over time.

None of these things is absolute, of course. Yet immobility is a persistent feature of human life and capitalist production. The issue is actually the *relative* mobility of capital and labour, of one kind of production process versus another. The mobility of capital is highly developed today, thanks to such innovations as electronic money transfer, telephone communication and the multinational corporation.[53] None the less, capital has not freed itself of the necessity of taking a material form as instruments of production. Similarly, capital is not normally invested in wholly new plants, but is added to or drained from existing facilities. There are other barriers to capital mobility, as well, such as small firms with little investment search capacity, poorly developed information or financial linkages, and personal allegiances to place. Industries also vary considerably in their material fixity, from the vagabond character of construction and transport activities to the long life of some mines or large steel complexes.[54] Labour migrates, too. While this is often triggered by, or directly mobilised by, movements of capital,[55] labour migrations have a dynamic of their own once a stream is established, which may come to bear little relation to job prospects.

Further, industries differ in the degree of stability needed for a successful employment relation. Some employers, such as automobile companies or machining firms, desire a stable, low-turnover workforce on which they can rely for predictable, knowledgeable long-term performance. Many working-class communities come to be based on such stable employment, on which long-term financial commitments for houses, etc, are made and to which successive generations will return. On the other hand, many industries are characterised by an in-built variability in employment, as in the seasonability of nineteenth century shoemaking in Lynn, Massachussetts, the war-spending swings of modern jet production or the persistently high turnover of workers in electronics assembly.[56] Associated with such industries one finds workforces and working-class communities with a high degree of adaptation to the unstable conditions of employment, whether through finding counter-seasonal work in other sectors, moving from job to job and place to place within the same industry, temporarily returning to housework, moving on, or recruiting a whole new workforce, as needed. Of course, 'successful adaptation' in such situations can mean acceptance of lower living standards or of profound instability in familial and personal life. One should not, therefore, always associate the regularity of employment practices with stability in a literal sense.

Whatever the degree of personal or market stability involved, every employment relation rests on some degree of regularised practices in time and space. But every employment relation inevitably becomes subject to destabilisation, erosion and either termination or reconstruction in a new form. The sources of destabilisation are, broadly: those originating with changes in the external circumstances of capital, such as macroeconomic cycles, inter-firm competition, or product markets; those originating with labour outside the workplace, such as dwindling supplies from the locale, growing militancy in the community, or changing nationality of immigrants; and, finally, those deriving from the contradictions of the employment relation itself, such as the exchange leverage of skilled workers, high turnover because of oppressive control systems, or rigidity of habitual practices in the face of an ongoing need to introduce new technology to remain competitive. There is, therefore, an inevitable tendency in the nature of capitalism and employment for employment relations to have to be dissolved and reconstituted in the course of industrial evolution.

Employment in space thus has two dimensions: allocative (cross-sectional) and temporal. The former refers to geographical *matching* of capitalist labour demands in each workplace to available labourforces. This sort of matching takes place regardless of whether capital moves to a pre-existing labour supply or labour migrates to sites of employment. Allocation is a relatively static conception of the problem, however, which takes us only one step away from conventional neo-classical theories of industrial location. Adding the temporal dimension of employment, the making and breaking of specific employment relations, makes the question of location not only one of *where* to go, but of *when* to go. Furthermore, the concept of where to go, or of 'matching' labour demands and labour supplies, takes on a more rich and subtle aspect. The qualities desired by an employer derive as much from the currently-lived experience of work as from prior skills, attitudes, and so forth. (And background characteristics derive strongly, in turn, from prior work experience.) Employers do not simply choose appropriate workers for a technically-given labour process, except in their dreams when a new plant is opened; most workers are recruited for and socialised into ongoing employment relations, often via connections with old workers. As a result, one can never be sure of the goodness of fit or the internal stability of the employment relation before the fact; it is an ongoing site of struggle.

The location process thus becomes a strategic part of the employment of labour by capital. Looking at it from a simplified perspective of a 'war of position' between the classes, we see that spatial manoeuvre is a fundamental tactic, especially of management, but also of labour. Yet that 'war' still operates under the restraints of the practical problems presented by production in different industries, or the division of labour, as well as the restraints of practical consciousness, which is something less than the 'rationalist' model of decision-making.

The result of the location process is, at any time, a mosaic of workplaces and associated communities. This mosaic is literally a spatial division of labour. That spatial division of labour is necessarily uneven in its development because of the differences among labour processes and the idiosyncratic element in workplace employment relations. And the mosaic shifts continually over time as industries evolve and labour relations are reconstituted, with the new overlaying the old in a rich criss-cross of industrial and class history.[57]

As the sands of capitalist development shift and slide, so do the fortunes, actions and beliefs of the people trying to build on them. I am not concerned here with a critique of the social costs involved in this.[58] Rather, I wish to point up the implications of this spatial flux of employment for the way people constitute themselves as classes and reproduce the class structure of capitalist societies, that is, to take a step beyond showing that the location of industry involves a 'spatial division of labour' to showing that it is part of the socio-spatial construction of class.

In short, adding another 'layer' of structural determination – the dialectic of fixity and mobility in space over time – to the three layers previously identified – class, division of labour, and the employment relation – adds another degree of richness to the analysis of social life under capitalism. There is much that this leaves untouched, of course, but it illustrates the direction in which we should be going. And in particular, it adds an essential element to an understanding of class formation, to which we now return.

Conclusion: class formation as a geographic process

I have tried here to advance the idea of class structuration a short step by adding three additional layers of structure – division of labour, employment, and space – to class analysis. The focus of this effort has been to portray the employment relation as an open system in which class relations are actively constituted through the practical activities, interactions and power struggles of people on the job. A second purpose has been to argue that given the inherent geographic element in production, class manoeuvre and the reproduction of capital and labour, classes are necessarily constituted in and through the use of space.

This way of looking at things, it should be added, grew out of the practical exigencies of a research effort that was seeking to comprehend the logic of industrial location for a group of specific industries, with specific differences in technology, labour relations, and locational patterns. At the same time, the construction of this model in no way entails rejection of any basic tenets of the Marxist analysis of capital. Indeed, each level of structuration in a sense grows out of the previous ones: division of labour out of the capitalist drive to accumulate, the employment relation out of the class encounter within the division of labour, and the spatial division of labour out of the employment relations in various industries.

The conclusions that flow from this view of class formation are likely to be controversial. It appears, at first glance, to introduce a strong element of class fragmentation along the lines of the division of labour and the regional unevenness of employment. Indeed, it implies a somewhat weaker concept of class and process of reproduction of class structure than most Marxist approaches. But it accords much better with the findings of geographic differentiation in the working class by historians and geographers.[59] The problem is to account for such observable variations in class formation without having to abandon the principle insights of Marx. It is only certain romantic notions of a revolutionary working class 'for itself' that are damaged by this view of things, not class theory itself. This view also does not accord well with other popular but oversimplified theories of working-class 'bourgeoisification', bifurcation, degradation (deskilling) and the like.

On closer inspection, however, asking whether classes are 'fragmented' begs the prior question as to how classes take shape through human experience and practical activity. It presumes an empiricist or structural–functionalist notion that class is a singular 'thing' which is less real if it is less unified, that is, one can make fewer empirical generalisations about it.[60] But class does not exist in this sense. Class is a dimension of life that people feel more or less strongly depending on circumstances. Even the worker who lives out his life as a coal-miner in the most despotic company town is never fully defined by his working-class status. People experience class as it is built into their lives in particular ways and come to realise the force of class in and through the immediate circumstances they can experience and understand directly. As Giddens puts it '[c]lass boundaries [cannot] be settled *in abstracto*: one of the specific aims of class analysis in relation to empirical societies must necessarily be that of determining how strongly, in any given case, the class principle has become established as a mode of structuration.'[61] *Thus the only way people can develop a practical understanding of class relations is in a fragmented form.* From that base, of course, they may or may not make the leap to class as an abstract, discursive concept.

It has been said that structure is enabling as well as limiting to human action; it might just as well be said that agency is enabling as well as limiting to structure. This applies as well to the various substructures that at first appear to weaken the force of class structuration. That is, while competing structures such as the division of labour or spatial relations have a certain attenuating effect on the force of class in everyday life, they also may have a galvanising effect, as in the case of nationalist class formation. Spatial contiguity and the traditions of place-bound groups, both in workplaces and in communities, are very important bases for the kind of experience and knowledge that clarify class relations – which is why one finds that coal-miners are frequently the most class-conscious of workers.

The issue, then, is not whether or not classes are fragmented but whether the fragments of everyday life provide a basis for weaker or stronger formation of class-oriented institutions, practices and insights. Do people encounter the capital–labour relation in ways that emphasise or hide the class dimension of their existence? And do they encounter it in a manner that makes it possible to build more strongly class-oriented organisations, activities or politics, and hence to reproduce class structure in a progressively stronger fashion? Certain simple and habitual acts, such as going to work for profit-making firms, create the reality of class structure in the weak sense, but no more. The making of a coherent working class or a polarised class society is a cumulative historical process which depends on both existing material sources of commonality and the creation of further resources from those at hand. Hence, crucial defeats of efforts to build up class organisation, class politics or class culture actually weaken the force of class structuration.[62] This approach does not deny that class polarisation can take place very fast, given the right circumstances. But it suggests that, in human as in physical geography, it is often the slower, less dramatic processes of building up and tearing down that have the greatest effect in the long run.

Notes

1. See Przeworski (1976) and Wright (1980) for reviews.
2. Lukács (1971).
3. Thompson (1968).
4. Anderson (1980).
5. Przeworski (1976).
6. See Connell (1979); MacKenzie (1982); Wright (1976) and (1978).
7. Wright (1976), (1978) and (1980). See also Carchedi (1977).
8. MacKenzie (1982) p. 74.
9. This discussion is based on Giddens (1979); Bhaskar (1978); Sayer (1982); Bourdieu (1977) and Harvey (1973).
10. Bourdieu (1977).
11. Dahrendorf (1959).
12. Wright. (1983).
13. Sayer (1982).
14. Wright (1982); Roemer (1982).
15. Przeworski (1976).
16. Wright (1980).
17. Braverman (1974).
18. Wright (1976) and (1980).
19. Harvey (1982).
20. Carchedi (1977). See also MacKenzie's (1982) sympathetic critique of Carchedi and Connell's (1979) unsympathetic lambasting, as well. I must

admit my own previous conception of class has been too static. See Walker and Greenberg (1982).

21. For a critique of functionalism, see the work of Giddens and his followers, for example, Giddens (1979) and (1981b).
22. Wright (1982).
23. cf. Cohen (1978).
24. Marx (1967) ch. 14.
25. Marglin (1974).
26. Wright (1980) p. 354.
27. Giddens (1981a).
28. Marx (1967) ch. 14 and 15. Braverman (1974).
29. Wright and Perrone (1977).
30. For example, Poulantzas (1975). See discussion in MacKenzie (1982); Wright (1978) and (1980).
31. Weber (1978).
32. This is a position I once favoured: Walker and Greenberg (1982). MacKenzie (1982) and Giddens (1981a) fall into the same trap in trying to use labour market segmentation to explain class inequality.
33. Wright (1976).
34. Wright (1980).
35. Thompson (1978).
36. Carchedi (1977).
37. Walker (1979).
38. The following discussion is based on Storper and Walker (1983) and (1984).
39. Marx (1967) ch. 24.
40. Nichols and Beynon (1977).
41. Rosenberg (1976).
42. Edwards (1979).
43. Aronowitz (1978).
44. Giddens (1979).
45. Burawoy (1979).
46. See Storper (1982).
47. In emphasising capital reproduction over labour reproduction, I am open to all the criticisms made by McDowell (1983).
48. Storper (1982); Storper and Walker (1984).
49. Storper and Walker (1983) and (1984).
50. Walker and Storper (1981).
51. Bleitrach and Chenu (1981); Massey (1978a).
52. For example, Giddens (1981a).
53. Bluestone and Harrison (1982); Walker and Storper (1981).
54. Walker and Storper (1981).
55. Clark and Gertler (1983); Piore (1979).
56. Storper (1982).
57. Massey (1978a).
58. See for example, Bluestone and Harrison (1982).
59. For example, Gregory (1982b); Walkowitz (1978).
60. See again Sayer (1982).
61. Giddens (1981a) p. 110.
62. Davis (1980).

9
Spatial Change, Politics and the Division of Labour

ALAN WARDE

This paper addresses some puzzles in the historical geography of British politics. It is concerned with the rhythms of the rise and fall of political practices which are spatially concentrated within the nation-state. What makes for the formation of 'Red' Clydeside, or the 'Socialist Republic' of South Yorkshire? How can we account for the resurgence of Celtic nationalism, whose explanation has defeated political scientist in recent years? What are we to make of analyses which identify the growth of urban and local social movements as a key political development of the last fifteen years? An adequate explanation of these developments would appear to require theoretical reference simultaneously to space, time and social mechanisms with causal powers. However, as Sack has pointed out,[1] explanations which successfully embrace all three elements are extremely rare. He maintains, reasonably, that this is because explanation in social science is generally weak: despite recent endeavours,[2] no theory satisfactorily encompasses the interrelationship between spatial, temporal and substantive social processes. In the meantime, for want of adequate theory, social scientists have tended to resort to the use of metaphor. This paper teases out one metaphor of change in the spatial patterning of social and economic relations, that conceptualised by Doreen Massey. Her metaphor, influential in British studies of Marxist, Marxisante, or 'structural' persuasion,[3] represents the patterns in location of manufacturing industry in terms of the effects of successive rounds of capital accumulation, which are deposited in layers one upon another in such a way as to create qualitatively different economic sites across each national territory. In each new round, capital makes optimal location decisions primarily in the light of the labour force characteristics of different locales. I examine some limitations of this fruitful metaphor. Then, noting ways in which other writers have tried to explain the incidence of locally-specific political practices, I attempt to specify the criteria which an adequate theory of spatial change would have to meet, suggesting tentatively an approach based upon an extended metaphor of the geology of social relations.

Babel

Although by now many people may be tiring of the lament that social scientists ignore space and time, it can hardly be denied that there is no corroborated theory concerning historical trends in spatial patterning. No agreement exists as to the mechanisms which distribute significant social artefacts across space over time. Nor is there even consensus about how to describe the spatial patterns. Questions about the causes and the directions of spatial change are answered with considerable assurance but little consistency.

Consider, on the one hand, Lojkine's account of the tendencies in spatial change in contemporary society:

The social division of labour under the effect of monopolistic accumulation engenders two contradictory spatial phenomena, both of which, however, result from the common search of all capitalist firms for a location enabling them to reduce indirect production costs as much as possible. These phenomena are, on the one hand, the increasing underdevelopment of the regions least well-equipped in urban infrastructure (material means of circulation and collective means of consumption) and, on the other hand, the growing congestion of the gigantic 'megalopolises' in which the most varied and densest means of communication and collective means of consumption are already concentrated. Concentrations within which the same process of spatial differentiation between the best-equipped areas, which will become even better equipped – business districts, residential districts for the dominant classes – and the least well-equipped areas, will be reproduced, with a tendency for the gap between them to grow ever wider.[4]

Lojkine's projection is entirely contrary to that of Williamson who, in what has become a classic essay, argues that although 'in the initial stages of national development regional inequality is likely to increase', we should expect 'the elements which tend to cause divergence to diminish over time, allowing the more classical equilibrating effects to make themselves felt'.[5] In the first case the effect is one of cumulative spatial inequality in economic practices at both regional and local levels; in the second, the trend is toward spatial homogenisation in the division of labour. Lest it be thought that this disagreement is a mere function of a difference between neo-classical and Marxist economics, it should be noted that the Marxist historian Hobsbawm endorses Williamson's view, at least with respect to the British case. Hobsbawm, addressing the question of whether there are spatial divisions among the working class in the UK, says:

> Local and regional differentials were high and probably growing one hundred years ago; but have tended to diminish since 1900, though at times when some regions were relatively prosperous and others very depressed as between the wars, they could remain very large in practice because of unemployment. In theory the rise of state monopoly capitalism and employment in the public sector has also tended to even them out. In practice things are more complicated.[6]

Evidence concerning political change in a spatial context is more sparse and more unsatisfactory than that regarding economic development. The orthodox sociological position probably remains that of Durkheim, who maintained that the increasing division of labour caused spatial homogenisation. As a famous passage from *The Division of Labor in Society* put it, in 1893:

> Geographical divisions are, for the most part, artificial and no longer awaken in us profound sentiments. The provincial spirit has disappeared never to return; the patriotism of the parish has become an archaism that cannot be restored at will. The municipal or departmental affairs affect and agitate us in proportion to their coincidence with our occupational affairs. Our activity is extended quite beyond those groups which are too narrow for it, and moreover, a good deal of what happens there leaves us indifferent.[7]

This view, that as time passes so too do local and regional cultural differences, is inherent in classical sociology's central distinction between *Gemeinschaft* and *Gesellschaft* and enshrined in recent theories of modernisation, mass society, mass media studies, decline of community, and many more. Yet it is not clear that this trend is either so preponderant or so advanced as is often imagined. Rose and Unwin, for example, analysing regional support for political parties in capitalist states in 1945 and 1970 – a study parallel in intent and scale to that of Williamson's comparative international study of economies – showed only a marginal tendency for regional differences to diminish, regional parties survived, and regional voting patterns persisted.[8] The evidence for the United Kingdom has been most closely examined by Hechter in his attempt to explain the phases in the development of Celtic nationalism.[9] He found tendencies towards a decline in spatial differences in England, but considerable distinctiveness in Wales, Scotland and Ireland. Having standardised for industrial structure, he discerned a large 'cultural residual', as he called it, in the Celtic regions which prevented the explanation of political differences in terms of an economic division of labour. There are some difficulties with Hechter's analysis, not least the fact that neither of the two theories he was testing, a diffusion thesis and the internal colonialism thesis, remotely accounted for his data. But if nothing else he casts serious doubt on the existence of trends towards homogenisation.

The existence of fundamental inconsistencies in the descriptions and explanations of economic and political trends is incontrovertible. One source of this chronic confusion derives from the difficulty of demarcating meaningful and comparable spatial areas. Whether one detects specialisation or diversification depends to a degree upon which level of spatial disaggregation one chooses to use. Analyses variously refer to putative nations, regions, sub-regions, counties, urban systems, localities and neighbourhoods. Some of these are meaningful economic units, others are meaningful political units; but rarely is a single unit amenable to both political and economic analysis for any length of time. Nor is it necessarily the case that trends at each level move in the same direction: it has been suggested, for example, that statistical aggregation makes it appear that regions are converging, whilst component sub-regions remain as diverse as ever.[10] Unsurprisingly it remains a matter of controversy among spatial theorists at what level the most important spatial effects occur.

A second set of problems arises from the understandable fervour of social scientists who have painstakingly collected time–series data to detect trends, even if the evidence be ambivalent. In the case of British economic development, the empirical indicators regularly in use tend to be inconclusive. Lee's figures for the regional distribution of industry at the Censuses of 1881, 1921 and 1961 show a marginal propensity toward specialisation in the first period, and a marginal propensity towards diversification in the second.[11] Chisholm and Oeppen, who sought to analyse exactly the question of whether there was regional specialisation or diversification, concluded that there was a slight tendency towards diversification between the 1930s and the 1970s but on evidence that they acknowledged to be weak – the changes were statistically insignificant using their initially preferred statistical technique.[12] Such evidence does not fit well with either neo-classical or Marxist projections: the tendencies involved are too slight. A further problem of whether the standard indicators are appropriate also pertains and has been an issue in the evaluation of regional policy:[13] some indicators show one trend, others another.

Some recent authors would contend that this confusion necessarily arises from false expectations about the capacity of a positivist or empiricist social science to deliver generalisations about spatial patterns. Some would argue that space is simply an invalid object of study;[14] others, more moderately, merely claim that the 'geometric' space which is the normal object of positivist geography is a 'chaotic abstraction' so that searching for empirical generalisations about space is futile.[15] Instead, it is often suggested that a realist conception of social science will direct attention toward rational abstractions, toward the uncovering of the unified mechanisms which generate phenomenal appearances. The promise is that the one feature of spatial change to which the existing evidence does bear witness – the uneven emergence and distribution of social artefacts in space – might be explained in terms of the effects and counter-effects of one, or more, underlying mechanism or contradiction. This appears a cogent enterprise, but one which is still more often invoked as a desirable project than put to explanatory use. Nevertheless there have been some notable achievements in developing this route out of Babel, works which have nominated mechanisms which do have pertinent spatial effects. It is to those that I turn in the hope of isolating those mechanisms which will explain uneven internal de-velopment and its political effects.

The basic metaphor

One theoretical strategy for specifying the contours of intra-national spatial differentiation has been to apply models which have registered

some success in illuminating uneven international economic development. But, as several critics have observed, models of centre and
periphery, unequal exchange, internal colonialism, etc., have proved
recalcitrant to the analysis of the spatial division of labour in
metropolitan countries.[16] Having recognised this, exponents of structural theory have turned to trying to account directly for that division
of labour. The explanatory mechanism most frequently adduced
is that of imperatives associated with accumulation in capitalist *production*. Despite a considerable degree of difference in detail,[17]
there is a fairly clear basic theory of cumulative regional inequalities
advanced by European Marxists. The work of Lojkine, already
quoted, is one example, considering the analysis of production
processes to be sufficient to the explanation of both urban and
regional structures.[18] Lipietz in another article examining the growth
of services in the French space economy is satisfied, on the basis of
regional statistics on employment by sector, to affirm the emergence
of four distinct kinds of region classified by their function for production.[19]

In Britain, one of the principal contributors to the exercise of
generating an explanation of regional uneven development has been
Doreen Massey. She too considers the process of accumulation
associated with capitalist production to be the key element of an
explanation of spatial change. Less a theory, more a heuristically
valuable metaphor, Massey has presented a schematic view of how
cycles of accumulation in a single country can, with reference to
world economic conditions, be conceived as producing spatially
uneven effects as a result of historically prior social uses of space. Her
work, sometimes in co-operation with Richard Meegan, now constitutes a substantial body of empirically supported analysis of
modern Britain's industrial geography. Beginning from a realist
critique of the inadequacies of traditional regional theory, deficient
because solely concerned with spatial explanation,[20] she has argued
steadily for recognising the importance of economic production
processes in generating spatial forms. Initially she insisted on the
importance of understanding production at a sectoral level in the
context of international and national competition.[21] Increasingly,
though, she has insisted also on disaggregating production in terms of
a spatialised hierarchy of functions within the firm.[22] Her contention,
like that of Lipietz, is that different functional levels require different
qualities of labour, the activities of different branches within the same
firm or sector become specialised by the proportions of different

qualities of labour power required. In this respect she distinguishes three types of labour: professional–scientific engaged in control and development functions; skilled manual; and unskilled manual labour. On this basis Massey argues that although some employment indicators may suggest a convergence between regions in the recent period, specialisation continues, but along new dimensions.[23]

The logic of Massey's account is that capital has come to use spatial differentiation as a resource in the competitive search for profit. There is a search for spatial advantage. Such advantage is most readily obtained by discriminating between available labour forces. This, a point of general agreement among recent structural accounts,[24] acknowledges that capital is nowadays highly mobile, and certainly more mobile than labour, thus implying that many constraints on location which pertained in previous epochs have been overcome.[25] Interested in the pattern of job-loss in manufacturing industry in Britain and its relation to the process of the restructuring of capital in Britain since the mid-1960s, Massey distinguishes three predominant strategies of capitalist reorganisation – rationalisation, technical innovation and centralisation of capital through mergers. The third, the consolidation of the market position of the merging enterprises, has no direct or necessary impact on labour. But the first two – the closure of plant and the saving of labour costs through the introduction of new technology – are important.[26] In both instances the spatial division of labour power is of primary significance. Rationalisation, and technical innovation because it de-skills the labour force, are both liable to provoke resistance. Massey notes various ways in which resistance may be averted. For example, one repeatedly used strategy is to shed skilled jobs in one location and replace them, when necessary, with unskilled jobs in another location. Thus, premises in the inner cities, often employing workers who would resist de-skilling, will be closed down and the production process, with perhaps new technology, will be shifted to, or expanded in, other areas where new, unskilled, often 'green' and often female, labour will be engaged.[27] These three different types of labour are not necessarily unevenly distributed among *regions*, though by implication the South-east must increasingly have attracted the first type. Labour may be locally specialised.[28]

Massey's account, specified and documented for the period 1965–80, provides the basis for the metaphor which Massey uses more generally in order to understand changes over time in the location of production processes. The metaphor is geological; successive rounds of accumulation deposit layers of industrial sediment in geographical space.[29] That sediment comprises both plant and persons, the qualities of the latter, deposited in one round, being of primary importance at the beginning of the next round. Such a proposition clearly has implications for the connections between production and politics in localities and regions. As yet, however, Massey has not taken steps to integrate her work on the hierarchical restructuring of labour within the firm with an analysis of its political consequences. Of course her stress on strategies designed to alter control over the labour process resonates with that body of literature on working-class politics which was inspired by the publication of Braverman's *Labor and Monopoly Capital*. But despite this, her first sortie in this arena, the essay 'Industrial restructuring as class restructuring',[30] although stimulating, exposes the limits of the basic metaphor. Here, she examines post-war changes in the industrial structure of three coalfield areas in terms of their effects on regional class structure, the characteristics of these areas being briefly contrasted with those of the very different Cornwall. The chain of reasoning about the political effects of industrial change was a direct one, from industrial structure, through occupational structure, to regional class structure. This is not necessarily an objectionable initial procedure, but it renders all spatial effects as class effects. This is unfortunate since in an earlier essay Massey announced that regions were generally unimportant as political units:[31] unless there are political forces operating to unify social classes in a given spatial area, or there are independent spatial effects, it is difficult to see why regional class structures are worthy of isolation. It is doubly unfortunate because she hovers on the brink of admitting other spatial effects. She acknowledges their existence. On the first page of her paper she says:

> Broader social structures of community, changing patterns of consumption, the restructuring of spatial forms, the changing national ideological and political climate and the market patterns of geographical cultural differentiation – all of these will combine with changes in the social relations of production in determining both the overall pattern of class structure and the more detailed internal characteristics of those classes.[32]

However, that is the only reference to such phenomena; subsequently they are ignored. This is almost certainly an effect of being reluctant to envisage an explanatory mechanism other than relations of production. There is thus a certain elegance is her theoretical parsimony, but it remains uncontaminated by the reciprocal relation with cultural forms at the cost of a reduced capacity to grasp historical processes. This is perhaps manifest in some of the substantive work on Wales which has attempted to apply such an explanatory framework to regional change in the UK: that Welsh nationalism should become virtually inexplicable is a serious limitation.[33] It is my contention that the metaphor is too restrictive, and I now want to spell out the reasons.

The limits of simple geology

There are, I think, three limitations to Massey's metaphor. First, an unsolved problem concerns an adequate account of historical changes in location patterns – to be fair, not Massey's problem. The notion of layers raises the issue of whether the mechanisms which generate one layer are the same as those which generated previous layers. Should we expect different layers to be formed by different forces, or simply by the same forces successively over time? The intimation of Massey's work seems to be that the search for spatial advantage has always been one associated with the qualities of local labour forces, but she is ambivalent about the implications. It may be merely the consequence of the spread of multinational corporations with a new global geographic mobility which renders labour the critical factor in the location of production facilities. If so, it is reasonable to assume that earlier layers were sedimented on the basis of distinctive, alternative logics of location. Indeed, in the early stages of the industrial revolution, many people would agree, access to sources of power and transport costs were principal considerations. But for the period since the later nineteenth century there are no obvious explanations of why layers differ, whether the search for spatial advantage was especially important, or what importance labour had in locational logic. The first step in extending the metaphor should then be to specify what might be called the transformation rules between the logics of location in each layer. It is necessary to know when, and for what reasons, one layering process subsides and another takes its place.

Second, consider the character of the surface, the top layer, at any point in time. That surface will be irregular, since it is the effect of several previous forces: elements of the most recent round will coexist with others from the previous round, etc. If that surface is to be evaluated, either by firms contemplating location or by theorists, in terms of the quality of its labour force and the local balance of class forces, there arises a problem of defining what might be called class combination rules. Decisions to locate, expand or cease operations at a given site will depend upon the combination of characteristics like skill profiles, historical experiences of class conflict, etc. It is then necessary to determine the rules of combination between various class residues in any place, since different combinations will produce different political effects. At present we know about the political propensities of some highly distinctive locales: places with a high proportion of manual workers in mining have different political cultures from agrarian areas or retirement zones on the south coast. But the political outcomes of a much wider range of local or regional class formations need to be delineated. In this respect Massey's formulation is highly indeterminate since she tells us little about what typical combinations produce what effects.

Third, it is necessary to qualify Massey's assumption that the only relevant local effects are class effects. The basic metaphor presents a very truncated view of what comprises a spatial division of labour. No contemporary account of the division of labour can afford to ignore the broad range of social relationships which derive from the process of the (re-)production of labour power.[34] There is significant disagreement among Marxist accounts on the importance of state intervention in the process of the reproduction of labour power, and on how effects of that intervention should be conceptualised – hence the debate over collective consumption. But even those who consider reproduction important take almost no notice of variations among social institutions of civil society which produce labour power – households, families, neighbourhoods, etc. Yet there are considerable temporal and spatial variations in the conditions under which labour power is produced, and different sets of social arrangements appear to have pertinent political effects.[35] These effects are germane to the formation of a local surface.

The recognition of this aspect of local differences prompts further attention to the question of local specificities. In Massey's metaphor space is denied any autonomous properties. The critique of orthodox geography's 'fetishisation of space' is tightly embraced in the metaphor. It seems correct to accept that space has no causal powers: as Sack put it, only social entities of 'substance', which occur in space, have effects.[36] Yet different kinds of spatial structures remain necessary general conditions of certain kinds of action. Minimally, it is hardly controversial to say that the dispersal of agricultural workers and the concentration of coal-miners identifies some causes of their respective trade union practices. In this example, the spatial property of 'density' summarises the conditions of variable industrial practices. But we can go further and plausibly postulate the existence of 'emergent spatial effects', social practices which are irretrievably connected to spatial arrangements of proximity or distance. For example, the overall importance of the 'neighbourhood effect' in determining the outcome of a general election may be limited,[37] but it does account, in terms of spatial distribution, for voting in an area favouring a dominant party disproportionately, given the other social characteristics of that area. It is worth recalling that one of the more persuasive philosophical defences of the existence of 'emergent social properties' was that of Nagel who showed that a series of numbers had properties over and above those of each number taken separately.[38] Contiguity was a source of qualitative difference! Of course the range and importance of such emergent spatial effects may be contested. It seems probable that a *perfect* social theory would be able to account for all spatial effects in terms of generalisations which make no separate reference to spatial entities; although it seems equally probable that a perfect theory of spatial distribution would implicitly subsume generalisations about substantive social practices. Pending the social scientific millenium, however, we might do worse than endorse Gregory's exhortation 'to abandon the search for some general theory of spatial structure, and instead to consider whether there are any general spatial concepts which might help to identify a specific social structure and which might reveal the transformations within it'.[39] We might then be in a better position to explore the spatial aspects of social phenomena – like, for example, differences in behaviour in towns and factories related to their size, the cultural distinctiveness of the Celtic periphery which gives rise to neo-nationalism, the existence of community spirit and civic pride, and the varied traditions of municipal politics – without prejudice to whether or not they be, ultimately, emergent spatial effects. It must be unsound for any approach seeking to explain spatial distribution to exclude on principle spatial effects. Giddens's proposition that 'the locales of collectivities are integrally involved with the structural constitution of social systems',[40] if somewhat imprecise, would be granted general assent if applied to nation–states. Within the nation-state there is the same potentiality for emergent regional or local institutions, practices and consciousnesses to play a significant part in the reproduction of areal social networks. To the extent that such potential is realised even sometimes a theory of spatial changes must be able to incorporate it. Some localities and regions develop collective identities and solidarities, others do not. Such identities are not independent of class structure, but nor are they reducible to class structure. In other sociological discourses these identities might be described as local cultures.[41] (It is interesting that Lojkine in a recent article has been apologising for having previously tended to 'reduce ... the question of local autonomy to its class content' whereas he now considers that local class consciousness 'is a result of a far more complex bundle of factors arising from their place in the relations of production, the political and cultural situation of their class, and even their individual family, professional and cultural experiences'.)[42] Thus, though space is no first cause, it should not be dismissed from analysis. Metaphorical local surfaces are blemished by past local political practices, household organisation, social protest movements and local customs, as well as their industrial histories. Cumulative local, cultural effects cannot be omitted.

Towards an extended metaphor

The basic metaphor is, then, limited by its inability to produce a historical periodisation, to anticipate the differential effects of types of class combination, and to allow any locally-specific, non-class effects. I propose to explore ways of extending the metaphor, deliberating whether other mechanisms which have been said to have spatial effects can be used to give a more complex understanding. I discuss four such mechanisms, compatible with the basic metaphor, which have been employed to explain excessive spatial effects: class struggle over the labour process, labour markets, collective consumption and reproductive practices in civil society.

Struggle and the labour process

The main elements in Massey's own account which would explain local specificity were class struggle and the labour process. In the recent period, while it was capital's need to transform the labour process which accounted for some of the more impotant locational moves, Massey did not attribute any systematic theoretical importance to struggles over the labour process. Rather it was to class structures that she turned when wishing to anticipate differential regional political activities in South Wales and Cornwall. By contrast one American theorist, Gordon, managed to generate approximate transformation rules for the phases of industrial location from the mechanism of struggle over the labour process. His essay, 'Class struggle and the stages of American urban development', purports to give a schematic explanation of the rise of the sunbelt cities.[43] He argues that there were three distinct phases in the historical development of the urban industrial landscape, and that transitions between phases were caused by struggles arising out the contradictions of the previous phase. He also links the internal ecology of cities – typical patterns of land use – to each phase of accumulation.

The first phase was the commercial, where the city centre, unsegregated by district, harbours all social classes except the poor and the vagrant who live outside, literally on the periphery. This pattern was disrupted by the central contradiction of commercial capital accumulation: the merchants' privileges appeared unjust, because their wealth derived not from labour but merely from profitable exchange, but could not be concealed, since they shared the same residential space with the productive classes. This situation was conducive to class conflict.

Concentration of production in the large industrial city constituted a temporary solution to these conflicts, for there, at first, workers were isolated in an anonymous milieu. In the early industrial period, Gordon argues, militancy and strikes were rare in the big cities and much more frequent in smaller cities. However, capital's control over labour in the larger cities soon declined. By the 1890's employers were beginning to desert the industrial districts of the city centre because organisation and militancy increased there. This resistance was attributed by some employers to a contagion induced by the spatial concentration of both industry and working-class residence. The response was a preference first for location in the suburbs, and then in new towns on the metropolitan fringe. In this phase, without denying other advantages such as agglomeration economies to firms from metropolitan location it was again industrial class struggle which impelled capital to alter its spatial location. Gordon consolidates his argument by observing that the move from the city-centres considerably pre-dated technological changes in transportation.

The third phase, the corporate era, is one in which industry and working-class residence were further decentralised. With the exception of a tendency for the hierarchies of business to remain in the central business districts of the biggest American metropolises, economic activity has decentralised. Sunbelt cities are ideal, not primarily because they tap a fresh, unorganised labour force, but because they can be designed with industry widely dispersed and mingled with equally dispersed residential quarters for labour. By contrast, the old industrial cities built in the phase of industralisation are unfit to be restructured. The rise of the sunbelt cities is thus a response to the search for more effective, qualitative control by capital over labour.

Gordon's schema is promising. It discriminates between periods in history, it contains a dual spatial reference (to regional economies and urban ecologies) and it contains a dynamic mechanism – industrial class struggle. To what extent it could be applied to Britain is a matter of speculation. There seems to have been some similar correlation between industrial militancy and city-size in nineteenth-century Britain.[44] British industry did move toward suburban locations, though at a considerably later date than in the USA, though that may well be because Britain was much slower to transform the labour process, scientific management techniques not having been introduced until the 1930s.[45] Similarly, residential segregation in the British city seems to have occurred at a different stage of industrial development and not to have changed much over the past hundred years.[46] Also, some authors have considered that the visibility of the bourgeoisie in the British towns was conducive to conflict, though others have attributed the same outcome to the absence of a bourgeoisie.[47]

Regarding theoretical issues some reservations should be registered. First, Gordon conflates contradictions and struggles: contradiction and conflict are logically and historically separable, contradictions not necessarily leading directly to struggle.[48] Second, the historicity of the scheme is dubious. Gordon's scheme is rather unilinear, accounting for uneven development by a very even logic. It would seem to imply, for instance, a strong tendency towards uniform, nationwide spatial differentiation within each phase. Third, spatial effects are specified with almost exclusive reference to labour militancy and capital's search for control, to the neglect of other processes. Finally, and incidentally, the explanation of the rise of the sunbelt is not wholly convincing, as it is unclear why just any greenfield would not have been satisfactory, or why the sunbelt emerges as a part of the emergence of the corporate era of accumulation.

Labour markets

Although both Massey's and Gordon's accounts implicitly refer to labour markets as a result of focussing on the quality of labour power available in a given location the concept itself is spurned.[49] Admittedly the analysis of labour markets is problematic. Defining meaningfully the spatial limits of a labour market, and obtaining data for other factors in the same area, present difficulties, although some recent work has begun to construct a typology of labour markets on the basis of typical social relations under certain market conditions.[50] It is also difficult to make links between labour market structures and political effects: explanations of historical change in struggle at the workplace in terms of labour markets, while interesting, have found the making of a plausible theoretical connection intractable.[51] Furthermore there is almost no historical analysis of changes in labour markets. Despite many historical studies of local economies and local class structures, which in principle might be drawn together, there is no general framework within which to make historical comparisons.

Apart from the very recent publication by Storper and Walker of a complex formal model specifying relationships between the labour market, the labour process and sectoral growth, labour markets have been largely ignored as elements of the spatial division of labour.[52] This is a great shame since labour markets offer some illuminating connections in the geological metaphor. First, the structuring of labour markets in particular places is a direct effect of rounds of capital accumulation, since capital moulds the surface of a new layer by offering only certain kinds of employment to local residents. That is the principal means by which successive rounds of accumulation recreate local class structures. Second, it should be appreciated that types of labour market are more easily mapped and classified than is 'labour force quality' in the basic metaphor. Third, attention to labour markets picks up aspects of gender inequalities: some of the most valuable applications of dual and radical labour market theory have been in the area of explaining patterns of women's employment. Finally, position in the labour market remains a key determinant of the process of distribution of rewards, a factor which should not be entirely forgotten in the rush of enthusiasm for studying the labour process.

At the same time, it should be recognised that labour market theory is potentially subversive of the basic metaphor of Massey. If labour markets be segmented, than capital might be expected, in its search for spatial advantage, to consider only the character of the particular segment of a local labour force which it seeks to employ. If a firm is seeking unskilled labour, for example, it need not explore the ambience of the entire labour market, but only the capacity of the secondary market to provide the required labour power. That is, *unless* the organisation and militancy of workers in the primary market tend to encourage similar behaviour among secondary workers. The basic metaphor is ambiguous, in this respect. If it be the entire labour force which is relevant, it would be imperative to seek rules of combination between, *inter alia*, primary and secondary workers in a locality in order to determine this influence. For an important attribute imputed to segmentation in the labour market is that it constitutes a basis for gender divisions, as it is systemic that the primary sector is predominantly male, the secondary sector female. Thus, neither an identity of interests nor a similarity of disposition toward industrial resistance between primary and secondary workers can be assumed. This line of cleavage within localities too often goes unremarked.

Collective consumption

The work of Castells is sufficiently appreciated to obviate detailed exposition. It contains some clues for the discovery of a more complex metaphor. Castells is primarily concerned with the determination of social practices within urban systems, which he delimits in a fashion similar to the British geographers' notion of a metropolitan labour area, constructed 'on the basis of a map of commutings'.[53] The distinctive characteristic of urban systems in advanced capitalism is that they are structured in accordance with a logic of collective consumption. Cities are the loci for the provision of services which socialise the process of the reproduction of labour power, thus minimising the costs to capital of transport, health-care, education and housing, such necessary services being wholly or partly financed and organised by the state. It is unclear whether this has been the principal role of cities throughout the period of the dominance of the capitalist mode of production – explicitly it was not so in pre-capitalist modes.[54] Castells postulates a qualitative change in the period since 1945. He implies that the requirements of production previously determined urban form, but that currently the spatial horizon of the productive enterprise is the region. Sites are sought in an appropriate region, industry being indifferent to locality.[55] Hence, like other French Marxists,[56] Castells describes a tendency toward regional specialisation in economic production. Meanwhile, the urban system becomes primarily a repository of labour power wherein the state supervises its effective reproduction.

Formally, Castells expresses this change – that is, advancing regional specialisation and localities responding to a logic of consumption – by proposing that the complete process of capitalist production and reproduction comprises several elements. In *The Urban Question* five elements are distinguished: production, consumption, exchange, administration and the symbolic.[57] Castells argues that these may each be primarily effective at different times in different spatial units. Consumption is dominant in the contemporary city, as is demonstrated by the examination of 'urban problems'. Urban problems are nothing other than instances of the 'fundamental structural tendencies of monopoly state capitalism'. In response, new forms of social conflicts emerge which present 'the claim of the dominated classes for more and more "indirect wages" in so far as this is assuming an increasing place in their process of simple and extended reproduction'.[58] Castells is now busy classifying and analysing, in terms of urban struggles and urban social movements, the ways in which such 'claims' are filed, on the assumption that they are distinct, analytically, from struggles organised around production.[59] This analytic separation is, of course, one which has attracted vehement criticism from adherents of the basic metaphor.[60] In brief, Castells offers a two-stage model of the history of spatial change, and attributes relative autonomy to spatially-definable social processes which generate political practices which are not directly reducible to production activities.

Castells' notion of an historical shift whereby capitalist firms seek regional rather than local locations has met with some scepticism: it appears to be an imprecise formulation of the complex calculations of multinational corporations. However, this does not necessarily vitiate his conclusions about the determinant place of consumption in generating urban struggles.

Believing that a 'growing political stake ... is represented by the management of *local and regional governments*',[61] Castells has gone to enormous trouble to understand new social movements in terms of their effects, their relationship to the state and their relationship to class struggle. The extent to which these concerns have led Castells himself to postulate autonomous, spatial, political effects remains ambiguous. It is never clear to what extent urban social movements are locally-specific with cumulative political consequences, or are mere instances of movements thrown up, society-wide, by the modern system of collective consumption. Movements must be localised in the sense that the concrete issues over which they are struggling have only a local relevance: the inhabitants of Bordeaux are unlikely to show much interest in tenants' movements in the *Square Gaieté*, Paris. However, the movements may be the particular outcome of a national mechanism – if the same conditions pertained in Bordeaux, then the same kind of movement would emerge. In earlier works Castells seems to veer toward the former, seeking to avoid reducing urban social forces to class forces, urban stakes to class stakes. But in, for example, the summary articles in the volume, *City, Class and Power*, Castells seems to suggest that the significance of urban struggles should be assessed only in the context of class struggles.

This relates to a second indistinct element in Castells' work. He always contends that it is contradictions of capitalism which generate urban politics, but is frustratingly imprecise about what these contradictions comprise, and under what conditions they become effective. Hence it is difficult to disentangle the relative impact of production and consumption logics in generating political outcomes. It is an important aspect of Castells' early work that he stresses that production is the sole element determining political outcomes, thus leaving analytic space for popular struggles against the state over matters irreducible to occupational class. However, the interaction between the forces generated in each separate sphere needs defining if the surface of any geological layer is to be accurately described.

Castells' emphasis on the role of the state in the determination of spatial patterns through collective consumption is valuable and has had the effect of inspiring studies of urban politics in Britain, increasingly with some historical focus.[62] However, if the reproduction of labour power is the objective of state intervention in urban issues then the state's role must be considered in association with the domestic provision of services which also produce labour power.

Civil society and household organisation

Castells should not have neglected the role of private and household consumption when addressing the problem of the effects of social arrangements for the production of labour power. The spatial implications of variations in women's economic activity are considerable. Though it has reduced markedly since the Second World War, local and regional variations in the extent to which women, and especially married women, were engaged in the formal economy were very great. For example, within Lancashire in 1911 the proportion of single women economically active varied from 30 per cent (in Widnes) to 80 per cent (in Rishton); and the proportions of economically active married women ranged from 2 per cent (in Haydock) to 48 per cent (in Great Harwood).[63] Furthermore it is known that the size of labour markets for women is much smaller than those for men, that is, women's activities are more spatially concentrated.[64] There are also considerable spatial variations in fertility rates, illegitimacy ratios, etc., which suggest a weakness in spatial analyses which ignore gender divisions and household practices.[65] Moreover, recent inquiries into de-industrialisation have posited important local differences in access to the informal economy which, it is predicted, will play an increasingly important part in the production of labour power in the near future.[66] One account which draws together aspects of de-industrialisation, household consumption, local class structure and local politics is that of John Urry.

Urry employed a strategy similar to that of Castells in disaggregating some elements of the total process of the reproduction of capitalist societies in order to generate an historical periodisation in which different mechanisms generate different spatial effects at different times. In *The Anatomy of Capitalist Societies* he distinguished three distinct spheres, the economy, civil society and the state. Civil society was denoted the sphere of circulation, reproduction and struggle; and it was hypothesised that over time there was a movement within civil society from the domination of the sphere of circulation to the domination of the sphere of reproduction. On this basis, Urry identified a movement in types of political struggle. In the first period struggles revolved around the establishment of formally equal exchange and, typically, generated class struggles. In the second era, struggles over the distribution of rewards and the consumption of commodities led to a decline in the importance of class: other movements grew in importance, movements of 'women, youth, blacks', and class struggle became less intense as the state intervened to help socialise the costs of the reproduction of labour power.[67] A general tendency was diagnosed for the emergence of struggles concerned with the consumption of use–values and the manner of their provision, whether commodified or not.

In subsequent essays concerned with de-industrialisation and politics Urry has attempted to specify the spatial consequences of this scheme.[68] Adopting a view of spatial change in production owing much to Massey, Urry generates a view of increasing local differentiation of political conflicts. The new patterns of industrial location have produced local class structures of great variety, the responses of which may be complex especially since the politics of both production and reproduction in a period of industrial decline will tend to encourage non-class, local, social movements.[69]

There are some problems with this schema, the most obvious perhaps being its wayward periodisation. There does not seem to be much historical justification for asserting that struggles over circulation were replaced by struggles over distribution, for example. But it is important to inquire into the relationship between class and popular struggles over consumption. Urry's focus permits analysis of the politics of consumption without restricting its scope to state intervention in urban system. Thus, the metaphor is extended to involve not merely production (in many accounts only manufacturing production, at that) but also to a generalised conception of consumption which generates spatially differentiated political movements.[70] How the struggles over production and consumption mesh together remains problematic: the 'combination rules' are still unwritten. But by stressing the combined importance of local differences in labour markets, household forms and industrial structure, distinctive spatial aspects of struggle are drawn into focus.

Conclusion

In conclusion, I would suggest that any satisfactory account of the geology of social relations, whether as extended metaphor or social theory, should satisfy four criteria with respect to the analysis of uneven development. First, it should be able to explain the origins of historical phases in the location practices of capital, and would provide the transformation rules which structure the industrial layers deposited in any given area. Second, it should be able to specify determinately the political outcomes contingent upon different kinds of localised systems of social relations. This would entail being able to classify the typical effects of different combinations of class, gender and popular forces. Third, it should be able to recognise autonomous spatial effects, whether regional or local, where they exist. This is no more than to take seriously the capacity for interaction networks to create emergent spatial effects, which in some argots would be nominated as local culture or community. Such effects may arise from distributive mechanisms, consumption practices and political intervention as well as from production processes. Finally, the condi-

210 Spatial Change, Politics and the Division of Labour

tions under which mechanisms or contradictions have effect must be sufficiently elaborated and precisely specified to permit reconnection with historical evidence. An inherent danger of a realist approach is that mechanisms, their effects, and their mutual modification in concrete conjunctures, become dissociated so that appearances can no longer discriminate between one realist theory and another. Adequate explanation requires that it be demonstrated exactly which mechanisms, in which combinations, account for the composition of the geological layers of social relations.

It would be unduly optimistic to suggest that attention to these additional mechanisms producing spatial effects would be sufficient to produce a theory of the connections between space, time and social relations adequate to meet Sack's stringent criteria of a social scientific theory. It is not proven that the mechanisms briefly examined are mutually compatible. Nor have the theoretical connections between them been specified. But they do suggest ways in which the basic metaphor might be extended and, since neither the basic metaphor nor any single mechanism seems capable of giving a faithful account of the unevenness of development, this cannot but be useful. There is good reason to believe that, together with capital in search of profit, labour processes, labour markets, collective consumption arrangements and household organisation, all contribute to the generation of spatial variation in social relations and political practices. The geological formation of local social relations is a complex process.

Notes

1. Sack (1980) p. 59.
2. For example, at a general level, Giddens (1981b).
3. Storper (1981) usefully distinguishes a modern *systems* approach to location analysis from a *structural* approach which is often, but not necessarily, of Marxist inspiration.
4. Lojkine (1976) pp. 134–5.
5. Williamson (1968) pp. 102, 106.
6. Hobsbawm (1981) pp. 11.
7. Durkheim (1964) p. 28.
8. Rose and Unwin (1975) attribute the lack of movement to the fact that a shift to the 'nationalisation of politics' had occurred in a previous period which they did not study.
9. Hechter (1973; 1975).
10. For example, Fothergill and Gudgin (1980).
11. Lee (1971, appendix).
12. Chisholm and Oeppen (1973).

13. See the criticisms of Keeble (1977) by Massey and Meegan (1978) about the validity of alternative economic indicators.
14. For example, Saunders, in this volume.
15. For example, Sayer (1982).
16. See Union of Radical Political Economics (1978) pp. 1–12; Lovering (1978); and the summary by Massey (1978a).
17. See the comprehensive survey of Lebas (1982).
18. Lojkine (1976). But note that his position seems to have modified considerably of late (see Lojkine, 1981).
19. Lipietz (1980a).
20. Massey (1973; 1979).
21. Massey and Meegan (1978; 1979); Massey (1978a).
22. Massey (1978b; 1979); Massey and Meegan (1982).
23. Massey and Meegan (1978); also the conclusions of Massey and Meegan (1982).
24. For example, Walker and Storper (1981) who argue a strong case for labour as the basic source of competitive advantage, but who stress that the conditions of its reproduction are critical in respect of location strategies.
25. Such propositions are made on the authority of the influential work of Fröbel *et al* (1980).
26. Massey and Meegan (1979; 1982); Massey (1978b).
27. Massey and Meegan (1982).
28. It may thus be possible to explain the relatively strong urban–rural shift in employment in Britain, most recently and comprehensively documented by Fothergill and Gudgin (1982).
29. See Massey (1979) pp. 234–5 for the clearest description of her 'schematic way of approaching this . . . historical process'.
30. Massey (1980).
31. Massey (1978a).
32. Massey (1980) p. 1.
33. See for example some of the work of Lovering (1978); Cooke (1981); Day (1982).
34. See Gittins (1982).
35. See for example Liddington and Norris (1978); Macintyre (1980) and Gittins (1982) for some preliminary suggestions of how domestic arrangements and political effects vary over space and time.
36. Sack (1980) passim.
37. Taylor and Johnston (1979) pp. 221–69.
38. Nagel (1955).
39. Gregory (1978a) p. 46.
40. Giddens (1981b) pp. 39–40.
41. For example, Johnson (1979); Homans (1969).
42. Lojkine (1981) pp. 97–9.
43. Gordon (1978a); or see, alternatively his similar argument (1978b).
44. Lees (1982).
45. Littler (1982).
46. Ward (1980); Shaw (1979).
47. See Anderson (1976) note 59.

212   *Spatial Change, Politics and the Division of Labour*

48. See the argument of Giddens (1979).
49. It is surprising that Gordon makes no use of the concept since it is one he has used effectively in other works, for example, Gordon (1972); Gordon, Edwards and Reich (1982).
50. See Norris (1980); also Lever (1979). For a summary of the limits of recent approaches to the comparative study of local labour markets see Warde (1982) pp. 25–35.
51. A principal example is Edwards (1979); for a critique of Edwards' labour market apprach see Penn (1982).
52. Storper and Walker (1983). *Prima facie*, the model appears so complicated that its application to the explanation of historical instances seems unlikely to succeed.
53. Castells (1977) p. 445.
54. Castells (1977) p. 443.
55. Castells (1977) p. 444.
56. For example, Lojkine (1976); Lipietz (1980a).
57. Castells (1977) pp. 129–233.
58. Castells (1977) p. 451.
59. Castells (1978) pp. 93–151.
60. For example, Mingione (1981) p. 66.
61. Castells (1978) p. 178.
62. Byrne (1982); Duncan and Goodwin (1982); Smith (1983).
63. Census 1911, *Report for the County of Lancashire*, Table 25.
64. Ball (1980).
65. See, for example, the fascinating discussion of Smout (1976) on regional variations in illegitimacy ratios in nineteenth century Scotland.
66. For example, Gershuny and Pahl (1979); Pahl (1980).
67. Urry (1981a) pp. 125–32.
68. Urry (1981b; 1982; 1983a); Murgatroyd and Urry (1982).
69. Urry (1982; 1983a).
70. See esp. Urry (1981b; 1982); also Pahl, Chapter 11 of this volume.

10
Class Practices as Regional Markers: A Contribution to Labour Geography

PHILIP COOKE

Introduction

Between the generality of aggregate social structure, on the one hand, and the uniqueness of *locale*, on the other, there is a socio-spatial scale at which it is possible to place in focus the specificity of particular class formations. Moreover, such an apparently narrow focus can still shed light upon the mechanisms that tend to have a global effect upon the nature of class practices. In this study I will attempt to show how this scale, which for purposes of simplicity I shall call *regional*, not only helps considerably to clarify the relationship between social and spatial processes but also, because of the uneven nature of capitalist develoment, represents a more generally useful point of entry to the study of classes in modern society. In one respect the whole of what follows is an attempt to define the vexed concept of 'region', and I attempt to do so by arguing that regional boundaries are largely coterminous with the limits of dominant class practices. Such practices are as capable of being dominated at the level of culture, also, to a marked extent politically, and even, in lmited ways, economically, by the interests of labour, as they are by those of capital.

I have chosen to illustrate the argument by examining an area of Britain which has been referred to (perhaps over-ambitiously) as one of her few 'Red Belts',[1] but which can more reasonably be referred to as having been, traditionally at least, something of a radical region. The region in question is South Wales, a centre of rapidly-declining coal-mining and steel manufacture. Inevitably then, this study places the accent upon the class practices of workers, although some attention is paid to the owners of capital too. This is by no means an arbitrary decision; for too long the ways in which the working class has constructed modes of resistance to the under-cutting of both its social and spatial bases of collective identification have been, at best, ignored, and, at worst, no less in orthodox economics than in certain government policies, perceived as a friction effect hindering efficiency in the space-economy. So what follows is subtitled 'a contribution to labour geography' in the hope that others may wish to help develop a form of analysis of socio-spatial processes in geography which begins to balance the array of studies that perceive spatial development as the unproblematic outcome of the decisions of capitalists.

Regions as practices: theories of socio-spatial diversity

I begin with an examination of some theoretical work on the importance of space to the understanding of social diversity. This will assist in moving towards a working definition of the category 'region' which can be used in the subsequent analysis. Perhaps the best place to start is with some of the relatively few thoughts on the relationship between space and society provided by Gramsci. In various writings on the historical role of Italian cities, the importance of the Piedmont in the *Risorgimento*, and the Southern question,[2] Gramsci pointed to key markers of regional and sub-regional differentiation that retain their value for contemporary socio-spatial analysis. Four points are of importance here.

The first of these is that simple status distinctions as between, for example, manual workers and entrepreneurs tell us very little about the interest that each kind of worker may have in changing the general social relations of a given productive system. Rather, Gramsci argues, it is in specific social relations and conditions for exchange within the more general complex of social relations of production that the key distinctions lie. He then goes on to show how specific, spatially distinctive social relations of domination and subordination could lead, for example, to profound quiescence amongst rurally-based manual workers – as in the South – or surprising radicalness amongst middle-managers in certain Northern engineering centres.

The second point, which helps us understand such socio-spatial variations in habituation to the hegemony of domination and subordination, refers to the practices of intellectuals. These practices are precisely the means by which the contraints of structure and the opportunities for individual action are communicated and reinforced. Whichever class is spatially (that is, locally, regionally, nationally) dominant has an interest in and pursues practices which seek to sustain and reproduce that dominance. Gramsci noted how the urban entrepreneurial class created conditions for subaltern strata of different kinds of intellectual to sustain it and give it homogeneity. These ranged from researchers, technicians and accountants to organisers of cultural innovation and, more thoroughly, of new legal codes to facilitate contractual relations, and so on. Such strata grew 'organically' as the entrepreneurial class grew. The peasantry, by contrast, lacked dynamism partly because its intellectuals were conveyed in significant numbers into the clergy, the 'organic intellectuals' of the landed aristocracy. Other strata reinforcing this traditional subaltern class included local administrators, lawyers, doctors, teachers and so on. The peasantry was a class, in other words, which produced the means of its own hegemonic subordination and thus, for Gramsci, could not play a transformative role as long as this state of affairs continued. Neither, for the same reason, could this intellectual-producing capacity be turned to the advantage of the other great subordinate class, the urban working class. Its essential problem of organisation and resistance was the difficulty of developing its own 'organic intellectuals'.

The third point noted by Gramsci was the way the functions of intellectuals varied between the rural and urban contexts. The relevance here is in the spatial variation of structural constraint and degree of openness for individual agency that Gramsci's analysis opens up. In the rural context there was an almost constant interaction between the peasantry and the professional petty-bourgeoisie of the small towns. This reinforced the aspirations of the peasant towards achieving higher status for family members, not least for the easing of the economic life of the peasant which connection to higher status networks was expected to bring. In the industrial cities, by contrast, the entrepreneurial 'subalterns' did not have this social control function in relation to labour. This was assumed to be substantially supplied by the wage-relation. Thus, Gramsci argued, entrepreneurs would only seek indirect controls on workers. Even in his discussion of the technologically more advanced Americanism and Fordism this was seen as being achieved by selective recruitment, high pay,[3] the use of transfer-machinery, and the procurement by the state of a climate of responsibility outside work, in the family and community. Hence, to the extent that labour had developed organisations of resistance to the disciplines of the accumulation process, and, crucially, its own strata of organic intellectuals, Gramsci could see that intermediate workers such as technical staff might come under the political influence of organised labour rather than capital. Lastly, Gramsci points to the importance of spatially variable cultural practices in contributing to differentiated socio-spatial relations. In making the point that during the *Risorgimento* the cities were more progressive politically than the countryside he stresses the fact that it was industrial cities, not all cities which displayed this characteristic. In the non-industrial 'cities of silence' there was a parochial culture of dominance practised towards the despised and subordinated countryside. This antipathy derived, paradoxically, from the material dependence of such centres of consumption upon rurally-created wealth, and was bolstered by specific ideological practices, notably in the forms of idealistic philosophy and notions of classicism. The few, great Northern industrial cities, untrammelled by the accretions of deference and stasis found in the South, contained entrepreneurs and workers each working to new practices. Ideologically positivist rather than idealist, and futurist rather than classicist they were also linked from civil society to political society (the state) along distinctive lines. Trade associations, trade unions and political parties replaced the church and the aristocracy as means of interest-representation.

Into this field of political forces, divided between Southern conservatism, Northern entrepreneurial liberalism and proletarian proto-socialism were inserted the two large island blocs of Sicily and Sardinia. These culturally distinctive, ethno-regional formations were prone both to fissile pressures from separatist interests and to equally powerful unitarist counter-pressures. Hence, despite their marginality and rurality, these islands triggered off a sometimes leaderless and anarchic turbulence within the South which had important political repercussions throughout Italy.

The usefulness of Gramsci's analysis in the context of this study is that it clearly pinpoints the spatially uneven nature of social relations and explains this in terms of different means of controlling the basic structure of dominance and subordination characteristic of the urban and rural forms of class society. The obvious contradictions between the two sets of class relations were subsequently shown by Gramsci to have been the basis for the formation of a power bloc between industrialists and workers in the North and urban *rentiers* in the South centred upon political liberalism. By enlarging – or perhaps entrapping – a large, semi-colonial market in the South behind tariff walls, the expansionary economic interests of the North could be furthered. At the same time the maintenance of traditional class relations in the South gained perceived justification in the wider interests of the Italian state. Gramsci thus provides an illuminating portrayal of the mechanisms responsible for systematic reproduction of spatially uneven development.

Moreover, it is the breach in such institutionalised spatial power relations, as signified by the formation of a combative and organised rural proletariat in Central Italy, following the penetration of capitalist agriculture into that region, that Gramsci shows to have ushered in the extreme authoritarianism of the Fascist era. The danger posed to the viability of the fledgling Italian state, its burgeoning capitalism and its class base by the prospect of an alliance between rural and urban proletariats provoked a deeply nationalistic and populist response from within diverse sections of civil society. These proved powerful enough to take over and modernise the apparatuses of the state wholesale.

Gramsci's insight into the nature of spatial variations in social relations, the role of ideology in forming and reproducing consciousness, and the social practices which mark off distinctive spaces in terms of degrees of freedom from structural constraint, are of considerable value to the project of the present study. However, it contains weaknesses which need to be avoided. One of these is his adherence to an excessively deterministic theoretical contradiction between the city and the countryside. It is quite clear that rural social relations can be antagonistic and non-deferential though Gramsci tends not to make much of this important point. Equally, while he distinguishes usefully between the progressiveness of industrial cities and the reaction of those devoted to consumption rather than production, he overlooks variations in political awareness and organisation between industrial sectors. It is normally the case, for example, that steel-manufacturing towns or cities in different countries require massive provocation to stir from political quiescence.[4]

A second weakness is Gramsci's under-emphasis upon the practices of workers in the sphere of production. This is to some extent understandable given his concern to examine and theorise the role of ideas in enabling a social class, once it was consciously formed and organised, to maintain or secure dominance. But this does make huge assumptions about the underlying processes by means of which individuals in the aggregate perceive the rational case for acting collectively, or not, as the case may be. The probability that such motivations have some basis in production-related issues, including wage-struggles, is at least worthy of some investigation. Such an approach might have enabled Gramsci to pin down some part of an explanation of the apparently motiveless 'turbulence' to which the South was so prone.

The question of when and for what reasons apparently firm structural constraints upon social practices cease to operate, thereby opening up substantially the scope for individual action, is by no means well understood. However, the recent work of Giddens has helped somewhat to formulate the nature of this core relationship of social theory.[5] In elaborating his theory of structuration he gives a central position to the concept of social practices. These are both constrained and facilitated by structure which, in turn, is reproduced by the actions of practising individuals and collectivities. The structures, as for example those of dominance and subordination of social classes, cease to be reproduced when practices no longer conform to them. Interestingly Giddens incorporates a spatial (and temporal) dimension into this theory of social action arguing that social systems may be more or less tightly controlled according to the level of development of integrative institutions – such as the law or the state. Where there is a relatively less well-developed system of structural control there may be instances of spatially distinctive social practices that are also temporally uneven. Cities are seen by Giddens as having been crucial to the degree of 'distanciation' present in a given social system. This was due to their powers of control through surveillance and information-gathering, functions since taken up by the state in contemporary societies.

Unfortunately, Giddens' account does not get us very much closer to those forms of structuration and disassociation from structural constraint that have operated beyond the purview of specifically city or state administration, in the factory or the landed estate. Moreover, in the last two kinds of setting it is quite conceivable that levels of surveillance, or at least knowledge about the practices of workers inside work, were and remain quite high. Yet in both settings there are plenty of examples of counter-structural practices. By contrast, where counter-structural practices were able to take root and form the basis for quite socially widespread though often spatially-contained ideologies and actions, the level of control exercised by the initiators of such practices was often woefully weak. It is clear that there are means by which powerful ideas can be formed and transmitted, with important effects on the relation between structure and agency, that are not in themselves administratively powerful nor well-equipped to engage in information-gathering or surveillance activities. The generalisability of the notion of a 'moral economy' amongst a disenfranchised and powerless historical class-grouping is one example, the articulation of the unacceptability of female disenfranchisement or lack of civil rights for racial minorities are others. The spaces and times in which such moral sensibilities are expressed and transformed into practices, when structures cease to be reproduced by actions, are not determined by 'distanciation'. But they are to be understood in terms of some combination of their specific social relations, their particular cultural and historical practices, and the moral strength of their case.

This line of reasoning is pursued to some extent in the research conducted into processes of social recomposition in the Marseilles sub-region by Bleitrach and Chenu[6]. They refer to the area as a stronghold of 'Mediterranean culture', one which, although sustained by a declining, craft-dominated industrial base in shipbuilding and ship-repairing, owes its origin to a productive base, sets of property and social relations, and everyday institutional structures established in a different space–time conjuncture. Their description of the working-class culture of Marseilles as exclusive, strongly socialist, where the family was a key mechanism both for the recruitment of labour into skilled occupations and for transmitting working-class consciousness, and above all, internally open and egalitarian in the conduct of everyday life, contains echoes of that found in nineteenth century Provence, especially in 'Red Var.'[7]

The rural radicalism of the Var owed a good deal to the combination of what was produced and where it was marketed, the nature of local property relations, the way in which the labour process was organised, gender relations in and out of the workplace, the extent of housing concentration, and the degree of formal social and political organisation capable of being achieved. In Var, in particular, wine-production predominated in the later nineteenth century. Its market was metropolitan rather than local and the scale and risk involved in production were that much greater. The Var peasantry was in exclusive possession of the small plots which supported the vineyards, there were no feudal rents to pay. But as small, independent proprietors they could only meet market demand and make a reasonable living by organising the wine-production process (as distinct from vine-growing) on a co-operative basis. Moreover, vine-growing was so labour-intensive that women were fully engaged in the labour process, normally on the basis of family-membership. Because land was scarce and valuable, and plots were small, villages were concentrated in isolated, dense clusters. Social life was characterised by a high level of formal and informal interaction, an open and communal mode of discourse, and active political debate. These social characteristics are usually summed up in the term *Provençal sociability*.

What Bleitrach and Chenu do for the Marseilles sub-region is to trace the tension between a socio-spatial formation and its practices on the one hand, and the interests of capital and the Gaullist state in breaking them down, on the other. The point here is that such integrated formations as these act as obstacles to the accumulation process. Such obstacles may be overlooked until, as in the case of the French state-planning apparatus, a reason is identified for developing a neglected region in the greater interest of the French economy. The Marseilles region was seen as ideal as a growth pole concentrating on heavy industry (steel, chemicals) for export to the relatively undeveloped but ripening Southern European market and beyond. At the same time state and private sector investment in this and other growth poles would modernise French heavy industry, making it competitive on a world scale.

They show how, as a result of regional development planning, the social life of the sub-region has been divided up as three kinds of firm, with their associated labour processes and forms of capital ownership, have come to restructure the industrial labour market quite radically. First, there are what Bleitrach and Chenu refer to as Fordist concerns, the large monopolies employing migrant labour either from previous centres of (for example, steel) production or from North Africa, indifferent to the availability of local labour pools and the supervision of work practices. They comment on the overt consumerism which management inculcates in such workers, and as in Gramsci's discussion of Fordism, the managerial strategy of rewarding 'responsible' workers and weeding out 'trouble-makers' so that self-supervision is more closely approached. Such workers develop no significant oppositional institutions and are thoroughly incorporated.

Second, they refer to Taylorised, unskilled piecework being carried out under labour-intensive conditions by poorly unionised, low-wage and marginalised workers amongst whom women form a substantial grouping. Some of this work is sub-contracting for the Fordist sector locally, or similar large concerns elsewhere, or simply sweatshop work for direct consumption. These enterprises are small and locally-owned and though workers may be conscious of their exploited condition they are so exposed to unemployment that they can do little about it. The third category is the traditional craftwork sector where relatively autonomous skilled workers have both a tradition of cohesiveness and a reasonable income enabling them to secure a degree of control over working and living conditions not shared by the other labour sub-markets. For example, Bleitrach and Chenu speak of the pauperisation by space and time imposed by the long journeys to work of steel and chemical workers to their free-standing growth-pole, and by marginalised workers to their small town and rural workplaces where reproduction costs are low.

Clearly, this approach is not unproblematic: it works with a too rigid theory of the state and of the labour market to make its points thoroughly convincing.[8] The presentation of the state acting smoothly to further the direct interests of French monopoly capital may be less unbelievable than it would for other developed economies, but it still comes over as rather too slick an account of the growth pole programme. The extent to which Gaullism, with its intensely patriotic strand, was simply being expressed in economic modernisation, or, as well, in a quest to unify a politically diverse society by responding to pressure for development 'from below', is unexplored here. Similarly, one wonders how far the formalism of the triple labour market model captures the agency effects of organised labour in addition to those of the different kinds of capital which seem so neatly to have sewn up the regional economy.[9] Nevertheless, these formalisms do not entirely obfuscate some of the useful findings of the research. The methodology employed has usefully sought to link together production relations and certain relations of civil society – family, locality, cultural and ideological practices – in explaining the nature of a specific socio-spatial formation and elements of its deformation.

In conclusion, therefore, each of these contributions helps to establish the importance of the spatial dimension to the understanding of differentiation in the characteristic social _practices_ conducted by particular class-groupings. The spatial edges of these social practices can be quite marked as combinations of the structural factors which have been discussed take on a different emphasis. It is important to see such changes as clear ones rather than in terms of an imperceptible merging of practices along some kind of continuum. This is because – as will be seen in the section which follows – even superficially cognate practices such as, for example, agrarian political radicalism and industrial political radicalism involving culturally identical groups, become thoroughly disconnected when the dominant social relations found in the different regional settings reveal themselves as distinctive forms of appropriation of surplus labour: although, as I will indicate, such a formulation is already too restrictive with its economistic accent.

In the following section I will schematise the salient points of the foregoing review into a series of five factors which I think are crucial to explaining variations in the regional practices which designate distinctive socio-spatial formations.

The specificity of the regional: the example of South Wales

It is important that the following five threads are disentangled from the multiple structural influences upon socio-spatial diversity if we are to move towards an analytical framework for studying and comparing the geography of class relations:

1. *the productive base* (that is, the nature and extent of definite forms of appropriation of surplus value, the precise commodities which are produced, and the natural conditions for their production);
2. *the labour process* (that is, degree of autonomy of direct producer, extent of supervision, intensity of skill, mechanisation and level of workforce organisation resistance);
3. *the ownership of capital* (that is, industrial capital, finance capital, large or small scale; local, national, international; private or state);
4. *specific social relations* (that is, regional, urban, rural alignments/ cleavages of interest, gender relations, wage relations, consumption relations, popular (including ethno-regional) struggles);
5. *institutional specificities* (that is, cultural, intellectual, cognitive (for example, information/knowledge) and ideological practices).

In order to make fully adequate use of such a schema it is plainly desirable for a range of different kinds of region or locality to be compared (for example, regions dominated by different industrial sectors, rural smallholdings versus wage-labour communities, ethnically heterogeneous versus homogeneous regions and localities, and so on), but in what follows the framework will be given a trial run on the somewhat rugged terrain of industrial South Wales.

The productive base

Superficially South Wales has much in common with other basic industry areas of the older industrialised world: it developed in the later nineteenth century as a major coal-mining and steel-producing centre. But it did not develop a substantial secondary manufacturing capacity such as in shipbuilding or heavy engineering. It remained, after a period of rapid industrialisation, a relatively underdeveloped region in terms of industrial diversification and capacity for sustained economic growth. This was an effect of a range of complex determinations, three of which can be briefly mentioned as contingent upon characteristics of the productive base, others of which are aspects of the other four main factors to be considered.

First, the natural, geographical and topographical setting of the coalfield and iron towns of South Wales was one of relative remoteness from other major centres of capital accumulation in Victorian and Edwardian Britain. Also, the coal was extracted from narrow, deeply-incised valleys in an upland plateau in which centralised urbanisation, with all that is thereby implied for speeding-up the circulation of capital and its further valorisation through diversification[10], was impossible. Iron and steel production was interspersed throughout the coalfield in similarly small and fragmentary units.

Secondly, in both coal and iron production, a substantial amount of production was absorbed directly into the transport and packaging industries: the coal was ideal for stoking the massive British military and merchant fleet; much of the iron was used for the production of rails, plates, sections and so on used in the shipping and railway industries outside Wales; and tinplate was used in the canning and domestic utensil industries, again often away from the point of production.

Third, both the main industries of coal and iron/steel were organised according to the highest principles of Victorian industrial capitalism. There were regular efforts by owners to raise absolute surplus value through the extension of the working-day and the reduction of necessary as compared with surplus labour with only relatively limited efforts to increase relative surplus value by increased mechanisation.[11] The repercussions, in terms of class relations, of these productive characteristics included the formation of highly solidary, protective trade union organisations, albeit with markedly different structures of interest-mediation, in the two dominant industries.

The labour process

The differences in the forms of interest-mediation and representation derived reasonably straightforwardly from the differences in the technical process of production of the principal commodities as expressed in the organisation of the respective labour processes. The key mediating role between capital and wage-labour was performed by craft-workers who dictated the timing and pace of work and negotiated the rates of pay in the coal and steel industries. Both industries were characterised by the system of production by sub-contracting. Contracts were struck between craft-workers and owners (or more usually, managers) of steel-mills or coal-mines. Wage-labour was consequently employed by craft-workers rather than directly by capital. Hence, direct supervision of the labour process by the representatives of capital was negligible: the subordination of labour to capital was formal rather than real, therefore, in the two key industries of the region.[12]

However, beneath this surface similarity there were crucial differences in the mode of control between the two industries. Moreover, the relationship between the skilled mining sub-contractor and management on the one hand, and his underhands, on the other, was different from the production relations operating throughout much of nineteenth and early twentieth century industry in Britain. As Littler has shown,[13] the sub-contracting system (with variations) was near-universal until the inter-war period, a fact which has made other theories of British industrial organisation, such as direct owner-manager control or craft-control, look threadbare. Littler identifies two key systems of control which nicely encapsulate the differences between coal and steel industries in South Wales. The first is the *gang-work* system (more commonly known as the butty-system) typical of coal-mining and other extractive industries; the second is the *craft-work* system, common in the steel and other metal trades.

Now, Littler argues that the power of the craft-worker rested on his special technical knowledge of the manufacturing process, something which neither the owner, manager nor underhand normally possessed. This gave the craft-worker, classically in iron and steel, an exclusivity and status which separated him markedly from his employees, and gave him a closer-to-equal relationship with management. One effect of this, which was borne out in the South Wales steel industry as elsewhere, was that the industry was, and remains, remarkably strike-free. Nevertheless, because of their subordinate position, underhands quickly became conscious of their need to unionise, as much to protect themselves against craft-unions as against owners and managers. The history of the South Wales steel industry is dotted with instances of intra-plant disputes between craft and general unions and between craft unions, but the industry as a whole has remained quiescent. Of key importance to that quiescence was the institutionalisation of internal arbitration procedures conducted by representatives of management and unions from distant regions. This institution, known colloquially as 'the neutrals', was the product of a settlement between craft-unions and steel-owners in 1869 after severe conflict between them which nearly bankrupted the industry over wide areas. The South Wales steel industry is, therefore, a good example of the craft-work system of control of the labour process in operation.

However, the same cannot be said of the South Wales coal industry *vis à vis* Littler's definition of the gang-work system. He argues that, because he was the direct employer of wage-labour the ganger naturally sought to justify his separate status on the grounds of special expertise just as the craft-worker could. Nevertheless, because of the relatively unsophisticated nature of the relevant technology (at least by comparison with steel-making) and the over-supply of labour which often ensued, the ganger was unable to establish a true craft-status for himself. As a result, he was obliged to develop a close personal relationship with the manager or owner to gain, for example, information about good working-places, which would help to maintain his exclusivity and, importantly, his wage differential over his underhands.

But in South Wales the definition of skill based on *exclusivity* implicit in Littler's analysis was absent. Rather, the collier (that is, the skilled sub-contractor) expressed his expertise and thus his status by the fact that he could and would habitually perform *all* the tasks involved in mining coal, not just the most skilled. The self-definition of skill was thus an *inclusive* not an exclusive one. Moreover, the relationship between the collier and the relevant management deputy was fraught with conflict. This was because of the issue of 'deadwork', that is, time used in removing the rock preventing access to a coal seam. The geological conditions of the coalfield were such that up to a quarter of the average collier's earnings actually derived from deadwork. Not surprisingly deadwork was closely scrutinised by the deputies, and the daily haggling over the extent and rate to be paid for deadwork was a constant source of tension. Another source of tension was the shift-system which in South Wales, unlike elsewhere, remained as a single nine to ten hour period of work. Even after the 1908 Mines Regulation Act was passed, reducing the working day to eight hours, South Wales colliers completely rejected the coal-owners desire to institute double eight-hour shifts for coal-cutting. The reasons successfully advanced by the colliers were that: (i) deadwork could not be evenly divided between shifts, so one collier might easily gain a disproportionate reward from the unproductive work performed by the preceding one; (ii) sharing of income with the second shift would threaten the privacy of the wage packet; and (iii) dividing the day into two shifts would disrupt their family lives and opportunities for sociability outside work.[14]

All this was very different from the position obtaining in Northeast England. There, a strict division of labour existed such that faceworkers worked exclusively on coal-cutting, clearers on clearing, fillers on filling, and hauliers on hauling. This fact led directly to a more finely differentiated social structure within the community, based on the clear income differentials between the various grades of worker. An indicator of the acceptance within the wider community of the privileged status of the coal-hewer was the fact that he frequently received a rent-free house from the coal-owner, something unheard of in South Wales.[15] Daunton argues persuasively that these controls and privileges accrued by the North-eastern collier, and the hierarchised social structure within the working class which grew in its wake, are crucial to our understanding of the lack of a militant reputation amongst miners there. It was certainly the case that, as in the steel industry, the miners' union in the North-east operated an internal system of arbitration and conciliation on behalf of the coal-owners from as early as the 1870s.[16]

The question is, does the lack of equivalent hierarchisation in the South Wales coalfield help to explain why it developed a reputation for industrial militancy? Clearly the conflicts between colliers and deputies over deadwork, and between colliers and coal-owners over shift-work show that there was little of the incorporated tradition such as could be observed in the North-east between skilled workers and management. Also, the non-exclusivity of the definition of skill on the part of the collier would seem to point to a more egalitarian labour process and, perhaps, everyday life. This might be supported by the evidence that the family was an important source of recruitment for hewers and hauliers in South Wales, where, in 1906 for example, 15 per cent of coal-cutters were boys under 16 years of age, while in the North-east there were none. On the other hand, this set up tensions which were absent in the North-east where hierarchisation also meant that there was a career structure from haulier to hewer. Perhaps the best indication that social relations of production were more egaliterian comes not from looking for the even-handedness of the collier, but rather at the combativeness of the underhands.

Because the South Wales coalfield was closely-tied to the world market its output was subject to large fluctuations in price over short periods, sometimes as little as months. To offset losses the coal-owners introduced the 'sliding scale' system of payment to colliers whereby for every shilling change in the price per ton of coal, earnings were changed by 7.5 percent.[17] Colliers were paid by the ton but hauliers were paid by the day. If the price dropped colliers could work harder and make up the deficit whereas hauliers clearly could not. Hauliers' wages declined therefore, while simultaneously they were required to work harder to remove the colliers' increased output. This issue lay behind the massive strike in South Wales during 1893 when 1 500 000 working days were lost. The strike ushered in the formation of the general union, the South Wales Miners Federation, which sought to minimise these internal work-group conflicts and in the process of achieving this aim contributed enormously to the solidarity of South Wales miners in the workplace and outside after 1898.

To return, finally, to the iron and steel industry it is noteworthy that even though the model of underhands achieving improved payment in the coal industry existed, their own capacity to achieve similar improvements was blocked successively by the craft unions. Even though a sliding scale system of payment also operated in the steel industry, whenever tonnage payments fell craft-workers were able to make good their own deficits by laying-off the poorly-organised underhands. Eventually, towards the end of the inter-war years the unskilled workers were better-organised and able to resist lay-offs to a greater extent, in part because the power of the craft unions had entered substantial decline with changes in technology and the growth of semi-skilled work. Hence, the marked unevenness in the development of solidaristic labour organisations between the coal and steel industries, and their distinctive social structures of work and everyday life emerged as the sub-contracting system unfolded differently in the two industries. Nevertheless, the recognition that formal organisation was the keystone of resistance to exploitation was widespread throughout the industrial region from the late nineteenth century onwards.[18]

The ownership of capital

Although the predominant scale of capital ownership was initially relatively small, the process of capital concentration led, by the interwar years, to the existence of some very large units of industrial capital, the biggest of which such as the Powell Duffryn Steam Coal Company in coal, or Guest, Keen and Nettlefold in steel, now operate as medium-sized transnational corporations. Despite this apparently similar tend to concentration it is essential to note the diametrically-opposed origins and deployment of the source of capital in coal and steel respectively. In the coal industry the early sources of capital formation (up to 1875) were primarily local and small-scale. That is, mining ventures were normally embarked upon by the local petty-bourgeoisie (shopkeepers, lawyers, teachers) pooling their limited resources with a view to modest investment in joint ownership and operation of a single mining enterprise. While the coal-measures under exploitation remained close to the surface such ventures could be reasonably profitable, although lack of technical knowledge meant that such a pattern of mining tended to be highly inefficient and productivity levels were low. As and when mining had, perforce, to become deeper, the technological and engineering expertise developed in older British deep-mine coalfields such as Durham had either to be bought in or established by immigrant coal-owners and managers. In the late Victorian/Edwardian period, therefore, levels of capitalisation increased manyfold and, although much of this capital was raised from within the personal resources (retained profits, private borrowings) of the owners, rather than through the issuing of equity,[19] the owners themselves were increasingly non-local and occasionally foreign-based. Relations between owners and workers tended to become progressively distant, less paternalistic, and more conflict-ridden during this period, culminating in 1926 with the General Strike, sparked off by coal-miners' resistance to wage cuts and extension of the working day.

The iron, and later, steel, industry in the region was established almost exclusively by individual, non-local capitalists, some possessing financial and technical resources from involvement in iron manufacture elsewhere in Britain, others seeking an outlet for surpluses gained in agriculture or commerce. Both groups borrowed substantially from London and Bristol banks to supplement investment capital, purchase a competitor's faltering enterprise, or simply keep the business going during the early, competitive stages of the industry's development. As the iron industry stagnated in the late nineteenth century a further external stimulus was provided by a considerable transfer of the British iron and steel industry from the landlocked Midlands of England to coastal South Wales from which the imperial export trade could be more effectively managed. It was only the tinplate industry of the western part of the region which was established and remained in the ownership of local capital, and even this occurred only to a limited extent, despite the fact that one locally-owned concern (Richard Thomas and Co.) eventually came to play a dominant role in the regional steel industry.

Another factor worth noting is that, in the earlier period of development of the coal industry, paternalistic control of the workforce was often associated with small, local capital but declined somewhat with concentration in the industry. Also in the iron and steel industry paternalism was mostly obviously to be found in the smaller, more dispersed tinplate mills than in the larger iron and steel works. However, far from explaining this as a simple function of scale and isolation it is likely that paternalistic control in the coal industry was a response by local owners to profound class conflict in the early nineteenth-century coal industry, as represented by such institutions as the 'Scotch Cattle' and other embryonic working-class organisations. Similarly, the later paternalism of the iron and steel industry is likely to have been forced upon the heirs of the early non-local ironmasters whose abrasiveness towards workers in the industry had led to serious rioting and subsequent military intervention.[20]

It should, finally, be noted that capital ownership in these two key industries was socialised by the state following the Second World War. This reflected *inter alia*: (i) the failure of heavy industrial capital to compete on world markets; (ii) its failure to sustain the representation of its interests in the form of government support for continued private ownership; (iii) the failure of both paternalistic and overtly antagonistic labour relations strategies to undermine the capacity of organised labour to defend *its* interests; and (iv) the more general recognition by dominant class forces of the importance of making concessions to labour during post-war reconstruction as the basis of a settlement without which revived accumulation would be difficult to sustain.[21]

Specific social relations

While heavy industry regions may be thought of as archetypally the locations of the core elements of the classic working class, the practices often associated with such formations are highly unevenly developed.[22] Thus, a clearly-perceived class consciousness, a marked degree of organisational solidarity or a heritage of industrial militancy can by no means be attached to all such regions. I have already indicated the importance of labour process variations to intra-class social hierarchisation, and this may well be a necessary condition for the difference between class assertiveness and deference to develop. In a later part of this sub-section I want to explore other sources of specificity in social relations, and the practices which define them, which are of a more contingent nature. But first I want to examine a feature of industrial South Wales which, in its heyday as a heavy industry region up to the end of the first half of the twentieth century, was generalisable to other similar regions – its characteristic gender relations.

Although employment in the coal industry had not always been a male preserve it became exclusively so in South Wales after the First World War. Women had been excluded from underground employment by the Mines Act of 1842, although the extent and intensity of its implementation varied considerably. Subsequently, they were employed as surface workers engaged in hauling coal-trucks, coal-washing and shifting pit-props. After the 1914–18 period these jobs were subsequently taken by boys and old miners, suggesting that it was not the arduousness of the work which determined that women should relinquish it. The most appropriate explanation for the extrusion of women from waged work in the South Wales coalfield is a combination of the conditions of labour over-supply which were endemic in the years leading up to the First World War, the effects of these conditions on wages, and the availability of better-paid work for women outside the coal industry during the war, especially in transport and munitions work. The key problem for male colliers at the time was the influx of unskilled miners and, especially, boys into mining, as Smith makes clear:

> The more practical need for trade defence led to the boosting of the notion of the skilled, craftsmanlike collier, whereas, in fact, the rapid promotion of youths was effectively undercutting the reality of apprenticeship.[23]

Smith is writing of South Wales in 1910, but Macintyre shows that this pressure was still observable after 1921.[24]

In conditions such as these, it was in the interests of both male colliers and underhands to remove the elements in the labour market that contributed to a further depressive effect on wages. Boys, as we have seen, were engaged in skilled work underground for part of their time, and as such enabled the collier to maximise returns for minimal outlay. Old miners were protected by union-negotiated seniority rules which ensured them lighter surface work in their later years. Women were the principal alternative source of cheap labour and they were the category dispensed with, under the guise of patriarchal arguments based on the impropriety of women working as miners.[25]

In the iron and steel towns within the coalfield, the situation of women as employees was completely polarised. Although in the earliest period of the development of the industry women had worked alongside men, especially in unskilled work, they had largely withdrawn from steel employment in the central and eastern parts of the industrial belt by the early twentieth century. However, at the western end where the specialised tinplate industry was concentrated, women were employed as production workers until after the Second World War. The tinplate industry was scattered in small hand-worked mills which rolled and cut the steel. This was then dipped in vats of liquid tinning material for subsequent use in the canning and domestic utensils industry. Women were employed in the latter stages of this process, which were also the most dangerous. The cutting of steel-strip into manageable proportions resulted in large, razor-sharp pieces of steel being slid or passed from worker to worker at some considerable speed. The women's only protection was a pair of heavy gauntlets and work-boots. As can be imagined these gave only limited protection against industrial injury either in the form of lacerations or scalds from the molten tin.

One interesting feature of women's non-exclusion from heavy industry in west South Wales is that there was not the same pressure from immigration there as was the case further east. Trade unionism was not as well-organised and relations between management and workers were highly paternalistic. The industry was also, however, located in a part of industrial South Wales which remains ethnically and linguistically the most distinctively Welsh area in the region. As such it also has the strongest nonconformist religious tradition. It might be anticipated that such 'conservative' practices would radically reject women's work of the kind described, but this simply was not the case.[26]

A deduction that can be drawn from the absence of exclusion of women from heavy and dangerous work in a part of industrial South Wales where unionisation was relatively weak, paternalism was strong and labour supply was not over-abundant, is that the control of the female labour supply is a source of male bargaining power in a context of antagonistic capital–labour relations. The basis for this power is the fact that labour power reproduction is not, in the final analysis, something over which capital has direct control. Rather, labour power is produced in the domestic sphere and, as such, is subject to controls other than the mere demands of capital. In a context where capital is capable of impoverishing a workforce generally through depressing the average wage rate by employing women, it makes sense for men to use the defensive institution of the trade union to exclude the source of wage-rate reduction and then argue for a family wage. Of course, had patriarchy not been the condition upon which the convention was established that income-disparity by gender was an appropriate practice, organised labour would not have been so vulnerable to this problem in the first place. This seems, in conclusion, to cast considerable doubt on the notion that the domestic division of labour is somehow essential to the development of capitalist relations of production.[27] If anything, the domestication of women, at least as far as South Wales is concerned, was an outcome secured by organised male labour to fight income erosion. It was then sustained by its capacity to enforce patriarchal relations in the home, in part through the institutionalisation of the family wage.

A final point concerns the role of women as supporters of militant trade union practices despite their confinement to the domestic sphere. Their assertiveness outside the domestic sphere leads to a questioning of their acquiescence within it, and Macintyre's allusion to the power of patriarchy as expressed through the medium of male violence towards women seems a plausible, if partial, explanation.[28]

There are three other factors which deserve special attention in considering the determination of specific social relations in the context of industrial South Wales. The first of these is historical and concerns the nature of the transition across Giddens' 'time–space edges' or between different modes of social relations, expressions of distinctive productive bases under the same general relations of market exchange and production for profit. A key marker of this transition is represented by the distinction between the categories 'rural' and 'urban' where forms of life in the first category come to inform social practices in the second. To illustrate; the populations which largely constituted the first wave of urban, industrial workers in South Wales came from an agrarian society already characterised by turbulence, radicalism and egalitarian practices deriving from *inter alia*: (i) the nature of agricultural production: (ii) ethnolinguistic alignments and cleavages; (iii) popular religious dissent; and (iv) relatively under-determined relations of class domination. Consider the following:

> The main financial returns came from the sale of store cattle and of casked salted butter. But no holding had calves to rear for sale or milk for butter-making without the services of a bull. Bulls however are expensive animals to keep, and only on holdings of some 65 acres (or more) could they be kept. Five holdings out of every six were smaller than this, so that every five holdings depended on the sixth for a bull's services. And payment for these services was not in cash but in labour at the hay harvest...local idiom ... indicates that people saw the society in which they lived in terms of the three main divisions of 'gwyr mawr' (gentry), farmers and 'pobl tai bach' (cottagers)... *but in certain contexts they (farmers and cottagers) were both of them 'pobl gyffredin' (ordinary people) vis à vis 'y gwyr mawr'* and the threefold division of society seems to become twofold.[29]

What is implied here is that the subjective conception of class membership by small farmers was indeterminate precisely because of the exploitative relationship which existed between the landed aristocracy and all smallholders. This applied even though there were reasonably distinctive gradations between those few, more prosperous farmers who possessed resources, and presumably income, which were the basis for a non-cash, seasonal exchange relationships, and the less prosperous smallholders who were dependent upon those resources but paid for them in the collective form of communal labour power. Objectively, because neither farmers nor, certainly, cottagers would be significant purchasers of wage-labour in the conventionally understood sense, and because each would own means of production in varying degrees, both categories belonged to the same class. Thus in objective terms, the class system from which most of the earliest migrants to the South Wales coalfield sprang was a two-class system of gentry and smallholders. Subjectively, on the part of the smallholding class, differences in endowment existed but the barriers between strata were by no means exclusive. The importance of this for the later development of an egalitarian, proletarian consciousness is twofold. In the first place there was a relative absence of deferential attitudes towards the landed class where it was also the capitalist class, and second, the least-equipped workers were not inclined to be acquiescent in their relations with better-skilled, or at least, better-placed colliers, as has already been seen. These practices should be compared, once more, with those of the Great Northern coalfield where the coal-mining industry virtually reproduced *en bloc* the class structure of the preceding agricultural economy. This was a three-class system divided between landed aristocrats who were also coal-owners, wage-labour employing farmers and a proletariat of agricultural labourers. The semi-feudal deference and dependency structures built into that system provided the basis for the social hierarchisation within the working class that, as Daunton shows,[30] has been such a characteristic element of the working-class culture of the North-eastern coalfield.

A second factor of great importance to this under-determination of classes in South Wales is the intermeshed question of language and religion. Both farmers and cottagers spoke Welsh while the gentry (despite being ethnically Welsh) habitually spoke English. Paralleling this cleavage was that centring upon religion which separated the two class groupings into nonconformists (farmers and cottagers) and Anglicans (gentry). These two powerful bases of collective identification combined with important effects for consciousness and practice:

> [Welsh] was the language of the common people in the sense that it was incorporated into their own institutions. The chapels had originated as their institutions: it was they had provided the élite, and for nearly a century there had been harmonious understanding and an implicit realisation that they – the common people – could exert some kind of control. After all, this was why they were nonconformists and not Anglicans.[31]

This is perhaps as clear an indication as any of the crucial breach between the dominant class and its subaltern intellectuals. For, whereas in Gramsci's account of the *Risorgimento* rural intellectuals drawn from peasant stock functioned as relayers of aristocratic hcgemony, in rural Wales they were actively involved in its undermining. When this culture was transmuted into the urban–industrial context radicalism was mediated in complex ways. While the proletariat and owners of means of production were predominantly Welsh, institutionally and linguistically paternalist social relations in the workplace were traded-off for reformist political representation under Liberalism. But once a falling away in religious adherence developed with, *inter alia*, the escalating scale of industry, new and massive influxes of English-speaking workers from rural areas characterised by poverty and conflict, intensified industrial conflict associated with price and wage fluctuations and the increasing appeal of socialist ideas and personalities, the hitherto harmonious class relations of the coalfield disintegrated for ever in the first decade of the twentieth century.[32] If this break with Welshness provided conditions for aggravated social turbulence and conflict in the coalfield region it is unquestionably the case that the sparking mechanism for particular conflicts lay not in the cultural sphere but in the spheres of exchange and labour power reproduction (rather than in production *per se*).

The third factor contributing to the specificity of local social relations was the peculiarity of the Welsh markets, in both coal and steel (expanding American and European heavy industries, fuel for the imperial fleets, both naval and mercantile, and for Latin American railways). Such markets were unlike those of any other world coalfield of the Edwardian era and they further accentuated the inevitable supply and demand fluctuations of competitive market relations. In both main industries it will be recalled, the sliding scale system of payment was implemented. This, as much as anything, helps to explain the intense conflicts in industrial South Wales from 1898 to 1926. Six- and seven-month strikes and lockouts were not uncommon, workers were blacklisted, scab labour was recruited at regular intervals and unionisation itself was at issue as coal-owners, in particular, sought – with some success – to establish company unions. In virtually every case these conflicts arose around issues of wages and conditions such that by 1926, at the time of Britain's only General Strike, that struggle had been distilled into the South Wales colliers' demand for 'not a minute on the day, not a penny off the pay'. By this period the space–time distanciation between rural, nonconformist and Liberal Wales on the one hand, and urban, militant and Socialist South Wales on the other, was objectively enormous despite a continuing fluidity of movement between the families and communities which continued to straddle the divide geographically.

Institutional specificities

Out of this turbulence emerged institutions which sustained important elements of a prefigurative proletarian culture, in the sense of a coherent set of intellectual, cultural and ideological practices. These were widely understood and reproduced during a period when the dominant culture and ideology of imperial Britain was militaristic, nationalistic and individualistic.[33]

Only three of these can be noted here; trade unions, health associations, and educational institutions, although others such as recreational and leisure practices, popular entertainment, but above all, political practices, are clearly important. One reason for playing down political practices is that through the development of Labourism from its earlier strands in the Independent Labour Party, the chapels and early trade unions, South Wales is not especially distinct from other heavy industry regions in Britain. However, the mass support which the British Labour Party gained from industrial South Wales was constructed on a far more thoroughgoing basis of resistance to ruling ideas and practices than was normal in such regions.[34] Trade unionism, as we have seen, was initially the province of craftworkers who had effectively lost control in the coal-mining industry by 1900, but retained it until the 1960s in the steel mills. Initially trade unionism in South Wales was fragmentary (organisation in coal being centred on eight small, local unions, five of which possessed no funds). But with the massive growth in numbers of unskilled workers flooding to the coal, transport, steel, construction and retailing industries as coalfield production took off at the end of the nineteenth century they gained in stability. A key factor in this process was the integrating influence provided by trades councils located in the larger urban centres. Interestingly, it was often the railway workers who took a leading role in defence of the right to strike and in demands for industrial unionism at this time.[35]

However, so large was the mining workforce (270 000 in 1920) that it exerted an overwhelming dominance over the political and social life of the region. This is exemplified in the ways in which, once localism had been overcome and the South Wales miners had joined the Mining Federation of Great Britain and affiliated to the Labour

Party, the union itself became the major cohesive force in the regional formation:

> From the chapels to the free libraries, from the Institutes to the sports teams, the control was a popular and a democratic one. The organisation of politics in the localities had a similar intent (diverse ideologies notwithstanding), and in all this the primary organization was the Union . . . the SWMF was, literally, the fount of control in other spheres as well as that of the industry itself.[36]

As an illustration of the ways in which wider community life was improved by the implementation of progressive, popular services in the absence of either privatised or state socialised equivalents, it is instructive to consider the establishment of local systems of health-care in parts of the coalfield during the inter-war years. Because of the unhealthy conditions of the work available in such communities, the poverty and frequent destitution which accompanied industrial conflict, and the damp climate of the upland coal-mining towns and villages, there was a high incidence of diseases such as turberculosis, pneumoconiosis, silicosis, diphtheria, scarlet fever, and the effects of malnutrition such as high infant mortality rates.[37] One early response to this situation, which was copied elsewhere in the coalfield, was the Tredegar Medical Aid Society.[38] The miners' and steelworkers' unions also established convalescent homes and rehabilitation centres for injured and invalided members from the 1920s onwards.

These local welfare institutions sprang from the collective responses of ordinary workers to the needs and suffering of their communities, as a means of improving the day-to-day conditions of life in such localities. However, it was clear to many that such patching-up could do little or nothing to bring about systematic changes in the exploitative social relations of which poor health was only one symptom, along with inadequate wages, lack of employment security, and primitive housing conditions. Coal-miners in South Wales, especially, sought to establish throughout the coalfield the means for acquiring and disseminating scientific socialist analyses of the market system and alternatives to it. This was done through each union lodge (branch) establishing, as far as possible, its own library, reading room and pedagogy within the local miners' institute.

By the mid-1940s a network of well over a hundred working-class educational centres had developed, holding classes, discussions and lectures, sending students on to working-men's colleges such as

Ruskin College, Oxford, and, later, the Central Labour College. Working-class self-education was systematised through an activist association known as the Plebs League with its own journal, newspaper and pamphlets. One of the best known of the latter was the celebrated syndicalist manifesto produced by the Rhondda rank-and-file movement and entitled *The Miner's Next Step* (1911) which called for a single, decentralist, international union, rejected state ownership of the coal industry, and demanded workers' control for the communally-owned means of production, exchange and distribution.

For all the progressive purpose and achievement contained in these practices and institutional forms it is an ironic feature of the social relations that developed in this region that those centring upon gender remained so reactionary. South Wales is, of course, not alone in having possessed this particular blind spot; patriarchy has been a transcendent feature of capitalist society in general. However, the somewhat aggravated form which patriarchy has taken, and continues to take in supposedly politically progressive regions elsewhere, suggests that the condemnation of women to a plainly secondary role may well be the price that well-organised labour has been content to pay to exercise leverage against capital and to maintain an area of control, in the domestic sphere, beyond the 'dull compulsion of economic forces'.

Concluding remarks

This study has been premised on the notion that uneven spatial development is not merely an economic phenomenon which distributes industrial sectors around the space-economy in heterogeneous fashion but with relative homogenising effects upon the class relations which are formed in the diverse parts of the system. On the contrary, it assumes there to be important socio-spatial variations that are contingent upon the uneven character of capitalist development. These variations arise from a combination of particular, spatially-distinctive conditions of production, on the one hand, and spatially-delimited social practices on the other. These practices express the relative domination and subordination of classes which form the most necessary condition of production for profit.

Rather than provide merely a reprise of the theoretical, analytical and empirical argument which has been offered in justification of that conclusion, I will draw attention to the three features which, I think, emerge as the strongest elements in the formation of the relatively solidaristic region which has been described. These are class relations and their pre-industrial popular lineaments, the ways in which a non-deferential working class remained only formally subordinated to the hegemony of production for profit, and the institutional structures by means of which resistance was reproduced through a popularly-controlled, oppositional self-education system.

For nearly fifty years a popular socialism which consisted of far more than Utopian recipes existed as an alternative culture within the (admittedly loose) interstices of capitalist production relations.

Most important of all, in the context of the theoretical instruments which helped bring this analysis to fruition, is the strong evidence that the 'Gramscian' organic intellectual was a material force in the South Wales coalfield. Such institutional structures as the system of adult education established, probably uniquely, with the conscious aim of developing an informed mining leadership capable of articulating the widespread desire of removing the industry from private ownership were seen as being of central importance. The point here is that we are not observing some random or spontaneous process by which 'Primitive Rebels' emerge at an appropriate hour. Indeed, as Gwyn Williams has put it 'for many of the Welsh movement which would occupy us under this head Sophisticated Rebels would be a more suitable title'.[40]

Thus, the South Wales coalfield was able to sustain itself as a centre of relatively strong resistance to the dominant social relations of its time through the rich interaction of economy, community, culture and history, turning these connections into *practices* of the most everyday and taken-for-granted kind, the more powerful for being perceived as unexceptional. However, it was the selectively reflexive rather than the unreflexive character of such practices, which Bourdieu has taken to be the defining character of 'habitus' or cultural specificity,[41] that is also responsible for the oppressive gender relations on the basis of which some of the achievements of South Wales radicalism have been built. Practices such as those that have been discussed here ossify into conventions in the absence of intellectual scrutiny, organic or otherwise.

Notes

1. See Williams, G. (1982) p. 185. Although South Wales was clearly socialist in the sense that the coalfield was uniformly represented by Labour in

Parliament from the 1920s (either by the Independent Labour Party or the Labour Party) Communist Party strength, with which the notion of the 'red belt' is normally associated elsewhere in Europe, was confined to the leadership of the mining union (see Francis and Smith, 1980) or localities within the coalfield, as described by Macintyre (1980).

2. The historical role of cities is discussed at various points in Gramsci (1971) while the importance of the Piedmont is dealt with in Gramsci (1971; 1977). The Southern question is extensively discussed in Gramsci (1978).

3. A similar point is made by Price (1983).

4. Good explanations for this are found in Metzgar (1980).

5. Giddens (1979; 1981b).

6. Bleitrach and Chenu (1979; 1981). For a review (in English) of the French language book of 1979 see Coing (1981) and discussion in Lebas (1982).

7. See, on this, Loubère (1974): Judt (1979); Agulhon (1982).

8. Why, for example, is consideration only given to production and consumption when, presumably, circulation, into which the wage-relation fits, is some importance to the construction of the everyday life of the worker?

9. For discussion which moves beyond this position see Kreckel (1980); Berger and Piore (1980); Cooke (1983a; 1983b); Taylor and Thrift (forthcoming).

10. For elucidation of this argument see Harvey (1982).

11. See Williams, J. (1973); Williams, G. (1980).

12. For theoretical discussion see Lazonick (1978).

13. Littler (1982).

14. Details of this successful opposition to the temporal restructuring of the working day are given in Daunton (1981).

15. On rent-free housing for colliers in the North East of England see Daunton (1980; 1981).

16. Daunton (1981) p. 579.

17. Noted in Morgan (1982) p. 174.

18. A fuller account of the sub-contracting system and its implications is given by Cooke (1982b) pp. 150-1.

19. See Walters (1980).

20. An extensive account of rioting which crossed over into a political rising is provided for the iron town of Merthyr Tydfil by Williams, G. (1978). 'Scotch Cattle', an underground, prefigurative trade union movement with terrorist overtones was based in Southern Monmouthshire, although its origins are to be found in an extra-legal, communal disciplinary ritual in the agrarian communities of West Wales, as described by Williams, G. (1982) pp. 46-82.

21. This is discussed in the study of corporatism in Britain by Middlemass (1979) especially ch. 14. Morgan, K. J. (1984) explores the implications of post-war reconstruction policy for development in Wales from a non-corporatist perspective.

22. See Cooke (1982b) pp. 151-6.

23. Smith (1980) p. 161.

24. Macintyre (1980) p. 114.
25. A related but more general argument along these lines can be found in Walby (1983).
26. The persistence of female employment in heavy industry in areas which were also noted centres of nonconformist religion is by no means confined to this small corner of South Wales. The clothing regions of Northern England and even Massachusetts would be comparable instances. See Dawley (1976); Joyce (1980); Hareven (1982).
27. This functionalist view has been argued by some Marxist feminists. See Himmelweit and Mohun (1977); Beechey (1977): Molyneux (1979).
28. Macintyre (1980).
29. Jenkins (1980) pp. 80–124 (emphasis added).
30. Daunton (1980; 1981).
31. Jones (1980) p. 67.
32. Morgan, K. O. (1982) p. 46.
33. Blanch (1979) p. 104.
34. For detailed accounts of oppositional consciousness and organisation see Francis and Smith (1980); Smith (1980).
35. The Taff Vale case is notorious in trade union history, being named after a railway linking the coalfield to the principal coal exporting centre in Cardiff. See Saville (1960).
36. Francis and Smith (1980) p. 34.
37. Even as late as 1937 when the average death rate for England and Wales was 9 per thousand, in the core of the coalfield it was 13 per thousand, with nearly 15 per cent of children officially declared to be undernourished. See Morgan, K. O. (1982) p. 233.
38. Foot (1962) p. 63.
39. Egan (1978).
40. Williams, G. (1982) p. 1.
41. Bourdieu's definition of *habitus* as:

> systems of durable, transposable dispositions, structured structures predisposed to function as structuring structures, that is, as principles of the generation and structuring of practices and representations which can be 'objectively regulated' and 'regular' without in any way being the product of obedience to rules, objectively adapted to their goals without presupposing a conscious aiming at ends or an express mastery of the operations necessary to attain them (Bourdieu, 1977, p. 72)

is a good *description* of the uncritical acceptance of gender inequality in the South Wales region, but is unhelpful in *explaining* the selectivity involved in such practices.

11
The Restructuring of Capital, the Local Political Economy and Household Work Strategies

R. E. PAHL

It is now a commonplace to recognise that the national and international restructuring of capital is producing rapid and dramatic changes in urban and regional economies.[1] This has led to yet a further shift in focus amongst those ever in search of a 'new' urban sociology.[2] An earlier debate shifted the focus from the misplaced concreteness of the spatially-defined local area, to what was considered to be the sociologically more significant arena of the politically defined State.[3] However, the emphasis on the State as the source of 'managing everyday life' through the way it provided the means of collective consumption[4] was relatively shortlived.[5] The process of sloughing off public expenditure in Britain and the United States or, in more fashionable terminology, the re-commodification of collective consumption, has re-emphasised market mechanisms and the importance of the individual as opposed to the social wage. At the same time, the growth of trans-national or multinational companies has encouraged a new international division of labour to develop so that local collusion between capital and labour is more likely than conflict.[6] The threat that a plant might simply leave the country, should the circumstances cease to be entirely agreeable, can have a remarkably de-radicalising influence.

Szelenyi's call for more precise analysis of the regional implications of this restructuring of capital is surely right, but he is not, of course, alone in pursuing such a line of thinking.[7] In a series of stimulating papers, Massey has drawn an outline of the spatial consequences of the uneven development associated with the restructuring process, but, as she would be the first to admit, this is not to emphasise the novelty of uneven development *per se* – historically that is simply a fact of capitalist development – but rather the implications of such restructuring in terms of a broader understanding of inequality, particularly in terms of class and gender relations.[8] Thus, it is relatively unexceptional to observe that there has been substantial interregional decentralisation from the conurbations and intraregional shifts to peripheral areas. This has occurred in both Britain and the United States. However, there has been rather less emphasis on the characteristics of the *jobs* so redistributed; as Massey points out, they are more likely to be classified as being semi-skilled or unskilled, they are frequently in branch plants, they are likely to be low paid and, most significantly, they are likely to be jobs done by women. Not only may the relative position of labour to capital be diminished but there may be a shift in gender relations as well. The decline in male employment in manufacturing industry has been partially matched by an increase in female employment in that sector, yet these national changes have very marked variations in operation and impact between one area and another. As Massey puts it 'the structures of local economies can be seen as a product of the combination of "layers", of the successive imposition of new "rounds of investment", representing in turn the successive roles the areas have played within the wider national and international division of labour'.[9] She demonstrates that the same 'layer' or 'round of investment' may have different effects in different areas, since it comes into contact, as it were, with different pre-existing structures, each a product of a distinctive set of investment practices and historical experiences. Furthermore, these local structures do not passively receive whatever is done to them from outside but can, in turn, interact with, and to some extent moderate or modify, these external forces differentially.

The research by Massey is supported and to some degree modified by Urry, Rees and others working in distinctive local or regional contexts.[10] This work is important and it is not our purpose to dispute the significance and strength of its line of analysis. Spatial restructuring implies social restructuring, and analyses at the level of local labour markets need to consider in considerable detail the pattern of waged work – its pay, skill, level, and whether it is full-time or part-time, seasonal, etc. Some areas are heavily dependent on local capital, others more heavily dependent on international capital: the permutations and combinations can be highly complex and different strands need to be teased out.

This analysis of the regional implications of the restructuring of capital can be extended to encompass in a more explicit way land, property and rents, as well as capital, employment and all forms of work, and local as well as national government actions. This conception of the local political economy would involve as much historical understanding of, for example, the development of the local land market as of the local labour market. Inevitably, most analyses of so-called 'local labour markets', especially when limited largely to formally recorded full-time or part-time wage-labour, is of only modest sociological interest – as Blackburn and Mann have convincingly demonstrated.[11] To know that certain kinds of employment are growing or other kinds are declining is obviously relevant, but so too is knowledge about other resources in the area: the fertility of the area as a seedbed for other new industries or forms of employment, the potential for building or improving dwellings and the strength of informal support networks and other means of getting by are only some of the significant elements of which some understanding is needed if a full assessment of the social-structural implications of the restructuring of capital are to be explored in detail.

A more complex, but perhaps more appropriate, model would focus on *all* forms of work and employment and would involve bringing together ideas and arguments which have been kept in separate spheres for separate audiences. One set of arguments has focussed on the work which is done within the domestic dwellings, focussing on a group of tasks conventionally seen as 'women's work' and described as domestic labour. Debate has been vigorous about whether this is appropriately conceptualised as being fundamentally the means for reproduction of surplus value:[12] the issue has usually been posed in terms of identifying the source of oppression at an abstract level and exploring its implications for an understanding of the nature of a social formation. Little attention is given by those engaged in these debates as to how all forms of work may be changing: in the same way that the restructuring of capital produces changes in the pattern of waged work, so the pattern of domestic work may change. Indeed, Gershuny and others have now shown that the amount of time spent in domestic labour correlates negatively with the level of participation in formal employment.[13] It may be the case that certain domestic tasks do not get done when women are in full-time employment or it may be that men do more of them. The issue is an empirical one; but what is not in doubt is that the formal economy and the domestic division of labour by gender are interrelated. Massey and others who point to the connection between layers of capital

investment and gcnder relations do not extend their analysis to the
market and those who focus on the market do not always extend their
analysis to the local labour market or region. In Britain, it is true,
some connection is made between women's employment and the
changing structure of local labour markets by using terms like the
'reserve army of labour',[14] but as conditions of employment have
become more insecure for other social categories so these concepts
have come to lose whatever precision they once had.

Certainly, detailed analysis of the 'reserve army' in different contexts is not without interest, but there has been little attempt to
account for the size and composition of this army in different areas
and to relate this systematically to the restructuring argument. Furthermore, there has been relatively little attempt to link systematically
the restructuring of the domestic division of labour and other kinds of
work outside employment with structural changes in the formal
economy and the changing technology of the household. In an
attempt to do this, the following distinctions between spheres of work
may be made:

1. In the *first* sphere, the social relations of work are determined by
   the way the formal demand for labour is constructed or determined: wage-labour may be recorded or unrecorded, protected or
   unprotected, and the social relations of wage-labour may be more
   or less modified or moderated by the actions of the State. Where
   wages and salaries are exchanged for labour, there may be little
   difference in the actual social relations of work, whether or not
   that work is formally recorded in the national accounts. Within
   this sphere there may be petty commodity production with its
   distinctive social relations of work and which again has its undc-
   clared, darker side or shadow. How far this 'shadow' wage-labour
   and *a fortiori* petty commodity production is accurately recorded
   in national accounts is to a degree arbitrary, depending on the
   State policies at the time.
2. The *second* sphere of domestic work includes all the production
   and consumption of goods and services undertaken by members of
   the household within the household for themselves, irrespective of
   the pattern of motivations determining these activities and the
   pattern of constraints under which they may or may not be done.
   Here the emphasis is on *who* does the work and *where* it is done.
   This is essentially the sphere of self-provisioning.
3. The *third* sphere refers to all those activities carried out by and for

members of *other* households, whether or not they are related to them. By and large this work does not depend on payment or, if it does, the payment is not based on strictly market principles. More likely, goods and services are exchanged according to norms of reciprocity which may, in particular localities, be extremely forceful and binding. However, again, the concern is with all this activity, irrespective of the pattern of motivation or the pattern of constraints under which the work may or may not be done. Here the work is defined by the distinctive social relationships and the local context in which it is embedded.

These three spheres are neither mutually exclusive nor should they be considered to relate to distinct physical contexts. Evidently, petty commodity production very often takes place in the household and reciprocal exchanges can take place at the formal workplace. However, the analytical distinctions between these three spheres are important as a means of understanding more clearly all forms of work taking place in distinct territories. The intention is to understand how these three spheres of work interrelate and how the whole assemblage of work in distinctive milieux relates to the restructuring of capital.

The informal economy question

Szelenyi has referred to the informal economy as 'an alternative to capitalism', a position which seems hard to sustain since there is only *one* economy, although parts of that economy are not always recorded completely in national accounts. It is certainly true that wage-labourers may receive less money and protection if their labour is unrecorded (and this is a common theme in discussions of the 'hidden' or 'black' economy) but they may, in other circumstances, receive more money and more protection. Nevertheless, it is evident that unrecorded work is, by definition, not publicly accountable, thus removing a crucial defence of the vulnerable. The particularistic and 'weak' ties in the sphere of informal work may provide a degree of security and support over long periods,[15] but this is likely to involve asymmetrical patterns of power and dependence. Unrecorded work varies in its range and extent from one area to another, but this is generally ignored in studies focussing on the territorial impact of the restructuring of capital.

There has been substantial, scattered and unsystematic debate about the supposed disproportionate growth of this informal work in relation to formally accounted work.[16] This has frequently referred to the same process as if it applied to all forms of informal work, whereas the different strands are, I think, better considered separately. The discussion which follows attempts to do this for the British case.

The growth of informal work in the formal economy

First, it is evident that the growth of various forms of employment protection legislation, compulsory pension payments and union protection encourages employers not to give full accountability of their employment practices. Second, the lowering of the tax threshold and the imposition of Value Added Tax on services and goods purchased considerably increases the incentive for the self-employed and for small businesses to under-declare their levels of economic activity. One way or another, this changing State involvement in labour relations and in taxation produces the relative growth of unrecorded, or what was previously termed 'shadow' wage labour. Opportunities for 'shadow' waged or salaried work depend crucially upon the structure of capitalist enterprise in a given social formation. In Britain, the concentration of capital has proceeded further than in any other Western capitalist state, and the undergrowth of family capitalism has been almost all cut down and, where it does still exist, is sparsely and patchily developed. Some areas of some cities have been receptive to immigrants and small, highly self-exploiting family enterprises have been established in certain industries, such as clothing and manufacturing, and in certain services, such as restaurants and take-away food bars. But in other countries, such as Italy, a separate sphere of family capitalism flourishes, much of it undeclared and unrecorded.[17] Whilst there is a range of different kinds of *work* which can be aggregated under the term 'informal', however, there is nevertheless only one economy as such, with one system of currency and one banking system, and there is thus no need to postulate a separate *economy* which can be labelled 'informal'.

Informal work for domestic self-provisioning

In addition to paid informal work, there has been a similar growth in unpaid self-provisioning work in the home. A number of factors may be adduced to account for this. First, the number of hours which workers perform in the formal economy has consistently declined, providing what is seen to be 'free' time to do other work.[18] This allows people to engage in second jobs, often referred to as 'moonlighting', but this cannot be described as 'informal' work, unless it is undeclared. (Second jobs are not in any way illegal and are formally recorded in the national accounts.) This growth in free time has been coupled with a similar growth in home ownership, and in cheap and effective power tools and other do-it-yourself equipment. In addition, the rising cost of providing small-scale domestic repair and maintenance in the formal sector creates strong economic incentives for this work to be done within the household.[19] To this could be added the fact that many people feel that they can do better and more painstaking work for themselves: they then have the satisfaction of exercising a craft or skill and of adding to the value of their property. (It is as well to recognise, however, that most individual owners of domestic properties are obliged to maintain their property by the terms of their mortgage agreement.) Other goods and services are increasingly provided in the home because of the differential productivity of labour in manufacturing. With new equipment capital can be substituted for labour, goods or services can be provided more cheaply and there may also be gains in time and other satisfactions. There is no need here to attempt a detailed cost–benefit analysis of every consumer durable, nor it is likely that the consumers themselves all make these types of calculations. In any case, there is undoubtedly a strong incentive in the manufacturing sector to devise more technological aids for self-provisioning. As a result of these and other factors, people are encouraged to produce goods and services for themselves, often more cheaply but certainly taking up more time in unrecorded domestic production. The growth of this domestic self-provisioning has a reciprocal effect on the formal economy in respect of certain services and facilities: for example, the decline in the number of laundries and cinemas, and an increase in do-it-yourself shops and the like.

Values and ideological practices affect the range and incidence of informal work and these change over time between different countries and social categories. A section of the middle class currently has a value set which affirms the 'wholesomeness' or 'healthiness' of home-produced bread, jam or beer, the satisfaction of cooking fruit or vegetables which have been grown in one's own garden or allotment, and the pleasure in pottery, carpentry or weaving which can add practically and aesthetically to the home. Paradoxically, practices which were once the coping resources of the poor – for example, making jam or keeping chickens – have now been adopted by more affluent strata seeking a more 'natural' life-style, but using advanced technology where appropriate. The very forces which would seem to encourage the development of the electronic home have produced a reaction which stresses the value of craft production. A bourgeois reaction against mass-production mirrors in a curious way necessary activity for the needy. For the working class, the stripping of a car engine or the production of a giant marrow may serve to support a masculine identity in a way which perhaps waged labour no longer can. So deskilling in the formal sector is matched by re-skilling in informal work.

Furthermore, the effect of economic recession may be to encourage people who have the time and resources to use their own facilities to produce more goods and services for themselves as publicly provided services and facilities decline. It is important to recognise, therefore, that the same overall tendency has been seen by some commentators as a coping response of an increasing proportion of the poor,[20] while others see it as a reflection of greater affluence, more free time and greater technological skill and resources.[21]

Informal reciprocal work outside the household but in the locality

Finally, there is informal work which is unpaid but which does not take place in the household but is still connected with self-provisioning. This includes the reciprocal services for friends and neighbours, and there is clearly some connection between fluctuations in this kind of work and changes in the formal economy. Thus, if women with young children have the capacity to find paid employment, the value of informal support networks will increase. Again, where unemployed men get taxed at 100 per cent on everything they earn over £4, there is a strong incentive to build up reciprocal support by doing favours rather than getting cash. The role of the State is also important because the reduction of public provision of certain welfare services and facilities can lead to more inter-household work.

The distinctive and contradictory functions of informal work   It has been suggested that informal work may:

● be a valuable coping strategy for the poor;
● allow people to use or develop skills which are not available to them in the formal economy;

- serve as an element of social control: if people are mending each others' cars they are not generally planning a revolution;
- save the State expenditure when, for example, the care of the elderly is taken over by kin rather than welfare state institutions;
- provide a seedbed for the establishment of small capitalist enterprises;
- provide cheap training for a reserve army of workers who do not receive the privileges of employment protection legislation, but who learn to suffer long hours of work for low pay;[22]
- express particular cultural patterns which cannot, seemingly, be expressed in other ways;
- have the effect of driving down the wages in local milieux since shadow-work wage-rates typically undercut those in the recorded sector. Thus, whilst the work may get shared more widely, the spreading of resources between households may reduce the collective wealth overall.

The exact mix of informal work is an empirical question as is the establishment of the *functions* of such work in specific territories: the full implications for class and gender relations have not so far been adequately analysed. Different configurations reflecting the way all work is done will arise in different territories. Access to different kinds of work – formal and informal; in the household or in the locality – is unevenly distributed, and strength in one sphere may not be paralleled in another, nor in the same sphere for men and women equally. If informal work is growing disproportionately in relation to the work which is formally recorded, however, it should be understood that informal work takes place *in all three spheres*. Although glib dichotomies provide apparent clarity, in practice they generate confusion: the notion of 'the informal economy' obfuscates the issue because it distracts attention from a concern with rational concepts. The barrier between the formal and the informal then becomes harder to bridge. And yet as scholars have come to recognise, 'the informal economy' is a concept which is both remarkably difficult to use and remarkably difficult to escape.[23]

The local political economy and household work strategies

In the previous section I emphasised the danger of discussing imputed causes or consequences of the growth of informal work *tout court*, without disaggregating this in terms of specific *kinds* of informal work for specific *categories* of the population in specific *contexts*. If the way work is done is changing, then one needs to know what work is done, by whom, when and where.

There is, of course, a limit to the amount of theorising that can be done without empirical investigation but, since most work outside employment is unrecorded, one cannot rely on official sources. Even time-budget data, so ingeniously analysed by Gershuny and others, have the crucial limitation of abstracting the task from its context. This usually makes it impossible to understand anything about the social relations and relationships in which given work tasks are embedded.[24] A respondent may record that she is simply 'ironing', but, without knowing more, one cannot even be sure in which sphere of work that task should be placed. Even if we knew that she was sometimes engaged as an outworker in some form of petty commodity production, we could not be sure whether, on that particular occasion, that was the kind of work on which she was engaged.

In both the household and the communal spheres of work the range of tasks and activities will vary substantially, both over space and across society. Relating these patterns of household provision of goods and services to other work in the formal economy in local areas has rarely been effectively achieved, but there may be significant shifts in the amount and distribution of work in these three spheres in particular territories. Wage-labour, household production and communal reciprocal work have, of course, been carried out in a country like England for many hundreds of years, but the relative balance between them may now be changing, although that is very difficult to demonstrate. There is nothing new in the *types* of work: what is distinctive is rather the way that one type grows at the expense of another, as when wage-labour and social reproduction came to dominate other forms of work in early large-scale capitalist industrial production.

In order to analyse these distinctive mixes of work further and to explore how these may be changing in relation to each other, the term *household work strategies* has been adopted. This term refers to distinctive *practices* adopted by members of a household collectively or individually to get work done. Distinctions between spheres of work should not, of course, be interpreted too rigidly. Wage-labour in the form of outwork can take place in the dwelling and reciprocal exchanges can be undertaken at the workplace. However, the social relations in which the work is embedded can be analytically separated. The same task – caring for children, for example – can be wage-labour, shadow wage-labour, biological reproduction, social reproduction, communal work, and so on. Whilst each household is in some way unique in the way it allocates its time and resources to get work done, distinctive patterns emerge, dominated, of course, by the need to get money from land (rent), capital (interest), labour (wages) or the State (benefits and allowances). Hence the markets for land, labour and capital together with the nature, range and style of State intervention and provision crucially determine the potential for household work strategies. Furthermore, these factors change in emphasis and importance over time: the changing market for land and the changing availability of skilled labour may be crucially important in, as it were, 'allowing' a given style of household work strategy to emerge. Once a given pattern has emerged with its distinctive practices, this in turn reflects back upon and partially creates the material conditions for a later period. However, it should be emphasised that the centrality of the household work strategy is not intended to imply that the actions of households are the central determinants of economic and social life; rather, they may be viewed as tracers of the effects of the restructuring of capital in specific milieux. The same process of investment, as Massey points out, can have different consequences in different milieux and this is both revealed in and perhaps partially caused by household work strategies, particularly in generating female part-time employment.

It is also important to recognise that there is no discussion here of the processes and conflicts taking place *within* households. Household work strategies may be based on more or less direct conflict, whether latent or manifest. In general, as I noted above, women have unequal access to formal employment and also, almost certainly, to informal waged work in most local territories. Part of the process of restructuring of capital is, as Redclift points out, to exploit undervalued and underwaged women workers.[25] Working-class women may spend less time in household work [26] but they also spend more time at lower wages in formal employment. Whilst this may be true for given populations as a whole, however, it still requires detailed analysis of specific household work practices in specific milieux to see how the balance of all forms of work is changing or being renegotiated. Figure 11.1 indicates some of the connections which are being suggested.

The local political economy encompasses, therefore, much more than simply the traditional concept of a local labour market: it also includes local land and housing markets and how these are inter-

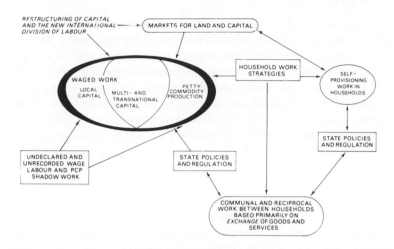

FIGURE 11.1 *Renegotiation of divisions of labour within households by age and gender*

related with the policies and practices of both local employers and local and national government. Other, unrecorded, work in the household and between households should also be considered and opportunities for doing this involve further considerations such as the age and tenure of the housing stock, access to alternative sources of food and raw materials and so on. These other elements of a local milieu have generally been disregarded by geographers and regional economists over the past thirty years. A previous generation was perhaps more sensitive to the nuances of the local, particularly those influenced by Vidal de la Blache, Jean Brunhes, H. J. Fleure and others. It might not be too fanciful to return to a concept coming directly from de la Blache, namely the *personality* of place. This emphasis on cultural diversity is a useful corrective to an approach which, perhaps over-deterministically, attempts to relate local practices of survival and 'getting by' to shifts in the global process of capital accumulation. Certainly, one would want to resist the suggestion that a given set of material conditions produces a direct response through specific household work practices. Such would be a naïve and over-deterministic position. Nevertheless, one must equally resist a completely voluntaristic and culturally-specific response, implying that people have more control over their life chances than can possibly be the case. The stance which is being adopted here attempts to hold a middle position between these two extremes, not out of some pragmatic desire for compromise but rather because such a position carries greater theoretical persuasion. It is claimed that household work strategies are not a direct response to material conditions, simply because these very material conditions are partly created by the practices of previous generations. Indeed, cultural lag is an extremely important concept for understanding the practices of everyday life. Working-class culture is a slippery concept, to be sure, but, however hard to handle, that is no excuse for denying its reality. Local cultural practices and traditions do vary from one milieu to another and help to create the conditions which encourage new, and distinctive, forms of capitalist penetration. Patterns of deference or of militancy, traditions of married women's employment, distinctive strategies of getting by, forms of collective communal action, whether instrumental or expressive, and many other such practices and traditions have distinctive geographical distributions. Massey's notion of 'layers' of capital is similar to the notion of a political generation as a means of understanding contemporary configurations. A given milieu needs to be understood, therefore, in terms of these layers of capital investment, but also of micro-cultural styles, political generations, waves of house-building, immigration, local and national government policies and much else besides. Geographers will, perhaps, be more ready to accept such a stratigraphical analogy, the erosion of some strata and the stubborn resistance of others to the attacks of eroding agencies. Perhaps 'social geomorphology' would be a better basis for analogy than sociography: at least the former carries with it implications of historical process.

The personality of Sheppey

In what follows I propose to illuminate some of these notions within the particular milieu of the Isle of Sheppey in Kent (Figure 11.2) where five years of research have provided an extraordinarily rich set of materials. There is no space to review these in any detail here; my comments are therefore partly illustrative.[27]

Initial impressions of the Isle of Sheppey suggested that it was isolated and neglected: with a population of between 30 000 and 35 000 concentrated in the two industrial towns of Sheerness and Queenborough and with a declining holiday-camp industry fourteen miles away at Leysdown, it seemed more distinguished for its lack of public investment by central and local government. Nevertheless,

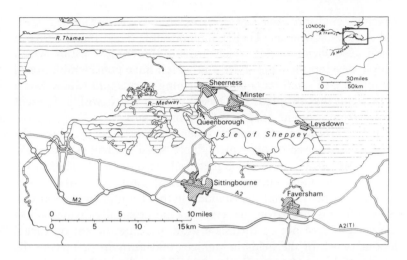

FIGURE 11.2 *The Isle of Sheppey*

there has been substantial investment over the past twenty years in the establishment of a deep-water port at Sheerness, which is now one of the main ports of entry for imported Japanese cars, and the development of plants for Sheerness Steel and Abbotts Laboratories (making pharmaceutical products) financed by Canadian and American capital. Such foreign investment means that half of the main industrial employment is controlled from outside Britain. The unemployment rate is now just under 20 per cent. Opportunities for employment for school-leavers are very limited as there is hardly any development of service industries and married women compete for semi-skilled factory work, increasingly on a part-time basis. Men made redundant from the older, declining industries generally find it impossible to get employment on the Island. The highly-paid stevedores in the docks are mostly young men who have effectively secured their own jobs, but, with mechanisation, fewer are needed and natural wastage is not replaced. Similarly, the steel mill is reducing rather than recruiting labour: early in 1983 there were fears about its future viability. Sheppey is not part of the newly-created Enterprise Zone which includes Gravesend but not Chatham. The holiday industry is also in decline.

Away from the main industrial areas, there are wide open pastures and saltings with geese, ducks and rabbits; the sea can provide fish and pleasure in summer and there is a large new private housing development for relatively prosperous white-collar and affluent manual workers at Minster. There is a remarkable range and diversity of small-scale social worlds which provide the context within which people develop their life-styles and which have considerable social significance in reinforcing and confirming norms and values. Some even claim that people from Queenborough speak with a different accent from those at Sheerness three miles away.

In the early twentieth century, when the Naval Dockyard was the focus for the island's employment, there was a resident skilled workforce, a technical school which prepared entrants for the dockyard's apprenticeships and a host of working men's clubs, many of a respectable and improving nature. Islanders in that tradition were respectable, conformist and strong believers in a hierarchically-divided working class. Those not so fortunate were more dependent on casual labour: work in the fields in summer and autumn or serving the holidaymakers who, until the mid-1970s, doubled the island's population in the summer. This was a casualised workforce, little socialised into the time-disciplines of industrial capitalism.

The political culture of the island is hard to describe with any precision. The traditions of the Naval Dockyard were based on a hierarchical and divided workforce in which individual mobility through craft apprenticeships was a more effective strategy than collective action. The state was a reliable, paternalistic if ungenerous employer. It is understandable, then, that a strong sense of collective shock was experienced as the expectations built up over two centuries were shattered once the dockyard was closed in 1958. In the eighteenth century Sheerness was remarkable for having one of the largest concentrations of manual workers in the country (along with other Naval Dockyards). Perhaps the people of Sheerness had been well trained in dependency; certainly the attitude now is one of gratitude rather than resentment towards employers. When the Canadian-owned Sheerness Steel Company came to the island, every effort was made to reinforce the benefactor role. Everything was done to create dependence on the mill and up to 800 workers expected to find permanent employment there. During the national strike in the steel industry, steel-workers at Sheerness were exceptional in refusing to join the strike, despite considerable pressure from visiting pickets and attention from the media. Wives of some steel-workers staged a counter demonstration supporting their husbands for staying at work and notices in pubs and shops announced that pickets would not be served. Mrs Thatcher commended the Sheerness workers for what she claimed was their good sense. Unhappily the loyalty of both management and workers was not rewarded: the British government refused to provide assistance when the company began to suffer from the limitations of the EEC restrictions on steel production, and the men who had been promised job security began to be laid off.

This unhappy experience, first of the dockyard workers and later of those in the steel mill, was paralleled in smaller ways when other companies which had been encouraged on to the island in the 1960s with subsidies and cheap premises began to collapse in the late 1960s. Some were taken over by larger corporations and then closed under a rationalisation policy; others had cash-flow problems or simply bad management. The history of employment and unemployment over the past twenty years was, until the late 1970s, an erratic pattern of rises and falls as firms came and went. More recently unemployment has simply continued to rise.

Realistically, the people of Sheppey know that there is absolutely nothing that they can do to increase their employment prospects. British managers of multinational organisations have to explain to their workers that if they object to what is proposed – redundancies, rationalisation or whatever – the plant will simply close altogether or move elsewhere. A long history of such closures easily persuades the workers that the threat is not idle. The island workforce is geographically imprisoned. Women accept 60 pence an hour to do simple component assembly work in their homes. There is little alternative and there are as many on the waiting list to do such work as there are already employed. Almost anything is accepted. Hundreds of acres of land behind one of the housing estates are covered with Japanese cars: the people were offered £300 toward their local community centre by the company concerned. Even if the economy picks up, Sheppey people know that the most efficient employers will continue to substitute machines for labour: they see as clearly as any academic analyst the logic of their own disaster.

What, perhaps, they do not see yet are the cleavages based on gender which are becoming more pronounced. Thus, women, classified as semi-skilled workers, are cheaper and more skilled than men who are classified as skilled, and many of the manufacturing companies prefer to have a more easily controlled workforce. Rarely is it necessary to make a woman redundant; natural wastage provides a painless way of adjusting labour supply and demand. This may be related to the domestic cycle, but some women resign not because they want to but because the taxation system very seriously depletes any income they earn if their husbands are unemployed. Many firms and their women workers prefer the flexibility of part-time work, which carries with it the assumption that another member of the household is the chief earner.

Although the pattern of employment is gripped in a downward spiral, not all households are equally penalised. One of the paradoxes is that the wives of those men in employment may find it easier to be employed. For example, stevedores earn very high wages – certainly in the island's terms – and by and large their work is more boring than tiring, involving sitting in a fork-lift truck when there is a ship to unload. However, they have the time and very often the skills to do most of the home decoration, maintenance and improvement that is required. Hence their homes are likely to be in good order, well-equipped with consumer durables and thus very easy to keep clean. Their wives are then free to enter employment once their children enter full-time education. Such households are, comparatively, extremely well-off, and it is likely that these divisions will intensify: increasingly those in employment speak for other members of their household when they hear of vacancies. A polarisation is developing between those households with multiple earners and those with none.

The interrelations between different forms of work

So much, then, for a brief account of the pattern of employment. How is this pattern related to all the other work that households do in the other spheres which are described in Figure 11.1? There is, perhaps, a conventional expectation that a household doing less in one sphere will do more in another: less time in employment would mean more time for communal work or shadow wage-labour. Unhappily, this is *less* likely to be the case. Work outside employment needs more than time: it needs tools, equipment, materials and the social contacts to find it: it also needs the will, spirit and enthusiasm to provide appropriate incentives. Money makes more money more easily than time makes money. Analysis of survey results which attempted to define the relationships between various characteristics of households and various forms of unwaged domestic and other work connected with the household showed a positive correlation between number of earners and amount of domestic work done. The more there is of one kind of work, the more there is of another.

In 1977 when research first began on the island, there was almost certainly more opportunity for work outside employment. At that time, fruit, meat and Japanese radios were imported through the docks and I quickly gathered a host of anecdotes in the pubs and on the doorsteps. A respectable old lady walking by the walls of the docks told of sheep flying through the air in front of her, and in some cafes, it was said, steak and chips were cheaper than egg and chips. Everyone seemed to know someone in the docks and people had deep-freezes in sheds and garages stuffed with meat. The honest ones would boast that they only had the 'odd crate of oranges' as if that did not count. Certainly free bananas never counted as pilfering. At the same time there were many painters, window-cleaners and home car-tuning experts who advertised in the local paper. Materials were relatively easy to come by. People laughed at a case reported in the paper of a man who appeared in Court for receiving stolen property. His defence was that he had done no more than ask in the local pub where he could buy 'cheap bricks'. His mistake was that he gave someone his address. He woke up one morning to find a load of bricks outside his house. Or so he said. The joke was the feebleness of his excuse.

At that time the pubs were full most nights of the week – and with over 140 licensed premises on the island that meant a lot of drinking. The local brewers in Faversham saw Sheppey as one of their best markets. People were busy doing up their houses, making extensions to nineteenth-century cottages and doing up and selling old cars. Sometimes this work was for money (shadow wage-labour), sometimes it was simply to do a favour for a friend (communal work). Many working-class people went away for a holiday for the first time in their lives. They came back with Spanish dolls and guitar-shaped wall decorations and they make a cocktail bar in their front room like the one they saw in the hotel.

Those who were unemployed *at that time* were in a favoured position. There was still a reasonable amount of fish to be caught in the local waters, there were duck or rabbits to be shot and people had money to pay for odd jobs being done. 'Cheap' goods were available to circulate round the island, holiday-makers still brought a lot of money to spend in Leysdown each summer, and the owner who lives above the amusement arcade and is said to be a millionaire, hired youngsters straight out of school every summer. The ordinary school-leaver from Sheppey Comprehensive School traditionally never con-sidered employment until the autumn – leaving at Easter he or she would 'go down Leysdown' in May and either clean chalets or take the money for machines and fair ground 'attractions'. People I met and interviewed at length were getting by with considerable verve and style in 1977 and 1978. Parents were worried that it seemed so easy for youngsters to make money on the side that they would be encouraged to leave school early rather than stay on for better qualifications and the better job that would surely ensue.

However, it now seems likely that the project was being established at the very time that work outside employment and outside the dwelling was beginning to decline. The police made a vigorous attempt to control pilferage from the docks and many people became frightened. Those who had been chief suppliers of 'cheap meat' were disowned as being 'too greedy'. Many went out at night and threw meat and radios over the cliffs (or so I was frequently assured). At the same time the nature of the goods imported through the docks changed: no meat, much less fruit and no electronics goods. Instead, importing cars became much more important and security in the docks was substantially tightened. The holiday trade also declined dramatically and teenage unemployment became a serious problem. All this happened in a very short space of time. From 1978 to 1981 the whole stye of economic life in the island changed. The policies of the new Conservative Government helped to produce a drastic increase in registered unemployment and, as the surplus money dried up, so also did the opportunities for making extra money. There were too many unemployed. Fewer people had spare money for paying neighbours to paint or to build. Even the fish in the sea got harder to find. By the time I was in a position to quantify informal, communal work it had all but disappeared. A new suspicion developed in ordinary working-class streets: if unemployed people were seen to run a car or appeared to leave the home too regularly each day they were 'shopped' to the local Social Security Office. Even the little corner shops, of which there are many in Sheerness, are no longer the discreet supporters of an erratic cash flow: people were 'shopped' by the shopkeepers if they appeared to have too much money. When my colleague and I interviewed unemployed men in the summer of 1982 they were more likely to be disconsolate and depressed, and quite unlike the quick-witted men I had interviewed five years earlier. Despite this decline in informal work outside the household, the 1981 survey provided evidence of a truly astonishing amount of work *inside* the household. This self-provisioning work seemed to be very widespread amongst those households based on married or living-as-married couples under retirement age. People painted, made cakes or beer, fixed their own cars and dug their allotments, seemingly irrespective of their social class. In order to measure the quantity and range of this activity a *Self-Provisioning Scale* was built up from the following tasks: regular vegetable growing, home maintenance, car maintenance, home renovation and improvement, regular production of jam, beer, wine or cakes and, finally, the production of personally-made clothes. A six-point scale was constructed which simply aggregated any two, three, four, etc. tasks. It is clear from Table 11.1 that the more earners in the household, the greater the amount of self-provisioning.[28]

TABLE 11.1 *Earners and self-provisioning by households*

Number of earners in each household	Self-provisioning in each household		
	1-4	*5-6*	*N = 100%*
0	79	21	245
0.5	71	29	31
1	49	51	207
1.5	40	60	73
2	45	55	109
2.5	36	64	22
3	30	70	23
3.5	30	70	10
4	25	75	8
5	–	100	2
All	57	43	730

Conclusions

The Sheppey research project has documented a growing polarisation between households with a number of earners which are also likely to do other work outside employment and those households with no earner, no opportunities for local communal work (whether paid or not) and also unable to engage in work within the home – often for lack of such relatively small things such as the cost of paint or an essential tool. Household income is not a simple reflection of social class, but it is also correlated to number of earners: variations of household income may be relatively modest between social classes but differences in life-styles remain. This suggests that whilst the strategies for *getting* money are becoming more similar (more earners in the household), the ways of *spending* that money remain distinctive. These class-cultural distinctions seem less closely linked to present material circumstances, but rather have developed in characteristic ways over a number of generations. Whilst it is true at one level to say the inhabitants of Sheppey united as 'consumers' in some highly general and abstract way, more detailed interviews indicate very specific and distinctive ways of getting by in the sphere of self-provisioning. Some people have designed and built their own homes, others have moved to a degree of self-sufficiency in food production. These strategies are clearly bound by the opportunities for getting cash in the formal economy. However, within these broad limits there is remarkable diversity. The processes may be similar and in certain respects so may the responses. However, an over-deterministic materialist conception should be rejected. People cannot be so readily dehumanised: strategies and practices of survival, getting by and developing life-styles are much more creative than that.

This process of polarisation between multiple-earner households and the rest is brought about through the interaction of many distinct elements: the increase in female activity rates has been commonly attributed to the economic needs of the household, attempting to maintain or gradually increase its standard of living. Perhaps less well understood is the way these shifts in the involvement of household members in wage-labour affect the amount and distribution of all forms of work within and between households. This is a highly complex matter: the shift of some resources from the public to the private leads, for example, on the one hand to more home-ownership and on the other to more community – that is, female – responsibility for the elderly.[29] Those households based on couples at certain stages of the life-cycle are more effective in getting by, not simply because of their dual earning capacity, but also because of an improved capacity to maintain high levels of self-provisioning through the sexual division of tasks and skills. The combination, therefore, of high earning-potential matched with appropriate position in the domestic cycle and balance between the genders produces the best unit for high output in all spheres of work.[30] These new patterns of polarisation have direct implications for systems of class and gender-based stratification. However, as I have accentuated throughout this chapter, *these stratification orders are manifested in specific local milieux.* The local political economy, the personality of the place and wider national and international economic and political forces combine to produce a distinctive opportunity structure of patterns and constraints. Household-work strategies thus reflect the dialectical relationship between material conditions and cultural values mediated in specific milieux.

Acknowledgements

I am glad to acknowledge that this work is funded by the British Social Science Research Council, Grant No. G00230035.

Claire Wallace has contributed substantially to the formulation of the general argument of this paper. An earlier draft under joint authorship was read at the World Congress of Sociology in Mexico City in August 1982. Since then that paper has been divided and Claire Wallace is publishing a new paper on self-building as a distinctive household work strategy elsewhere. I also wish to thank Jan Pahl, Chris Pickvance and Nanneke Redclift for reading earlier drafts. Such informal work is best rewarded informally, but I must formally acknowledge that all deficiencies in the paper are my responsibility alone.

Notes

1. Cox (1978); Dear and Scott (1981); Harvey (1981); Massey (1978a; 1979; 1982a); Massey and Meegan (1982); Mingione (1981); Urry (1981c).
2. Szelenyi (1981).
3. Castells (1977); Harloe (ed.) (1977; 1981); Harvey (1973); Lojkine (1977); Pickvance (1976); Saunders (1979; 1981).
4. Castells (1977).
5. Lebas (1981; 1982).
6. Fröbel *et al*; (1980); see also Elson and Pearson (1981).
7. Szelenyi (1981).
8. Massey (1978a; 1979; 1982); Massey and Meegan (1979a).
9. Massey (1982).
10. Urry (1981c); Rees and Lambert (1981); Cooke (1982a).
11. Blackburn and Mann (1979).
12. Molyneux (1979); Sokoloff (1980).
13. Gershuny and Thomas (1980); Gershuny (1982; 1983); Meissner (1975).

14. Beechey (1977; 1978); Kenrick (1981).
15. Granovetter (1973).
16. Gershuny (1979); Henry (1981).
17. Bagnasco (1979; 1981).
18. Alden (1979; 1981); Gershuny and Thomas (1980; 1983); Sekscenski (1980); Stafford (1980); Thomas and Shannon (1982).
19. Gershuny (1978; 1982).
20. Caplovitz (1981).
21. Gershuny (1983).
22. This is perhaps more typical of Mediterranean and Third World countries: see Elson and Pearson (1981).
23. Bromley (1978); Moser (1978).
24. But see Nissell *el al*, (1982).
25. Redclift (1983).
26. Gershuny (1982).
27. See Pahl (1980); Pahl and Dennett (1981).
28. For more detailed discussion, see Pahl and Wallace (1983).
29. Harloe (1981); Ungerson (1981).
30. Pahl and Wallace (1983).

12
Time, Space and Regionalisation

ANTHONY GIDDENS

Most social analysts treat time and space as mere environments of action, and accept unthinkingly the conception of time, as mensurable clock time, characteristic of modern Western culture. With the exception of the recent works of geographers – of which more in a moment – social scientists have failed to construct their thinking around the modes in which social systems are constituted across time–space. I want to argue that investigation of this issue is one main task of what I call the theory of structuration; it is not a specific type or 'area' of social science, which can be pursued or discarded at will. It is at the heart of social theory, and should hence also be regarded as of very considerable importance for the conduct of empirical research in the social sciences.

Time-Geography

Fortunately, we do not need to tackle these issues *de novo*. Over the past few years there has been a remarkable convergence between geography and the other social sciences, in which geographers, drawing upon the various established traditions of social theory, have made contributions of major significance to social thought. I think it would be true to say that most such writings remain unknown to the majority of those working in the rest of the social sciences, although they contain ideas of very general application. Some of these contributions are to be found in the work of Hägerstrand, but they are by no means confined to his writings and those of his immediate colleagues.[1] In previous analyses of the theory of structuration I have mentioned the significance of this approach without confronting it directly or trying to point out its limitations. But in this exposition I shall do so.

Time-geography, as formulated by Hägerstrand, takes as its starting-point the routinised character of daily life. This is in turn connected with features of the human body, its means of mobility and communication, and its path through the 'life–cycle', and therefore with the human being as a 'biographical project'. Hägerstrand's approach is based mainly upon identifying sources of constraint over human activity, given by the nature of the body and the physical contexts in which activity occurs. Such constraints provide the overall 'boundaries' limiting behaviour across time–space. Hägerstrand has formulated these in various different ways, but his characteristic emphasis is upon the following factors:[2]

1. The indivisibility of the human body, and of other living and inorganic entities in the *milieux* of human existence. Corporeality imposes strict limitations upon the capabilities of movement and perception of the human agent.
2. The finitude of the life-span of the human agent as a 'being towards death'. This essential element of the human condition gives rise to certain inescapable demographic parameters of interaction across time–space. For this reason if no other, time is a scarce resource for the individual actor.
3. The limited capability of human beings to participate in more than one task at once, coupled with the fact that every task has a duration. Turn-taking exemplifies the implications of this sort of constraint.
4. The fact that movement in space is also movement in time.
5. The limited 'packing capacity' of time–space. No two human bodies can occupy the same space at the same time; physical objects have the same elemental characteristic. Therefore any zone of time–space can be analysed in terms of constraints over the two types of objects which can be accommodated within it.

These five facets of 'time-geographic reality' express the material axes of human existence and underlie all contexts of association in conditions of co-presence.[3] Examined as resources, such factors condition the webs of interaction formed by the trajectories of the daily, weekly, monthly and overall life-paths of individuals in their interactions with one another. The trajectories of agents, as Hägerstrand puts it, 'have to accommodate themselves under the pressures and the opportunities which follow from their common existence in terrestrial space and time.'[4]

Hägerstrand's generalised conception of time-geography originated in a long-term series of studies of a local parish in Sweden. The area in question boasted comprehensive population statistics, enabling him to trace all the individuals who had lived there and moved in and out of the area, for a period of something like a hundred years. Ordering these data as lifetime biographies, he sought to analyse them as composing life-paths in time–space that could be charted using a particular form of notation. The typical patterns of movement of individuals, in other words, can be represented as cycles of routine activities across days, or longer spans of time–space. Agents move in physical contexts whose properties interact with their capabilities, given the above constraints, at the same time as those agents interact with one another. Interactions of individuals moving in time–space compose 'bundles' meeting at 'stations' or definite time–space locations within bounded regions (such as homes, streets, cities, states). Hägerstrand's dynamic 'time–space maps' are of definite interest, and provide a graphic form that has relevance to situations well beyond those for which they have been used so far.

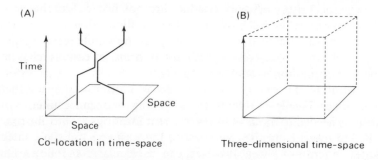

FIGURE 12.1 *Time–space maps*

The diagrams in Figure 12.1 show this in its simplest guise. Two individuals live, say, a mile apart in a neighbourhood; their time–space paths during the course of the day bring them into contact in an encounter of short duration, for example, a restaurant, after which their activities again diverge. If the daily activities of a specific individual are recorded, it is easy to build up a gross characterisation of his or her routine activities, insofar as these comprise trajectories in time and space. As a portrayal of a life-path, this would involve generalised patterns of time–space movement within the 'life-cycle'. A person may live in the house of his or her parents, for example, until establishing a new residence on marriage. This may be associated with a change of job, such that both home and workplace as 'stations' along the daily trajectory become altered. Mobility within the housing market, marital separation or career progression, amid a host of other possible factors, may influence typical life-paths.

The encounters into which individuals enter in the trajectories of daily life are subject to constraints deriving from the list indicated previously. Hägerstrand acknowledges, of course, that agents are not merely mobile bodies, but intentional beings with purposes or what he calls 'projects'. The projects which individuals seek to realise, if they are to be actualised, have to utilise the inherently limited resources of time and space to overcome constraints which they confront. 'Capability constraints' are those of the sort listed above. Some affect primarily time-distribution – for example, the need for sleep, or for food at regular intervals, ensures certain limits to the structuration of daily activities. 'Coupling constraints' refer to those that condition activities undertaken jointly with others. The volume of time–space available to an individual in a day is a prism bounding the pursuance of projects. Prisms of daily conduct are not just geographical or physical boundaries, but have 'time–space walls on all sides'. The size of such prisms, of course, is also very strongly influenced by the degree of time–space convergence in the means of communication and transformation available to agents.

The notion of time–space convergence was introduced by another geographer, Janelle, to refer to the 'shrinking' of distance in terms of the time needed to move between different locations.[6] Thus the time taken to travel from the east coast to the west coast of the United States, in terms of available media, can be calculated as follows. On foot, the journey would take more than two years; on horseback eight months; by stage-coach or wagon, four months; by rail in 1910, four days; by regular air-serivces today, five hours; by the fastest jet transport, just over two hours. Time–space convergence can be plotted to describe the outer bounds of daily prisms. However it is obvious that there are major discrepancies between and within social communities in terms of the constraints on mobility and communication affecting different groups and individuals. Seriality and turn-taking are built into most forms of transportation. Thus, for instance, an express train may connect two cities in a time of three hours. But the availability of seats may be limited, even for those able and willing to pay. Moreover, if a person misses the train, there may be only local trains for several hours until the next express, giving time–space convergence a 'palpitating' character.[7] Finally, for those in most societies, and for most of the days in an individual's life, mobility takes place within relatively constricted time–space prisms.[8]

Hägerstrand has made a particular effort to employ time-geography to grasp the seriality of the life-paths or 'life-biographies' of individuals. A life-biography, he says, is made up of 'internal mental experiences and events . . . related to the interplay between body and environmental phenomena.'[9] The conduct of an individual's day-to-day life entails that he or she successively associates with sets of entities emanating from the settings of interaction. These entities are: other agents; indivisible objects (solid material qualities of the *milieu* of action), divisible materials (air, water, minerals, foodstuffs) and domains. Domains refer to what I prefer to call the regionalisation of time–space: the movement of life-paths through settings of interaction that have various forms of spatial demarcation. But the properties of domains can be subjected to direct study in terms of the coupling constraints which a given distribution of 'stations' and 'activity bundles' creates for the overall population whose activities are concentrated within those domains. Thus the nature of interacting social patterns within domains of time–space is limited by the overall organisation of capability and coupling constraints. There are 'ecological' constraints which, as Carlstein has tried to show in detail, derive from three modes of 'packing':

1. the packing of materials, artefacts, organisms and human populations in settlement space–time;
2. the packing of time-consuming activities in population time-budgets;
3. the packing of bundles of various sizes, numbers and durations in the population system, that is, group formation because of the indivisibility and continuity constraints of individuals.[10]

Critical comments

The interest of time-geography to the theory of structuration is surely evident.[11] Time-geography is concerned with the infrastructural constraints that shape the routines of day-to-day life, and shares with structuration theory an emphasis upon the significance of the practical character of daily activities, in circumstances where individuals are co-present with one another, for the constitution of social conduct. Hägerstrand's concentration upon everyday social practices is very pronounced and clear; he wishes to use time–geography, as he insistently says, to understand 'the impact of the ordinary day of the ordinary person' upon the overall organisation of social systems.[12] But time-geography has some very distinct shortcomings. It cannot serve as a basis for time–space analysis as I want to conceive it, although it provides some indispensable conceptual clues for such analysis.

The main reservations one must have about time–geography are the following:

First, it operates with a naïve and defective conception of the human agent. In stressing the corporeality of the human being, in structured time–space contexts, Hägerstrand's ideas are admirable and important, but he tends to treat 'individuals' as coming into being independently of the social settings which they confront in their day-to-day lives. Agents are regarded as purposive beings in the sense in which their activities are guided by 'projects' which they pursue. But the nature and origin of projects is left unexplicated.

Second, Hägerstrand's analyses therefore tend to recapitulate the dualism of action and structure, albeit in rather novel form because of his pre-eminent concern with time and space. 'Stations', 'domains', etc., are themselves taken as givens, the outcome of uninterpreted processes of institutional formation and change. Unsurprisingly in this type of viewpoint little emphasis is given to the essentially transformational character of all human action, even in its most utterly routinised forms.

Third, concentration upon the properties of the body, and its movement through time–space, only in terms of constraints, is unwarranted. All types of constraint are also types of opportunity, media for the enablement of action. The specific way in which Hägerstrand tends to conceptualise 'constraint', moreover, betrays a certain culture-bound element in his views. For capability constraints, coupling constraints, and so on, are typically discussed by him in terms of their operation as scarce resources. It is not difficult to see here a possible link with a version of historical materialism. There is more than a hint in Hägerstrand's writings of the notion that allocation of scarce resources of the body and its media have some sort of determining effect upon the organisation of social institutions in all types of society. Such is only a feasible proposition, I think, in the case of contemporary societies, in which a premium is placed upon the 'efficient' use of resources.[13]

Finally, time-geography involves only a weakly-developed theory of power. Hägerstrand does talk of 'authority constraints', which he links to capability and coupling constraints. But these are both vaguely formulated, and invoke a zero-sum of conception of power as a source of limitations upon action. If power is conceived of as generative, on the other hand, the 'constraints' of which Hägerstrand speaks are all modalities for the engendering and sustaining of structures of domination.

In order to develop such ideas more adequately in respect of spatial concepts in particular, we have to look again at the notion of 'place' as ordinarily used by geographers. Hägerstrand's time-geography represents a very effective critique of 'place' in respect of demonstrating the basic significance, in studying human social conduct, of analysing the organisation of time–space. But his emphasis is very much upon integrating temporality into social theory. He does not subject the notions of place or location to a close conceptual scrutiny, and uses such terms in a relatively unexamined fashion. The term 'place' cannot be used in social theory simply to designate 'point in space' any more than we can speak of points in time as a succession of 'nows'. What this means is that the concept of presence – or rather, of the mutuality of presence and absence – has to be explicated in terms of its spatiality as well as its temporality. In developing the theory of structuration, I have introduced two notions that I consider to be of some importance here: the concepts of *locale* and of *presence-availability* as involved in the relations between social and system integration.[14]

Locales refer to the use of space to provide the *settings* of interaction, the settings of interaction in turn being essential to specifying its *contextuality*. The constitution of locales certainly depends upon the phenomena given pride of place by Hägerstrand: the body, its media of mobility and communication, in relation to physical properties of the surrounding world. Locales provide for a good deal of the 'fixity' underlying institutions, although there is no clear sense in which they 'determine' such 'fixity'. It is usually possible to designate locales in terms of their physical properties, either as features of the material world or, more commonly, combinations of those features and human artefacts. But it is a basic error to suppose that locales can be described in those terms alone – the same form of error which is made by behaviourism in regard of the description of human action. A 'house' is grasped as such only if the observer recognises that it is a 'dwelling' with a range of other properties specified by the modes of its utilisation in human activity.

Locales may range from a room in a house, a street-corner, the shop-floor of a factory or towns and cities, to the territorially demarcated areas occupied by nation-states. But locales are typically internally *regionalised*, and the regions within them are of critical importance in constituting contexts of interaction. Let me develop a little further the notion of context. One of the reasons for using the term 'locale' rather than that of place is that properties of settings are employed in a chronic way by agents in the constitution of encounters across space and time. An obvious element of this is the physical aspect of what Hägerstrand calls 'stations' – that is, 'stopping-places' in which the physical mobility of agents' trajectories is arrested or curtailed for the duration of encounters or social occasions – as locales in which the routine activities of different individuals intersect. But the features of settings are also used, in a routine manner, to constitute the meaningful content of interaction. Context thus connects the most intimate and detailed components of interaction to much broader properties of the institutionalisation of social life.

Modes of regionalisation

'Regionalisation' should not be understood merely as localisation in space, but as referring to the zoning of time–space in relation to routinised social practices. Thus a private house is a locale which is a 'station' for a large cluster of interactions in the course of a typical day. Houses in contemporary societies are regionalised into floors, halls and rooms. But the various rooms of the house are zoned differently in time as well as space. The rooms downstairs are characteristically most used in daylight hours, while bedrooms are rooms to which individuals 'retire' at night. The division between day and night in all societies used to be perhaps the most fundamental zoning demarcation between the intensity of social life and its relaxation – ordered also, obviously, by the need of the human organism for regular periods of sleep. Night-time was a 'frontier' of social activity as marked as any spatial frontiers have ever been. It remains a frontier, as it were, that is only sparsely settled. But the invention of powerful, regularised modes of artificial lighting has dramatically expanded the potentialities of interaction settings in night-hours. As one observer has remarked:

> The last great frontier of human immigration is occurring in time: a spreading of wakeful activity throughout the twenty-four hours of

the day. There is more multiple shift factory work, more police coverage, more use of the telephone at all hours. There are more hospitals, pharmacies, aeroplane flights, hostels, always-open restaurants, car rental and gasoline and auto repair stations, bowling alleys, and radio stations, always active. There are more emergency services such as auto-towing, locksmiths, bail bondsmen, drug and poison and suicide, gambling 'hot lines' available incessantly. Although different individuals participate in these events in shifts, the organisations involved are continually active.[15]

Zerubavel's study of the temporal organisation of a modern hospital, where zoning is very tightly controlled, is relevant here. Most of the services of medical care in the hospital which he studied are provided by nursing staff working on rotating shifts. The majority of nurses work for set periods on different wards, moving around the different sectors of the hospital; and they are also called upon to alternate day and night shift work. The cycle of movement between wards coincides with that between day and night work, so that when someone 'goes on days' they also change to another sector. The scheduling of these activities is complex and detailed. While nurses' work is regulated in standardised four-weekly periods, the rotation of interns and residents is variable. Nurses' rotations always begin on the same day of the week, and since they are of twenty-eight days they do not coincide with calendar months. The activities of medical house staff, on the other hand, are organised in terms of calendar months, and hence begin on different days of the week.

Weekly and daily zones are also punctiliously categorised. Many routines occur at precise, seven-day intervals, especially those involving nurses. Nurses' 'time-off' is also counted against a weekly schedule. Time-off can be split into a number of segments taken separately, but each segment has to be a multiple of seven days; and each has to begin on Sunday and end on Saturday, to co-ordinate with the rotations of work activities. 'Weekdays' are not identical to 'weekend' days, however, because although operating upon a continuous basis various kinds of services are restricted in the hospital during the weekend. As laboratories are closed, for example, the hospital staff know that they cannot get certain sorts of tests carried out. They try to admit as few new patients as possible on weekend days, and to avoid initiating new treatment programmes for existing inmates. Saturdays and Sundays are usually 'quiet' days, with Monday being the busiest day of the week. In day-to-day life in the hospital, the alternation of 'day' and 'night' resembles the division of the week into weekdays and weekends. As the author notes, the fact that working at night is still considered unusual, and unusually demanding, is indicated by the term used to refer to it: 'night duty'. There is no corresponding term, 'day duty'.[16]

A useful classification of modes of regionalisation might be offered as shown in Figure 12.2.

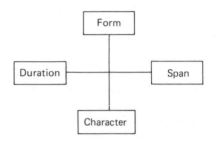

FIGURE 12.2 *Modes of regionalisation*

By the 'form' of regionalisation, I mean the form of the boundaries that define the region. In most locales, the boundaries separating regions have physical or symbolic markers. In contexts of co-presence, these may allow a greater or lesser number of features of 'presencing' to permeate adjoining regions. In social gatherings the regionalisation of social encounters is indicated usually only by body posture and positioning, tone of voice and so on. In many such gatherings, as regionally bounded episodes, encounters may be nearly all of very short duration. Walls between rooms, on the other hand, may demarcate regionalisation in such a way that none of the ordinary media of co-presence can penetrate. Of course, where walls are thin, various kinds of interruptions or embarrassments to the closure of encounters can occur. Ariès, Elias and others have pointed to the ways in which the internal differentiation of the houses of the mass of the population since the eighteenth century has been interrelated with changing aspects of family life and sexuality.[17] Prior to the eighteenth century in Western Europe, the homes of the poor frequently had only one or two rooms, in which various communal living and sleeping arrangements were found. The grander houses of the aristocracy had many rooms, but these usually connected directly with one another, without the hallways which in modern houses permit types of privacy which were previously difficult for all classes of society to achieve.

Regionalisation may incorporate zones of great variation in span or scale. Regions of broad span are those which extend widely in space and deeply in time. Of course the intersection of 'spans' of space and time may vary, but regions of considerable span necessarily tend to depend upon a high degree of institutionalisation. All regions, as defined here, involve extension in time as well as space. 'Region' may sometimes be used in geography to refer to a physically demarcated area on a map of the physical features of the material environment. This is not what I mean by the term, which as used here always carries the connotation of the structuration of social conduct across time–space. Thus there is a strong degree of regional differentiation, in terms of class relationships and a variety of other social criteria, between the North and the South in Britain. 'The North' is not just a geographically delimited area, but one with long-established distinctive social traits. By the 'character' of regionalisation I refer to the modes in which the time–space organisation of locales is ordered within more embracing social systems. Thus in many societies the 'home' – the dwelling – has been the physical focus of family relationships, and also of production, either carried on in parts of the dwelling itself or in closely adjoining gardens or plots of land. The development of modern capitalism, however, brings about a differentiation between the home and the workplace, this differentiation having considerable implications for the overall organisation of production systems and other major institutional features of contemporary societies.

Front regions, back regions

One aspect of the character of regionalisation is the level of presence-availability associated with specific forms of locale. The notion of 'presence–availability' is an essential adjunct to that of co-presence. The 'being together' of co-presence demands means whereby actors are able to 'come together'. Hägerstrand's time–geography draws our attention to some of the basic factors typically involved here. Communities of high presence-availability in *all* cultures, until as recently as a hundred years ago, were groupings of individuals in close physical proximity to one another. The corporeality of the agent, the limitations upon the mobility of the body in the trajectories of the *durée* of daily activity, together with the physical properties of space, ensured that this was so. The media of communication were always identical to those of transportation. Even with the use of fast horses, ships, forced marches, etc., long distance in space always meant long distance in time. The mechanisation of transport has been the main factor leading to the dramatic forms of time–space convergence noted previously as characteristic of the modern age. But the most radical disjuncture of relevance in modern history (whose implications today are very far from being exhausted) is the separation of media of communication, by the development of electronic signalling, from the media of transportation, the latter always having involved – by some means or another – the mobility of the human body. Morse's invention of the electromagnetic telegraph marks as distinctive a transition in human cultural development as the wheel or any other technical innovation ever did.

The different aspects of the regionalisation of locales already indicated shape the nature of presence-availability in varying ways. Thus the rooms of a dwelling may ensure that encounters can be sustained in different parts of the building without intruding upon one another, providing a particular symmetry, perhaps, to the routines of the day for its incumbents. But living in close proximity within the house also means, of course, high presence-availability: co-presence is very easily secured and sustained. Prisons and asylums are often associated with enforced continuity of co-presence among individuals who are not ordinarily accustomed to such routines of daily life. Prisoners who share the same cell may rarely be out of each other's presence for the whole of the day and night. On the other hand, the 'disciplinary power' of prisons, asylums and other types of 'total institution' is based upon disrupting the gearing of presence-availability into the routines of daily trajectories 'outside'. Thus the very same inmates who are forced into continuous co-presence are denied the availability of easy encounters with other groups in the prison, even though those others may be physically only on the other side of the walls of the cell. The enforced 'sequestration' of prisoners from the 'outside world', limiting the possibilities of co-presence to those within a single locale, is of course a defining feature of a 'total institution'.

We can further draw out the relevance of regionalisation to the structuration of social systems by considering how zoning is accomplished in different settings, as shown by Figure 12.3. 'Face' and 'front' are related first of all to the positioning of the body in encounters. The regionalisation of the body, so important to psychoanalysis – which, in Lacan's phrase, explores 'openings on the surface' of the body – has more than a spatial counterpart in the regionalisation of the contexts of interaction. Regionalisation encloses zones of time–space, enclosure permitting the sustaining of distinctive relations between 'front' and 'back' regions which actors employ as integral to the contextuality of action and to the sustaining of ontological security. The term 'façade' in some part helps designate the connections between face and front regions.[18]

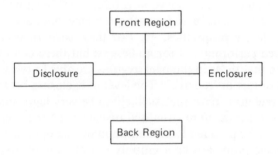

FIGURE 12.3 *Zoning*

The differentiation between front and back regions by no means coincides with a division between the enclosure (covering up, hiding) of aspects of the self and their disclosure (revelation, divulgence). These two axes of regionalisation operate in a complicated nexus of possible relations between meaning, norms and power. Back regions clearly often form a significant resource which both the powerful and the less powerful can utilise reflexively to sustain a psychological distancing between their own interpretations of social processes and those enjoined by 'official' norms. Such circumstances are likely to approximate most closely to those in which individuals feel themselves to be playing parts in which they do not really 'believe'. But it is important to separate two types of situation in which this may hold, because only one approximates at all closely to the dramaturgical metaphor – such as used by Goffman.[19] In all societies there are social occasions which involve ritual forms of conduct and utterance, in which the normative sanctions regulating 'correct performance' are strong. Such episodes are usually set apart regionally from the rest of social life, and specifically differ from it in requiring homology of performance from occasion to occasion. It seems especially in these circumstances that individuals are likely to feel they are 'playing roles' in which the self is only marginally involved. Here there is likely to be tension in the style and continuity of performance, and style may be focalised much more than in day-to-day social activity.

Disclosure and Self

Back regions involved in ritualised social occasions probably often do fairly closely resemble the 'backstage' of a theatre or the 'off camera' activities of filming and television productions. But this backstage may very well be 'onstage' so far as the ordinary routines of social life, and the ordinary proprieties, go. For these sorts of occasions do involve fixed performances for audiences; but there is no necessary implication that those in the back regions are able to relax the usual courtesies of tact or 'repair'.[20] The level of enclosure between front and back regions is nevertheless likely to be very high, since it very often holds that the more ritualised or continued the occasion, the more it has to be presented as an autonomous set of events, in which the backstage props are kept entirely out of view of audiences or observers. It is worth pointing out that there is much more to the distinction between 'public' and 'private' activities than might appear by the seemingly mutually exclusive nature of these categories. Ceremonial occasions are distinctively, protoypically public events, often involving 'public figures'. But the backstage of such occasions is not a 'private sphere': the chief figures in the drama may be able to relax even less when, leaving the ceremonial arena, they move among their inferiors, the individuals who are merely 'behind the scenes'.

Ritual occasions seem for the most part distinctively different from the range of circumstances in which back regions are zones within which agents recover forms of autonomy which are compromised or treated in frontal contexts. These are often situations in which normative sanctions are imposed upon actors whose commitment to those norms is marginal or non-existent. The forms of enclosure and disclosure which allow agents to deviate from, or flout, those norms are important features of the dialectic of control in situations involving surveillance. Surveillance connects two related phenomena: the collation of information used to co-ordinate social activities of subordinates, and the direct supervision of the conduct of those subordinates. In each respect, the advent of the modern state, with its capitalist industrial infrastructure, has been distinguished by a vast expansion of surveillance.[21] Now 'surveillance', by its very nature, involves disclosure, making visible. The garnering of information discloses the patterns of activity of those to whom that information refers, and direct supervision openly keeps such activity under observation in order to control it. The minimisation or manipulation of conditions of disclosure is thus ordinarily in the interests of those whose behaviour is subject to surveillance – the more so according to how far their required activity in such settings is regarded as uninteresting or noxious.

Back regions in, say, settings of the shop-floor include 'odd corners' of the floor, tea-rooms, toilets and so on – as well as the intricate zonings of displacement of contact with supervisors which workers can achieve by bodily movement and posture. Descriptions of the use of such zoning in order to control properties of the setting (and thereby sustain modes of autonomy in power relationships) are legion in the literature of industrial sociology. For instance, here is a worker talking about a characteristic incident on the floor of a car factory:

I was working on one side of the car and the boot lid dropped. It just grazed the head of the fella working opposite me. I can see it now. He stopped working, had a look round to see if anyone was watching. I was pretending not to look at him – and then he held his head. He'd had enough like. You could see him thinking 'I'm getting out of this for a bit'. He staggered; I could see him looking round. You know what it was like in there. Paint everywhere. He wasn't going to fall in the paint . . . so he staggered about ten yards and fell down with a moan on some pallets. It was bloody funny. One of the lads saw him there and stopped the line. The supervisor came chasing across. 'Start the line . . start the line . . .'. He started the line and we had to work. We were working one short as well. It took them ages to get him out of there. They couldn't get the stretcher in. It must have been half an hour before they got him. Him lying there y'know with his one eye occasionally opening for a quick look round: 'What's happening?'[22]

The regional zoning of activities in many contexts of this sort connects closely, of course, with the seriality of encounters in time–space. But again it does not clearly converge with a division between public and private activity. The worker makes no attempt to disguise from his workmate that the act of malingering is directed towards temporarily escaping from the pressures of the assembly-line. Such front/back differentiations – ordinarily occurring in circumstances of marked imbalances of power – can be distinguished in a general way from those in which – in Goffman's terms – the situational proprieties of interaction are weakened or allowed to lapse. These are situations in which front, the details of bodily control, and some 'repair' procedures of care for others, can all be relaxed. At least *one* connotation of 'privacy' is the regional isolation of an individual – or of individuals, for privacy does not seem inevitably to imply solitude – from the ordinary demands of the monitoring of action and gesture, whereby 'infantile' types of conduct are permitted expression. The zoning of the body seems in most – perhaps all – societies to be associated with the zoning of activities in time–space in the trajectories of the day within locales. Thus eating usually occurs in definite settings at definite times, and is usually also 'public' in the restricted sense of involving gatherings of family members, friends, colleagues and so on. The dressing or adornment of the body may not be universally regarded as 'private', but at least in most cultures seems to be so regarded. In spite of Elias's claims that sexual activity was carried on in an unconcealed way in medieval Europe,[23] genital sexuality seems everywhere to be zoned as a back-region phenomenon – with many variations, of course, in intersecting modes of public and private behaviour.

It seems plausible to suppose that the intersections between regionalisation and the expressions of bodily care are intricately bound up with the continuity of personality. Back regions which allow the individual complete solitude from the presence of others may be less important in this respect than those which allow the expression of 'regressive behaviour' in situations of co-presence. Such regions may permit

> profanity, open sexual remarks, elaborate griping . . . rough informal dress, 'sloppy' sitting and standing posture, use of dialect or substandard speech, mumbling and shouting, playful aggressivity and 'kidding', inconsiderateness for the other in minor but potentially symbolic acts, minor physical self-involvements such as humming, whistling, chewing, nibbling, belching and flatulence.[24]

Far from representing a diminution of trust, these types of behaviour might help to reinforce the basic trust in the presence of intimates originally built up in relation to the parental figures. They are not marked by the sort of upsurge of anxiety brought about by critical situations, but the reverse – a dissipation of tensions deriving from the demands of tight bodily and gestural control in other settings of day-to-day life.

Regionalisation as generic

The differentiations between enclosure, disclosure, back and front regions, apply across large spans of time–space, not only in the contexts of co-presence. These are, of course, unlikely to be as directly monitored reflexively by those whom they affect, although such may be the case. Regionalisation within urban areas in contemporary societies have been much studied since the famous early work of the Chicago sociologists Park and Burgess. In most Western societies, the zoning of cities into neighbourhoods with markedly different social characteristics is strongly influenced by the operation of housing markets, and by separations between individually-owned homes and state-operated housing sectors. Neighbourhoods may not be as symmetrically zoned as some of the 'ecological' urban analysts suggested, but their distribution certainly has the consequences of creating various sorts of front/back contrasts. Industrial areas in northern towns and cities in England were once the most visible features of the built environment – factories and mills, as it were, proudly displayed. But the tendency in urban planning in recent years has been to treat such areas as unsightly, as back regions to be hidden away in enclosed enclaves, or transferred to the edge of town. Examples can easily be multiplied. The access of those in more affluent sectors of housing markets to relatively easy transfer of property underlies the 'flight to the suburbs' that has helped to transform city centres from regions of frontal display to back regions of urban decay, which the 'respectable classes' avoid. Ghetto areas may be rendered 'invisible' by their regional enclosure in neighbourhoods having both very low rates of property transfer and of daily mobility from those neighbourhoods into other parts of the city. As always, various types of time-series phenomena underlie such spatial regionalisation.

Regionalisation across long spans of time–space has been analysed by many writers in terms of familiar notions such as 'uneven development' and distinctions between 'centre' (or 'core') and 'periphery'. These notions however, can be applied across the whole range of the settings of locales, from large to small. Rather than discussing the theme of uneven development here, however, I shall develop the differentiation of centre and periphery by relating it to 'embeddedness in time'. If the world economy has its centres, and cities have their centres, so too do the daily trajectories of individual actors. In modern societies, for the majority of males at least, the home and workplace form the two main centres in which the day's activities tend to be concentrated. Locales also tend to be centred regionally. For example, some rooms in a house, such as spare bedrooms, may be only used 'peripherally'.

Distinctions between centre and periphery tend frequently to be associated with endurance over time.[25] Those who occupy centres 'establish' themselves as having control over resources which allow them to maintain differentiations between themselves and those in peripheral regions. The established may employ a variety of forms of social closure to sustain distance from others who are effectively treated as inferiors or outsiders.[26] The 'established' industrial nations

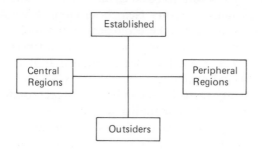

FIGURE 12.4 *Centre–periphery distinctions*

of the Western 'core' maintain a central position in the world-economy on the basis of their temporal precedence over the 'less developed' societies. The geo-political regionalisation of the world system may be changing – with, for example, shifts in centres of manufacturing production to erstwhile peripheral zones in the East – but the factor of priority in time has so far decisively influenced preeminence in space. Within nation-states, centre/periphery regionalisation seems everywhere to be associated with the prevalence of 'establishments' that lie at the core of the structuration of dominant classes.[27] Of course, there are a variety of complex relations involved in these phenomena, and I offer these examples as purely illustrative.

Time, Space, Context

Let me at this point offer a summary of the main points in this chapter so far. The discussion has been concerned with the *contextuality* of social life and social institutions. All social life occurs in, and is constituted by, intersections of presence and absence in the 'fading away' of time and the 'shading off' of space. The physical properties of the body, and the *milieux* in which it moves, inevitably give social life a serial character, and limit modes of access to 'absent' others across space. Time-geography provides an important mode of notation of the intersection of time–space trajectories in day-to-day activity. But it has to be inserted within a more adequate theorisation both of the agent and of the organisation of the settings of interaction. In proposing the ideas of locale, and of regionalisation, I wish to begin to formulate a scheme of concepts which help to categorise contextuality as inherently involved in the connection between social systems of smaller and larger scope.[28] The graphic techniques de-

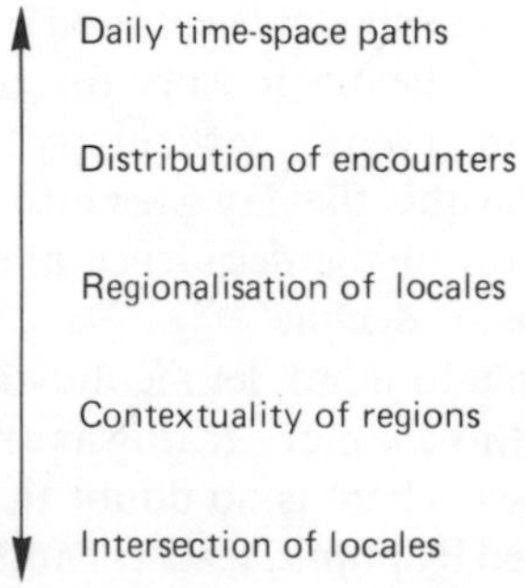

Daily time-space paths

Distribution of encounters

Regionalisation of locales

Contextuality of regions

Intersection of locales

FIGURE 12.5 *Contextuality and its categories*

veloped in time-geography have already proved their fruitfulness in several areas of research. There is no reason at all why those working in a range of fields in the social sciences should not adopt – and adapt – Hägerstrand's method of notation. But the limitations of time-geography as indicated above must certainly also be borne in mind. Moreover, 'clock time' should not be accepted as simply an unquestioned dimension of the construction of topographical models, but must be regarded as itself a socially-conditioned influence upon the nature of the time–space paths traced out by actors in modern societies. The point may on the face of things appear to be a banality, but is actually very far from being so. What is at issue is not just different means of reckoning time, but divergent forms of the structuration of daily activities.

Consider, for instance, Bourdieu's well-known discussion of time and time-reckoning in Kabylia. Here the year is considered to run from autumn towards summer, and the day from evening towards noon. This scheme expresses, however, a conception of time as eternal recurrence, which is in turn part of the basic composition of day-to-day activities. Night is symbolically a time of death, marked by regular taboos – against bathing, coming into contact with stretches of water, looking in a mirror, anointing the hair or touching ashes.[29] The morning is not just 'daybreak', but a triumph in the struggle between day and night: to be 'in the morning' is to be open to the light, to the beneficence that is associated with it. The 'opening' of the day is thus a time for going out, in which people pour from their houses to their work in the fields. Getting up early means putting oneself under favourable auspices, to 'do honour to the angels'. It is not just a transition in time, but a keying of events and practices. Nevertheless, the creative potential of the day must be fostered by magic, or other malignant forces can intervene – particularly following the zenith of the sun's rise. For after this the day goes into decline, signalling the immanent arrival again of the decadence and decay of night, 'the paradigm of all forms of decline'.[30]

Bearing this example in mind, let me illustrate some of the main notions developed in this chapter – taking as an example schooling in contemporary societies. There is no doubt that mapping the time–space patterns followed by pupils, teachers and other staff in a school is a useful topological device with which to begin to study that school. Rather than using the exact forms of representation formulated by Hägerstrand and his co-workers, however, I would propose to emphasise the 'reversible time' of day-to-day routine conduct. Hägerstrand usually portrays time–space paths as having a 'linear' movement through the day. But a more accurate representation of the repetitive character of day-to-day social life is given if we emphasise that most daily time–space paths involve a 'return'. Instead of adopting the form of the diagram on the left of Figure 12.6, we might take as exemplary that of the diagram on the right. The left-hand diagram is of the sort favoured by Hägerstrand, in which we look at time–space 'laterally' and where the 'time' arrow makes out a specific

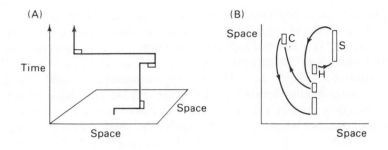

FIGURE 12.6 *Time–space maps*

temporal sequence (usually equivalent to the working day). I do not propose to abandon this type of notation, but to supplement it – conceptually if not figuratively – with the one on the right. In the right-hand diagram we are looking 'down', as it were, rather than laterally. The lines marked with the arrows represent paths of time–space movement. The length of the lines refers to the amount of time, measured chronologically, spent moving between 'stations' in the course of a particular day by a particular or typical individual; the degree of elongation of the boxes indicates the length of time spent within a specific locale. Thus a child's day in the school term looks something like the scheme indicated in the diagram. The child may spend three discrete periods in the home (*H*) per day – sleeping there from the middle of the evening until the early morning; returning there from school (*S*) in the late afternoon; and coming back again after having been out to the cinema (*C*) in the evening. Some aspects of the child's day are no doubt strongly routinised (the journey to school and back) whereas others (going out to the cinema) may be less so. The most routinised types of activity can be represented as a profile of time–space paths embedded in reversible time.

A school, in Hägerstrand's terms, is a 'station' along the converging paths traced by clusters of individuals in the course of the day. He is certainly right to point out that the conditions which make it possible for individuals to come together within a single locale cannot be taken for granted, but have to be examined as an 'infrastructure' of daily life. But a locale is of course more than a mere stopping-point. 'Stations' tend to be black boxes, as it were, in time-geography, because the main focus is upon movement between them. As a type of social organisation, concentrated upon a locale having definite physical characteristics, the characteristics of a school can be under-stood in terms of three features: (i) the distribution of encounters within it; (ii) the internal regionalisation that it displays; and (iii) the contextuality of the regions thus identified.

Modern schools are disciplinary organisations, and their bureaucratic traits clearly both influence and are influenced by the regions they contain. Like all forms of disciplinary organisation, the school operates within closed boundaries, its physical borders being cut off rather clearly from day-to-day interaction outside. A school is a 'container', generating disciplinary power. The enclosed nature of school life makes possible a strict co-ordination of the serial encoun-ters in which inmates are involved. The segments of children's time that are spent in school are spatially and temporally sealed off from potentially intrusive encounters outside. But this is also true of the divisions between different classes – or at least, is usually so. Schools are internally partitioned. There may be some areas in a school, and some times, when heterogeneous or unfocused forms of interaction tend to occur – for example, at the beginning and end of classes. But for the most part the distribution of encounters within a school contrasts dramatically with sectors of social life in which the nor-mative regulation of activity is looser. Disciplinary spacing is part of the architectural character of schools, both in the separation of classrooms and the regulated spacing of desks that is often found inside them. There is no doubt that spatial divisions of this sort facilitate the routinised specification and allocation of tasks.

The school time-table is fundamental to the mobilisation of space as co-ordinated time–space paths. School administrators normally do not face the same problems of 'packing' as do their counterparts in hospitals. But like all disciplinary organisations schools operate with precise economy of time. It is surely right to trace out the origins of school discipline in some part to the regulation of time and space which a generalised transition to 'clock time' makes possible. The point is not that the widespread use of clocks makes for exact div-isions of the day, but that time enters into the calculative application of administrative authority. Time becomes the very exemplar of a scarce resource.

The contextual features of classrooms, as the main 'areas of application' of disciplinary power, obviously vary widely. But in more severe forms of classroom spacing, the specification of bodily positioning, movement and gesture is usually tightly organised. The spatial positioning of teacher and pupils in the context of a class is quite different from most other situations in which face engagements are carried on. Indeed it usually signals a collapse in the teacher's control if spatial positionings are subverted. The seeming *minutiae* of bodily posture and mobility to which Goffman draws attention are far from incidental here. The classroom, like the school, is a power container. But it is not one that merely churns out 'docile bodies'. Contexts of co-presence can be described as *settings*, and settings have to be reflexively activated by authority figures in the course of making that authority count. Discipline through surveillance is a potent medium of generating power, but it none the less depends upon the more or less continuous compliance of those who are its 'subjects'. The achievement of such compliance is itself a fragile and contingent accomplishment, as every teacher knows. The disciplinary context of the classroom is not just a 'backdrop' to what goes on in the school class; it is mobilised within the dialectic of control. A school class is a face engagement which has to be reflexively managed, like any other.

Consider the following strip of interaction, described and discussed by Pollard:[31]

Bell for 9.0 a.m. goes, about half class in, mostly reading books. Teacher enters breezily – 'Morning – ah, that's good, getting those books out'. Teacher sits at desk, tidies up, gets register out. Meanwhile most of the other children have come into the classroom. The later arrivals talk, swap some football cards, occasionally glance at the teacher.

Teacher: Right, let's do the register, then, hurry up and sit down you football maniacs – I see that Manchester United lost again.

Manchester United Supporters: Oh yeah, well they're still better than Liverpool.

Teacher: (jokey sarcasm in voice): Really? It must be all the spinach they don't eat. Now then ... Martin ... Doreen ... Alan ... Mark (calls register and children answer).

A child comes in late, looking sheepish, and walks to his seat. Other children point and laugh.

Child: Hey, Duncan, what are you doing?
Teacher: Duncan, come here. You're late *again*, three minutes late to be exact. Why?

Duncan: Sorry Sir.
Teacher: I said 'Why?'
Duncan: I slept in, Sir.
Teacher: Well, are you awake now?
              (Other children laugh.)
Duncan: Yes, sir.
Teacher: Well you'd better stay behind for three minutes at 4
              o'clock and don't go to sleep again after that.

More laughter, Duncan sits down. Teacher finishes register.

What is going on here? We have to recognise, as the teacher does, that registration has a particular significance for the ordering of the day's activities. It is a marker that signals the opening of the day's activities. It is a marker that signals the opening of the brackets in an encounter, and it is the first salvo fired in a battle that is joined daily between teacher and pupils. The teacher recognises it as the first occasion to test the mood of the children, which the children also recognise in respect of the teacher. The teacher's maintenance of directive control depends upon ensuring that the children assume the routines involved in the classroom setting. On entry to the classroom in the morning the children are expected to sit in their assigned places, get out their reading books, and answer to their names when they are called out. Pollard interprets the teacher's joking and teasing as a front performance, which is intended to set the tone of the day as one of co-operative work. However this strategy has its risks, as is indicated by the response to a late arrival of one of the children. Another feels able to tease the latecomer. The teacher at once recognises this as the first test case of the day, in respect of which his superior authority must be demonstrated. His bantering rebuke to Duncan mixes appeal with firmness, a tactic shown to be successful by the laughter of the children. Thus the events of the day move on. If the teacher had been more overtly disciplinarian, and sent the miscreant to the head, the response could have been judged too severe by the rest of the children. The result then might have been an escalation of threat and punishment more ineffective in sustaining routine than the 'effort bargain' which teacher and pupils have implicitly concluded as part of a more co-operative atmosphere.

The very nature of classrooms, in which most things both teachers and children do are visible each to the other, means that back regions usually have a strong temporal as well as spatial definition. For children, these lie in some part along the narrow temporal boundaries between classes, whether or not they involve physical movement from one classroom to another. Although the weight of discipline normally bears down most on the children, it is often felt more oppressively by teachers. Teachers usually have a back region to which they can retreat – the staff room – which children ordinarily do not enter. The staff room is no doubt a place for unwinding and relaxation. But it is also somewhere in which tactics of coping with teaching tend endlessly to be discussed, formulated and reformulated.

It is in the nature of disciplinary organisations that the intensity of surveillance inside inhibits direct control from outside. This is a phenomenon which can be seen both in the internal regionalisation of the school and its situation as a locale within other locales. Inside the school, the concentration of disciplinary authority in separately-partitioned classrooms is the condition of the high level of control over bodily positioning and activity which can be achieved. But this circumstance also inhibits the direct supervision of the supervisor. The head is 'in authority' over the teaching staff, but such authority cannot be exercised in the same way as teachers endeavour to control the conduct of children in their classes. Schools therefore tend to have a rather sharply opposed 'double line' of authority. The control which teachers seek to exercise over their pupils is immediate, involving the teacher's continuous face-to-face presence with the children. Supervision of the activity of teachers, however, is necessarily indirect, and proceeds by other means. One might hazard a guess that it is only in organisations in which a considerable amount of autonomy from direct supervision is given in which a graduated line of authority can be achieved. The enclosed nature of the school, and its clear separation in time and space from what goes on in surrounding locales, also inhibits supervisory control from the outside. Thus inspectors may visit schools regularly to check upon their operation; boards of governors and parents' associations may make their power felt in influencing policies that help shape the life of the school. But it is intrinsic to disciplinary power that what goes on in the 'power container' of the school has a significant degree of autonomy from the very outside agencies whose ethos it expresses.

Against 'micro' and 'macro' : social and system integration

The foregoing considerations are of key importance in examining the relations between the immediate contexts of interaction and larger social systems. I do not employ the more familiar terms, 'micro-' and 'macrosociological' study for two reasons. One is that these two are not infrequently set off against one another, with the implication that we have to choose between them, regarding one as in some way more fundamental than the other. In Goffman's studied refusal to be concerned with issues of large-scale social organisation and history, for example, there seems to lurk more than a hint that in what he sometimes calls microsociology is to be found the essential reality of social life. On the other hand, advocates of macrosociological approaches are prone to regard studies of day-to-day social activity as being concerned with trivia – the most significant issues are those of broader scope. But this sort of confrontation is surely a phoney war if ever there was one. At any rate, I do not think that there can be any question of either having priority over the other. A second reason why the micro/macro division tends to conjure up unfortunate associations is that, where there is no conflict between the two perspectives, an unhappy division of labour has tended to come into being between then. Microsociology is taken to be concerned with the activities of the 'free agent', which can safely be left to theoretical standpoints such as those of symbolic interactionism or ethnomethodology to elucidate; while the province of macrosociology is that of analysing the structural constraints which set limits to free activity. Such a division of labour leads to consequences that are at best highly misleading.

Why should the issue of the relation between 'micro-' and 'macrosociological' study be seen as so problematic by many writers? The conceptual division of labour to which we have just referred is undoubtedly the most significant cause. Reinforced by a philosophical dualism, it cannot be escaped except by a more thoroughgoing reformulation of social theory than most authors are able or willing to contemplate. It will help to develop this point by looking briefly at one of the more interesting recent discussions of the issue, offered by Collins.[32] Collins points out that the schism between micro- and macrosociological approaches, as these terms are ordinarily understood, has become accentuated over the past decade or so. While social theory was dominated by functionalism and Marxism, or some combination of the two, social relations in situations of co-presence were typically regarded as substantially determined by broader 'structural' factors. However, as led especially by ethnomethodology, microsociology has become a burgeoning field of interest, and one in which the presumptions of these approaches have been taken to task in a fairly radical fashion. In Collins's view:

The newer, radical micro-sociology is epistemologically and empirically much more thorough than any previous method ... I would suggest that the effort coherently to reconstitute macrosociology upon radically empirical micro-foundations is the crucial step toward a more sociological science.[33]

How should this effort be made? According to Collins, the proper path forward is via a programme of the 'micro-translation' of 'structural phenomena'. Such translation is likely to eventuate in theories which have a stronger empirical basis than existing macrosociological theories. Those who are concerned with macrosociological issues are not called upon to abandon their endeavours, but to recognise that their work is theoretically incomplete. There are, in Collins's eyes, only three 'pure macro-variables': time, space and number. Thus a concept such as 'centralisation of authority' can be translated into accounts of micro-situations – how situated actors actually exert authority in describable contexts. However the 'pure macro-variables' enter in as the number of situations of such a sort, in time and in space. 'Hence structural variables often turn out to be sheer numbers of people in various kinds of micro-situations.'[34] 'Social reality', then, is 'micro-expreience'; it is the numerical temporal and spatial aggregations of such experience which makes up the macrosociological level of analysis. The 'structural' qualities of social systems are the 'results', Collins says, of conduct in micro-situations, insofar as they do not depend upon number, time and space.

Collins is right to hold that generalisations linking 'structural variables' can always in principle be interpreted in terms of the intentional conduct of cognitively sophisticated agents, acting in contexts the properties of which are not always transparent to them. But in other respects, Collins's view is wanting. As I have consistently stressed, to treat time and space as 'variables' is to repeat the characteristic error of most forms of orthodox social science. Moreover, why should we assume that 'structure' is only relevant to macrosociological issues? Activity in micro-contexts has strongly defined structural properties. I take this, in fact, to be one of the main claims which ethnomethodological research has successfully sustained. Also, why hold that time as a 'variable' is only relevant to macrosociological concerns? Temporality is as inseparable from a small strip of interaction as it is from the longest of *longue durées*. Finally, why propose that structural properties consist only of three dimensions, time, space and number? The reason, I assume, is that Collins still has in mind that 'structure' must refer to something 'outside' the activities of social agents if it is to have any sense at all in sociology. Dispersion in time and space seems the only phenomonen left – given that Collins accept a good deal of the criticisms that have been levelled by 'radical micro-sociologists' against the collective concepts with which their macrosociological antagonists usually operate.

But the most important confusion in Collins's account is the assumption that 'macro-processes' are the 'results' of interaction in 'micro-situations'. According to Collins, the 'macro-level' consists only of 'aggregations of micro-experiences'. Now it can be agreed that generalisations in the social sciences always presuppose – and make at least implicit reference to – the intentional activities of human agents. However it does not follow from this that what is described as the 'macro-level' has a rather sham existence. This only takes us back to the phoney war. Social institutions are not explicable as aggregates of 'micro-situations', nor fully describable in terms that refer to such situations – if we mean by these circumstances of co-presence. On the other hand, institutionalised patterns of behaviour are deeply implicated in even the most fleeting and limited of 'micro-situations'.

Let us pursue this thought by asking why the micro/macro distinction is not a particularly useful one. What is a 'micro-situation'? The response might be: a situation of interaction confined in space and time – seemingly Collins's view. But this is not very helpful. For encounters 'slide away' in time; once we start being concerned with the way encounters are carried on by their participating actors, it becomes clear that – even if it is plainly bracketed, temporally and spatially – no strip of interaction can be understood on its own. Most aspects of interaction are deeply sedimented in time, and sense can be made of them only by considering their routinised, repetitive character. Moreover, the spatial differentiation of the micro- and macro- becomes inprecise once we start to examine it. For the forming and reforming of encounters necessarily occurs across broader tracts of space than that involved in immediate contexts of face-to-face interaction. The paths traced by individuals in the course of the day break off some contacts by moving spatially to form others, which in turn are broken off and so on.

It is apparent that what is being talked about under the heading of micro/macro processes is the positioning of the body in time–space, the nature of interaction in situations of co-presence, and the connection between these and 'absent' influences relevant to the characterisation and explanation of social conduct. These phenomena – the anchoring concerns, in fact, of structuration theory – are better dealt with as concerning the relations between 'social' and 'system integration'. Now some of the questions at issue in the micro/macro debate are conceptual problems to do with the long-standing controversy over methodological individualism. Other aspects of the problem, however, do not rest upon solely conceptual considerations. They can only be resolved by directly analysing particular types of society. Because societies differ in their modes of institutional articulation, the modes of intersection of presence and absence that enters into their constitution can be expected to vary.

Social integration has to do with interaction in contexts of co-presence. The connections between social and system integration can be traced out by examining the modes of regionalisation which channel, and are channelled by, the time–space paths which members of a community or society follow in their day-to-day activities. Such paths are strongly influenced by, and also reproduce, basic institutional parameters of the social systems in which they are implicated. Tribal societies tend to have a heavily segmental form, the village community being overwhelmingly the most important locale within which encounters are constituted and reconstituted in time–space. In these societies, relations of co-presence rather than influences of a more remote kind tend to dominate. It makes sense to say that in them there is something of a fusion of social and system integration. But such a fusion is obviously never complete: virtually all societies, no matter how small or seemingly isolated, exist in at least loose connection with wider 'inter-societal systems'.

Since we now live in a world where electronic communication is taken for granted, it is worth emphasising what is otherwise a self-evident feature of traditional societies – of all societies in fact up to a little over a century ago. This is simply that all contacts between members of different communities or societies, no matter how far-flung, involve contexts of co-presence. A letter may arrive from an absent other; but of course it has to be physically taken from one place to another. Very long journeys were made by specialised categories of people – sailors, the military, merchants, mystics and diverse adventurers – in the traditional world. Nomadic societies would roam across vast tracts of land. Population migrations were common. But none of these phenomena alter the fact that contexts of co-presence were always the main 'carrying contexts' in interaction.

What made possible the larger time–space 'stretch' involved in what I shall call class-divided societies was above all the development of cities. Cities establish a centralisation of resources – especially administrative resources – that makes for greater time–space distanciation than is typically the case in tribal orders. The regionalisation of class-divided societies, however complicated it may be in detail, is always formed around the connections – of both interdependence and antagonism – between city and countryside.

We tend to use the term 'city' in an encompassing fashion to refer both to urban settlements in traditional societies and to those convergent with the formation and spread of capitalist industrialism. But this is an obfuscating usage if it is taken to imply that in modern times we merely have more of the same – as if today's urbanism is only a denser and more sprawling version of what went before. The contextualities of traditional cities are in many respects different from those of modern urbanism. Rykwert, for example, points out the symbolic form that many cities had, in widely removed parts of the world, prior to modern times:

> It is difficult (for us today) to imagine a situation where the formal order of the universe could be reduced to a diagram of two intersecting co-ordinates in one place. Yet this is exactly what did happen in antiquity: the Roman who walked along the *cardo* knew that his walk was the axis around which the sun turned, and that if he followed the *decumanus*, he was following the sun's course. The whole universe and its meaning could be spelled out of his civic institutions – so he was at home in it.[35]

Such cities, we could say, do not yet exist in commodified time and space.[36] The buying and selling of time – as labour-time – is surely one of the most distinctive features of modern capitalism. The origins of the precise temporal regulation of the day may perhaps be found in the chime of the monastery bell; but it is in the sphere of labour that its influence became embedded in such a way as to spread throughout society as a whole. The commodification of time, geared to the mechanisms of industrial production, breaks down the differentiation of city and countryside characteristic of class-divided societies. Modern industry is accompanied by the spread of urbanism, but its operation is not necessarily fixed in any particular type of area. Traditional cities, on the other hand, are both the main locus of disciplinary power in class-divided societies, and as such set off from the countryside – very often, physically and symbolically, by the city walls. Together with the transformation of time, the commodification of space establishes a 'created environment' of a very distinctive character – expressing new forms of institutional articulation. Such new forms of institutional order alter the conditions of social and system integration, and thereby change the nature of the connections between the proximate and remote in time and space.

Notes

1. See Hägerstrand (1970; 1973; 1975); also Gregory (1978; 1982a) and this volume; Carlstein (1980); Pred (1977); Parkes and Thrift (1980); Thrift (1983).
2. Hägerstrand (1975); cf. Parkes and Thrift (1980) pp. 247–8.
3. Pred (1978).
4. Hägerstrand (1967) p. 332; cf. Hawley (1950) ch. 13–15; Ericksen (1980).
5. After Parkes and Thrift (1980) p. 245.
6. Janelle (1969).
7. Forer (1978).
8. Palm and Pred (1978).
9. Hägerstrand (1978) p. 123.
10. Carlstein (1978) p. 159; Carlstein (1980).
11. cf. Carlstein (1981).
12. Hägerstrand (1970) p. 8.
13. Giddens (1981b).
14. Giddens (1981b) pp. 161 ff.
15. Melbin (1978) p. 100.
16. Zerubavel (1979) p. 22; cf. Clark (1982) and Zerubavel (1981). One might point out that while the 'year', 'month' and 'day' have links to natural events, the 'week' does not: see Colson (1926).
17. Ariès (1973); Elias (1978b).
18. Hall (1966) p. 98.
19. Goffman (1959).
20. Goffman (1959) ch. 3.
21. Giddens (1981b) p. 169.
22. Beynon (1973) p. 76.
23. Elias (1978).
24. Goffman (1959) p. 128.
25. cf. Elias and Scotson (1965).
26. Weber (1978) pp. 341–4.
27. Giddens (1979) ch. 9.
28. Giddens (1981b) ch. 5 and *passim*.
29. Bourdieu (1977) pp. 143–52.
30. Bourdieu (1977) p. 153.
31. Pollard (1980).
32. Collins (1981b); see also Collins (1981a).
33. Collins (1981b) p. 82.
34. Collins (1981b) p. 99.
35. Rykwert (1976) p. 202.
36. Giddens (1981b) ch. 5.

13
Suspended Animation: The Stasis of Diffusion Theory

DEREK GREGORY

Shortly after ten o'clock the singing-boys arrived at the tranter's house, which was invariably the place of meeting, and preparations were made for the start....

Mellstock was a parish of considerable acreage, the hamlets composing it lying at a much greater distance from each other than is ordinarily the case. Hence several hours were consumed in playing and singing within hearing of every family, even if but a single air were bestowed on each. There was Lower Mellstock, the main village; half a mile from this were the church and vicarage, and a few other houses, the spot being rather lonely now, though in past centuries it had been the most thickly-populated quarter of the parish. A mile north-east lay the hamlet of Upper Mellstock, where the tranter lived; and at other points knots of cottages, besides solitary farmsteads and dairies....

'Times have changed from the times they used to be', said Mail, regarding nobody can tell what interesting old panoramas with an inward eye, and letting his outward glance rest on the ground because it was as convenient a position as any. 'People don't care much about us now! I've been thinking we must be almost the last left in the county of the old string players? Barrel-organs, and the things next door to 'em that you blow wi' your foot, have come in terribly of late years'.

Thomas Hardy, *Under the Greenwood Tree*

Introduction

Concepts of spatial structure are at the centre of many contemporary writings in social theory, where they engage with two fundamental questions: the problematics of *structuration* and *anatomy*. The first of these is concerned with the relations between human agency and social structure, and here Hägerstrand's time-geography has been drawn on by a number of authors to show the ways in which the production and reproduction of social life depends upon knowledgeable human subjects tracing out routinised paths over space and through time, fulfilling particular projects whose realisations are bounded by structures of interlocking capability, coupling and steering constraints. The geometry of these space–time interactions is not incidental to their social outcomes, and Giddens in particular has argued that 'it is useful to think of the daily lives of individuals in a social system as a series of "time–space paths" conjoining at intersections that can be represented topographically', as Hägerstrand's web-model suggests, because the Hobbesian 'problem of order' which gave sociology its classical *raison d'être* turns on showing 'how form occurs in social relations or (put in another fashion) how social systems "bind" time and space'.[1] But this 'weaving dance in space and time', to use Pred's phrase, quite literally *takes place* within a wider frame, and is itself bound in to what Urry calls 'the anatomy of capitalist societies': to the changing time–space relations between economy, civil society and the state.[2] The contributions to this second debate are more diverse, and they are not confined to capitalist societies, but some examples can indicate their general direction. The efforts of Harvey, Massey, Storper, Walker and others to link the dynamics of capital accumulation to emergent geographies of combined and uneven development and the restructuring of class relations to successive divisions of labour have done much to clarify the heterogeneous 'logics of location' through which historical eventuation is instantiated in human geography.[3] To be sure, these 'logics' are not limited to the narrowly economic, which is why they are conveyed through a distinctively political economy, and parallel excavations of the political matrices of capitalism by Clark, Dear, Scott, Soja and others have started to reveal the role of the state, of surveillance and territoriality in constituting material frameworks for these divisions of labour within different modes of production.[4]

To cut through a complicated cluster of mediations, we can say that the first problematic is broadly concerned with transformations within the spatial structures of societies, and the second with articulations between them. These are rough and ready distinctions, of course, and the relations between them are of central importance to the discussion which follows. Most authors have recognised these bonds, even if they have rarely been able to provide a wholly satisfactory explication of them. Giddens is no exception. Although the primary focus of his theory of structuration is the topography of time–space routines, he also discusses what he terms 'time–space distanciation' and connects this to combined and uneven development and to the administrative space of the nation–state.[5] But his writings seem to me to marginalise the importance of locational structures, and in seizing upon Hägerstrand's time–geography he has seized upon the least 'geographical' of all geographies: or so I shall claim.[6] This is not to say that an unreconstructed location theory can offer much guidance, however, and contemporary theorisations of locational structure are embedded in much more inclusive theorems about the production and reproduction of society than the 'separatist' formations of conventional spatial science usually allowed.[7] Even so, these modern endeavours remain strategically incomplete in so far as they continue to confine human agency within a theoretical grid which represents the changing configurations of capitalism as moments in the unfolding of an immanent 'logic'. There are naturally some exceptions, since these enclosures are far from necessary ones, but in large measure the contingencies of 'struggle' seem to be subordinated to the structural compulsions of 'capital' in ways which tremble on the very edges of the functionalism so strenuously repudiated by Giddens and others.[8]

The integration of these two problematics is thus an urgent task, but it cannot be tackled on a meta-theoretical level alone.[9] Partly for this reason, the present discussion is confined to a critique of diffusion theory and centres on Hägerstrand's seminal contributions over the last thirty years. There are, of course, older traditions of diffusion research, both inside and outside human geography. Some of them, like the classical investigations in rural sociology during the 1920s and 1930s, are open to many of the same objections as Hägerstrand's early writings;[10] others, and particularly Sauer's much less formal reconstructions of evolving cultural morphologies, derive from an anthropology whose discriminations between 'different levels of reality' are at least partially congruent with the rejection of methodological individualism entailed by a relocation of diffusion theory within the philosophy of realism which I seek to explore in this essay.[11] Although I shall not discuss these other traditions in any direct way, therefore, they are not completely absent from the argument: if such a circumscription is limiting, then it is not, I think, disabling. Indeed, it facilitates what is sometimes called 'de-construction', and by so to speak 'unpacking' Hägerstrand's conceptual apparatus and setting out some of the continuities and changes of emphasis between his early formalisations of innovation diffusion as a 'chorological' or 'spatial process' and his later accommodation of innovation within the framework of time-geography, I hope to prepare the ground for a preliminary (and necessarily programmatic) reformulation of diffusion theory: one which has at its heart the connective imperative between 'history' and 'geography' which is all but severed by Hägerstrand's twin projects.

Barrel-organs and harmoniums

Torsten Hägerstrand's *Innovationsförloppet ur korologisk synpunkt* was first published in Swedish in 1953, but it was fourteen years before it was translated into English as *Innovation Diffusion as a Spatial Process*, a title with which Hägerstrand is evidently uncomfortable. He insists 'I never said that diffusion is a "spatial process"; this expression was introduced in translation'. Certainly such a title seems to indicate a close conformity with the canons of spatial science, whereas the text was rooted in a continental European tradition which reached back to Ratzel's magisterial *Anthropogeographie*. Furthermore, its immediate intellectual genealogy was highly complex – the influences of Karl-Erik Froberg, Sten de Geer, David Hannerberg, Edgar Kant, George Lundberg and Sigfrid Svensson were all especially formative – and the subsequent spread of its ideas through the English-speaking world was similarly complicated.[12] Yet its starting-point was deceptively simple: like Hardy's Mail, Hägerstrand wanted to know 'how does the adoption of an innovation become widespread?'. He arrived at his answer through a series of diffusion studies in the districts of Kinda and Ydre in southern Östergötland, where he examined both specific innovations (which were confined to the agricultural community, like the grazing subsidies shown in Figure 13.1)[13] and general innovations (which could in principle be adopted throughout the population). From these detailed descriptions Hägerstrand concluded that the pattern of adoptions did not correspond to farm size or tenure categories 'in any obvious way' and that although a 'strict spatial sequence from farm to farm' did not exist, nevertheless a contagious, distance-bound 'neighbourhood effect' emerged 'again and again' as 'the dominant feature of the innovation processes'. This only made sense, so he

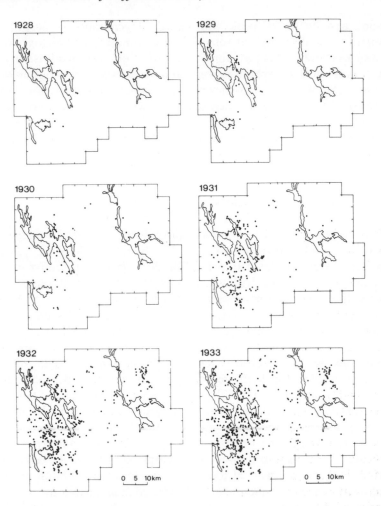

FIGURE 13.1 *The diffusion of grazing subsidies in central southern Sweden (after Hägerstrand)*

claimed, if private rather than public information – person-to-person 'pairwise tellings' – was regarded as 'the most important driving force behind the innovation diffusions under study'. The contrast between the rapid spread of grazing subsidies through farms in the west of Kinda-Ydre and their slower, more restricted progress in the east, for example, coincided with marked differences in the distribution of contact surpluses and deficits between the two sub-regions (Figure 13.2).[14] As Hägerstrand was to say later, then, 'diffusion of innovation is by definition a function of communication'.[15] His final model

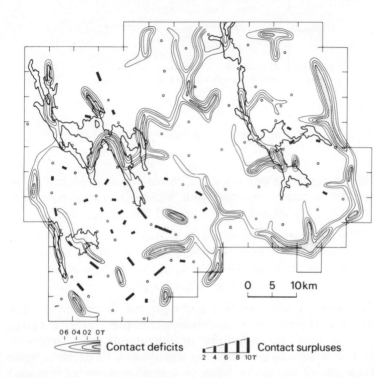

0   5   10km

0·6 0·4 0·2 0·T Contact deficits   Contact surpluses
                                      2 4 6 8 10T

FIGURE 13.2 *Contact fields in central southern Sweden (after Häger-strand)*

is summarised in Figure 13.3. There, an interaction matrix constitutes a generalised or 'mean' information field which structures the way in which information circulates through a regional system. These flows are modulated by both physical barriers and social resistances, which together check the transformation of information into innovation and so shape successive diffusion waves which break onto the adoption surface.

The details and developments of this theoretical scheme need not detain us,[16] but there are four cumulatively reinforcing comments I wish to make about its construction.

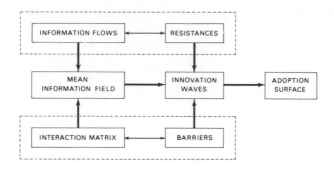

FIGURE 13.3   *The Hägerstrand model of innovation diffusion*

1. Hägerstrand's procedures are directed towards *generalisation*: they are primarily concerned with 'whether it is at all possible to detect any spatial order in the general diffusion process'.

   The [innovations] are not in themselves of any special interest. The same is true of the specific area within which the [innovations] are examined. Our aim is not to describe or analyse a region but to throw some light on a general pattern.

   The objective was thus 'not that of trying to determine which factors have produced the distribution of an [innovation] at a given point in time', but rather that of illuminating those factors involved in the change from one distribution to another: hence Hägerstrand repeatedly refers to the innovations as *indicators* 'whose scope would lend itself to the drawing up of generalisations'.[17]

2. Hägerstrand's procedures are conducted under the sign of *empiricism*: they assume that the leading edge of scientific advance is observation and that the empirical particulars of scientific discourse are *events*. Hägerstrand suggests that:

   The process concealed behind a synoptic growth curve can be divided up into a large number of events, which occur simultaneously in different parts of the area.

   According to this view, science characterises such a 'process' by connecting one event with another – here, 'pairwise tellings' with 'adoptions' – and depends upon an essentially Humean model of causation in which events of one kind are regularly followed by events of another kind. These 'constant conjunctions' are usually given in the form 'if *A*, then *B*', so that explanation becomes symmetrical with prediction (replication). Thus Hägerstrand regards 'the accuracy of the prognosis' as the 'final criterion' of success.[18]

3. Hägerstrand's procedures fasten on what Durkheim called a *social morphology*: the diffusion process is defined as the change from one distribution to another. This is supposed to consist of a cascade of systematic 'spatial regularities': local concentrations of initial acceptances; radial dissemination and the rise of secondary concentrations; saturation.[19] To be sure, Hägerstrand acknowledges that 'the diffusion of an innovation propagates in two dimensions, the spatial and the social', but he declared at the outset that he intended 'to examine only the spatial sides of the matter'. This separation is of the utmost significance, for Hägerstrand insists that:

> The introduction of model territories in the theoretical [section] of this work puts space *per se* in a position of more fundamental importance than would be so if analysis were restricted to a given part of the earth's surface, i.e. a geographical area.

The 'explanation' is then a strictly morphological one, in which the geometry of the mean information field (an exponentially bounded contact array) is mapped onto the geometry of the adoption surface (the 'neighbourhood effect'). The circularity is clear-cut: one distance-decay curve is transformed into another.[20]

4. Hägerstrand's procedures are symptomatic of a *formalism*: the transformation from one distribution to another, and from one distance-decay curve to another, is effected through the mathematical theory of *stochastic processes*, which is used to describe the conjoint probabilities of 'pairwise tellings' and 'adoptions'.[21] Although this incorporates elements of both contingency and determination, however, the dependencies which are contained in such simulations are purely formal characterisations of a statistical series: they have nothing to do with any substantive theory of historical structuration. They necessarily represent time as a logical structure – what Lévi-Strauss called a chronological code – rather than an ontological history: its sequences alone 'make it possible to abstract the structure which underlies the many manifestations and remains permanent through a succession of events'.[22] In the original model time is 'decomposed into a row of

regularly spaced and chronologically ordered points',[23] and these decompositions become especially intrusive in those extensions of Hägerstrand's work which treat it as a special instance of the simple epidemic model. For example:

> One of the major problems associated with many ... studies of diffusion is that ... they tend to be idiographic. Historical events rarely repeat themselves exactly, farmers can accept a given innovation only once, and so on. If we are to be able to model a diffusion process adequately, we need one data set upon which to calibrate it and another data set upon which to test it; thus, we need a process that repeats itself in time and space in a way that cultural events rarely do.[24]

This distinction between 'time' and 'history' evidently parallels the previous one between 'space' and 'geography': and it is these twin partitions which confine Hägerstrand's diffusion theory to the identification of empirical regularities and the replication of events.

Taken together, I suggest that the cumulative weight of these comments tips the scales of classical diffusion theory towards a basal concern with what Boudon terms 'reproductive processes'.[25] Its inability to explicate historical transformations is not a quirk of stochastic modelling, but is written into its own theoretical prospectus through two exclusion clauses. First, Hägerstrand offers no serious discussion of the structures of social relations and systems of social practices through which innovations filter. The only concessions to these questions are gestural – 'information flows' and 'resistances' – and (even when properly specified) these scarcely exhaust the *conditions* of innovation diffusion. Second, Hägerstrand similarly offers no serious discussion of the *consequences* of innovation diffusion. These are limited to the 'chorological' – a sequence of 'distributional changes' – and are severed from the production and reproduction of 'emergent' social structures and systems. In place of these multidimensional social processes, Hägerstrand substitutes the geometry of locational structure as simultaneously a space of description and of explanation.[26]

In case this is misunderstood, let me say at once that I do not mean to deny the importance of quantitative work; on the contrary. But here is Hägerstrand himself, writing some twenty years after these first formalisations of diffusion theory. We need, he says:

to close the gap between detailed story-telling and simplified statistical model-building. Each side has to give up some of its present ambitions... But still further adjustments are needed. In order to locate the full picture of an innovational process in the broader context of prerequisite *conditions* and of following *consequences* we need a way of mapping the whole chess-board on which the game takes place.[27]

This is exactly what his time–geography is supposed to provide, of course; and it is also in this very symmetry between *condition* and *consequence* that Giddens sees the fundamental 'recursiveness' in the relations between agency and structure, contingency and determination, which allows him 'to bring temporality into the heart of social theory'.[28]

The Mellstock Quire

The first explicit discussions of time–geography appeared in the mid-1960s, and were subsequently extended in the course of a collaborative research project on 'Time use and ecological organization' directed by Hägerstrand at the University of Lund. Some commentators have viewed this as significant departure from his previous work, but Hägerstrand himself considers that 'there is more continuity in the growth of my world picture – or maybe ontology – than appears from my occasional essays' and in my view, certainly, the continuities are as remarkable as the contrasts. They are in some measure empirical – many of Hägerstrand's exemplifications continue to be drawn from central southern Sweden, and especially from the parish of Asby in the west of Kinda-Ydre,[29] but here I want to tease out two more abstract threads which can be woven together to show the basic design of the time–geographic model.

Time–space paths

Hägerstrand's diffusion theory had its origins in an investigation of what he termed the 'population archaeology' of Asby. 'My attention', so he recalled, 'was not to count anonymous numbers but to excavate the individual biographies of everybody who had breathed the air of Asby from 1840 and onwards up to 1940'.[30] It was then that he conceived 'of depicting a biography as a time–space path', but he had yet to devise a formal notation to capture the intricacies of what he saw as ' "forests" of biographies':

> My problem . . . was that I had far more in my files in an ordinary historico-geographical sense than I could handle from the point of view of available theory as well as elementary description. But I had learned one thing and that was the surprising stability of the movement patterns of people over [their] life-times and, as I believed I could conclude from that, of their social networks. My main interest then became the geographical shape of the network of social communication. I saw this in my mind as a rather stable structure seen over space and time. People were born into it and on the whole had to accept it as given. It struck me that the network, seen in this way, must form a sphere which is . . . important for human geographers to investigate . . . It was only then that I began to look for 'indicators' of how 'information' possibly moved through the network, and so the book on innovation diffusion came into being.[31]

In his derivation of the mean information field, which was the mainspring of his diffusion theory, Hägerstrand suggested that:

> Virtually every individual possesses his own unique field of movement, with his residence in the centre and with places of work, shops, places of recreation, residences of intimate friends and other similar locales serving as nodal points.

In so far as these fields of movement are strongly routinised and repetitive, then Hägerstrand believed that it was possible (in principle) 'to symbolise the individual by a system of isolines indicating the probability with which he could be expected to be found at various points'. These probability contours, marking movements 'inseparable from the fleeting and more permanent contacts that develop between an individual and his fellow men', would have provided 'an ideal basis for interpreting the innovation processes'; but Hägerstrand also accepted that it was virtually impossible (in practice) to reconstruct complex sociometric nets 'for an entire region with its thousands of inhabitants and millions of personal relations'. Instead, he had to derive 'the approximate values and types of private information fields' by subsuming them within the generalised interaction matrix and mean information field of the diffusion model.[32]

But he returned to his original conception in a series of transitional studies of population migration. There, 'each individual has a moving pattern of his own, with turning points at his home, his place of work', and it was then that Hägerstrand developed an elementary space–time notation from standard Lexis-Becker diagrams to display this 'intricate, but far from unordered fabric' of space–time movements.[33] These notions were later formalised in the *web model* shown in Figure 13.4, which represents the social system as a closely-knit web of continuous 'paths' of people flowing through a set of discrete 'stations'. This three-dimensional co-ordinate system is intended to emphasise the fundamental 'meshing' of space and time in the conduct of everyday life: just as Hardy's church choir was destined to spend several hours tramping for miles around the farms and cottages of Mellstock 'playing and singing within hearing of every family' in the parish, so all systems of social practice are supposed to depend upon similar space–time discriminations within and between their constituent projects:

> Distance between components [of a project] is important . . . because the necessary movements take time. If too much time is

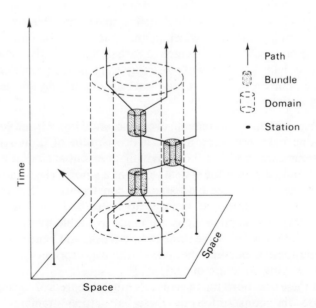

FIGURE 13.4 *Hägerstrand's web model*

consumed by movement it may not be possible to maintain the order within the project necessary for its survival.

These space–time interdependencies are the means through which social life is given a *coherence* – what Hägerstrand sometimes calls a 'grain structure' – which is produced and reproduced as a 'never-ending packing process' of projects in space and time. For this reason Hägerstrand explains that when he speaks of a web model 'this is not just a metaphoric expression but a way of indicating what kind of mathematics one would need in order to handle it'. By this he means a *combinatorial* mathematics, capable of conveying 'a world of incessant permutations', although he also (and significantly) commends conventional simulation techniques 'until more general mathematical tools become available'. In a non-technical sense, however, these space–time trajectories can be 'ordered' – their 'structure' disclosed – through the superimposition of a tripartite theoretical grid:

1. space and time are *resources* on which individuals have to draw in order to realise particular *projects*, subject to:
2. three *constraints*:
   capability constraints which define space–time paths;
   coupling constraints which define space–time bundles;
   steering constraints which define space–time domains.
3. these constraints are interactive rather than additive, and their prisms delineate a series of *possibility boundaries* in space and time which correspond to (or map out) an underlying and evolving 'logic' or 'structure'.

The empirical problems remain, of course, and Hägerstrand concedes that 'one risks becoming lost in a description of how aggregate behaviour develops ... without arriving at essential clues toward an understanding of how the system works as a whole'. His solution is to inspect the 'time–space mechanics of constraints' rather than the intersections of paths and projects: 'to try to find out what choices and behavioural combinations are made available by the "geographies" ... that people have come to be part of' and hence to disclose 'the relationship between the space–time trajectories of people and the underlying structure of options'.[34]

But these questions then become as much theoretical as empirical, because the constitution of these 'structures' remains deeply problematic. I think it wrong to suppose that Hägerstrand's 'constraints' are simply social extensions of the 'barriers' in his diffusion model, however much some of his preliminary formulations of the web model appear to invite such a reading. When he suggests that 'the population forms a kind of traffic flow in a road net with generally rusty gates', for example, it is easy to see how they can be dismissed as 'pseudo-structures' which amount to no more than 'an institutional system of barriers and restrictions'.[35] Although some commentators inculpate time–geography in the failings of structural functionalism, Carlstein represents it as a 'time–space structuralism'. Hägerstrand's later formulations seem to mimic its methodologies, and the distinction between a repertoire of possible space–time paths and a configuration of trajectories realised within these structural templates is, so Carlstein claims, formally equivalent to de Saussure's distinction between *langue* and *parole*. The objections to the linguistic model are well known, of course, and Carlstein draws upon the anthropologies of Friedman and Godelier to re-cast these equivalences within a materialist framework in which technology and technical change mediate between 'economy' and 'ecology'.[36] But, as I must now show, the continuities which can be traced through Hägerstrand's writings – from 'probability contours' to 'possibility boundaries' – have rather more to do with the natural than the social sciences.[37]

Naturalism

Hägerstrand's diffusion theory was imbricated in a physicalism which ultimately derived from Carnap and Neurath, and which was part of the Vienna Circle's attempt to demarcate science from metaphysics. In their view, scientific discourse was to be conducted through 'one unified language which spoke about physical things and their movements in space and time' and which took modern physics as its model. Physics and psychology were seen as opposite poles: 'Physics is, altogether, practically free from metaphysics, thanks to the efforts of Mach, Poincaré and Einstein; in psychology, efforts to make it a science free from metaphysics have hardly begun.' According to Popper, a fierce opponent of the physicalist programme:

> Everything was to be expressible in this language, or translatable into it, especially psychology in so far as it was scientific. Psychology was to become radically behaviouristic; every meaningful statement of psychology, whether human or animal, was to be translatable into a statement about the spatio-temporal movement of physical bodies.[38]

Hägerstrand's original 'behavioural geography'[39] conformed to these protocols. He claimed that his concept of the 'private information field' stood in the closest possible association to that of the 'social atom' which had been developed in some versions of behavioural psychology:

> The smallest constellation of psychological relations which can be said to make up the individual cells in the social universe. It consists of the psychological relations of one individual to those other individuals to whom he is attracted or repelled and their relation to him all in respect to a specific criterion (as living in proximity).[40]

But Hägerstrand's physicalism was much more direct than this. Froberg, an old school-mate and an associate professor in the physics department at Lund, introduced Hägerstrand to Monte Carlo simulation, and Hägerstrand's subsequent attempts to recreate the 'structural ties of Kinda-Ydre's social atoms' paralleled Froberg's simulations of the paths of atomic particles through various shielding materials: 'here was the origin of the Monte Carlo simulation idea, substituting the spread of an innovation for the dispersion of an atomic particle'.[41] And, as Jensen-Butler has demonstrated, physicalism continued to be the explicit basis for time-geography.[42] Much later, for example, in his programmatic critique of human geography and its 'surprisingly arbitrary' conceptual structure, Hägerstrand was still arguing that 'it seems very reasonable to consider man to be . . . a central elementary particle' and for human geography thus to concern itself with 'a unified space–time recording of events . . . [in] a sort of landscape like the bubble-chamber of the physicist'.[43] Human geography was no stranger to social physics, of course, but whereas many of these classical models (especially the abstractions of 'macro-geography') were based on Newtonian mechanics, both Harvey and Rose have equated Hägerstrand's time-geographic notation ('micro-geography') with the analytic geometry developed by Minkowski to describe the space–time manifolds of Einstein's relativity theory.[44]

Even so, time-geography is not confined to the penumbra of the physical sciences; it also depends, crucially, on the biological sciences. Hägerstrand considers himself 'more interested in seeing how the human world is emerging from the natural world that how various sorts of societies (capitalist or socialist) have become shaped', and so, for him:

A time–space web model in the sense of a flow of life-paths, controlled by given capabilities and moving through a system of outside constraints which together yield certain probability distributions of situations for individuals, should, in principle, be applicable to all aspects of biology, from plants to animals to men.[45]

Its central objective, therefore, is 'to incorporate certain essential biotic and ecological predicates' within social theory, 'to bridge the gap between biological and human ecology', and so Hägerstrand describes its theoretical armature as a *socio-technical ecology*. From this perspective, space and time are viewed as resources with a limited 'carrying capacity' and innovations are seen as 'invasions' which restructure pre-existing configurations of space–time utilisation. A simple example is given in Figure 13.5, which shows how a project consists of a sequence of operations taking place in a series of space–time 'pockets'. These are hooked together as a cascading system of storages and transfers which form intricate space–time webs of inputs and outputs. Innovations secure 'niches' or 'slots' in this web; they 'carve out some share from the limited supply of fibres

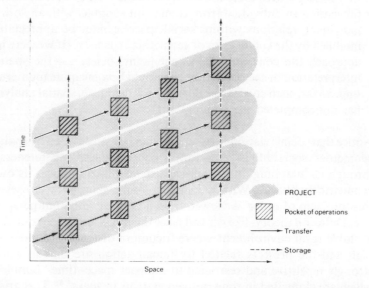

FIGURE 13.5 *Projects as space–time sequences (after Hägerstrand)*

and spaces in the fabric of [their] period and place' and are 'slotted or fitted into certain parts of more or less cyclical activity systems.' This means that they transform coupling periodicities, and through these 'displacement effects' set in motion a round of repacking activities in space and time. In this way, the conditions and consequences of innovation diffusion are written into what Hägerstrand calls the space–time 'scores' of co-existing and competing projects.[46]

These continuities set important limits to Hägerstrand's own project, but I now want to draw out three contrasts between diffusion theory and time-geography. As I hope will become clear, these changes of emphasis are closely interlocked and provide a series of keys which, when filed down and polished, eventually open the doors to a more rigorous social theory.

Space and time

Hägerstrand prefaced his original thesis about diffusion in the following way:

> In a society where there are no appreciable time or cost obstacles preventing an individual from coming into contact with any other individual, relations within 'social space' cannot be appreciably modified by the constraints of geometrical space . . . [If we were to] approach the conditions of a 'one-point society' . . . the spatial interpretation of social phenomena would become quite uninteresting. So far, such conditions do not exist; therefore, spatial analysis has not completed the playing of its role.[47]

Notice that social relations are supposed to be transformed by spatial geometries: social life is given form – coherence and concreteness – through its 'mapping' into a physical space which imposes its own geometric disciplines. Within the optic of time-geography, however, this 'problem of order' is viewed from a radically different perspective. Diffusion theory, like central place theory, is seen to be rooted in a 'stable rural environment where friction of distance is immensely high and the projects related to human action are on the whole strongly repetitive and restricted to compact space–time "bubbles" which are elongated in time but very narrow in space'.[48] This arises not only because these classical models grew out of the pre-war agrarian landscapes of Hägerstrand's southern Sweden (and Christaller's southern Germany), important though these periods and places undoubtedly were, but also because the genesis of coherent spatial patterns depends upon distance-bound processes. If the contact distribution within the mean information field of the Hägerstrand model is not exponentially bounded, for example, and the frequency of interaction does not decline with distance, then the diffusion wave disintegrates and advances are made by spatially irregular contacts.[49] It is no longer possible to map one distance–decay curve into another; as the bounds are relaxed, so the patterns dissolve.

In a later essay, however, Hägerstrand sharply questions this hypostatisation of distance:

> I wonder if it is not true to say that we have been so exclusively interested in the distributional arrangements of things and quantities in a relative locational sense that we have tended to overlook the space-consuming properties of phenomena and the consequences for their ordering which these properties imply. The frequently-quoted definition of human geography as a 'discipline in distance' – which in its way is a good one – gives no hint of a concern for spatial competition, for the 'pecking-order' between structures seeking spatial accommodation ... The notion of space as made up of distances has overtaken the notion of space as a provider of room.[50]

Time-geography reverses these priorities. Its sense of space resonates with what Hägerstrand calls 'an inward-directed finitude': otherwise, clearly, it could hardly carry the constellation of meanings required of its definition as a scarce resource. In a thoughtful commentary on the words *space* in English and *rum* in Swedish, Gould has shown how in Hägerstrand's usage 'the emphasis of meaning is upon constraint, packing, allowing and forbidding'; its domain is 'the adult world where my actions constrain yours, where our interdependencies jostle and compete, demand and require' and where 'we have lost the innocent freedom of the child in the sun-lit meadow' capering through the infinitude connoted by the English sense of *space*.[51] This 'loss of innocence', a metaphor through which so many writers have, in different guises, unmasked the modern world – and thereby seriously distorted the historical geographies of what Raymond Williams summarily describes as 'the country and the city'[52] – marks for Hägerstrand too a *rite de passage*:

In the urban–industrial world the competitive accommodation of projects is much more complex [than in the rural–agrarian world] and above all much more spread out over terrestrial space. But still these projects must be well ordered in time, since order in time is the fundamental condition for survival of a project.[53]

Notice that it is now *order in time rather than order in space* which gives shape and substance to social life. Some commentators have objected to this reading: to Parkes and Thrift, for example, it is a 'fundamental misconception' of the nature of time-geography.[54] But here is Hägerstrand himself:

This kind of understanding gives prominence to the sequential relations of events across the whole population (the time-dimension if you like). The prominence of domains in the channelling of trajectories makes us see space, first and foremost, as a provider of room (and only secondarily as a maker of distances).[55]

This new prominence was signalled by the title of the Lund School's original project, of course, and can be indexed in all sorts of ways: perhaps most strikingly by the frequent collapse of the three-dimensional co-ordinate system of the web model into a graph – 'a two-dimensional plain or even a one-dimensional island' – and the conversion of complex trajectories into simple vectors (compare Figures 13.4 and 13.5). These reductions are of considerable significance, as I must show, but they allow Hägerstrand to distinguish 'two diverse systems in interaction':

One is the predominantly *time-directed* warp of individual life-paths, which make up the population of an area and the concomitant capability constraints. The other is the more *space-oriented* set of imposed [coupling and steering] constraints [which define the] bundles and domains to which the individual may or may not have access.[56]

Whenever this spatial grid – the weft, so to speak, rather than the warp – is reduced to a graph, however, it becomes exceptionally difficult to explicate its developing historical geography. And it is vitally important to do so because the casting and recasting of webs of interaction is clearly *not* independent of the production and reproduction of the locational structures which contain them. These are *not* constants, and Carlstein notes that even in the short term 'elements in the settlement system would change in size, some would cease to exist, while others would be added to the landscape'.[57] The locations of these stations – the 'spatial bases for activity' – are supposed to be 'strongly determined by the sequence of events in time' and in particular by the 'conditions of connectivity' which exist within and between projects.[58] In so far as these coupling periodicities are transformed by technical change (which Hägerstrand regards as 'the prime mover'),[59] then spatial configurations are likely to be *inherently unstable*: according to Carlstein 'when innovations are adopted, the settlement system is almost invariably rearranged to accommodate them'.[60] But these arrangements and rearrangements need to be accorded a much more central place within time-geography, because without a proper theorisation of the instability of these locational structures – what Harvey sees as the chronic tension between 'fixity and motion' within the 'structured coherence' of spatial configurations[61] – space–time paths become moments in the continuous, routinised reproduction of an 'enormous maze': confined within a 'categorial' framework, their webs can only spin in an endless stasis.[62]

This is patently not what Hägerstrand intends, but the fact remains that to 'give prominence to the time dimension' does *not* necessarily mean that 'studies of change and of development trends . . . take precedence over examinations of equilibria and steady states'.[63] If, as Giddens has shown, it is an elementary error to identify the elapse of time with transformation, then it is no less misleading to identify space with stability.[64] On the contrary, I want to say that models of transformation require theorisations of spatial structure, not as flat, frozen lattices – 'the most solid of all geometries' – but as hierarchically ordered arenas of social practice.[65] This in turn demands a reworking of conventional location theory and its incorporation within a wider set of theorems about the production and reproduction of society. In many ways, of course, Hägerstrand's various discussions of the concept of *domain*, of 'survival and arena', speak directly to such a project, since they connect through to an understanding of *domination* in terms not of 'the relations between actors' but rather of 'the conditions for action imposed by arrangements on the stage'.[66] These notes are programmatic rather than definitive, clearly, and I shall return to them shortly; but given a proper 'prominence' they seem to me to gesture towards the constitution of what Foucault calls the *société disciplinaire*, in which, in the first instance, 'discipline proceeds from the distribution of individuals in space'. This gives the 'problem of order' a much sharper edge, as I have shown elsewhere, and it is partly for this reason that Foucault urges that:

> A whole history remains to be written of *spaces*, which could at the same time be the history of *powers* (both these terms in the plural): from the great strategies of geo-politics to the little tactics of the habitat.

I do not intend this to be read as an unequivocal endorsement of Foucault's problematic, but the parallel with Hägerstrand's work could surely not be clearer; and if it is to be pursued then, just as clearly, the hypostatisation of space (within diffusion theory) must not be exchanged for the hypostatisation of time (within time-geography). Whatever one thinks of Foucault's analytics – and his dissections of the 'anatomies' of the spatial grid are extraordinarily suggestive – he has established, I think decisively, the case for the repudiation of the tradition in which:

> Space was treated as the dead, the fixed, the undialectical, the immobile. Time, on the contrary, was richness, fecundity, life, dialectic... The use of spatial terms seems to have the air of an anti-history. If one started to talk in terms of space that meant one was hostile to time. It meant, as the fools say, that one 'denied history'... They didn't understand that [these spatial configurations]... meant the throwing into relief of processes – historical ones, needless to say – of power.[67]

Information and resources

In his original formulation of diffusion theory, Hägerstrand represented innovation as a function of information. 'Information' was conceived in a very restricted sense, however, because he was primarily concerned with the transmission of signals rather than the meaning of messages: in other words, the model was essentially syntactic rather than semantic.[68] Information flows were supposed to be homogeneous and undistorted, therefore, so that diffusion theory depended on what Blaut calls a 'cognitive purism'. By this, he means a methodological *epoché* which brackets all structural asymmetries and conjectures a 'uniform cognitive region'. In Blaut's view, such a procedure is only admissable in very special circumstances. Thus:

[Hägerstrand] was working (in the rural heartland of Sweden) with a culturally uniform space, with a population of potential adopters who possessed quite generally the technical and economic means for adoption, and with a set of innovations which had a demonstrable utility. Information was, in essence, the only missing variable, the only element needed to set the diffusion process in motion.[69]

We must suspend judgement on the empirical validity of these sentences, I think, but a number of writers have objected to the 'information axiom' (Blaut's term) on more general theoretical grounds. In its most basic form, it involves a double claim: 'first, that geographical processes derive from decisions, and second that decisions are fundamentally determined by the presence or absence of information available to the decision-maker'. These twin assumptions stake out a simple voluntarism which encloses a Platonic realm within which knowledge is given 'a space of its own' and protected from any structural determinations.[70] In Hägerstrand's case these protocols are reinforced by what I take to be a methodological individualism: although Cox has argued that the communication network makes 'the social' central to the model, the primacy of 'pairwise tellings' in the diffusion process, structured only by 'the constraints of geometrical space', suggests otherwise.[71]

Such a behavioural calculus is a common one – indeed, Blaut regards it as 'one of the pervasive paradigms of modern geography' – and yet authors from the Chicago School to the Frankfurt School have sought to link together communication, power and the social order.[72] Taken together, these writings describe a wide intellectual arc, and the differences between them should not be minimised; but they all testify to the social relations embedded in even the simplest categorisations of 'information'. These extend far beyond the constitution of 'meanings' within structures of *signification* (although this is undoubtedly a major lacuna in Hägerstrand's model) and Foucault in particular has shown that the circulation of information is bound into the production and reproduction of structures of *legitimation* and *domination*.[73] When Braudel peers over Philip II's shoulder at the correspondence crossing the desks of his functionaries, he reminds us that 'the speed of news and the passage of letters' marked the front-line in 'an unremitting struggle against the obstacle of distance' and (like Hägerstrand) reconstructs 'waves of communication' in which isotropic surfaces are transformed into 'elastic' information networks; but he regards these unpredictable triumphs over distance as moments in the maintenance of a political and commercial hegemony throughout the Mediterranean world, 'sixty days long' in the sixteenth and seveteenth centuries.[74] As this example suggests, there is a series of strategic mediations between surveillance and the state which makes 'information' a much more highly-charged category than Hägerstrand allowed: so much so, in fact, that Giddens regards them as primary sources of time–space distanciation and hence as fundamentally implicated in the generation of power.[75] The complexities of such a structural nexus are barely captured by the sort of dualism proposed by Blaikie:

> The ruling class (which broadly controls the institutions of the state to serve its own interests), particularly in social formations where the level of development of productive forces is low, employs a hierarchical, space-leaping and relatively efficient system of channels of communication, as opposed to [the] exploited classes who are forced to use a slow, contagious structure of communication, which is unreliable for transmitting and receiving complex messages.

This is unsatisfactory in several respects, and the correspondences which Blaikie posits between circuits of information and circuits of surplus value involve an essentialism in which these spatial configurations are derived directly from the 'inner logic' of a mode of production.[76] But the recognition of heterogeneous determinations which extend beyond the reach of the knowing subject is nevertheless of immense importance, because (macro-)structures of any complexion are conspicuously absent from Hägerstrand's early writings and, as I have already argued, this severely limits the ability of his diffusion theory to account for historical transformations. Here is Blaut again:

> In Hägerstrand's landscape, the structural units were individual, microgeographic, entrepreneurial decision-makers. A theory of structural change for this granular region can be said to coincide with a theory of spatial diffusion within the region. This is a rare situation in cross-cultural terms; the pure case would be a sort of Adam Smithian landscape, one totally without macro-structure. Contrast this with the condition of peasants [for example] . . . whose decision-making power is limited by a general exploitative structure at the macrogeographic level.[77]

This ought to be put both more strongly and more subtly: *all* social life goes forward within structural determinations, but these cannot be understood in terms of a simple micro/macro distinction. Although Yapa is thus correct to call for a model of *biassed innovation* – one in which non-adoption is not a passive state where the 'friction of distance' applies a brake to innovation, so to speak, but rather 'an active state arising out of the structural arrangements of society'[78] – these 'arrangements' ought to be conceived as a *hierarchical ensemble* of structures whose topographies mark out differential access to the means of production and reproduction. This should not be taken to imply an Althusserian trilogy of 'levels' and I have already rejected the essentialism which this entails. Neither should it be assumed that these ensembles are independent of human agency, since I take the 'causal powers' possessed by their constitutive structures to be exercised through social struggles whose outcomes are never fully determined. If social structures are both conditions and consequences of the social practices which are sustained through them, therefore, their symmetries are always contingent. It may well be that, as Yapa notes, 'initial income inequalities usually are exacerbated by technological innovation, leading to a circular and cumulative transfer of a disproportionate share of the economic surplus from one class to another': but the explication of these 'conditions and consequences' does not involve the substitution of an ontology of structures for an ontology of events.[79]

Class notations in any form are foreign to Hägerstrand's diffusion theory, of course, but in so far as his time-geography is supposed to incorporate a 'resource dimension' it ought to be capable of responding to some of these criticisms. Certainly, Hägerstrand continues to insist that 'one of the most problematical aspects of any project is to get access to suitable information exactly when and where it is needed'; but he also concedes that 'to see this process [of innovation] as predominantly a question of communication' is to adopt a 'restricted perspective'.[80]

In looking to the 'time–space mechanics of constraints', therefore, Hägerstrand seems to be recognising the importance of *differential access* – according to Blaikie, 'central' to any reformulation of diffusion theory[81] – and rejecting his earlier framework in which 'indicators [innovations] were avoided where it was obvious that economic or technical factors could impede their [diffusion] to a considerable degree'.[82] But matters are not so straightforward. As I must now show, Hägerstrand's 'constraints' are not identical to or even necessarily conformable with Blaut's 'macro-structures' or Yapa's 'structural arrangements'; their provenance is altogether different from political economy, and they do not provide quite the 'resource-based theory of innovation diffusion' which Blaikie envisaged.

For the most part, so Hägerstrand claims, actors have to draw upon the resources required for their projects 'in the close vicinity which is given by the situation at the start'. This arises because of the order-breaking effects of movement: no project 'can include more than a certain amount of movement before it must collapse'. Further-more, 'the limited capacity of space to accommodate trajectories at the same time means that every vicinity around every actor always has certain scarcity characteristics' so that the space–time arena becomes 'a battleground between projects'. Its front-lines are drawn by the mosaic of domains, and it is through their mediation that the 'problem of order' is peremptorily solved:

> A great number of institutions have come into being to deal with the conflicts which this overlap [between projects] creates ... [which] all come together as a system of barriers which prevent trajectories from making certain turns and let them move ahead in other directions.[83]

These 'institutions' are concretisations of the capability, coupling and steering constraints of the web model, and Hägerstrand describes these three groupings as simply 'large aggregations' which 'im-mediately present themselves'.[84] Although their conjunctural en-gagements are supposed to constitute 'structures', therefore, they do not in themselves provide an ordered *system* of concepts which corresponds to the usual *systematisations* of social theory. Indeed, Hägerstrand has very little to say about the production and reproduc-tion of such constraints, and the explanation for this remarkable relegation of historicity is, I suggest, to be found within his original prospectus.

There, Hägerstrand distinguishes between those constraints which are *constant* – 'circumstances which no policy or planning can do anything about' – and those which are *contingent* – 'which at least in principle are amenable to deliberate modification'. The first group provides the basis for what van Paassen calls Hägerstrand's 'existen-tial anthropology', which is founded on these 'fundamental con-straints' which circumscribe the human condition itself. They include indivisibility, finitude and the inescapable necessity for space–time 'packing' in the conduct of everyday life. The second group can assume any number of historically-specific forms, but its invariant function is taken to be the provision of collective regulations for the maintenance of an essential space–time coherence: a claim which evidently has much in common with structural functionalism.[85] *Both* groups thus stress structural continuity, and so can be combined to form an architectonics within which the thrust of investigation is directed towards the changing 'time–space mechanics' rather than their encircling 'constraints'. In fact, Hägerstrand's own writings make it plain that his primary purpose is to sieve out 'order' in the organisation of projects: to instantiate 'structure' in routinised systems of interaction and to inscribe its moments directly in the geometry of space–time trajectories, rather than in any structural field consonant with the categories of conventional social theory. 'Situations' we are constantly reminded 'are linked one to another in a complex web *which is not without structure*'[86]. When Hägerstrand talks about geography as '*the study of collateral processes within bounded regions*', therefore, and juxtaposes his own *contextual* theorems to conventional *compositional* theories, he is speaking of 'structure' in a language far removed from the standard scientific lexicon.[87] As he declares himself:

> I believe that being a geographer basically means to appreciate that when events are seen located together in a block of space–time they inevitably expose relations which cannot be traced anymore, once we have bunched them into [categories] and drawn them out of their place in the block.[88]

It is thus scarcely surprising that the 'resource dimension' of the web model should be calibrated not in terms of what Carlstein all but dismisses as the 'pecuniary bias' of traditional accounting procedures – which is precisely what most critics of Hägerstrand's diffusion theory demanded – but in a metric which represents *space and time* as 'universal resource inputs into all human activities'.[89]

The root problem, then, is obviously that of connecting the contextual to the compositional: of showing how space–time configurations of paths, projects and domains flow from and feed back into developing structures of social relations and systems of social practices. This is, in part, the same problem which Harvey confronted in an early discussion of the 'geographical' and 'sociological' imaginations and, as he came to realise in his progress towards historical materialism, it is not a uniquely linguistic one; it is also the analytical terrain on which Giddens, in the course of his critique of historical materialism, attempts to conjoin time-geography to his theory of structuration.[90] Thrift has juxtaposed these two movements to identify the *labour process* as 'probably the main link between the compositional and the contextual'.[91] It can function in this way, as what E. P. Thompson would call a 'junction term', because, as Harvey emphasises, 'the labour process is fundamental to the workings of any mode of production' and occupies a central place in the explication of spatial divisions of labour, through which in turn it dovetails with the reconstruction and resocialisation of contemporary location theory;[92] and while Giddens is sharply critical of Marx's writings, his own analysis of the commodification of space and time, and his insistence on its being 'focal to the nature of capitalism' and to the conduct of everyday life within it, is based on a view of the labour process and the labour contract which is not wholly inimical to Marx's original formulations.[93] Hägerstrand does not attempt to unravel this rich conceptual nexus, however, and his 'weaving dance' ignores the compositional implications of its own 'choreography'. So, for example, the inputs to the sequence of 'pockets' shown in Figure 13.5 are supposed to be space–time dependent, and as such their availability 'is completely determined by how [transfers] and storage have come to distribute potential inputs beforehand'.[94] But there is no sustained examination of these distributions; and yet – on Hägerstrand's admission – these 'arrangements on the stage' are not innocent primitives. Possession of or separation from the means of production provides a fundamental basis for the constitution of class relations, whose determination thus requires a careful analysis of the relations between 'pockets', their containing projects *and the wider systems of distribution of the conditions of production.*[95] It is for reasons like these that Blaikie is surely correct to say that 'differential access' assumes a strategic – and *structural* – importance, and without a theorisation of the labour process in such inclusive terms, which intersect with urgent debates over economic restructuring and the space–time periodicities of contemporary capitalism,[96] technical change remains a *deus ex machina.* The result, ironically, is that Hägerstrand's 'prime mover' is locked outside his own model.

Resistance and struggle

Hägerstrand's original diffusion theory took little or no account of competition and conflict. In even the most developed version it is axiomatic that 'resistance levels' will eventually diminish, and these are supposed to be a function of insufficient information – of ignorance – rather than of conscious, collective action. There is a strong presumption that innovations are *pro bono publico*, therefore, and that their adoption is as uncontentious as it is unproblematic. A good deal depends on the definition of that 'public', yet Hägerstrand closes his analysis around a pre-given population of 'potential adopters' so that the constitution of this class and its changing relations with other classes are left unexplored.[97] This is really the heart of the matter. For if diffusion theory is to engage questions of historical transformation it will have to widen its circle of intelligibility to include the space–time constitution of societies rather than simply the space–time conduct of segments within them; and in doing so, I suggest, it will be obliged to concede the centrality of *struggle* to structuration.

In some measure, of course, Hägerstrand attempts to bring these processes within the domain of human geography through his development of a 'situational ecology' whose very existence depends on a continuing recognition of the salience of competition and conflict to the production and reproduction of social life. For example:

> Each project would seem to try, between its beginning and end, to accommodate its parts, be they tangible or not, in the surrounding maze of free paths and open space–times left over by other projects or gained through competition with them ... *The interlocking of projects of different life-span, up and down the hierarchy and between hierarchies, is the central problem for analysis.*[98]

But, as I must now show, 'struggle' is treated in a highly restrictive sense. The 'interlocking' of projects is envisaged as a 'Darwinian' contest for scarce resources which ensures the survival of 'dominant' projects.[99] Even so, this is not intended as a narrowly ecological perspective, and Hägerstrand has himself explicitly linked these characterisations to Giddens's reconstructed social theory: 'When trying to understand ... "structuration", it is therefore an essential task to study the relative strength of projects in competition'.[100] But these interfacings are more problematic than they seem. Two issues stand out. First, Giddens counterposes the concept of conflict with that of *contradiction*. Conflicts are oppositions between individuals or collectivities, but contradictions are disjunctions of 'structural principles' and so connect back to the omissions identified in the previous paragraphs. Only Carlstein has made any serious attempt to delineate structural contradictions in time–geographic terms, but, as I have argued elsewhere, his proposals entail a covert functionalism. They depend on a concept of 'structural causality' derived from the writings of Friedman and Godelier which is flawed by the ascription of 'needs' to structures and systems, 'unacknowledged by the actors themselves'.[101] The second issue bears directly on this last point. For Giddens insists upon the integrity of the *knowledgeable subject*. The whole purpose of his theory of structuration is the development of a non-functionalist social theory which restores the subject without lapsing into a subjectivism.[102] Although Hägerstrand has endorsed the 'existentialist' programme of Anne Buttimer (and I have already drawn attention to his own 'existentialist anthropology') he admits to feeling 'safer at a somewhat greater distance from the minds of others'. Where Buttimer is 'in the first place concerned with individuals and groups,' he continues 'my thoughts are more preoccupied with how to understand the contexts in which individuals and groups are immerged [sic]'.[103]

Yet these preoccupations are much closer to existentialism than Hägerstrand acknowledges. He begins a brilliant autobiographical illustration of time-geography by sounding a note of exemplary caution:

> The fact that a human path in the time-geographic notation seems to represent nothing more than a point on the move should not lead us to forget that at its tip – as it were – in the persistent present stands a living body subject, endowed with memories, feelings, knowledge, imagination and goals – in other words capabilities too rich for any conceivable kind of symbolic representation but decisive for the direction of paths. People are not paths, *but they cannot avoid drawing them in space–time.*

The added emphasis is, I think, indicative. For Hägerstrand moves speedily away from 'people' and prefers to fasten on their 'paths' because, as he notes, 'there is no simple and straightforward relation' between intention and realisation. Whereas it is perfectly possible to glimpse 'the practical realisations of projects', at least in principle, and so to map their space–time trajectories, 'the configurations of underlying intentions' are, characteristically, opaque. Even if they were not, even if one could see 'the inside' from 'the outside', as Buttimer would say, Hägerstrand insists that 'situations [would still] evolve as an aggregate outcome quite apart from the specific intentions actors might have had when they conceived and launched out their projects from their different positions'.[104] Now it is, of course, exactly this problem which Giddens addresses in his theory of structuration, and his discussion of the 'unacknowledged conditions' and 'unintended consequences' of human action is an incisive critique of the interpretative tradition within the social sciences; but, as he also makes clear, the solution does not involve 'bracketing' the knowledgeable subject, since this would entail, among other things, a conceptual 'cutting into' the continuity of action.[105] This is extraordinarily important, because it means that Hägerstrand's repeated claims for the 'significance of continuity in the succession of situations' are compromised by his geometric closure: by the collapse of projects into paths.[106]

But this must be pressed still further. The relegation of the knowledgeable subject in this way reduces social life to a form of what Sartre called *seriality*. This is an exceptionally difficult notion to grasp in the abstract, and even sympathetic commentators admit to its obscurity, but (to simplify) people in 'series' are 'subjects who regard themselves and others as objects',[107] and it is noticeable that Sartre, like Hägerstrand, refers to them as 'social atoms'.[108] Even within the series actors have to draw upon various practical competences, of course, and the production and reproduction of social life continues to be a skilled accomplishment, but in this basic form of collectivity Eyles suggests that:

> Society rests upon dispersed individuals, each person transforming nature and the world through his [and her] own praxis. The unity of the series is imposed. People are dominated then not by the result of their own praxis, but by the entire material field which has been created by everyone at work.[109]

It is this 'material field' which, I suggest, is displayed in the first-stage constructions of time-geography, where its 'unity' – Hägerstrand would say its coherence – is 'imposed' by the 'fundamental constraints' entailed by the indivisibility of the individual and the finitude of space and time. Indeed, Sartre, like Hägerstrand, explains this 'univocal relation of surrounding materiality to individuals' as the product of an elemental *scarcity*. 'The whole of human development' so he claims, 'has been a bitter struggle against scarcity.'[110] It reaches its (profoundly disturbing) climax in the *institution*, the most developed form of the series, in which the collectivity 'becomes the subject and the members become its objects' and whose coherence is then further guaranteed through the imposition of authority.[111] This, I suggest, corresponds closely to Hägerstrand's second-stage scaffolding, the 'historically-contingent constraints' which provide collective regulations for the maintenance of structural continuity.

Numerous objections can be registered against these theses, I have no doubt, and many of them rebound on Hägerstrand's own theorems,[112] but the point of this excursion is not to suggest that Hägerstrand's problematic is identical in every particular to that of Sartre. That would be a nonsense, and there are clearly very considerable differences between them.[113] But the translations which are possible nevertheless reveal the restrictions placed upon the concept of 'struggle' in time-geography: for Hägerstrand, unlike Sartre, *does not move beyond the series*. A single example can only indicate the severity of the enclosure, but it is far from exceptional. In the same essay in which people are placed at the head of projects, Hägerstrand describes these designs as being for the most part 'standard patterns' whose physical 'shape' alone makes intelligible 'the coalitions and conflicts that emerge when the project paves its way forwards in time, negotiating with the situations that have to be coped with'. These phrasings – and others like them – are strongly suggestive of the 'alterity' and alienation which Sartre finds within the series, I contend, because it is *projects* that are supposed to jostle, compete and struggle: *not people*.[114] But Sartre interposes what he calls the 'fused group' between the primary 'series' and the tertiary 'institution'; its diagnostic is the supercession of the serial by the communal, and the development of a fully reciprocal subjectivity. In so far as its formation is presented as the precarious pivot of 'dialectical reason', then its absence from time–geography might perhaps effect a further separation between Hägerstrand's categorical paradigm and the 'dialectical' renderings which Pred and others have sought to provide.[115] But, much more important for my present purpose, it is through the 'fused group' that Sartre seeks to explore 'those historical situations in which oppressed classes struggle against domination', and so to disclose the ambit of *collective consciousness* which Poster picks out as the 'underlying thread' of Sartre's problematic.[116] And it is *this* which needs to be woven back into Hägerstrand's web model.

Struggles cannot be reduced to subjects, of course, and I have already stressed that their outcomes depend upon a range of structural determinations. It follows that they are not exclusively *class* struggles, and that, whatever the merits of Sartre's writings as a whole, he was entirely justified in connecting exploitation and domination to 'freedom' in the widest of senses. Interestingly, Hägerstrand once agreed that the human and social sciences 'have as their central problem the conditions of freedom'.[117] But this demands a sustained interrogation of the intersections between agencies and structures, from which it should be clear that an adequate analysis of the diffusion of innovations and of their incisions into the space–time fabric of social life requires a recognition of the capability of actors *outside* the privileged circle of 'potential adopters' to know a great deal about their circumstances – 'the contexts in which they are immerged' – and to *use* that 'information' as part of a solidary 'resistance' which is deeply implicated in historical structuration.

Conclusion

These comments carry a number of implications, and perhaps the most convenient way of bringing them together is through the summary distinctions between empiricism and realism made in Figure 13.6. I have argued that Hägerstrand's diffusion theory is located within the first of these philosophies: that it is concerned with discovering *generalisations* about sequences of *events* and framing them within a *morphology* whose spatial systematics depends upon an abstract *formalism*. Although time-geography maintains close con-

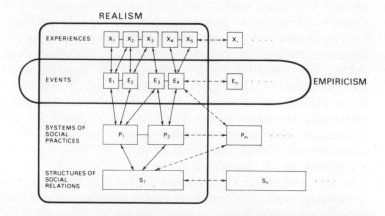

FIGURE 13.6 *Realism and the 'layers' of social life*

tact with some of Hägerstrand's original postulates, most notably in its individualism and physicalism, its domain is more properly described as systems of social practices than constant conjunctions of events. This edges Hägerstrand's project towards (theoretical) realism, but, as I have suggested and as the diagram shows, its completion involves incorporation of both the knowledgeability of human subjects and the authenticity of their experiences *and* of the structures of social relations within which and through which these are sustained. These twin requirements are *not* alternatives, and to differentiate between them in this way does *not* imply that 'experiences are less real than events, or events less real than structures' but, rather, that these 'internally related aspects may command, as it were, differential causal force'.[118] In contradistinction to Hägerstrand's early writings, therefore, any retheorisation congruent with theoretical realism – and removed from both empiricism and essentialism – must display four essential features.

1. It must be directed towards *abstraction* not generalisation. Many of the criticisms that have been made of both diffusion theory and time-geography can be shown to revolve around the need for what Sayer calls 'rational abstractions' rather than 'chaotic conceptions': in other words, they have failed to cut through the connective tissue of the world in such a way that its fundamental integrities are retained.[119] Obvious examples include the detachment of 'potential adopters' from their social moorings and the displacement of subjects from social struggles. The need for a more sensitive intellectual surgery is, I think, entirely compatible with Gould's explorations of polyhedral dynamics, and its urgency is both confirmed and complicated by the relations between the compositional and the contextual which are charted in these richly-textured, multi-dimensional spaces.[120] But Gould grounds these procedures in Heidegger's phenomenology,[121] whereas I prefer the protocols entailed by theoretical realism, which presumably Heidegger would repudiate: and in particular the specification of 'causal powers' (which roughly corresponds to the compositional) and of their 'fields of effectivity' (which roughly corresponds to the contextual).
2. It must depend, therefore, upon a concept of what Bhaskar terms 'ontological depth', which simply means that the world is conceived as a *multidimensional structure* and not 'squashed into a flat surface', pock-marked only by the space–time incidence of

events.[122] To claim that reality is 'stratified' is not to make any specific commitments about the nature of its social ontology, however, (although Bhaskar seems to think otherwise) and in differentiating between experiences, events, systems of social practices and structures of social relations Figure 13.6 offers no more than a highly schematic approximation which requires a much more nuanced set of discriminations.[123] Even so, it should be clear that explication, in the literal sense of 'unfolding', then consists of drawing out the chains of *causal articulation* which give this multidimensional structure its shape and substance – its 'anatomy' – and revealing the contingent and necessary relations which exist within and between its constituent domains.

3. At the same time, it must delineate the 'fields of effectivity' of each of these domains, which have distinctive geometries and temporalities within which their differential 'causal powers' are inscribed.[124] This does not turn on convening separate distance-decay curves (say, interaction, communication and adoption) within some plenary mathematical transformation,[125] because such a procedure depends upon a mathematical *function* which, as Gould is at pains to point out, 'crushes', 'distorts' and 'destroys' the very *relations* which constitute these complex fields.[126] This is therefore not a morphological question at all and instead requires the careful circumscription of what we might think of as *process-domains*. Because distance is then no longer used as a surrogate for unspecified conjunctures of causal processes, concepts of spatial structure and 'contextuality' cannot be severed from the social and reduced to abstract logics of space and time.

4. It follows that it must draw on *substantive theories of structuration* for its explications of contingency and necessity and not on purely formal characterisations of statistical series. These are not ready-made templates, of course, and to claim otherwise is to misunderstand the relations between the abstract and the concrete. In particular, the project of 'a general theory of landscape evolution' in which diffusion is supposed to have a primary role as 'one of the few primitive processes of concern to spatial analysis' is untenable:[127] the modalities of historical eventuation and structural transformation cannot be conveyed through such a singular formalism. This is also, in part, one of the weaknesses of existing formulations within the 'emerging consensus in social theory' and theories of structuration clearly need to specify the dimensionality of their own concepts. This does not mean using the 'material logic' of

time-geography to bind the abstract to the concrete, however; it means understanding the *hierarchy* of concepts involved in empirical work and moving patiently between the levels.[128] These requirements are clearly not confined to the recasting of Hägerstrand's problematic, and although I have used his writings as a series of pegs on which to hang my argument I believe that they are also minimal criteria for *any* social theory which seeks to inform the critical analysis of social relations and spatial structures.

Acknowledgements

I am deeply grateful to Peter Gould and John Langton for their exceptionally detailed comments on an early version of this essay, and to Ron Johnston, Allan Pred, Nigel Thrift, John Urry and Alan Wilson for their helpful responses. I owe a particular debt to Torsten Hägerstrand for his generous correction of a number of misconceptions on my part, and for allowing me to quote freely from our correspondence and his writings.

Notes

1. Giddens (1981b) pp. 196 and 30.
2. Pred (1977) p. 208; Urry (1981a).
3. See, for example, Harvey (1982); Massey (1984); Storper and Walker (1983); Walker and Storper (1981).
4. See, for example, Clark and Dear (1984); Scott (1980); Soja, this volume.
5. Giddens (1981b).
6. I am not alone in such a view: see Soja (1983); Urry (1982d). This 'marginalisation' arises, at least in part, through Giddens's debts to Heidegger and Marx: although both these authors commented on spatial questions – on notions of 'reach', for example, or 'combined and uneven development' – they remained peripheral to their primary focus on temporality. I discuss this in more detail in Gregory (forthcoming a).
7. Sack (1974); I say 'usually' because in their original formulations of location theory von Thünen, Weber and the members of the Chicago School were evidently far from indifferent to social theory.
8. See Wright (1983).
9. This is not intended as a dismissal of philosophy, and those who respond to its meta-theoretical discussions by jeering at the 'self-evidence' of its findings have to explain (i) their own grounds for believing what they do, and (ii) the difficulties which occur in translat-

ing these precepts into practice. An appeal to the 'intuitively obvious' will not help them then.

10. For a review, see Hudson (1972).
11. Cf. Duncan (1980).
12. Hägerstrand (1953); translation (1967); note also the preliminary sketch in Hägerstrand (1952). Hägerstrand's comments on the English title are contained in a letter, Hägerstrand to Gregory, February 1984. On the spread of Hägerstrand's ideas through Anglo-American geography, see Duncan (1974).
13. Hägerstrand (1967) p. 5; the map sequence is derived from pp. 58–62. These state subsidies for grazing improvements were introduced in January 1928 and followed a series of 'premature' and unsuccessful measures. They were only available to farmers whose holdings included less than 10 uncultivated hectares, irrespective of whether they were owner-occupiers or tenant-farmers, and the scheme was administered by the central Rural Economy Association (pp. 46–9). Hägerstrand considered that 'the grazing-improvement subsidy probably most closely approximates the ideal indicator – one whose diffusion takes place under constant conditions' (p. 70).
14. Hägerstrand (1967) pp. 163–4; the map is taken from p. 223 and is based on telephone calls between exchange areas: the derivation of the T-values is described in detail on pp. 221–2.
15. Hägerstrand (1966) p. 27.
16. For an extended commentary on the Hägerstrand model, see Amedeo and Golledge, 1975, pp. 227–56; the 'mean information field' is discussed in Morrill and Pitts (1967) and developed further – again through a Swedish case-study – in Wolpert (1966). For reviews of Hägerstrand's contributions to spatial modelling, see Haggett, Cliff and Frey (1977) pp. 232–47.
17. Hägerstrand (1967) pp. 11, 14 and 135.
18. Hägerstrand (1967) pp. 132 and 2. Cf. Hägerstrand (1983) p. 247, in which he recalls the resonance of Lundberg's claim that 'the ends of science are the same in all fields, namely, to arrive at verifiable generalisations as to the sequences of events.' At that time, Hägerstrand continues, geographers rarely spoke of 'sequences of events', and 'this new song sounded lovely in my ears.'
19. Hägerstrand (1967) pp. 133–4; see also Brown and Cox (1971).
20. Hägerstrand (1967) p. 6. Whether or not spatial autocorrelation was present in Hägerstrand's original maps is irrelevant to what is here a theoretical rather than a substantive claim; but for sophisticated statistical analyses of these maps, see Cliff (1968) and Haining (1983).
21. This is the basis of Hägerstrand's Monte Carlo simulations: see Hägerstrand (1965, 1967).
22. Lévi-Strauss (1969) p. 21.
23. Carlstein (1978) p. 146.
24. Cliff, Haggett and Versey (1981) p. 35.
25. Boudon (1981) pp. 86–90: Boudon uses this discussion of the Hägerstrand model as an exemplar of the analysis of 'reproductive processes'.
26. Cf. Sack (1972).

27. Hägerstrand (1974a) p. 3.
28. Giddens (1981b).
29. An area which he describes as 'my Montaillou' in his autobiographical essay: Hägerstrand (1982) p. 331; see also Hägerstrand (1983).
30. Hägerstrand (1983) p. 245.
31. Hägerstrand to Gregory, February 1984.
32. Hägerstrand (1967) pp. 8 and 166–7.
33. Hägerstrand (1957); Hägerstrand (1969).
34. Hägerstrand (1970) pp. 10, 11 and 21; Hägerstrand (1973) pp. 70 and 80; Hägerstrand (1978) pp. 129 and 144.
35. Hägerstrand (1970) p. 19; Jensen-Butler (1981) p. 47.
36. Carlstein (1982) pp. 55–60.
37. Lévi-Strauss's structuralism was not, of course, free from naturalism either.
38. Popper (1972) p. 265.
39. Hägerstrand's role in the development of behavioural geography is discussed in Golledge, Brown and Williamson (1972).
40. J. Moreno, cited in Hägerstrand (1967) p. 166; later, Hägerstrand recalled how he readily envisioned 'a projection of [Moreno's] concepts onto the population map and converted it in my mind into a huge structure of social atoms extending over regions, nations and continents': Hägerstrand (1983) p. 248.
41. Hägerstrand (1967) p. 167; Hägerstrand (1983) p. 248; Gould (1974). See also Gaspar and Gould (1981) p. 203: 'The basis is essentially a physical analogy, deriving from the work of von Neumann and Ulam on Monte Carlo simulations of particle absorption in heterogeneous shields around nuclear piles'.
42. Jensen-Butler (1981) p. 45.
43. Hägerstrand (1973) pp. 75 and 77; cf. Hägerstrand (1983) p. 241: 'I feel akin to chemists who built three-dimensional portraits of molecules with balls and pins'.
44. Harvey (1969) p. 226; Rose (1977) p. 45. Although Carlstein insists that 'time-geography is by no means inspired by relativity theory in physics and the four-dimensional space–time continuum', Hägerstrand himself concedes that 'it may well be that ideas derived from relativity theory and quantum theory are applicable also to everyday events at the human meso-scale', but prefers to leave this 'to others to think about': see Carlstein (1978a) p. 3fn; Hägerstrand (1975) p. 6.
45. Hägerstrand to Gregory, February 1984; Hägerstrand (1970) p. 20.
46. Hägerstrand (1974); Carlstein (1978).
47. Hägerstrand (1967) p. 7.
48. Hägerstrand (1973) p. 82. Central place theory seems to have had a powerful influence on Hägerstrand. He describes Christaller's work as a 'revelation' because through it 'comprehensible patterns became visible' in ways which prefigured the emergence of 'an ordering backbone' for the complexities of 'regional geography': Hägerstrand (1974a) p. 52. Note too that the construction of Christaller's hexagonal mesh also involved the use of telephone data, although this referred to installations rather than contacts: cf. Christaller (1966) pp. 143–7; Hägerstrand (1967) pp. 190–235.

49. For the statistical basis, see Mollison (1977); a convenient summary is Cliff (1979).
50. Hägerstrand (1973) p. 70.
51. Gould (1981) pp. 1–3; cf. Hägerstrand (1976) pp. 332–3.
52. Williams, R. (1973).
53. Hägerstrand (1973) p. 82.
54. Parkes and Thrift (1980) p. 276.
55. Hägerstrand (1978) p. 124.
56. Hägerstrand (1970) pp. 10 and 19.
57. Carlstein (1982) p. 44.
58. Hägerstrand (1973) pp. 80–1.
59. Hägerstrand (1970) p. 18.
60. Carlstein (1978a); cf. Carlstein (1982) p. 44.
61. Harvey, this volume.
62. For an account of the categorical paradigm, see Albrow (1974). Its hallmark is the representation of change as a combinatorial game – what Lévi-Strauss once described as 'an endless play of combination and recombination' of 'the same fundamental elements' – and Häger-strand clearly endorses this view through his own claim that 'the goal of science' is 'to find the terms by which we can see change as a constant permutation of a restricted number of invariants': see Gregory (1978b) p. 97; Hägerstrand (1974a) p. 52.
63. Hägerstrand (1970) p. 10.
64. Giddens (1981b) p. 17.
65. Gregory (1982a) p. 194.
66. Hägerstrand (1973) p. 85; Hägerstrand (1978).
67. Foucault (1980) p. 149. See also his 'Questions on Geography' *passim*, pp. 63–77, in which 'domain' is presented as a 'juridico-political notion', whereas Hägerstrand argues that 'the terrestrial domain can be seen as a human elaboration of the animal territory': Hägerstrand (1978) p. 143. There are, I think, definite continuities between Häger-strand's proposals and Ratzel's much earlier discussion of the concept of *Lebensraum*: see Gregory (forthcoming b).
68. Mayfield and Yapa, cited in Blaikie (1978) p. 275.
69. Blaut (1977) p. 344.
70. Blaut (1977) p. 344; Blaut (1980) p. 28.
71. Cox (1981a) p. 262; Boudon (1981) p. 86 also emphasises Hägerstrand's methodological individualism.
72. Blaut (1980) p. 28. In an essay entitled 'From the Chicago School to the Frankfurt School' Gouldner sketches out a series of connective themes which seem to have escaped the notice of modern human geography: see Gouldner (1976) pp. 118–37.
73. These three emphases are, of course, Giddens's characterisations of the structural dimensions 'that are combined in differing ways in social practices', Giddens (1979) pp. 81–2.
74. Braudel (1972) pp. 355–74; see especially Figures 28–30.
75. Giddens (1981b) pp. 169–81.
76. Blaikie (1978) p. 283.
77. Blaut (1977) pp. 347–8.
78. Yapa (1977) p. 359.

79. Yapa (1977) p. 351. On the relations between 'an ontology of structures' and 'an ontology of events' – and of the 'integrity' of these domains as 'differentiated features of social reality' – see Layder (1981).
80. Hägerstrand (1974) pp. 11 and 3.
81. Blaikie (1978) p. 274.
82. Hägerstrand (1967) p. 11.
83. Hägerstrand (1975) pp. 10–11; Hägerstrand (1973) p. 86.
84. Hägerstrand (1970) p. 11.
85. Hägerstrand (1975) p. 5; van Paassen (1976).
86. Hägerstrand, cited in Carlstein (1982) p. 56.
87. Hägerstrand (1976) p. 332; but Layder's discussion of 'interaction structures' speaks directly to Hägerstrand's concerns: see Layder (1981); Thrift (1983).
88. Hägerstrand (1974a) p. 53.
89. Carlstein (1978) p. 149.
90. Harvey (1973) pp. 22–49; Giddens (1979); Giddens (1981b). The relations between time-geography and the theory of structuration are complex. On the one side, Pred and Carlstein are clearly sympathetic to Giddens's project, but insist that this 'emerging consensus in social theory' has, for the most part, failed to identify the 'cement' which 'binds' space and time into the production and reproduction of social life (Pred, 1981a, p. 9), and that 'what has been done in time-geography so far is absolutely central to any structuration theory of the kind proposed by Giddens' precisely because it enables us 'to see its material logic' (Carlstein, 1981, p. 48). On the other side, Giddens is plainly drawn to the web model, whose 'general importance is that it emphasises the co-ordination of movement in time and space in social activity, as the coupling of paths or trajectories'; but he also claims that 'the interest of this conception of social activity' does *not* depend upon 'Hägerstrand's particular formulation of it, to which various objections can be made' (Giddens, 1979, p. 205). Although Giddens does not state these objections, I take them to be essentially theoretical: the relevance of these writings to his own project has much to do with Goffman's (1959) accounts of 'the presentation of self in everyday life', which draw attention to the *knowledgeability* of social actors in ways which, as I show below, Hägerstrand's formulations do not. The comparison which van Paassen makes between Hägerstrand's theses and Elias's 'figurations' is more instructive in this regard than he intends: van Paassen (1976) pp. 338–9; Elias (1978a). (Since completing this essay, I have read Giddens's contribution to the present volume, which seems to confirm the interpretation I offer here.)
91. Thrift (1983) p. 39fn. I have a number of reservations about this proposal. First, even if these 'links' can be given substantive meaning – which I doubt – they are clearly not confined to the labour process, and their identification requires an inclusive theorisation of the 'anatomy' of society. Second, I regard the connection between the compositional and the contextual as a *methodological* one, which is bound in to the relation between what I describe below as 'causal powers' and their 'fields of effectivity'.

92. Harvey (1982) p. 106; see also Massey (1984).
93. Giddens (1981b) p. 8; Wright (1983) p. 11.
94. Hägerstrand (1974) p. 10.
95. See Cutler, Hindess, Hirst and Husain (1977) p. 252.
96. These discussions centre on the causal relations between Kondratieff waves within contemporary capitalism and technical innovations within the space-economy. The theoretical filiations of these debates are remarkably heterogeneous, but for a review see van Duijn (1983).
97. Hägerstrand (1967).
98. Hägerstrand (1973) pp. 78–9.
99. Hägerstrand (1973) p. 86; on 'dominant projects', see also Pred (1981a; 1981c).
100. Hägerstrand (1982) p. 337.
101. Giddens (1979) p. 139; Giddens (1981) p. 231; Carlstein (1982); Gregory (1982a) p. 196.
102. Giddens (1979; 1981a).
103. Hägerstrand (1974a) pp. 53–4. See also Buttimer (1974); for her views on time-geography, see Buttimer (1976). Hägerstrand has since recorded that 'Anne Buttimer frankly told me that the world I depicted reminded her of a *danse macabre*': Hägerstrand (1983) p. 254.
104. Hägerstrand (1982) pp. 323–4; Buttimer (1974) p. 61.
105. Giddens (1976) p. 156.
106. Hägerstrand (1982) p. 323.
107. Poster (1979) p. 67.
108. Sartre (1976) p. 285.
109. Eyles (1981) pp. 1383–4; cf. Aronson (1980) pp. 259ff.
110. Sartre (1976) p. 123.
111. Poster (1979) p. 96.
112. Perhaps the most important is this: 'The transformation of societies is obscured from view as the Sartrean lens is focused on the microscopic world' (Poster, 1979, p. 102). Giddens (1981b) p. 196, claims that 'the development of societies' can *also* be conceived 'as a series of "time–space paths" conjoining at intersections that can be represented topographically', but he remains equivocal about Hägerstrand's 'particular techniques of representation' when 'adapted to such a purpose'. But there are very real difficulties in any such extensions; Giddens speaks of these 'time–space edges' as 'intersections between different planes of societal organisation' and as axes of 'social transformation' (p. 83) – from which it is but a small step to conventional notions of autonomy and dependency (p. 201).
113. The most striking is that 'the question of ecology' is 'completely suppressed' in Sartre's writings (Poster, 1979, p. 75).
114. Hägerstrand (1982) pp. 324–5. 'Alterity' is defined as 'a relation of separation, as opposed to reciprocity' (Sartre, 1976, p. 827).
115. Pred (1981c) p. 5fn; Pred (1981a) p. 31.
116. Poster (1979) p. 74.
117. Hägerstrand (1974a) p. 54.
118. Bhaskar (1978) p. 54; see also Bhaskar (1979). Agnew has argued that recent criticisms of diffusion theory entail a movement from instrumen-

talism (which stands in the closest association to empiricism) to realism, but his programmatic review says little about the wider and deeper implications of such a transition for human geography or social theory: Agnew (1979). But see S. Williams (1981).
119. Sayer (1981) pp. 69–72.
120. Gould (1982); Gaspar and Gould (1981).
121. See in particular Gould (1981) in which he acknowledges his debt to the philosopher Joseph Kockelmans and his writings on Heidegger.
122. Bhaskar (1978) p. 44.
123. See Keat and Urry (1982) pp. 242–3.
124. Cf. Harré and Madden (1975) pp. 164–84. This should *not* be confused with the 'field theory' formulations of spatial structure in Berry (1968).
125. See Olsson (1980) pp. 191b–3b; Taylor (1971).
126. Gould (1982) pp. 80–1; later in the same essay Gould notes that such a view 'throws a devastating light on the estimation of a Mean Information Field in conventional diffusion theory' because 'multidimensional complexity, and extreme variation in local structure, are simply crushed out and obliterated by the functional approach' (p. 93). An exemplification is provided in Gaspar and Gould (1981) where 'the functional language, borrowed from atomic physics, not only is incapable of expressing the reality of the situation, but distorts, to the point of masquerade, the actual unfolding of innovation adoption' (p. 204).
127. Gaile (1979).
128. Pred (1981c) p. 9; Carlstein (1981) p. 48: see note 88 in this set of notes. On the 'hierarchy of concepts', see S. Williams (1981); Keat and Urry (1982) Postscript.

14
The Social Becomes the Spatial, the Spatial Becomes the Social: Enclosures, Social Change and the Becoming of Places in Skåne

ALLAN PRED

Places and regions, however arbitrarily delimited, are the essence of traditional human geographic inquiry. Until recently, they have usually been conceptualised and treated in ways that selectively emphasise certain measurable or visible attributes of a circumscribed area during one or more arbitrary periods of observation. Thus, whether presented as elements within a spatial distribution, as unique assemblages of physical facts and human artefacts, as units interacting with one another in a system, or as localised spatial forms, places and regions have been portrayed as little more than frozen scenes for human activity. Even the 'new humanistic' geographers who see place as an object for a subject, as a centre of individually-felt values and meanings, or as a locality of emotional attachment and felt significance, in essence conceive of place as an inert, experienced scene. [1]

This chapter adopts a different position. The assemblage of buildings, land-use patterns, and arteries of communication that constitute place as what is scene cannot emerge fully-formed out of nothing and stop, grow rigid, indelibly etched in the once natural landscape. Place always represents a human product; it always involves an appropriation and transformation of space and nature that is inseparable from the reproduction and transformation of society in time and space. [2] As such, place is characterised by the uninterrupted flux of human practice – and experience thereof – in time and space. It is not only what is fleetingly scene as place, a 'locale' or setting for activity and social interaction. [3] It is also what takes place ceaselessly, what contributes to history in a specific context through the creation and utilisation of what is scene as place.

Using this conceptualisation of place (and region) as a point of departure, I have presented elsewhere a theory of place as a historically contingent process that emphasises institutional and individual practices as well as the structural features with which those practices are interwoven in usually unacknowledged ways.[4] The theory in question rests on an integration of the theory of structuration as developed by Giddens, Bourdieu, Bhaskar and others,[5] and the discipline-transcending language of time-geography.[6] It also indirectly owes much to the Vidalian tradition of *la géographie humaine*, with its emphasis on local practical life and its conceptualisation of *genre de vie* as a creative adaption to natural environment based upon the *civilisation* (or traditional attitudes, values, ideas, beliefs and psychology) of an area's decision-making and action-taking population.[7]

Since place is conceptualised partly in terms of the unbroken flow of what takes place locally, the proposed theory attempts to take into account both the material continuity of the people who participate in that process and the material continuity of any natural and social objects employed in time–space specific practices. Thus, the participating individuals, without whom there is no place as process, are not treated in the reified, fragmented, and atomised manner characteristic of conventional human geography and social science – regarded in one instance solely as producers, in another solely as residents, in another solely as consumers, and so on. Instead, process-participants are regarded as integrated human beings who are at once objects and subjects and whose thoughts, actions, experiences, and ascriptions of meaning are constantly *becoming*, through their involvement in the workings of society and its structural components as they express themselves in the becoming of places. I have discussed the details of this scheme elsewhere, and in what follows I therefore provide only a summary account of its leading theorems. I shall then work with them to interpret certain elements of the becoming of places in the Swedish province of Skåne under historically specific circumstances.

Place as a historically contingent process: a propositional summary

1. *Structuration*, or the process whereby practice and the structural properties of any social system dialectically reproduce and transform one another, *is materially continuous. The detailed situations and material continuity of the structuration process*, whereby social

reproduction and individual socialisation also uninterruptedly become one another, *are perpetually spelled out by the intersection of particular individual paths with particular institutional projects occurring at specific temporal and spatial locations.*

2. *The historically contingent becoming of any place,* all that is scene as place and all that takes place within a given area, *is inseparable from the materially-continuous unfolding of the structuration process in that place* (and any other places with which it is economically, politically, or otherwise interdependent).

3. As a place becomes under any given set of historical circumstances, power relations are at the heart of its social structure. No matter how they are conceptualised, power relations are usually institutionally embedded and always involve one or more acting individuals, groups, or classes together with actually-performed or potentially-executable behaviours.[8] Hence, at all levels, power relationships ultimately cannot be separated from the realm of action and everyday practices, from the direct or indirect control of who does what, when and where. Put otherwise, as a social relation power may be conceptualised not only as the capacity to define, require, permit, govern or somehow control the time–space specific *path* couplings of others for the purpose of bringing off some particular project, but also as the capacity to forbid, inhibit or restrict such path couplings. But, *the very nature of the structuration process as it unfolds in place is such that the power relations underlying routine and non-routine local practices are themselves established, reproduced and transformed by routine and non-routine practices.* Power-relation establishment and reproduction is in some measure equatable with:

a the establishment and repeated implementation of project definitions and explicit or unstated rules pertaining to project execution and admission;

b the accumulation of material or other resources either by the concerned institutional unit as a whole, or by its present or past power wielders;

c a predisposition – except where force is employed – on the part of power subjects to accept (willingly or grudgingly) the project definitions and rules confronting them.

Each of these preconditions is inseparable from previous path-project intersections since it is only through such time–space specific practices that:

    a the practical knowledge, situation-specific information, or ideology necessary to project definition and rule formulation can be obtained by power holders;

    b the competition or socialisation necessary to resource accrual can transpire;

    c the socialisation and personality development underpinning particular predispositions can occur.

By the same token, the transformation of power relations is rooted either in some form of conflict or consensus, and thereby in specific practical events or social interactions, or in contradiction (structural disjuncture) that is synonymous with the counter-final outcomes of specific practices.

4. By directly or indirectly limiting and enabling what people can do, power relations also directly or indirectly limit and enable what people know (and are able to say) and how they perceive and think. This means, in part, that *the constitution, reproduction and transformation of language and other sign codes is not only a prerequisite and consequence of institutional projects, but also a concomitant of the process whereby power relations become practices and practices become power relations.*

5. *The precise way in which the establishment, reproduction, and transformation of power relations is interwoven with the becoming of place depends upon the extent to which local institutions and their symbol systems are based upon non-local control and transactions.* In other words, the becoming of places is greatly affected by the degree of fusion between local face-to-face social interaction and the integration occurring within and between the institutions of a social system.[9]

6. Individual biography formation – including language acquisition, personality development, the evolution of a not-always articulated or self-understood ideology, and the development of consciousness – is one with the becoming of place. *Biographies are formed through the becoming of places, and places become through the formation of biographies.* Moreover, *in tracing out his or her unbroken path through time–space, in progressing from one institutional or 'independently' defined project to another, a connectedness is imparted to the formation of a person's biography through a complex 'external–internal' dialectic and a 'life-path – daily-path' dialectic.* (The 'external–internal' dialectic is meant to suggest the way in which a person's corporeal actions and mental

activities dialectically interplay with one another as (s)he intentionally and unintentionally contributes to social reproduction and the becoming of place[s]. The dialectic may be distilled down to three statements:

a External physical action, or project participation and any related travel, cannot occur without resulting in internal mental activity either as a consequence of a confrontation with specific personal contacts, elements of the environment, or information, or as the result of experiencing of specific emotions and feelings;

b Yet, the addition of external physical actions to an individual's path requires some internal activity – self-reflection, the recognition of scene-embedded codes, the performance of practical reasoning, the formation of intentions or unconscious goals, the imaginative creation of new project possibilities, or making choices between new or already existing project alternatives that do not violate basic time-geographic constraints;

c Such mental activity is itself intricately based on the experience and knowledge acquired by that individual through previous participation in time–space specific projects.

The 'life-path – daily-path' dialectic involves the interplay between long-term commitment and daily practice and is central to the local and wider reproduction of group, class and gender differences. Through the operation of this dialectic the long-term institutional roles among which a person may choose at any biographical point are, in essence, both walled-off and thrown open by the manner in which his or her previous institutional role commitments have affected, and been affected by, certain of his or her specific daily paths.)

7. *In any becoming place certain institutional projects are dominant in terms of the demands they make upon the limited time resources of the resident population and the influence they therefore exert upon what can be done and known.* Dominant institutional projects, by definition, account for the most significant path-project intersections occurring as part of the structuration process in place. As part of that process, they are at once the source and the outcome of the most important power relations within a place. Because of their time-allocation and scheduling priorities, dominant institutional projects periodically or persistently structure daily paths by influencing the sequence and pace of the other ins-

titutional and 'independently' defined projects which a person actually undertakes, and by time-geographically constraining participation in yet other projects.[10]

8. Dominant institutional projects are usually identical with the operation of a locally significant mode of production. Whether or not they are dominant, all the institutional production and distribution projects of a place or region involve a *spatial* division of labour, since they are not undertaken ubiquitously, and a *social* division of labour, since some people participate in different ways while others do not participate at all. *In the becoming of place neither the spatial nor the social division of labour can exist or emerge independently of one another.* In other words, the production and distribution projects contributing to the becoming of a place reflect a spatial and social division of labour that, in a variety of historically specific ways, is itself a consequence of the time–space flow of the structuration process.

9. Despite the tremendous associative and creative capabilities of the human brain, there are only a limited number of production and distribution activities and other cultural and social forms found in any becoming place. *The total array of locally-occurring institutional and 'independently' defined projects is inevitably constrained – but also enabled – in usually unseen ways by the ongoing dialectic between those practices and micro- and macro-level structural properties.* It is largely through the reproduction and transformation of language, knowledge, 'unknowing',[11] and power relations that the mix of residual, prevalent, and emergent cultural and social forms expressed within a becoming place is both constrained and enabled by the structuration process. In addition, once time has been allocated for physiologically-necessary activities and dominant institutional projects, there are only a limited number of other types of social interaction and culturally arbitrary practices that can be individually or collectively accommodated and mastered by the residents of a place because of the finiteness of their daily and longer-term time resources.[12] Hence, one of two situations must emerge when the dialectics of practice and structure lead to the creation, redefinition, or elimination of a particular institutional project. Either there will be an increased demand on time-resources resulting in a modification or total pushing aside of other existing activities, or a release of time resources permitting the expansion or appearance of other institutionally or 'independently' defined projects.

10. *Outer nature, or the physical environment, is perpetually transformed as places become through the structuration process and its associated flow of intersections between individual paths and institutional projects.* The role of humans in intentionally and unintentionally changing the face of the earth through place-bound ideology, knowledge application, and action is not confined to production projects and the construction and land-use projects that create what is seen as place. The local (and non-local) transformation of outer nature also is indirectly abetted by any of the countless everyday projects that involve the use of either humanly-made or still-natural objects. Moreover, as local outer nature is transformed – as land-uses, buildings, and communication links appear upon the landscape – certain events and projects are at least temporarily inhibited or prohibited by the scarcity of space, or the limited packing capacity of areal units, and the time investments required for moving from one fixed (and transformed) site to another. Normally, new projects cannot be accommodated locally unless the 'synchronisation' and 'synchorisation' of their component tasks is possible within the existing framework of transformed nature, or the existing spatial structure,

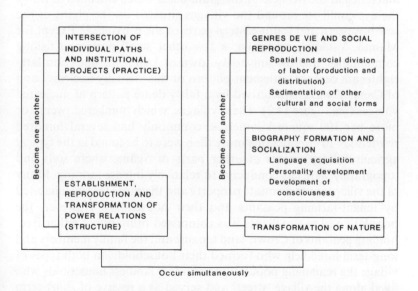

FIGURE 14.1 *Components of place (and region) as historically contingent process*

and the project demands already made by dominant institutions.[13] For this and the preceding reasons, 'the formation of spatial structure [is] a moment in social reproduction' (and the entire structuration process) just as 'social reproduction' (and the entire structuration process) is 'a moment in the formation of spatial structure'.[14]

Taken together (as in Figure 14.1) these overlapping positions mean that any place or region expresses a process whereby the reproduction of social and cultural forms, the formation of biographies, and the transformation of nature and space ceaselessly become one another at the same time that power relations and time–space specific path–project intersections continuously become one another in ways that are not subject to universal laws, but vary with historical circumstances.

Enclosures in Skåne: Background observations

While annotating his famed trip through Skåne in 1749, Linnaeus marvelled at the richness of the grain fields which extended as far as the eye could see around the villages situated on the plains of the south-western and south-eastern parts of the province.[15] Except for Malmö, Ystad, Landskrona, a few other small ports and fishing communities, and the university town of Lund, the mid- and late-eighteenth century settlement pattern of this virtually treeless 'Land of Canaan' was characterised by a fairly dense pattern of nucleated villages (see Figure 14.2). These villages, which numbered twenty or more per 100 square kilometres, commonly had several hundred residents,[16] or considerably more than were to be found in the typical agricultural settlements of other parts of Skåne, where soils and topography were less conducive to relatively intense farming. Many of the villages were on estate property and therefore largely inhabited by tenant-farming peasants and their households. However, the population of most villages was comprised primarily of either free-holding peasants or Crown-land tenants and the family members and long-term hired help who formed their households. In both types of village the remaining population included: landless households who lived along the village 'street' and served as a reserve of short-term agricultural labour; a blacksmith or two and a few other craftsmen; and crofters who had the use of small parcels of land but who lacked

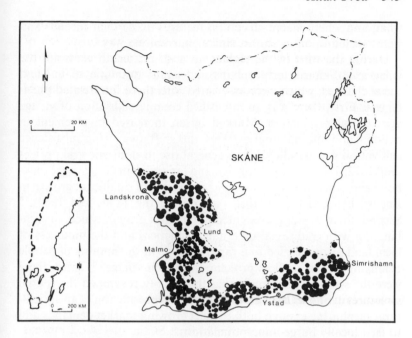

FIGURE 14.2 *Nucleated villages on the plains of Österlen and south-western Skåne. Trasition area borders determined by the extent of the three-field system prior to enclosures. After Campbell,* Skånska byg-der, *273; and Dahl,* Torna, *map facing 16. Cf. Gustav Ågren, 'Skånes jordbruksområden',* Sydsvenska Geografiska Sällskapet-Årsbok *(1926) 9.*

the right either to cultivate any of the numerous narrow strips in the village's three fields or to sit on the village council that co-ordinated and controlled major local agricultural projects.[17]

As a group these villages had much in common in terms of the agricultural, household, religious and festive projects through which socialisation occurred and social relations between groups and the sexes were reproduced. Certain common forms of agricultural co-operation among adjacent villages and of kinship links with nearby villages were also observable. In addition, there were case-to-case similarities with regard to the nature of economic contacts occurring between village residents and either urban businessmen or the rural inhabitants of the forested and more inland areas of Skåne.[18] However, each of the villages was a *distinctly becoming place* where the details of biography-formation and everyday life varied somewhat, and where macro-structural features made their inroads and were reacted upon in almost similar but unique ways.

During the turn of the eighteenth and nineteenth centuries the villages of Skåne's fertile plains underwent dramatic spatial and social changes, which were associated with three interrelated phenomena. First, there was an intensified commercialisation of village agricultural production. Marked by an increased involvement in national and international markets, this shift away from subsistence cultivation was paralleled by a general rise in domestic grain prices until 1812, a slowly mounting demand for grains in Göteborg, Stockholm and other Swedish cities, and a modest but significant growth in English demand for Swedish oats during the 1830s and 1840s.[19] Second, there was unprecedented population growth which, in combination with traditional inheritance practices and the finiteness of local land resources, led to a rapid upsurge in the number of people belonging to the landless proletariat of each village.[20] Third, there were the series of enclosures that thoroughly revamped the spatial structure of most villages and facilitated the production of an agricultural surplus big enough both to meet growing market demands and to feed locally burgeoning populations.

Legislated enclosures in Sweden took three different forms. The first of these was the so-called *storskifte* which was designed to overcome the obvious production inefficiencies which arose from each peasant household working many widely dispersed and quite narrow field strips. The *Storskifte Acts* of 1757 and 1762 specified that enclosures could be initiated at the request of a single village landholder and that under such circumstances the parcels of each peasant-farmer were to be consolidated into a maximum of four units of land. But the impact of *storskifte* enclosures upon the villages of Skåne's south-western plains was rather limited. Because every peasant was to have approximately the same quantity of land in each of the village's three fields – and because there were variations in soil quality, title rights and distance to the village centre – the surveyors responsible for reapportioning land seldom found solutions that left peasants with less than twelve to fifteen scattered strips. In fact, solutions where peasants were left with several times as many strips were not uncommon. Moreover, most villages on Skåne's south-eastern plains were never affected by the *storskifte* statutes.[21]

It was the next round of enclosures, referred to as *enskifte*, that most radically transformed the spatial structure of almost all the villages under discussion. Although no *enskifte* regulations were formally enacted for Skåne until 1803, a single large landlord, Rutger Maclean, innovated this type of enclosure in 1783 when he began replanning the four villages which comprised his estate on the south-western plains.[22] Maclean rearranged the holdings of individual peasants so that they no longer included from sixty to one hundred land parcels, but instead were confined to a single rectangular farm where fallowing was prohibited and a rotation of fodder roots, barley, and clover or vetches was mandatory. This replanning not only facilitated an increase in the number of peasant farmsteads, but it also required the construction of new buildings and roads *and was synonymous with the breaking-up of the settlement cluster at the core of each village.* While the drastic re-ordering which resulted from Maclean's exercise of power met with protest and resistance – half his tenants revoked their contracts – it eventually brought considerable economic success.[23] By the 1790s other estate owners in Skåne were inspired by this success to enclose the villages under their control. With the scattered incidents of peasant unrest that accompanied the bad harvests at the turn of the century, and with the French Revolution still echoing, some later imitators of Maclean were also motivated to break up the population concentrations of their estate villages in order to minimise the potential for future disturbances.[24]

According to the provisions of the 1803 *enskifte* decree, once a request for enclosure was forwarded to the county governor, a commissioned surveyor supervised by specially appointed civil witnesses was to work out as equitable as possible a reapportionment of property and of any previously uncultivated common lands. Although the configuration of new single-parcel farms resulting from *enskifte* varied from case to case, the general result was the same in the typical large village of the south-western and south-eastern plains. The village core was quickly thinned out, for only a few peasant homes persisted; many landless inhabitants remained but others had their small houses torn down and were completely displaced; and the great majority of landed peasant households now conducted most of their activities in relative isolation from one another (see Figure 14.3).[25]

At first there was widespread reluctance to undertake *enskifte*, particularly because of the village disintegration which it required. Although by 1812 individual resistance to this form of enclosures had not totally broken down, the number of peasants willing to initiate the often unpopular procedure was clearly increasing in the face of pronounced grain-price increases. (Between 1803 and 1812 the

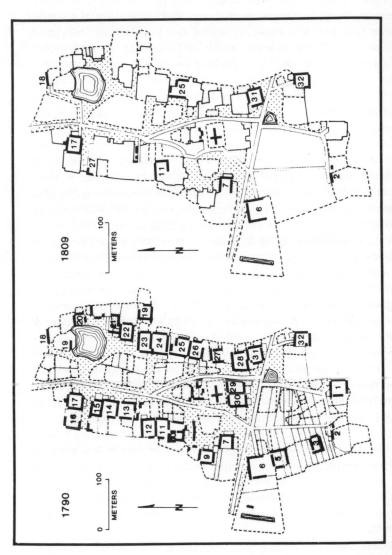

FIGURE 14.3 The core of the village of Hyllie, south of Malmö, before 1790 and after 1809 enskifte. Solid bars indicate buildings occupied and used by households, each of which is represented by a number. Note church and vicarage at centre. Modified from Nordholm, Skånes äldre

average market price for rye, barley and oats in Skåne more than doubled.)²⁶ With the help of state subsidies to cover the various costs involved, there were few villages remaining on the plains of Skåne that had not undergone *enskifte* by 1826.²⁷ Thus, the spatial organisation of that area was little affected by *lagaskifte*, or the final form of enclosures enacted the following year.²⁸

Informed questions

What were some of the basic components of the daily paths followed by landed-peasant household members during the decades immediately preceding *enskifte* enclosures on the plains of Skåne? What, in other words, were some of the general characteristics of the path-project intersections that were part of biography formation and the village-level unfolding of the structuration process? What were the power relations underlying daily paths? What characteristics of practice-based consciousness predisposed some landed peasants to initiate enclosure proceedings? How were daily paths and power relations altered as a consequence of *enskifte* enclosures? Or, to combine all these questions: how did the social become the spatial and the spatial become the social in the becoming villages of Österlen and south-western Skåne?

Most of these questions cannot be answered in a definitive manner, but there is a tremendous wealth of material available and what follows reflects but a small fraction of the available evidence and the reinterpretive arguments which can be developed from it.

Daily paths and agricultural projects of the landed-peasant household prior to *enskifte* enclosures

In the mid- and late-eighteenth century, the daily round of activities of peasant households was not normally confined to the landholder, his wife and any unmarried children who were not serving as hired help in another household. It typically also involved a teenage male farmhand, a somewhat older male farmhand and two young female servants.³⁰ While the activities incorporated into the daily paths of household members varied seasonally, throughout most of the year work-projects were interrupted frequently for eating, drinking alcohol and resting. During spring, summer and autumn, when the household was in motion from 3 or 4 a.m. until about 9 p.m., the day usually began with a sandwich and a shot of aqua vitae before all the males and some of the females left the house. Subsequent snacks and meals, each accompanied by a swig or two, occurred at 6 a.m., 7.30 a.m., 10 a.m., 12 noon to 1 p.m. (followed by a rest), 3 p.m., 5 p.m. and sometime during early evening.[31] When ploughing, sowing, harrowing, fertilising, harvesting or other field-centred dominant agricultural projects were undertaken, all but the last of these additional repasts were eaten at or near the work-site. Since most field-strips were highly elongated and at some distance from the homestead, it follows that a large amount of time was taken up by women and young boys bringing out food to the fields and, perhaps, by periodic down-field movement toward the village centre.

At one level, major agricultural projects required considerable daily path synchronisation and 'synchorisation' (or spatial co-ordination) among peasant household members as well as livestock and implements. Spring and autumn ploughing, for example, required the use of anything from three to seven pairs of horses and oxen, depending on soil characteristics and the crop to be planted. The large number of creatures needed to pull a plough in turn called for the presence of three or more adult males and any younger boys or girls in the household who might be available to help out or shout encouragement (Figure 14.4).[32] Fertilising projects, with their heavy labour inputs, constitute another good example. Manure was loaded and transported to various dispersed field-parcels and immediately spread out in late May or June, to be dug in some months later. In the south-east, at least, participation in the initial phases was not confined to household males and the draught animals and wagons necessary for transportation. The daily paths of female servants and daughters also had to be co-ordinated insofar as they were engaged in loading and spreading. (Because of the slowness of wagon movement over rudimentary roads and the volume of household time-resources diverted from other projects, fertilising activities decreased in intensity with increased distance from the village centre.)[33] Harvesting projects represented the extreme case of daily-path synchronisation and synchorisation, normally involving all a household's men and women (who were responsible for most of the raking, binding, and stacking) as well as draught animals, wagons and various hand-held implements.[34]

Seen in isolation, the household execution and co-ordination of ploughing, fertilising and harvesting projects, and attendant eating

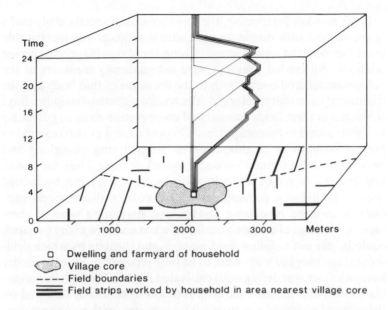

Time

24

20

16

12

8

4

0

0   1000   2000   3000   Meters

☐   Dwelling and farmyard of household
〰   Village core
– – – –   Field boundaries
▤   Field strips worked by household in area nearest village core

FIGURE 14.4 *Pre-enskifte daily paths of a hypothetical landed-peasant household during spring ploughing season. Field patterns and strip holdings generalised and simplified from maps contained in Nordholm,* Skånes äldre ekonomiska geografi II. *Food preparation, sheep-milking, poultry and swine-feeding, garden-patch tending, and other dwelling and farmyard projects involving women are not specified because of scale.*

and drinking activities, was inseparable from the reproduction of certain household power relations. Except where death had deprived the peasant household of its male head, patriarchal conditions reigned. The assignment of project roles and work details among the sexes, equally-treated children and servants, and any temporary help, was usually the province of the 'father' of the house. Likewise, unless authority had been delegated to the senior male hand, the male peasant more or less casually oversaw major agricultural projects, influencing the tempo and intensity of labour and the duration of rests and eating- or drinking-breaks.[35] However, although the male landed peasant of south-eastern and south-western Skåne were renowned for loafing about the house and being waited upon during winter months, the amount of direct power they exercised over domestic and farmyard projects was apparently limited.[36]

From another perspective, the spinning-out of specific daily paths in connection with dominant agricultural projects was inextricably bound up with the reproduction of long-standing village-wide power relations. All landed peasants were automatically members of the village council and bound both to the decisions of that body and the traditional rules that it enforced. The spatial pattern of strip-holdings splintered in three fields necessitated co-operation so as to guarantee everyone access to his own parcels. Co-operation was also required to prevent damage to neighbouring holdings during ploughing and harvesting and in connection with livestock grazing. Thus, the timing and content of major agricultural projects carried out by landed peasant households presupposed village council decisions on such matters as when ploughing, sowing and harvesting were to commence; the usage of common outfields; when and how many livestock could be put out to fallow-field pasture; and the date by which field-separating fences or walls were to be fully repaired in order to hinder livestock from wandering onto cultivated land.[37] Through its actions the council also dictated the crop rotation to be jointly followed on the strips of each field – normally fallow, barley (with some peas) and rye (or oats on heavy, less well-drained and more distant soils).[38] In addition, there were numerous project specifics prescribed by the *byordning*, or rules particular to each village, that had been passed on orally for centuries and eventually recorded as prescribed by a Royal Decree of 1742. Village rules normally addressed the details of fence, wall, gate and path maintenance. They were also usually precise as to grazing rights, shifting care of the village bull, and the fines to be meted out for damaging someone else's parcels of land. Outside the strictly agricultural realm, village rules covered project-related issues such as the role of the council leader or alderman, and its rotation each year; fire-safety measures and annual chimney check-ups; snow removal; and the care of indigent or incapacitated individuals and itinerant beggars.[39]

(The members of the village council affected the routine and non-routine daily paths not only of landed-peasant households. They also exercised a direct and indirect influence on the daily paths of other local residents, for example, by setting major agricultural project dates and thereby determining when short-term work might be found, by governing utilisation of the commons, by specifying which groups might attend any of the festivities associated with council activities and by limiting council participation for the landed. In bringing such power relations to bear council members accentuated the hierarchical social stratification that was becoming pronounced in the villages of south-eastern and south-western Skåne in the late eighteenth century as the number of people without prospect of inheriting any land increased.)[40]

From yet another angle, some of the daily-path segments traced out by the members of landed peasant households reflected power relations existing between institutions of the state and village inhabitants. The influence of the state was not only indirect in the sense that certain projects had to be undertaken in order for freeholding peasants to pay taxes or for Crown-land tenants to pay rent. For example, during the 1730s and 1740s provincial and national authorities took measures to alter the attention given to field-walls and fences in the hope of counteracting the forest resource problems of Skåne. In many villages this resulted in new practices that were firmly settled by the latter part of the century. In addition, groups of landed peasants were held responsible for constructing and maintaining specific bridges or stretches of road for the Crown. Moreover, the practice of home-brewing aqua vitae was subject to a series of restrictive laws and the location and time of annual and semi-annual markets attended by villagers was regulated by the state. In these and other realms of behaviour, the route of control from Stockholm to the village was often via the Lutheran parish church where, each Sunday, the presiding clergyman read announcements, statutes, and orders from state authorities.[41]

Practice-based consciousness and individualism

Until relatively recently many Swedish scholars held that the *enskifte* enclosures brought about an abrupt and fundamental change in the consciousness and personality of landed peasants. Prior to *enskifte* the landed peasants were supposedly 'completely free of individualism', their freedom to undertake land-use or other changes fettered either negatively by *bytvång* – the socially-based compulsion to co-operate – or positively by a sense of community. After *enskifte* and village disintegration, individualism supposedly blossomed among landholding peasants, their personal initiative to innovate no longer hindered by neighbours. One simple fact, however, indicates that the historical border between the presence and absence of individualism was not that clearly cut.[42]

While *enskifte* was reportedly unpopular because of the costs involved, the strength of tradition, and the security of village life as it was, in 'the overwhelming number of cases' such enclosures were initiated in south-eastern and south-western Skåne by one or a few landed peasants rather than by unanimous village councils, landowning clergymen, or estate proprietors.[43] Unfortunately, the pre-existing individualism that could have led to *enskifte* requests cannot be documented by the written testimony of specific initiators. All the same, there are several indicators pointing to the existence of self-centredness among some landed peasants before 1803.

It is known that personal disputes concerning the transgression of pasturing and fencing rules, the casting or removal of rocks from one field parcel to another and other matters, were constantly brought before the village council for settlement and the assessment of fines (usually in the form of beer or aqua vitae for council members).[44] While some of these interpersonal conflicts were probably anchored in laziness or neglect, it appears reasonable to speculate that the complaining party was often motivated to bring charges by a feeling that the productivity of his own property was being negatively affected.

Hanssen has argued that with the growth of the landless proletariat residing in villages, landed peasants could take on a larger number of long-term and short-term hands during the final pre-*enskifte* decades. This, in turn, supposedly inclined some of these men to act more independently of other households in carrying out major agricultural projects. Also, some were supposedly led to become less concerned with village-level co-operation in general, and personally to take on heavy-labour tasks no longer.[45]

More important, by the end of the eighteenth century landed peasants were becoming ever more involved in a variety of cash-economy and market-related practices. Far and away the most significant of these was the sale of surplus grains to wholesalers in Malmö, Ystad, Simrishamn, or Landskrona. (The surplus remaining after home consumption and any payments in kind were personally delivered by the landed peasant to the urban merchant who, in the face of limited local demand, exported almost all his purchases to domestic and foreign markets.) Income was occasionally derived on a much smaller scale from the urban sale of live or slaughtered oxen, pigs, poultry, and lambs or sheep, as well as field-grown peas, eggs, and lamb's milk or cheese. Garden plots also provided the landed peasant with cabbage, carrots and other vegetables, as well as cumin, fennel, anise and other herbs, to be sold in modest quantities in the nearest city. The landed peasant made sizeable cash purchases of wood for construction, implement-making, and repair purposes either directly from more inland forested areas or from urban merchants. The purchase of wooden shoes and hops originated in the northern part of Skåne and fish from coastal communities was also common. Hardware, rope and tar were bought periodically in the city, where the most economically successful also secured copper vessels, hats, gloves, and other conspicuous items of consumption. In addition, many landed peasants were by now accustomed to paying cash for the right to dig peat outside the village, for pasturing oxen at locations further inland, for auction purposes, and for drinks consumed at roadside inns when travelling.[46]

In short, at the time of the 1803 *enskifte* decree there were numerous landed peasants in south-eastern and south-western Skåne who were somewhat more than marginally integrated into a market and money economy, and who were at least incipient agrarian capitalists subject to developments in the wider economic environment.[47] It is quite likely that as a result some of them were prone to individualism in the sense that they made economic calculations in terms of their own concerns, entered into single-interest relations, and were sensitive to differences in wealth between themselves and their neighbours.[48] If all this is valid, it is not surprising that, as their unique external–internal and life-path–daily-path dialectics unfolded, certain landed peasants were predisposed to react to grain-price increases and the prospect of greater income by initiating enclosure proceedings.

Daily paths and agricultural projects subsequent to *enskifte* enclosures

As the land redistribution and new house, fence, and road construction required by *enskifte* enclosures was completed in any village, the daily paths of landed peasant households and the population as a whole were quickly altered – now stamped by new and modified agricultural projects.

Many of the path changes were connected with the more intensive cultivation of land that became necessary and feasible with the implementation of *enskifte*. The moving and construction costs incurred as holdings were consolidated forced some landholders to sell off a portion of their new property units. In more exceptional instances new landed peasant households were also formed because family property could now be split between two or more brothers or sons, whereas the pre-existing narrow parcels did not lend themselves to further division. Those who were confronted with a smaller total area of land to work and who desired to live at least as well as previously had no choice but to cultivate more intensively.[49] Those whose holdings had either not diminished, or had expanded slightly because of the allocation of limited common lands, found it feasible to cultivate more intensively and enhance their incomes through taking on more long- and short-term hands from among the burgeoning landless class, who were now without pasturing rights and often displaced.[50] In addition all landed peasants, regardless of the size of their holdings, could cultivate more intensively through the substitution of labour time for travel time and the more flexible co-ordination of individual paths which was now possible. After all, movement between widely separated parcels of land was no longer necessary and the average house-to-field distance was noticeably reduced (Figure 14.5).[51]

The extent to which agricultural projects were transformed or modified in any landed-peasant household depended in some measure upon how quickly either the imitation of others, the need to offset costs, or the desire to exploit favourable grain prices led to an abandonment of the traditional three-year rotation, which always left one-third of one's land in fallow, and the commencement of a six-year rotation which left about one-sixth of one's land in fallow.[52] With the adoption of a six-year rotation, which was almost universal in south-eastern and south-western Skåne by 1820,[53] each landholding household had to integrate five crop-project sequences rather than two. This set of circumstances must have compounded the need for additional hands on at least a temporary basis; for example, at harvest time when itinerant labourers from the neighbouring province of Halland frequently were taken on.[54]

Especially during the first years after *enskifte*, many peasant households seeking to bring all their land under cultivation were also forced to employ extra hands in order to drain portions of their property that had previously been in common meadows, marshes or fields with poor drainage. Prior to *enskifte* the execution of such labour-intensive drainage projects had been inhibited by the spatial pattern of field strips. (Once a drainage ditch was dug, draught animals could often only get from one end to the other end of the same parcel of land by crossing a specially-built bridge or by tramping on someone else's property.)[55]

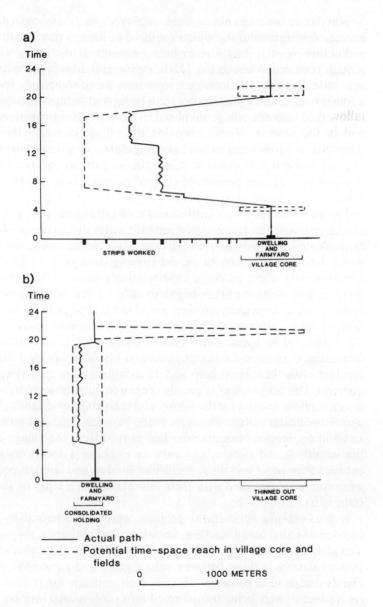

FIGURE 14.5 *The daily accessibility of a landed peasant to field and village-core projects (a) before and (b) after enskifte. Slow travel-time based on accompanying draught animals and poor roads or paths. Other project participants not indicated.*

Whether or not more hands were employed, the household's daily execution of agricultural projects required at least as much path co-ordination as ever. This was so because usage of the heavy wheel plough persisted as late as the 1850s, eating and drinking frequency was little changed, and livestock were now more commonly fed at home throughout the year, rather than being sent to the commons or fallow field with the village shepherd.[56] Under these circumstances, and in the absence of any need for the village council either to determine land-uses and project starting-dates, or to implement its grazing and parcel-protection rules, the importance of individual decision-making and household-centred power relations was magnified.

The increased project-definition and role-assignment power of the landed peasant within the realm of agricultural activities was gradually translated into new household interaction patterns and further social differentiation. Over a period varying from years to decades, and especially where holdings were relatively large, daily path-segments in and about the home began to reflect a new or strengthened sense of social superiority on the part of the landed peasant and his wife. In many instances she began to relinquish heavier tasks out in the fields and to spend more time around the house. It became increasingly common for the peasant and his family to stop eating together with their hired help and to establish their own sleeping quarters. The 'all-purpose' room also began to function less frequently as a meeting-ground for the family and their employed hands. As a corollary, clearer distinctions were made between child and servant. In addition, landed peasants who had moved from the village core presumably found it especially easy to establish a social distance between themselves and those small-plot holders and landless people who were not associated with their households on a long- or short-term basis.[57]

If post-*enskifte* agricultural projects were characterised by the exercise of individual discretion, initiative, and authority, they were also affected, at least indirectly, by the reproduction of another set of power-relations – those between urban grain and aqua-vitae merchants and landed peasants who, in their concern for profits and reinvestment, were being transformed into professional farmers. Insofar as self-determined operations enabled landed peasants to be newly or further enveloped in market-oriented production, and insofar as developing needs for prestige and self-esteem led them to include coffee, fine biscuits, pocket-watches, and other non-essential consumption items among their urban purchases,[58] their agricultural strategies were apt to become more influenced by the demands and conditions set by urban middlemen. In particular, since it was a common practice for grain wholesalers to extend credits and cash advances, the rural residents with whom they dealt were not likely either to neglect repayment schedules or completely ignore any inside market advice when choosing between the planting of rye, oats, and barley.[59] To the extent that he was himself influenced by price fluctuations and market circumstances in setting credit and cash-advance terms, the urban merchant functioned as an intermediary through whom new customs policies and other macro-structural changes filtered down to the everyday practices and consciousness of the landed peasant.

The spatial rearrangement of village settlements in Österlen and south-western Skåne further affected path-project intersections and biography-formation by leading to the elimination or dislocation of certain agricultural and non-agricultural projects. With common lands no longer in existence, village women could no longer co-operatively deliver geese to that location in the spring and co-operatively retrieve them in the fall. (Nor could some of the village's older women use those geese-tending days as an occasion for ritually checking the breasts of unmarried girls for milk in order to discover forbidden pregnancies.) Without common meadows communal hay harvests also disappeared along with the traditional festivities that occurred immediately afterwards.[60] Moreover, the spatial structure of the now dispersed village, coupled with the synchronisation and synchorisation demands of dominant agricultural projects, made it impossible or extremely difficult for children to participate in games on the village 'street', women from different households to card wool or work flax together, or adults of both sexes to exchange advice and engage in unplanned social interaction with their neighbours.[61]

The elimination or dislocation of these and other projects, together with the spatially-transformed village scene, must have greatly influenced the sense of place, structure of feeling and other elements of consciousness held by residents by breaking down the grammar of taken-for-granted codes. No longer did field-strip patterns communicate the relation of one village household to another. No longer did the sound of the alderman's horn signify that landholding males, *but not others*, were to assemble at the 'village stone' for a council meeting. No longer did unwed mothers have to wear special head-wear to indicate their 'shameful' position to others. And, sooner or later, locally prevailing folk clothing, with its status-communicating nuances, lost its significance and fell into disuse.[62] All of which is not to say that local social controls and all sense of community completely disappeared shortly after each village underwent *enskifte*. Church holidays and weddings continued to serve a cementing function for some time. The village council still occasionally convened, with meetings now held at the home of the current alderman after being called by a circulated message. And, for a few decades at least, numerous households would still co-operate in carrying out major construction and rebuilding projects and celebrate together upon completion.[63]

Variations in the becoming of place

Although all the villages of south-eastern and south-western Skåne shared a broadly similar physical environment and existed within the same wider context – interacting with the same state apparatus and in the same national and 'European world' economy – each of them became in a somewhat different way as macro-structural features made their local penetrations before, during and after *enskifte* enclosures. Despite the general similarity of events and consequences portrayed here, the finer grained details of everyday life and biography-formation in each village varied as the materially-continuous structuration process unfolded locally. In each place unique attributes were conferred upon local path-project intersections by practices and local power relations sedimented from the past. In each place agency and the 'external–internal' dialectic of specific individuals had its say. In each place the unavoidable distinctiveness of local becoming could be compounded either by opportunities resulting from micro-level variations in the physical environment, by narrowly circumscribed 'marriage fields', or by primitive road conditions that, as late as the 1840s, discouraged all but the most necessary travel between nearby villages.[64]

Aside from obvious differences in the exact timing of *enskifte* enclosures, variations in the becoming of individual villages were reflected, for example, by significant village-to-village dissimilarities in the mix of agricultural products sold to urban merchants, and by a diversity of locally predominant fence- and wall-construction practices.[65] Singularities in the local unfolding of structuration also were mirrored by sub-regional and place-specific differences in attire, hairstyle, diet and handicrafts, as well as by rhymes that caricatured the attributes of entire villages.[66] Perhaps most significantly, there were divergencies in the practice-based, practice-enabling, and thought-steering language employed by the inhabitants of different villages. 'Strictly speaking there [were] hardly two parishes [in Österlen] characterised by the same speech.' In fact, distinct dialects were known to be spoken by the residents of Borrby and Sandby, two neighbouring Österlen villages whose cores were separated by less than 3 kms. Also, subtle and pronounced differences existed among villages and sub-regions in the words used for vegetation, other landscape details, time designations, household articles, particular meals and dishes, fertilisers, and action-specific verbs.[67]

COD(E)A

First theme (*tout ensemble*)

The historically contingent becoming of any place, all that is scene as place and all that takes place within a given area, is inseparable from the materially-continuous unfolding of the structuration process in that place (and any other places with which it is economically, politically or otherwise interdependent). Or, any place is an ongoing process whereby the reproduction of social and cultural forms, the formation of biographies, and the transformation of nature and space become one another at the same time that time–space specific path-project intersections and power relations continuously become one another in ways that are not subject to universal laws, but vary with historical circumstances.

Second theme (*Swedish solo*)

The post-*enskifte* spatial configuration of villages in Österlen and south-western Skåne arose out of pre-*enskifte* practices and their underlying micro- and macro-level power relations. Spatial rearrangement – the replacement of scattered strips by consolidated holdings – led to new and modified daily paths and power relations.

Closing chords (*tout ensemble*)

SOCIAL
sSpOaCtIiAaLl
SsPoAcTiIaAlL
SPATIAL

Notes

1. For critical comments on the treatment of place and sense of place by the 'new humanistic' geographers, see Cosgrove (1978); Hudson (1979); Sayer, A. (1979a); Ley (1981); Pred (1983).
2. For other comments on places, regions and spatial organisation as a social product, see Soja (1980); Urry (1981c); Gregory (1981; 1982b).
3. Giddens (1979) pp. 106–7; Giddens (1981b) pp. 39, 45.
4. Pred (1984); see also Pred (1981c; 1981a; 1983).
5. There are a considerable number of authors who may be linked with the theory of structuration. The particular set of works influencing my own theoretical formulations are as follows: Berger and Luckmann (1967); Giddens (1976; 1979; 1981b); Kosík (1976); Bhaskar (1978a, 1979); Bourdieu (1977); Touraine (1977); Williams (1977); Shotter (1983). Note also the lucid introduction in Gregory (1982b).
6. A more detailed discussion of the language of time-geography will be found in Hägerstrand (1970; 1974); Pred (1973; 1978); Parkes and Thrift (1980); Carlstein (1982); Gregory, this volume.
7. For all its advantages, the Vidalian tradition is not without its limitations as a foundation for conceptualising places and regions in processual terms: see Gregory (1981); Pred (1984).
8. Although social theorists and philosophers define and interpret the elusive concept of power as a social relation in often disparate ways, the attributes specified here are normally explicitly or implicitly present.
9. Note related arguments about 'time–space distanciation' on the one hand and social integration and system integration on the other in Giddens (1981b).
10. Once a person makes a commitment to partake in *any* project at a given time and site it becomes impossible for them: (i) simultaneously to do something else somewhere else; (ii) to join any other spatially separate project which starts at another time but temporally overlaps with some portion of the project in question; or (iii) to join another project that presents no simultaneity conflicts but which is out of 'reach' because of travel-time requirements. Those unfamiliar with time–geography will find that these constraints are more readily understandable when depicted diagrammatically: see Lenntorp (1976); Mårtensson (1979).
11. Note comments on unknowing in Thrift (1983) and this volume.
12. Cf. Hägerstrand (1977); Carlstein (1982).
13. Cf. Hägerstrand (1974a).
14. Gregory (1982a) pp. 188–9.
15. von Linné (1959 [1751]) pp. 174, 177, 197, 238.
16. Dahl (1942) pp. 13–16 and map facing p. 16; Hanssen (1952) pp. 51–7. Although Dahl's data on village density are based on mid-seventeenth century sources, there was very little change in the number of settlements before the mid-eighteenth century.
17. For a much fuller and more nuanced account of the social composition of pre-enclosure villages on Skåne's fertile plains, see Hanssen (1952) pp. 48–61; Hanssen (1976) pp. 33–61. For related observations on

Swedish villages in general, see Hoppe (1981); Hellspong and Löfgren (1974) pp. 74–84.

18. See Hanssen (1952) pp. 63–83.
19. Åmark (1915) pp. 18–21, 44, 53–6; Fridlizius (1957) pp. 39ff. It was not until the 1850s, after the repeal of the Corn Laws, that grain shipments from Skåne to England really began to flourish.
20. Utterström (1957); Söderberg (1978); Winberg (1978); Löfgren (1974) pp. 17–52; Löfgren (1980). By 1800, if not earlier, the freeholding and tenant-farming peasant population of lowland Skåne was exceeded by that of the live-in hired help and landless households who constituted the agricultural lower classes.
21. For further observations on *storskifte* in general, see Helmfrid (1961) pp. 44–53. Regarding *storskifte* enclosures in Skåne, see Weibull (1923); Dahl (1941; 1942) pp. 84, 180.
22. Except for the provinces of Dalarna and Norrland, all of present-day Sweden was subject to *enskifte* laws by 1807.
23. Auberg (1953) pp. 65–72.
24. Åberg (1953) pp. 74–5.
25. Cf. Dahl (1942) pp. 186–8, 214; Utterström (1957) vol. I, pp. 574–5; Kristofferson (1924) pp. 96–9.
26. Åmark (1915) pp. 360–2. Although there was some fall-off and fluctuation after 1812, prices remained much above 1803 levels for several years.
27. Dahl (1941) map facing p. 96.
28. *Laga skifte* was a modified form of *enskifte*, intended to encourage enclosures in parts of Sweden where the local topography made it difficult to assign a comparable single parcel to each village resident. The *laga skifte* legislation permitted peasants to hold more than one piece of land where necessary.
29. For a fuller presentation, see Pred (forthcoming).
30. Solberg (1915–16) p. 391; Swanander (1958 [1796]) pp. 91–2; Bruzelius (1978 [1876]) p. 46. The number of hired hands present in a peasant household usually varied with the family cycle and time of the year (for example, extra threshing help was often hired during the winter). Larger peasant households commonly included two additional male hands and a third female servant. Cf. Hanssen (1976) p. 34ff; Löfgren (1974) pp. 23–4.
31. Solberg (1915–16) p. 404; cf. Nicolovius (1957 [1847]) p. 18; Bringéus (1971) p. 27; Utterström (1957) vol. 1, pp. 720–1.
32. von Linné (1959 [1751]) pp. 184, 204–6; Bruzelius (1978 [1876]) p. 64; Lönquist (1924 [1775]) p. 6; Solberg (1915–16) p. 392; Hallenborg (1910–13) pp. 297–8, 352; Hanssen (1952) pp. 24–6; Nordholm (1967) vol. I, p. 109; Campbell (1928) p. 41. Fresh grass and hay was in short supply because villages were typically so committed to grain cultivation that only a small area was set aside for common meadows. The accumulated undergrowth of unattended fallow fields also spurred the use of large draft teams. See also Nicolovius (1957 [1847]) p. 19; Lönquist (1924 [1775]) p. 6; Thunell (1952) p. 18; Hanssen (1952) p. 34.
33. Bruzelius (1978 [1876]) pp. 19, 62; von Linné (1959 [1751]) pp. 146, 246;

364   Enclosures and Social Change in Skåne

Hallenborg (1910–13) pp. 319, 339; Wigström (1891) p. 18; Dahl (1942) p. 123.

34. Lönqvist (1924 [1775]) p. 6; Bruzelius (1978 [1876]) p. 73; Löfgren (1975) p. 6.
35. Lönqvist (1924 [1775]) p. 6; Bruzelius (1978 [1876]) pp. 73–4; Hanssen (1976) pp. 35–49; Gustafsson (1956) p. 40.
36. Nicolovius (1957 [1847]) pp. 16, 45; Solberg (1915–16) p. 407; Wigström (1891) p. 10. If peasant wives had considerable power with respect to definition and role assignment in and around the home, they did not have much in the way of legitimate authority. Frykman (1977) p. 189.
37. Frostin (1932) pp. 1–22; Bruzelius (1978 [1876]) pp. 63–4, 73–5; Solberg (1915–16) pp. 394, 397; Nicolovius (1957 [1847]) p. 38; Åberg (1953) pp. 20–3.
38. Dahl (1942) pp. 98, 100, 130; Bruzelius (1978, [1876]) p. 62.
39. Engström (1928) pp. 24–35; (1927) pp. 18–39; Nilsson (1938) pp. 278, 282; Erixon (1978) p. 43; Frostin (1932); Bruzelius (1978 [1876]); Nicolovius (1957 [1847]) pp. 65–8. Although the Royal Decree of 1742 was intended to bring uniformity to village rules, considerable regional and local variations remained. Cf. Hellspong and Löfgren (1974) pp. 64–5.
40. Engström (1928) p. 22; Hanssen (1952) p. 50; Frykman (1977) p. 196.
41. Campbell (1928) pp. 18–33; Löfgren (1980) pp. 196–7; Åberg (1953) p. 20; Åmark (1915) pp. 301, 211–13; Hanssen (1952) p. 273.
42. See, for example, Heckscher (1946) pp. 45–51; Erixon (1956) p. 283; Sporrong (1970) p. 40; Campbell (1928) p. 51; Dahl (1942) pp. 84, 187, 211.
43. von Rosen (1908–9) pp. 197–8; Thunell (1952) p. 12; Dahl (1942) p. 188.
44. Erixon (1934) pp. 38, 43; Frostin (1932) p. 19; Engström (1928) p. 31; Lönqvist (1924 [1775]) p. 3; Bruzelius (1978 [1876]) p. 74.
45. Hanssen (1952) pp. 17, 49, 60.
46. von Rosen (1908–9) pp. 199, 302–5; von Linné (1959 [1751]) pp. 168, 207–8, 236, 389, 427; Hallenborg (1910–13) pp. 331–2, 336, 369; Swanander (1958 [1796]) pp. 87, 90; Barck (1904–8) p. 375; Solberg (1915–16) pp. 388–90; Bringéus (1971) pp. 44–5; Dahl (1942) pp. 154, 163; Hanssen (1952) pp. 139–383.
47. Cf. Østerud (1978).
48. Cf. Hanssen (1976) p. 50; (1952) p. 204.
49. Bringéus (1964) pp. 93–4.
50. Some of the landless were able to retain their small plots in the village care, while others secured limited patches on the poorer parts of the newly shaped holdings. Utterström (1957) vol. I, pp. 574–8; Dahl (1942) p. 214 ff. Note also Hoppe (1981) pp. 35–8 on enclosures and changes in the number of 'livelihood positions'.
51. Before enskifte the intensiveness of agricultural practices tended to decline with increased distance from the village core. Barck (1904–8) p. 374; Kristofferson (1924) p. 5; Åberg (1953) p. 48.
52. Lägnert (1955) pp. 133–4, 218, 227, 231.
53. Lägnert (1955) p. 212; Dahl (1942) p. 195.
54. Utterström (1957) p. 54.

55. von Linné (1959 [1751]) p. 269; Hallenborg (1910–13) p. 345; Barck (1904–8) p. 373.
56. Nicolovius (1957 [1847]) p. 20; Dahl (1942) p. 207; Bringéus (1971) p. 46.
57. Frykman and Löfgren (1979) p. 179; Frykman (1977) p. 197; Hellspong and Löfgren (1974) pp. 81, 138; Löfgren (1974) p. 31; (1975) pp. 7, 241, 28; (1978) p. 103.
58. Thunell (1952) p. 47; Frykman and Lófgren (1979) p. 30.
59. Fridlizius (1957) p. 59; Utterström (1957) p. 540.
60. Bringéus (1964) pp. 70–1, 74; Frykman (1977) pp. 112–16.
61. Wigström (1891) pp. 14, 23; Frödin (1946) p. 198. See also note 10.
62. Asplund (1983); Frostin (1932) pp. 9, 11; Bruzelius (1978 [1876]) pp. 59, 73; Frykman (1977) p. 131; Cf. Pred, 1983.
63. Engström (1928) p. 16; (1928a) p. 34; Frostin (1932) p. 11; Thunell (1952) p. 53.
64. Bruzelius (1978 [1876]) pp. 37, 40; Hanssen (1952) pp. 73–84.
65. Hanssen (1952) pp. 352, 362–82; von Linné (1959 [1751]) pp. 183, 203, 249, 267, 318–19; Hallenborg (1910–13) pp. 300, 318, 340, 359; Anckarsvärd (1910–13) p. 82; Campbell (1928) pp. 19–23, 44ff.
66. For example, Hanssen (1952) p. 85; Berg and Svensson (1934) p. 165; Frykman (1977) p. 123.
67. Areskoug (1949) p. 83; Hanssen (1952) p. 88; von Linné (1959 [1751]) pp. 82, 96, 252, 271, 290, 300, 308, 385; Ejder (1969) pp. 318, 405; Bringéus (1971) pp. 51, 54.

15
Flies and Germs: A Geography of Knowledge

NIGEL THRIFT

Introduction

> *Mother* We have to keep the screen door closed, honey, so the flies won't come in. Flies bring germs into the house with them.
> *Child (when asked later what the germs were)* Something the flies play with.[1]

This little vignette in which the child uses what knowledge is available to her to interpret her mother's interdiction, illustrates the central theme of this chapter, namely that what we know is an important constraint on what we can think and do. It also illustrates two other important themes which grow out of and into this central theme. The first is that knowledge is historically specific. Thus, before 1871, knowledge of 'germs' did not exist.[2] The mother could not have known of their presence and the child would not have had to answer her interrogator. Second, knowledge is geographically specific. Even now, the knowledge of germs does not stretch everywhere in the world and in these nescient places mothers do not have to tell their children something they cannot know.

   This chapter thus forms part of a continuing attempt to develop a theory of *situated* social action. Such a theory must continually intersect with both the presences and absences of social structure,[3] and with the continual turmoil of social groups in conflict in a complex process of 'structuring'[4] but I would argue that it still forms a relatively separate focus of attention.[5] Elsewhere, I have outlined the three most important elements of this project, which are the study of the process of personality formation, the study of the organisation of sociability and the study of the availability of knowledge (where knowledge is defined in its broadest sense as information about the world).[6] Since the availability of knowledge forms only *one part* of this project, and is inevitably linked to the others, its explanation necessarily involves some consideration of questions of personality formation and sociability, but in what follows, my primary focus is the 'geography of knowledge'.

The chapter is divided into four sections. The first considers, in very general terms, how 'stocks of knowledge' are continually being built up, and the second describes the types of knowledge from which such stocks have been constructed historically. A third section considers three case studies of the spatial availability of knowledge, and the final section traces some of the links between availability of knowledge and social action through a case study of political knowledge. Most of the illustrations are taken from Europe between the sixteenth and nineteenth centuries and are limited to knowledge disseminated through the medium of print. There are obvious disadvantages in such a restricted scope but they are, I hope, outweighed by a greater coherence. It follows of course that any illustration is evocative rather than exhaustive.

Two other qualifications are necessary. First, my emphasis on a situated theory of social action means that I will have rather less to say on the production, distribution and circulation of knowledge than on its availability.[7] This is not a derogation of these other elements but merely an effect of the emphasis I have chosen: *I am primarily interested here in what knowledge actors actually have at their disposal.* Second, and closely connected to this, the fact that knowledge is physically available does not mean that it has to be acted upon nor that it is unquestioned or undisputed. This entails important issues of 'ideology' and of 'hegemony' but again I will hardly touch upon them here.

Social knowing and social unknowing

'Social knowing' is the term I will use to denote the continual process of the creation of the *stocks of knowledge*[8] within a society upon which actors, who are always members of various social groups, can draw in the production of their life and the reproduction or transformation of the forms of life of social groups (their own and others) and ultimately of society.[9] I see this process as being an essentially recursive one, the result of *practices* that both provide the medium for and the outcome of social structure.[10]

From the perspective of the actor

All groups of actors have some degree of 'penetration'[11] of what is going on within the reciprocal flow of action and structure in which they are both constituted and constituting. But their ability to draw on and generate knowledge, whether this knowledge is discursively constructed or an unacknowledged reapplication of practical schemas, is simultaneously *limited* by the very experience of the production of practices and the continual monitoring and reinterpretation of this experience in the light of subsequent events. At least four closely interwoven limits are involved. First, all actors' knowledge is grounded in their biographically unique *experience* of practising a particular social system, and the power to reason can exist only relatively autonomously from this grounding in experience. The structures of domination, signification and legitimation that are woven into the patterning of this system resist the discovery of certain kinds of knowledge and can form unacknowledged conditions for action in the knowledge that is available. Second, all knowledge is the result of the particular *habitus* used to generate practices and monitor, interpret, reconstruct and ultimately confirm them.[12] Once again, the effect is to provide a particular horizon on upcoming experience and the conception of experience, and in this way to set a limit. Third, there is the basic fact that all practices are situated in *time and space*. The constraints of the human body and the extant physical infrastructure of society are such that knowledge must be generated from a finite series of practices (and experiences of these practices) that form part of an irreversible and repetitive form of conduct, one that usually sets quite severe limits on what can be thought – and on the amount of time available to think it – within each actor's allotted span of history. Finally, and as a result of these three limits, no two actors can *communicate* knowledge perfectly and this in turn sets a fourth limit. If the actors' experience (for example, of being a member of the same family), habitus (for example, being a member of the same social class) and position in time and space (for example, being an inhabitant of the same region) are the same, then communication will be easier and knowledge more likely to be disseminated than if any one of these factors is different (Figure 15.1).[13] To summarise, actors usually have only very partial knowledge of or access to knowledge that is available within a particular social group or society, let alone the time to produce the finished conceptual goods.

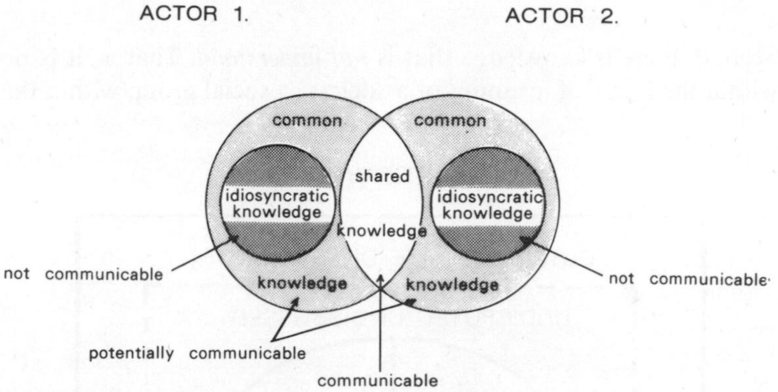

FIGURE 15.1 *Knowledge and communication (adapted from Kreckel, 1982, Figure 2, p. 227)*

From the perspective of society

Every society has an overall stock of knowledge and although some of this will be available to all its members, some will be differentially distributed amongst various social groups; there is thus a *social distribution of knowledge*. This distribution will be dependent upon all the numerous dimensions of social group structuration,[14] such as biological differentiation (gender, age, race, etc.), class (the capital–labour relation), the state, the region and all their cross-correlations.

Each society, and each social group within it, will have its own degree of penetration of the conditions of its existence dependent upon the stock of knowledge that is available to it. We can codify this penetration as five types of 'unknowing' (Figure 15.2).[15] First, there is 'knowledge' that is *unknown*. This is knowledge that it is simply not possible for members of a society to have because of its position in history and space.[16] As Castoriadis puts it:

> To have an experience of history as a historical being is to be *in* and *part of* more history, as well as *in* and *part of* society. It necessarily means thinking of history in terms of categories of one's own epoch

and one's own society (these categories being themselves the products of historical evolution). It also means thinking history in relation to some objective or purpose, which purpose is history itself.[17]

Second, there is knowledge that is *not understood*. That is, it is not within the frame of meaning of a society, a social group within that

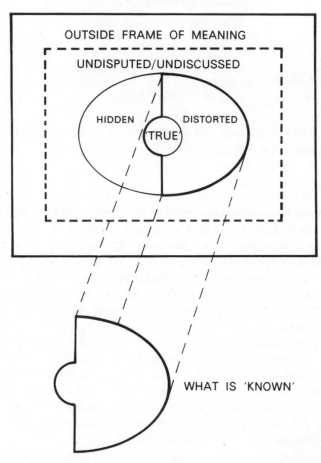

FIGURE 15.2 *The five kinds of unknowing (adapted from Thift, 1979, Figure 1, p. 27)*

society, or members of a social group living in a particular region. This lack of understanding can come about for a number of reasons. For example, a group whose form of life is essentially practical will have difficulties in grasping the form of life of a group based, at least in part, in discursive practices. This type of unknowing is well summarised in a passage from H. G. Wells:

> *Serpentine:* When I think to you, the thought, so far as it finds corresponding ideas and suitable words in your mind is reflected in your mind. My thought clothes itself in words in your mind, which words you seem to hear – and naturally enough in your own language and habitual phrases...
>
> *Barnstaple:* And that is why... when you soar into ideas of which we haven't a shadow in our minds, we just hear nothing at all.[18]

Third, and intimately related to the second type of unknowing, there is knowledge that is *undiscussed*. This is knowledge that is taken-for-granted either by a society, or a social group or the members of a social group living in a particular region. This form of unknowing is a prime characteristic of many systems of practical knowledge but it should not be seen as their exclusive prerogative. The acceptance by many scientists of 'the scientific method' as a model illustrates the use of a system of concepts that effectively 'conceals' the nature, causes and consequences of a set of practices as just that – a set of practices. Fourth, there is the type of unknowing that results from knowledge being actively and consciously *hidden* from a society, certain groups within that society or groups within a particular region. Fifth, there is the type of unknowing that results from *distortion*, in terms of being known in a distorted fashion by a society, social groups within a society or social groups within a particular region. Here, care must be taken to separate, *insofar as this is possible*, the distortion that arises from the history of the particular forms of life of social groups, with their 'traditional' systems of belief and knowledge, from the distortion that is part of an active process of manipulation by other social groups.[19]

The first type of unknowing can be seen as a historical constant. The other types come together in different combinations in different societies and social groups to produce a social distribution of knowledge (and non-knowledge).[20]

Types of knowledge

I want to claim that four main types of knowledge go to make up the stocks of knowledge that are available to social groups and to individual actors in modern society. These are (i) the unconscious (ii) practical knowledge (iii) empirical knowledge and (iv) 'natural philosophy'. These types of knowledge form loose clusters of information about particular *practices* ordered in particular ways, and this emphasis on practice has two important consequences. First, these types of knowledge are not meant to be seen as arising from distinctive forms of rationality,[21] nor are they meant to be depicted as the product of long-term changes in metaphysics or beliefs. The decline of witch-hunting in seventeenth-century Europe, for example, has been explained as a function of the rise of capitalism or of the new 'mechanical philosophy'. But:

> Two explanations seem more compelling. One is the loss of confidence in the ability of the courts to decide who the witches were, an increasing recognition of the weakness in the procedures of forensic demonology . . . The other is the stabilisation and territorialisation of religious authority which permits other and more regular and systematic means of disciplining flocks and the control of heresy. The success of the Counter-Reformation and the mutual exhaustion and stabilisation following the Wars of Religion bring heresy within the manageable limits of religious 'police'.[22]

Second, these types of knowledge do not form separate discourses or categories of belief. Human beings are *bricoleurs* and conventionally conjoin what may seem to be quite different types of knowledge. The very nature of human conduct as a compartmentalised stream of action and thought in space and time means that very few actors have a completely and consistently developed world view (while even fewer apply it to their actions). Thus, for example, the diary of Ralph Josselin (1617–83) an Essex clergyman, shows that he could quite confidently combine commercial capitalist calculation with Calvinistic religious practices and a degree of belief in witchcraft.[23] As Spufford puts it, it is 'extremely easy for academics to over-emphasize the degree to which the majority of ordinary people are either aware of, or bothered by, different categories of belief.'[24]

Unconscious knowledge

Unconscious knowledge is based upon forgotten practices still remembered in the limning of action. As Bourdieu puts it, 'the unconscious is never anything other than the forgetting of history which history itself produces by incorporating the objective structures it produces in the second natures of habitus'.[25] Interpreting the unconscious as a historically changing and geographically variable phenomenon, let alone the variations in the type of knowledge it provides, is the domain of a historical and geographical psychology that as yet hardly exists.[26]

Practical knowledge

Practical knowledge can be defined as that informal (but not therefore unstructured) type of knowledge that is learnt from the experience of watching and doing in highly particular contexts in direct mutual interaction. It still forms 'the massive central core of human thinking' that goes unrecorded in so many histories of social thought.[27]

Practical knowledge has four major components. First, it is *unarticulated*; that is, it is based upon practices that have, over the course of history, become naturalised so that much of its content now inhabits the realm of the undiscussed and, certainly, the uncodified. To have to ask about practical knowledge is to miss the point of practical knowledge.[28] Second, practical knowledge is part of a *continuous* and *repetitive* flow of conduct which takes place in finite time and which is oriented towards doing. This is a world in which 'I think' (*cogito*) is inseparable from 'I can' (*practico*) and in which long-term goals are submerged by immediate objectives. Third, practical knowledge is *local*, that is, it is knowledge produced and reproduced in *mutual interaction* that relies on the *presence* of other human beings on a direct, face-to-face basis.[29] Such knowledge is deeply imbued with both historical and geographical specificity, taking its cues from local contexts each with their own particular ensemble of practices and associated linguistic usages. Nowhere is this made clearer than in historical accounts of local communities which include glossaries of terms that describe practices (and the experience of those practices) now long past. These are words which not only capture the attributes of a particular practice but also begin to conjure up the ghost of the whole language of practice and practice of language associated with living a set of social relations in a specific physical setting. Finally, practical knowledge tends to be based upon *organic analogy* or *metaphor* and, following from the third component, these analogies or metaphors are usually based upon proximity.

The importance of analogy and metaphor in systems of practical knowledge should not be understated for they function as the correlates of patterns of bodily action and interaction which instantiate social relations. In the following passage, for example, it is possible to see how metaphors are used to fix the patterns of economic co-operation and exchange in an African village which form the material base of that community's life.

> The Kuranko of Sierra Leone use the word *kile* ('path' or 'road') as a metaphor for social relationship. For instance, the adage *nyendan bin to kile a wa ta an segi* describes the way a particular species of grass (used for thatching) bends back one way as you go along a path through it, and then bends back the other way as you return along the path. This movement to and fro of grass along a pathway is used as a metaphor for the movement of people and of goods and of services within a community; it is a metaphor for reciprocity. Thus, in Kuranko one often explains the reason for giving a gift, especially to an in-law, with the phrase *kile ka na faga*, 'so that the path does not die'. However, if relations between affines or neighbours are strained, it is often said that 'the path is not good between them' (*kile nyuma san tema*), and if a person disappoints a friend then people may comment *a ma kile nyuma tama a boma* ('he did not walk on the good path with his friend').[30]

Systems of practical knowledge are often sophisticated.[31] But the connections made between various phenomena in these systems have to be based upon the known world so that, once again, the limits to knowledge operate. Chapman provides the following example:

> Dutt lists a few of the beliefs or the omens of Bihar with respect to insect and pest attacks on their crops. In particular, he notes that there are many farmers who believe that certain caterpillars fall from the sky with the rain, and their cure for the attack is accordingly usually religious. The reason for the belief is that the caterpillars emerged from their eggs in cloudy, rainy conditions, and their life-cycle is not understood. That man is born of woman, and a calf of a

cow is well known, but that a moth or butterfly produces eggs which produce larvae which produce pupae which produce moths, going through great changes of shape and form, is not understood. It is intelligent to associate the pest with the weather conditions, and only someone in possession of a 'parity framework' which would reject this interpretation would be unsatisfied by it.[32]

Empirical knowledge

The stock of empirical knowledge is built up as a result of the general process of *rationalisation* of knowledge,[33] which has a double interpretation as the proffering of a rational explanation and the organisation of knowledge in a systematic fashion. Empirical knowledge, like practical knowledge (with which it continues to share many similarities), is bent towards the mastery of the conditions of existence, but it is exercised within a learning process which is not only cumulative but systematised and co-ordinated over large tracts of space and over longer time-horizons, particularly by modern state and economic institutions. The modern state is based upon the various practices associated with *surveillance* (that is, the accumulation of information on the population, the supervision of the population and the characterisation of the population in such a way that it can be supervised) and proceeds from the institution of regular armies and the systematic registration of births and deaths via the census and fingerprinting to modern computer data-banks. Similarly, the capitalist economy is based upon the co-ordination of the labour process and the complex exchange of commodities, both of which require the extensive collection of systematic knowledge, and proceeds from double-entry bookkeeping via modern accounting practices to – again – the computer. In both bases, the institutions engendered by these practices produce a network of space–time locations at which knowledge is stored, received and transmitted. The schooling system forms a particularly crucial set of nodes within this network.[34]

What, then, are the major characteristics of empirical knowledge? Above all, it is *heterodynamic*,[35] that is, it is acquired by virtue of an actor's membership of class and other social groups, and it is *distanciated*,[36] that is, it is removed in both time and space from the experiences and events it describes. Empirical knowledge does not depend for its acquisition upon the direct presence of people, but is transmitted through institutions and technologies which allow personal contact to be either by-passed or made specific to particular 'packets' of information. These two characteristics account for much of the *homogeneous* and *objectified* character of empirical knowledge.

The chief components of the stock of empirical knowledge are, I believe, crucially dependent upon the written word,[37] but also and more particularly, upon the practices engendered by the invention of printing (and the modern book). Since most commentators have underestimated the importance of this medium, I want to discuss it in some detail. The difference that the invention of printing made both to the stock of available knowledge *and* to the type of knowledge can be seen by considering what, historically, has been a transitory form between systems of practical knowledge and systems of empirical knowledge (and between oral and literate cultures), namely systems of *practical literacy*.[38] Before the invention of printing, these systems – usually associated with the collection of statistics and the transmission of orders by the emerging bureaucracy of an expanding state – were necessarily restricted by the strict limits imposed by the use of scribes.[39] 'Just as geographic space stopped short of the Pillars of Hercules, so too did knowledge itself appear to stop short at fixed limits set by scribal data pools.'[40]

The invention of printing changed all this.[41] First, and most obviously, the stock of available knowledge expanded rapidly, both in terms of absolute quantity and the amount of knowledge available in any one place. Second, the codification of knowledge became both possible and, with the expansion in knowledge, a necessity. Third, for many, consultation, comparison and choice between different items of knowledge became both possible and practicable for the first time. For example, a number of texts could be assembled in the same place and did not need to be transcribed. Fourth, knowledge became more accurate. Codification and comparison combined with the elimination of the errors that result from continual transcription ensured this. Finally, stocks of literature began to be built up which opened up the possibility of learning by reading, that is of learning skills at a distance instead of in mutual interaction. These are all key features of empirical knowledge.

Empirical knowledge can, of course, be divided further and I will now identify three main subsets in terms of their propinquity to practical knowledge. First, there is the empirical knowledge that now infuses a whole series of practices that were carried on before the advent of empirical knowledge (and which could, in principle, still be carried on without it). These practices have been systematised by the application of empirical knowledge and by learning about these practices via empirical knowledge. This knowledge stretches all the way from that found in gardening and cookery books to much of the knowledge disseminated via the media about politics and current events. Second, there is empirical knowledge that is oriented to the whole set of practices that are directly bent toward reproducing the state and the economy and whose existence is closely tied to the existence of empirical knowledge. This subset would include the aggregation and codification of knowledge about certain specific practices – for example, the law, town planning or engineering. This kind of empirical knowledge forms the basis of most of the 'professions', which is hardly surprising since the profession is, historically, one of the first devices used to differentiate a body of knowledge from practical knowledge, so bestowing on its practitioners a margin of respectability and economic and social recognition.[42] Third, there is knowledge generated by the restricted empirical model of the natural sciences (which is, effectively, a set of instructions on ways of proceeding *in practice*). This knowledge, which is generated by many of the social sciences (and especially economics and demography) as well as the bulk of the natural sciences, comes from practices whose conduct is resolutely oriented to the practical. It is the knowledge that arises from the practice of 'normal science':[43]

> Normal science is the linchpin of the scientific enterprise; it is how knowledge is developed and accumulated nearly all the time. Yet it is in no way a radically innovative activity. On the contrary, it is very much a routine carrying on of a given form of scientific life, employing accepted procedures along the lines indicated by accepted standards, and largely assuming the correctness of existing knowledge.[44]

Natural philosophy

The third type of knowledge (empirical knowledge) overlaps with knowledge gleaned from 'natural philosophy'. I use 'natural philosophy' in the most catholic of senses, to denote knowledge that attempts to unify a number of bodies of knowledge into one whole, as knowledge about knowledge.[45] It has at least three interrelated characteristics. First, it requires much time both to absorb a number of bodies of knowledge and to synthesise them.[46] As Kierkegaard put it, 'Life can only be understood backwards but it has to be lived forwards'. Second, although it may be a part of a practice, it is only indirectly related to immediate practical needs. Third, its content is related to what knowledge is available to be thought with, whether of the practical, empirical or natural philosophy types. For example, the types of analogy or metaphor upon which systems of knowledge can be built become more sophisticated as the objects that can be thought with become more sophisticated. Thus 'it is said that Aristotle thought of causal effects in terms of a horse drawing a cart and that Galileo thought of heavenly bodies as something like ships moving in an ocean without friction'.[47] But now the analogies of the steam engine (machinery), the microscope (the infinitely small), the telescope (the infinitely large) and a host of others are all available for use.[48] There has been, quite literally, a mechanisation of our world picture.

Types of knowledge and the availability of knowledge

That the availability of knowledge has a crucial effect on the form and content of natural philosophy and, indeed, on the other types of knowledge is worth establishing in some detail. I will do this by considering the base of magic, which, since it was evolved 'to fill in the gaps left by the limitation of techniques',[49] can be seen as an attempt to control the conditions of existence like any other.

At its most 'simple' magic is an integral part of the form of life of a community. It is part of a body of practical knowledge in which the explanations of magic are woven into the way of life of that community, the one reciprocally confirming the other.[50] The practice is the word and the word is the practice. This kind of magic still existed in England in the seventeenth century:

> Almost every English village had its 'cunning man', its white magician who told those who had been robbed how to recover their property, advised on propitious times and seasons for journeys and foretold the future. Nor were such beliefs limited to ignorant villagers.[51]

But, at the same time as this, there existed another magic in England, one enjoying a 'renaissance' in the universities and at court thanks to the discovery in the fifteenth century of texts attributed to Hermes Trismegistus.[52] The Hermetic tradition, meant to be based on the magical religion of the Egyptians, had spread rapidly (at least in part through the new medium of print). Alongside it the bodies of knowledge known as astrology and alchemy also still flourished.[53] The dividing line between these three bodies of knowledge and 'science' was problematic. On one side were the mages who incorporated scientific discoveries into their work: Giordano Bruno, who hailed the discoveries of Copernicus as proof of Hermetism; Tommaso Campanella, who was willing to allow of a category of 'real artificial magic' (such as mechanical statues);[54] the astrologer and herbalist Nicholas Culpeper, who made use of the recent invention of logarithms to aid his calculations; and the inventor of logarithms, John Napier, who 'was said to value them most because they speeded up his calculations of the mystic figure 666, the number of the Beast in *Revelation*'.[55] On the other side was Isaac Newton, who has been described as 'not the first of the age of reason' but 'the last of the magicians' and who left hundreds of pages of unpublished manuscripts on alchemy and turned to mathematics in order to understand astrology.[56] Tycho Brahe made the vast collection of observations which enabled him to redraw the map of the night sky, primarily for astrological purposes; and John Locke and Robert Boyle used astrological reckoning to find a time 'favourable for planting peonies'.[57] The connections are great enough for it now to be said that 'practical science can be seen to have developed, at least in part, out of the renewed interest in magic'.[58]

The reasons why magic, astrology and alchemy died out are complex. One was that they were opposed in England by a religion which had its own competing world system, and which had always been associated with a different kind of 'rationality'. A second reason was that it became obvious that, when *compared* with other systems (*which had not existed before*) magic did not work. A third reason is that systems of practical and empirical knowledge based upon 'science' were gradually slotted into place which began to confirm this view of the world, rather than the one based upon 'magic'. But we can legitimately wonder if:

> the circumstances of the acceptance of the mechanical philosophy allowed ideological elements to be incorporated into it from the start, which today have become hindrances to its further advance; total rejection of the ways of the *magi* may have closed some doors which might with advantage to science have been left open. Science, in Bernal's striking phrase, is not only 'ordered technique', it is also 'rationalised mythology'.[59]

The example of the rise and fall of magic illustrates two major themes. First, the connections between practical knowledge, natural philosophy and, later, empirical knowledge are by no means one-way: from natural philosophy to empirical knowledge and so on down to the person in the street. For example, practical knowledge can intervene in the building of empirical knowledge or natural philosophy, and this can happen in the most unexpected ways. Thus:

> In Bengal, as well as in China, there was a custom of imprinting letters and documents with a fingerprint tipped in ink or tar: this was probably a consequence of knowledge derived from divinatory practice ... In 1860 Sir William Herschel, District Commissioner of Hooghly in Bengal, came across this usage, common among local people, saw its usefulness, and thought to profit by it to improve the functioning of the British administration ... But really ... there was a great need for some such means of identification: in India as in other British colonies the natives were illiterate, disputatious, wily, deceitful, and to the eyes of a European all looked the same. In 1880 Herschel announced in *Nature* that after 17 years of tests, fingerprints had been officially introduced in the district of Hooghly and since then had been used for three years with the best possible results. The imperial administrators had taken over the Bengalis' ... knowledge and used it against them.[60]

Francis Galton saw Herschel's article in *Nature*, combined it with the theoretical work of Purkyné, and introduced fingerprinting to England and thence to the rest of the world. Second, the example of magic shows that all actors, including 'scientists' and natural philosophers, can only work with the knowledge they have and that knowledge shapes what they can perceive as and fashion into 'rationality'. As Thomas puts it:

> If magical acts are ineffective rituals employed as an alternative to sheer helplessness in the face of events, then how are we to classify the status of 'scientific' remedies, in which we place faith, but which are subsequently exposed as useless? This was the fate of Galenic medicine, which in the sixteenth century was the main rival to folk-healing. But it will also be that of much of the medicine of today. Sociologists have observed that contemporary doctors and surgeons engage in many ritual practices of a non-operative kind.[61]

Further:

> All the evidence of the sixteenth and seventeenth centuries suggests
> that the common people never formulated a distinction between
> magic and medicine . . . The modern working-class woman who
> remarks that she doesn't 'believe' in doctors is acknowledging the
> fact that the patient still brings with him an essentially unformed
> allegiance. Usually he knows no more of the underlying rationale
> for his treatment than did the client of a cunning man. In such
> circumstances it is hard to say where 'science' stops and magic
> begins . . . If magic is to be defined as the employment of ineffective
> techniques to allay anxiety when effective ones are not available,
> then we must recognise that no society will ever be free from it.[62]

In everyday life these types of knowledge are, more often than not,
unproblematically fitted together by each actor in an ongoing
bricolage, closeted away in the stream of each person's daily conduct.
This is not to say there are no *problems*, however; and these are
compounded by variations in the availability of printed knowledge
over space and by social group.

The geography of social knowing and unknowing

The purpose of this section is to establish, first, that spatial variations
in the distribution of the various types of knowledge (particularly the
empirical) exist and, second, that within the constraints set by those
broader patterns the different social groups present in each location
have different degrees of access to the types of knowledge which go to
make up their stock of knowledge: in short, that types of knowledge
are socially distributed over space. I will begin with two illustrations
from the seventeenth and eighteenth centuries, when the distribution
of knowledge was not complicated by the noise of media other than
print or the rise of mass state schooling systems. I will then try to show
how in the nineteenth and twentieth centuries there has been an
increase in the spatial variation of knowledge, which reflects changes
in the spatial organisation of society and in the social distribution of
knowledge.

In the mid-sixteenth century empirical knowledge began to become
widely available in the form of printed books. This new medium

transformed the technique and character of reading, writing and learning as well as what could be read, written and learnt. The rise of the printed book was rapid. It has been estimated that even *before* 1550, 20 million copies of books had been printed in Europe; a further 150 to 200 million books were published in the century after.[63] It is evident that these were not for the exclusive consumption of the upper classes, although consumption was just as evidently bent this way if only because of the constraints of cost and literacy. The books themselves covered a vast range of subjects from prayerbooks and devotional literature through scholarly texts and textbooks to books of hours and rewritten mediaeval romances. But by the 1490s cheap books or 'chapbooks' had made their appearance in France. They gained a wider audience in the early seventeenth century in the form of little blue paper-covered books sold at two *sous* a time by a vast network of vendors, pedlars, hawkers and packmen. Known as the *bibliothèque bleue*, these books are the subject of numerous historical studies in France.[64] Recently a comparable English literature has begun to grow up around the twopenny chapbooks of the sixteenth, seventeenth and eighteenth centuries, which makes it possible to say something about the spatial distribution of the various types of knowledge in England during this period.[65]

Caxton set up the first printing press in England in 1476. By the sixteenth century chapbooks were in circulation and by the seventeenth century there was 'a steady hail of printed pamphlets of news, political and religious propaganda, astrological prediction and advice, songs, sensation, sex and fantasy'.[66] The increase in circulation was spurred on, in particular, by the rapid rise in elementary schooling for the masses (at least until the Restoration), so that by the end of the seventeenth century English society had become one in which:

> a boy even from a relatively poor family might have a year or two's education to the age of six or eight. His almost invisible sister, historically speaking, sometimes was taught to read. If a boy was at school until seven, he could read, if he was at school until eight, or at the latest nine, he could write. Either way he would be able to make sense of whatever cheap print the pedlars brought within his reach. Either way his mental environment had undergone an enormous and very important change.[47]

The impact of this literature was twofold. First, it signified the beginning of a gradual transition from a predominantly oral to a print

culture and from practical learning and reckoning to a more rational-
ised, systematic and distanciated view of the world. But the transition
was very gradual; it must be remembered that many chapbooks were
meant for reading aloud and many were not much more than trans-
criptions into print of an oral tradition.[68] Second, chapbooks were a
means of disseminating the new type of empirical knowledge. The
example of the almanac is important here. It is estimated that by the
1660s some 400 000 almanacs were being produced in England
annually; one family in three was buying an almanac.[69] Such almanacs were not simply sources of astrological predictions and agricultural calendars. They provided information upon society and religion
and, more particularly, they 'played an important role, especially in
the seventeenth century, in the popularisation of the new science',[70]
especially by offering up information on astronomy (including advice
on building instruments and dials), mathematics and medicine. The
almanacs also provided almost the only systematic source of generally available information on politics, history (usually a single page
history of the world) and geography. Thus 'in the second half of the
seventeenth century *White* provided its readers each year with a crude
map of England showing the county boundaries'.[71]

But, as Figure 15.3 shows, the spatial distribution of this
knowledge was variable.[72] In general, those in the outlying districts
outside the major metropolises were more likely to suffer, not only
from a lack of schooling but also from a relative paucity of reading
matter. Their ability to compare and contrast, to break out of the
limits of the practical world, was therefore severely constrained,
although via the chapmen 'chapbooks were available to the reader
who wanted them, even in very remote areas'.[73]

Class considerations intrude more forcefully when we come to
consider empirical knowledge of a more systematic and less generally
available character than that offered by the almanacs. To illustrate
this point we must come forward in time to the eighteenth century and
to that remarkable enlightenment publishing venture, Diderot's *Encyclopédie*[74] which from the appearance of the first volume in 1751
was an attempt to:

> map the world of knowledge according to new boundaries, deter-
> mined by reason and reason alone. As its title page proclaimed, it
> pretended to be a '*dictionnaire raisonné des sciences, des arts et des
> metiers*' – that is, to measure all human activity by rational stan-
> dards and so to provide a basis for rethinking the world.[75]

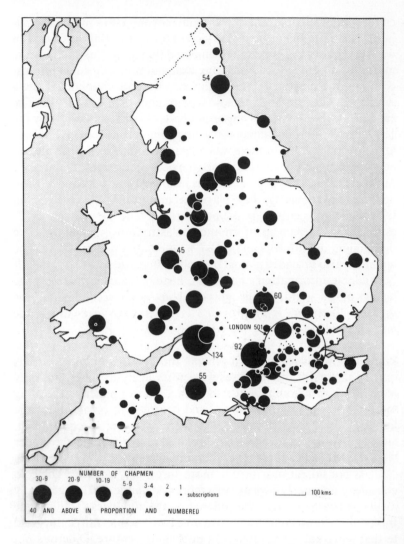

FIGURE 15.3 *The spatial distribution of chapmen licensed in England and Wales 1697–8*
SOURCE Spufford, 1981, Map 2, p. 119

The *Encyclopédie* is crucial in the history of the stock empirical knowledge because it represents a *de facto* attack on traditional learning which, it was implied:

amounted to nothing but prejudice and superstition. So beneath the bulk of the *Encyclopédie's* twenty-eight folio volumes and the enormous variety of its 71 818 articles and 2885 plates lay an epistemological shift that transformed the topography of everything known to man.[76]

The first four editions were luxurious folio publications that only a few could have afforded and, when taken together, account for only 40 per cent of the *Encyclopédies* in existence prior to 1789. The great mass of the *Encyclopédies* sold came from the cut-rate quarto and octavo editions printed between 1777 and 1782. Of those produced in France some 50 to 65 per cent were quartos and all these subscriptions can be traced, at least to the booksellers, so allowing Figures 15.4 and 15.5 to be drawn.[77]

The class-specific nature of these patterns can be elicited by the example of the town of Besançon.[78] In some respects Besançon does not seem the most fertile ground for the *Encyclopédie* – it was a provincial capital based upon religion and administration, a veritable bastion of Bourbon bureaucracy; but it also had a public library, a *cabinet littéraire* and four booksellers. Literacy rates were high (95 per cent for men, 60 per cent for women). In the event, the *Encyclopédie* sold well – to noblemen, to the military, to parliamentarians, to doctors and to lawyers. In contrast, the artisans, shopkeepers, day-labourers and servants who made up the other three quarters of Besançon's population do not appear at all amongst the subscribers, nor do the peasants and shopkeepers of the surrounding province of Franche-Comte. Certainly some of these may have consulted the *Encyclopédie* in the reading clubs of the area, but for the vast majority access to its knowledge was severely limited – by a whole host of closely interwoven factors such as distance, class, time and ability to read. Indeed, in France as a whole:

Although one cannot exclude the possibility that the *Encyclopédie* reached a great many readers in the lower middle classes, its main appeal was to the traditional élite – the men who dominated the administrative and cultural life of the provincial capital and small towns.[79]

Thus, the diffusion of the *Encyclopédie* is a record of the spatial differentiation of knowledge, one that is explicitly based, at least in France, in the class composition of the urban system. The *Ency-*

clopédie's store of empirical knowledge was, from its inception, marked 'reserved'.

In the seventeenth and eighteenth centuries the acquisition of knowledge (for all but *some* members of the upper and middle classes) was still dependent upon where a person was born (and subsequently lived out his/her life) and upon the corresponding local availability of

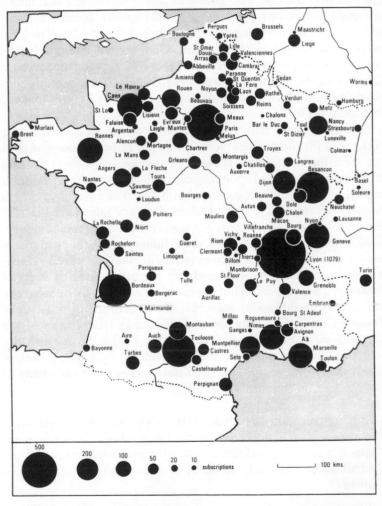

FIGURE 15.4 *The diffusion of the quarto edition of the* Encyclopédie *in France*
SOURCE Darnton, 1979, Figure 5, p. 279

schools, booksellers and other means of dissemination of empirical knowledge. The nineteenth and twentieth centuries, in contrast, can be interpreted as a period of rapid homogenisation in the degree of spatial variation of availability of empirical knowledge. At least three trends support such a stance. First, the coming of mass schooling systems and compulsory education means that a common level of knowledge was brought into existence. Second, improvements in the speed and efficiency of transport communications, the phenomenon of 'time–space convergence',[80] mean that more institutions which disseminate knowledge become potentially available. Third, mass circulation newspapers, radio, television and now computerised home information systems provide a large and generally available fund of common empirical knowledge.

But there are two countervailing tendencies, which can be traced

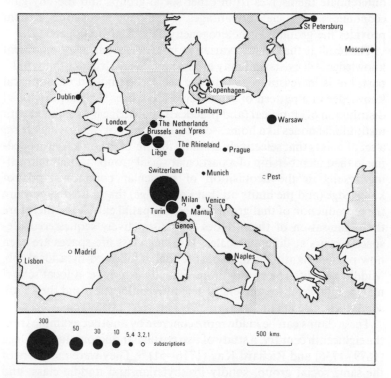

FIGURE 15.5 *The diffusion of the quarto edition of the* Encyclopédie *outside France*
SOURCE Darnton, 1979, Figure 8, p. 301

before the nineteenth century but which now become different facets of the same process of mobilisation of social groups around various specialised stores of knowledge. The 'constituency' of the various mass media is strongly differentiated by class and other social groupings to such a degree that the actual fund of knowledge common to all social groups (and likely to be spatially homogeneous) may well be quite small; the same point applies to mass schooling systems.[81] The first tendency is the explosion in the overall stock of knowledge in the nineteenth century as a result of the growth of the state, the capitalist economy and the various sciences which brings with it specialists in particular stocks of knowledge. The second tendency is the seizure by various social groups upon this growing body of knowledge (over and above that knowledge which becomes common to all or most of the population) as a fertile source of 'cultural capital'[82] with which to differentiate themselves from other social groups and thereby gain economic and social advantages. (Thus the education system provides the grounds of heterogeneity as well as homogeneity.)

The result is that spatial variation in the distribution of empirical knowledge still exists and may even be relatively stronger than in the past, but is increasingly tied to the *social* distribution of empirical knowledge in a pattern of sequestered life-spaces.[83] Thus, the social distribution of empirical (and practical) knowledge is associated with institutional nodes like home, school, university or office which form a set of points that selectively channel the life-paths of actors according to their membership of a particular social group.[84] This channelling results in the acquisition of particular common kinds of knowledge (and the limits on that knowledge) that ultimately ensure the reproduction of that group as a socio-spatial entity. Furthermore the organisation of these nodes into distinctively sequestered life-spaces occurs at different scales. Working-class life-spaces are even now predominantly local: a local school is followed by a local job. Middle class life-spaces are more spatially extensive: a local school may be followed by a university in a different location and then a job somewhere else again.

These claims can be made more concrete by another example from the eighteenth century, a study of two particular doctors, James Clegg (1679–1756) and Richard Kay (1716–51).[85] They were members of the same social group, solidly Presbyterian and middle class, and although they lived out their lives some kilometres apart they shared common interests, had friends in common[86] and had heard sermons preached by the same people. Indeed, they may even have met. Their respective life-paths and the daily-paths they rode and trod for a week in July 1745, are depicted in time-geographic fashion in Figure 15.6. Immediately the common nodes of this particular social group's form of life stand out – home, school, chapel.

What can we say about the stocks of knowledge upon which Clegg and Kay drew? First, they would have had a common pool of natural philosophy. Their upbringing was, in both cases, based upon a number of religious schools and dissenting academies. Second, they would both have had a common store of practical knowledge, a closed homodynamic code founded in and naturalised by the localised routines of family, farm and chapel. Third, they would both have had access to much the same supply of empirical knowledge – from school, from meetings of the Book Society and philosophical lectures and from various books and journals.[87] In particular, of course, they would have shared much of the same medical knowledge which was primitive but becoming more systematic as physiology and anatomy slowly developed.[88] Their diaries show they were well-versed in drawing blood, applying leeches and glysters, setting broken limbs and removing tumours. But there is one important change between Clegg's life-path and that of Kay. Clegg was essentially an ordained Presbyterian minister with a small farm who practised medicine to make ends meet, a practice common in remote rural areas of England but one that was already dying out in his lifetime. His medical knowledge was picked up by some reading, of course, but also through apprenticing himself to another doctor in Macclesfield. His right to practise without a licence was guaranteed by a medical degree obtained *in absentia* from Aberdeen on the recommendation of other (Presbyterian) doctors. In some respects Clegg was an 'amateur' doctor and the localised life-space of his life-path reflects this fact. In contrast, Kay had a year's formal training at Guy's Hospital in London, and his diary makes it clear that medicine was his first priority and that his living came from the practice of it. Here we see the beginnings of the formation of the medical profession as we now understand it, of a segment of a new professional middle class and of a new social distribution of empirical knowledge with the attendant qualifications serving as its cultural capital. We can also observe the corresponding change in Kay's life-space, when compared with that of Clegg – only a year in London perhaps, but soon to burgeon into a much longer period of formal training.

390

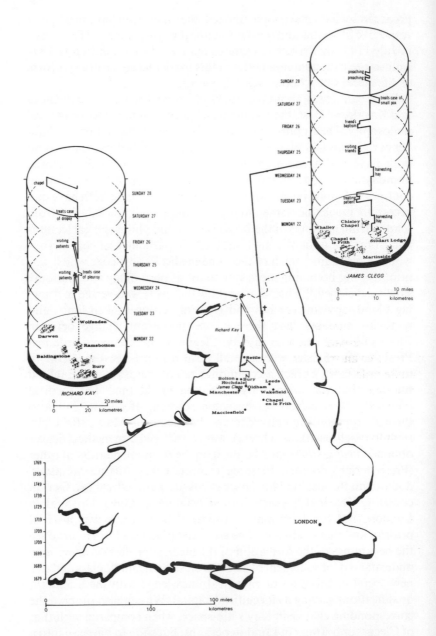

FIGURE 15.6 *The life-paths and daily-paths of James Clegg and Richard Kay during one week in July 1745*

The politics of knowing and unknowing

Finally, I want to turn to a more detailed discussion of the *links* between availability of knowledge and action by considering the implications that the availability of *printed* 'political' knowledge has for political organisation and action.[89] In order to anchor the discussion, I will limit my attention to how the 'working-class' was able to gain access to 'radical' literature in England in the early- to mid-nineteenth century. But four more general themes underly this particular experience: first, the physical availability of political knowledge, second, the relation of political knowledge to literacy and education, third, the organisational framework for the dissemination of political knowledge and, finally, the cognitive framework within which political knowledge is interpreted.

The physical availability of political knowledge

There is little doubt that the spatial distribution of knowledge has its effects. In particular, isolation takes its toll on what can be known. One partially doleful example of this is the Pentridge 'rebellion' of 1817 during which 200 or at most 300 men gathered in Pentridge and other villages at the foot of the Derby Peak, expecting their fellows in other centres to rise in revolt with them.[90] Their actions were, in part, predicated upon misinformation from the notorious *agent provocateur*, 'Oliver', whose success depended upon the isolation of these villages from news which in turn had much to do with their lack of contact with and access to the political organisations of London and the regional centres. But we should not make too much of the factor of isolation. It can also have the threefold counter-effects of fostering community cohesion, nurturing political traditions and making communities opaque to the surveillance of the authorities. Further, the evidence from early- to mid-nineteenth century England is that political knowledge does reach what might seem to be isolated rural communities surprisingly often. For example, in the early nineteenth century many of the dying breed of chapmen hawked not only the ordinary run of dying speeches and chapbooks but also political pamphlets and almanacs.[91] The latter had their accounts of political events which were often spiced with quite salty political commentaries. Other 'link men' provided political news and comment too,[92] particularly the carriers and coachmen who not only brought deliveries of newspapers, journals and radical books but also acted as conveyors of political opinion and as witnesses of actual events.[93] Of course, the spread of the radical press and of newspapers in general, as well as the unprecedented success of publications like Paine's *Rights of Man*, increased the level of available political knowledge in England dramatically. Thompson summarises the early- to mid-nineteenth century scene as well as anyone:

> Cobbett's 2nd *Register* at its meridian, between October 1816 and February 1817, was running at something between 40 000 and 60 000 each week, a figure many times in excess of any competitor of any sort. The *Black Dwarf* ran at about 12 000 in 1819, although this figure was probably exceeded after Peterloo. Thereafter the stamp tax (and the recession of the movement) severely curtailed circulation, although Carlile's periodicals ran in the thousands through much of the Twenties. With the Reform Bill agitation, the Radical press broke through to a larger circulation once more: Doherty's *Voice of the People*, and *The Pioneer* all had circulations above ten thousand . . . while a dozen smaller periodicals, like the *Destructive*, ran to some thousands. The slump in the sale of costly weekly periodicals (at anything from 7d to 1s.) during the stamp tax decade was to a great degree made up by the growth in the sales of cheap books and individual pamphlets . . . In the same period, in most of the great centres there were one or more (and in London a dozen) dailies or weeklies which, while not being avowedly 'Radical', nevertheless catered for this large Radical public.[94]

Nineteenth century developments in communications also played their part in the availability of political knowledge, but it was a part that, initially at least, was by no means entirely positive. Thus, in the rural areas:

> One factor in the relative quiescence of the period from 1830 to 1870 may have been the disintegration of the network of long-distance carriers and coaches after the coming of the railway. The railway may have united the urban proletariat but in rural areas it could not perform the role that the link men of the road had. Its network was much less integrated, sparse, and its stopping places much rarer. Indeed, initially, it isolated the rural labourer and artisans from regular and direct contact with the urban centres of political radicalism and with labourers in other areas. No wonder

Chartism barely touched the countryside. It is even possible that the village world of the 1840s and 1850s had a more restricted horizon than had the village in 1830. By the 1860s however, this horizon was beginning to widen again. Cheap daily newspapers, national networks of benefit societies, the penny post... all of which depended to some extent on a national railway network, gradually helped to restore the contacts between the village and the outside world that the railway had originally destroyed. The development of agricultural trade unionism on a national scale then became a possibility.[95]

The relations of political knowledge to literacy and education

Some degree of literacy is needed in a community that is to receive printed political knowledge and indeed by the early nineteenth century literacy had become widespread in England as the possibility of at least some education had become a probability. It has been estimated that, even at the beginning of the century, in the two most illiterate groups (agricultural labourers and servants) one in three possessed sufficient literacy to sign a marriage register and the proportion of tradesmen and artisans capable of signing on the register was about double the proportion of these two groups.[96] This degree of literacy was obviously spatially variable and, in general, literacy was greatest in the cities and towns and lowest in the agricultural villages and hamlets. Yet even in the rural areas most homes had a few books, albeit mainly religious.[97] And of course literacy was not a necessary prerequisite for acquiring political knowledge. Those amongst the working class who were literate (particularly the artisans) could act as scribes for their non-literate fellows and were often nominated to read out newspapers in public houses and other associative locations. James Dawson Burn provides one out of many similar autobiographical reminiscences:

There was a young man in Bellingham, named George Seaton, who had served his apprenticeship with a Mr Gibson, a saddler. Seaton was a person of studious habits, and an inquiring turn of mind: he was also a very good public reader. For some time after the *Black Dwarf* made its appearance in the village, Seaton was in the habit of reading it to a few of the more intelligent working people, at the old fashioned cross which stood in the centre of the village.[98]

The organisational framework for the dissemination of political knowledge

The institutional framework in which political knowledge is transmitted is clearly crucial, and just as clearly there is a sea-change in this organisation that begins in the early nineteenth century. In England, a whole network of new or adapted knowledge-disseminating nodes springs up at which newspapers, journals and books could be obtained. For example, newspapers were stocked in the new type of coffee shop, which sometimes even had a small library,[99] or could be heard being read aloud in the public houses and beershops. Artisans' libraries became common. Market stalls sold radical literature. Even the members of some workshops clubbed together to buy a journal or a newspaper. For those who were committed these nodes now formed an integral part of the routinised channel through which their life-path ran; they acted as the founts of a new popular sociability.[100] Thomas Carter (b. 1792), a Colchester tailor, was one of these committed men:

> The workshop employed a shopman, two apprentices, a foreman, and six journeymen, a sufficient number of individuals to combat the then high price of radical literature and to introduce Carter to contemporary politics . . . 'they clubbed their pence to pay for a newspaper, and selected the 'Weekly Political Register' of that clever man the late William Cobbett.' Later he moved to London and was able to avail himself of two more methods of extending the scope of his reading matter. He made a habit of taking his breakfast at one of the coffee shops, 'which were just then becoming general', on his way to work where he would read the previous day's newspapers, the contents of which he would relay to his fellow workmen. And in his spare time he found an opportunity for supplementing his own small library: 'At home I acquired increased facilities for reading, by means of a small book club, consisting of my landlord and a few of his friends. Of this I became a member; and thus had the means of becoming a little acquainted with works which I had not seen before'.[101]

The interpretation of political knowledge

It seems clear that the working classes in England in the early nineteenth century were, in many respects, still in the transition from an oral to a print culture, with print still only 'one of' rather than 'the major' means of disseminating and receiving political knowledge. Interpretation of print is concrete and literal. This is not so surprising. In England:

> the ability to read was only the elementary technique. The ability to handle abstract and consecutive argument was by no means inborn; it had to be discovered against almost overwhelming difficulties – the lack of leisure, the cost of candles (or spectacles), as well as educational deprivation. Ideas and terms were sometimes employed in the early Radical movement which, it is evident, had for some ardent followers a fetishistic rather than rational value. Some of the Pentridge rebels thought that a 'Provisional Government' would ensure a more plentiful supply of 'provisions'; while, in one account of the pitmen of the north-east in 1819, 'Universal Suffrage is understood by many of them to mean universal suffering' ... 'if one member suffers, all must suffer'.[102]

The relationship between political action (and inaction) by members of a particular social group and the availability of political knowledge must be related to the internal organisation of the institutions of that social group, the organisation of the (often intersecting) institutions of other social groups and the objective structural conditions which form the grounds of possibility.[103] The connections are often oblique and are continually changing over space and in time. But the fact remains that in many places in England during the early-to mid-nineteenth century access to political knowledge not only sensitised actors to current events but also helped to inspire them to action, however limited. For example, in 'radical Oldham' in the 1830s the cultural field sees:

> The biggest and most undeniable development of all – a mass readership of the radical press. While this cannot be precisely measured, the descriptive evidence indicates that the London and Lancashire working-class newspapers achieved something near a monopoly in Oldham.[104]

And such a process of getting knowledge is often cumulative for one part of a political tradition is to know how to know about politics.

The problems of making the connections between political action and the availability of political knowledge become even greater in the twentieth century when, for example, other media than print come into play (each with their own distinctive ways of disseminating, rationing and biasing knowledge),[105] when mass schooling systems guarantee a print culture's existence and when organised political parties hold sway. These changes are not within the scope of this chapter. But at the most general level, the difference between the nineteenth and twentieth centuries are probably not as great as might at first be assumed. In most social groups political commitment remains diffuse, those who read political books remain in a minority, those who know about politics and political institutions are relatively few.[106] It can be safely assumed that political knowing and unknowing remains differentially distributed amongst social groups, over space and in time.[107]

Conclusions

Four main threads can be teased out from this chapter. First, the availability of knowledge must be seen as an important component in the construction of a theory of situated social action. It is not the only component; it is probably not the most important component, but neither is it a component that can any longer be passed over. Ignorance may be no excuse in the eyes of the law, but it is a fact of social life that can no longer be overlooked. Second, the sociology of knowledge can be given a more coherent base, since it is now generally agreed that:

> an excessive interest in intellectual and intellectualised belief is a weakness of the conventional sociology of knowledge. Of much greater importance is the way that ideologies are represented and diffused in the relatively untheoretical 'ways of life' of whole social groups. It is notably difficult to provide a way of identifying these 'ways of life' or common-sense beliefs, and providing substantive studies of them . . . is a major task of a sociology of knowledge.[108]

I hope that this chapter goes some way towards beginning to overcome this difficulty. Third, epistemology must be seen for what it is. Thus, it:

> is not an emanation of 'reason' but is made up of doctrines and standards which themselves demand evaluation. One does not gain

exemption from evaluation by claiming to be rational, any more than by claiming to be scientific. In the last analysis a community evaluates all its cognitive authorities in relation to its overall way of life, not be reference to a specific set of standards.[109]

This is not an argument for an unalloyed historicism or a recalcitrant relativism.[110] But it is an argument for a situated or contextual epistemology, which acknowledges that people are historical, geographical and social beings.[111] Finally, a conclusion tinged with a certain amount of irony. We know very little about what people know and do not know. From the many indirect studies, we can expect there to be systematic variations in the knowledge available to and taken up by various social groups set in particular regions and times. Yet what is systematically known about these variations is restricted to a few desultory studies. This chapter is therefore at best a prelude to a pressing empirical task. It is the germ of an idea.

Notes

1. Cited in Kreckel (1982) p. 270.
2. According to the *Oxford English Dictionary* 'germ' in its modern meaning as a micro-organism did not come into existence until this date (although germ meaning a seed of disease as in 'germ of the smallpox' was current in 1803).
3. Giddens (1979; 1981b).
4. Social groups (which include classes) can be seen as the intermediate point in the process of 'structuring' between social structure and individual and between individual and social structure. The formation and reformation of social structure cannot be understood without considering this continual process of social group formation and reformation and neither can the formation and reformation of individuals. Thus a situated theory of human action must be built upon and necessarily intersect with an understanding of factors such as how such groups are continually organised and reorganised *in conflict* (and coalition) with other groups, how their distinctive spatial and temporal interaction structures (Layder 1981) produce, at a variety of scales, distinctive strengths and weaknesses and how these social groups are produced, reproduced or transformed by the actions of the individuals that are both constituted by and partially constitutive of them. This formulation makes it possible to reconcile 'way of conflict' with 'way of life' (Thompson, 1961) and 'economy' with what some Marxists continue to insist is a ragbag of superstructures but which is, in reality, an integral part of the production and reproduction of society, namely 'civil society' (see Urry, 1981a), a term which, of course, goes under

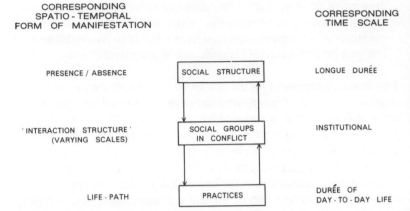

FIGURE 15.7 *The major components of the process of structuring (compare with Thrift (1983), Figure 2)*

many other names such as 'culture', 'civilisation', or '*mentalités*'.

5. See the remarks by Bhaskar (1980) p. 18.

6. See Thrift (1983); Thrift and Forbes (1983).

7. For a systematic account of the production, distribution and circulation system, albeit a rather abstract and partial one, see R. Williams (1981).

8. This term derived from the writings of Schutz and Luckmann (see, for example, Schutz, 1962; Schutz and Luckmann, 1973; Berger and Luckmann, 1967; Luckmann, 1982) is useful almost in spite of their work. Schutz, in particular, has an unfortunate tendency to reduce the social world to stocks of knowledge. See Hindess (1977) ch. 2 for a particularly hostile view of Schutz, and Abercrombie (1980) for a more sympathetic appraisal.

9. I want to use this term without its implications of a series of completely self-contained universes or of relativism. See Giddens (1976) p. 18.

10. See Giddens (1976; 1979; 1981b); Bhaskar (1979; 1980); Bourdieu (1977); Abrams (1982); Elias (1978b; 1982).

11. See Thrift (1983); my subsequent presentation is overwhelmingly biased to the negative side of knowing because we know so little about human creativity.

12. The term 'habitus' is taken from Bourdieu (1977) and refers to the cognitive structure of any social group which is the sedimented history of practices improvised to meet particular objective conditions which then tends to reproduce these conditions.

13. In modern societies media like books or television may complicate this picture but they do not fundamentally change the situation. Indeed we might think of these media as having some of the same qualities as human actors, in terms of their communicability of knowledge.

14. Urry (1981a) p. 70.
15. Thrift (1979; 1983); Thrift and Pred (1981).
16. Until quite recently in human history, of course, human societies were often still isolated from one another. Countries like China, for example, all but formed their own universes, devoid of outside influence or knowledge.
17. Castoriadis (1971) p. 217.
18. H. G. Wells, *Men Like Gods*, cited in Bourdieu and Passeron (1977) p. 71.
19. And which we might call 'ideology'. Habermas (1982a) p. 264, makes some similar observations in a rather different context.
20. It is important to guard against reductionism here, of course. Marxists have been particularly guilty, in that they too often *assume* direct connections between the capitalist economy and, for example, the division of the labour force into skilled and unskilled or into those with qualifications and those without. Abercrombie and Urry (1983) provide an excellent critique of this kind of tendency which is *still* apparent in many works (for example, Carchedi, 1983). However, there have been works which have avoided this tendency, for example, Zilsel (1942).
21. Such as those offered, most notably, by Habermas, but also by Willer and Willer (1973).
22. Hirst (1982) pp. 444–5. See also Hirst and Woolley (1982) ch. 14.
23. See Macfarlane (1970) ch. 12. The diary is available. See Macfarlane (1976).
24. Spufford (1981) p. 155.
25. Bourdieu (1977) p. 79.
26. Thus Freud's work is restricted to a particular class operating in a particular place and time. See Fromm (1981). But historical psychology is now receiving increasing attention with the impetus provided by Elias' work (1978, 1982).
27. Neisser's definition of practical knowledge is as good as any. Practical knowledge is:

    the human knowledge that is not based on a systematic knowledge of the laws governing nature or society but, though obtained pragmatically, possesses a high degree of certainty: for example, how to till the soil, how to make simple tools, how to care for a herd, how to hunt (Neisser, 1965, p. 24).

    But I would want to add to this definition, 'knowledge of social interaction', especially that gained in close-knit groups, such as the family. See Kreckel (1982).
28. See Bourdieu (1977).
29. Giddens (1979, 1981b).
30. Jackson (1982) p. 16.
31. See de Schlippe (1965); IDS Bulletin (1979); Brokensha, Warren and Werner (1980).
32. Chapman (1983). Note how the word 'belief' automatically denies that there is any truth in what is thought.
33. I mean 'rationaliation' to be taken here in the Weberian sense. For an

excellent reconstruction of Weber's theory of rationalisation see Habermas (1982b).
34. See Foucault (1977); Giddens (1981b).
35. Kreckel (1982).
36. I have taken this term from Giddens, who uses it to refer to distance in space and time.
37. See, in particular, Goody and Watt (1963); Goody (1968a); Goody (1977); Ginzburg (1980b); Giddens (1981b).
38. Goody (1968b); Tambiah (1968); Clanchy (1979). The form and extent of these systems should not be underestimated. For example, in England:

> By Edward I's reign serfs possessed seals to sign their names and they recorded their property transactions in writing. Thus the *nativi* – the natives, villeins and serfs – who had thought the Domesday Book to be the Last Judgement (according to FitzNeal in the twelfth century) had charters of their own (the Cartae Nativorum) by the 1300s (Clanchy (1979) p. 259).

39. These were particularly limits imposed by *time*. Thus in twelfth and thirteenth century England cursive script came into extensive use as pressure of business built up on scribes. Clanchy (1979).
40. Eisenstein (1979) p. 518.
41. The discussion which follows draws on Chaytor (1945); Febvre and Martin (1976); Hirst and Woolley (1982) and, in particular, Eisenstein (1979) Ch. 2. (There are, of course, many other effects of printing than those catalogued there. For example, the idea of the author dates from this invention). It is a worthwhile exercise to compare the four characteristics listed here with those characteristics of a 'knowledgeable society' listed in Lane (1966) pp. 653–7.
42. See the remarks on professions in Lane (1966) and in Ginzburg (1980b).
43. Kuhn (1970) p. 5 likens normal science to 'a strenuous and devoted attempt to force nature into the conceptual boxes supplied by professional education'.
44. Barnes (1982) p. 10.
45. Sohn-Rethel (1978) considers that abstract thought comes from the practice of commodity exchange. Whilst this may be a part of the picture, I remain to be convinced that it is anything like the whole explanation.
46. It is therefore debarred from many people. See Steiner (1978) on the death of the book.
47. Lane (1966) p. 654.
48. Lakoff and Johnson (1980); Hill (1982).
49. Bernal (1965) p. 40.
50. It should not be thought that magic is now the exclusive prerogative of the developing countries: see, for example, Favret-Saada (1980) on the Bocage of Western France. Hirst (1982) makes the point that the form of magic is intimately related to the spatial layout of a community. The Bocage area's form of magic, for example, relies on small family enterprises, settled residence and familial–patriachal relations. It would not work in a factory.

51. Hill (1982) p. 176. On 'cunning men' see Burke (1978).
52. Yates (1964). See also Yates (1972; 1979).
53. Rattansi (1973); Righini Bonelli and Shea (1975); Webster (1982).
54. Yates (1964).
55. Hill (1982) p. 177.
56. Webster (1982).
57. Hill (1982) p. 177.
58. French (1972) p. 109.
59. Hill (1982) p. 191.
60. Ginzburg (1980b) pp. 26–7.
61. Thomas (1971) p. 799.
62. Ibid, p. 800.
63. Febvre and Martin (1976).
64. See, for example, Mandrou (1964); Bollème (1971); Burke (1978) and the review by Martin (1978).
65. See, for example, Neuberg (1977); Burke (1978); Spufford (1981).
66. Spufford (1981) p. xviii.
67. Spufford (1981) pp. 36 –7. This conclusion is, of course, open to debate since it is based upon partial knowledge but I am sure it is correct. See also Spufford (1979); Schofield (1968; 1973) Cressy (1980).
68. See Goody (1977).
69. The account that follows is taken from Capp (1979).
70. Capp (1979) p. 180.
71. Ibid, p. 203.
72. There are obvious problems in using a surrogate variable like number of licensed chapmen to represent the patterns of distribution of cheap books. First, chapmen certainly did not sell only books. These were usually just one of their wares, although some were specialists in book-selling. Second, many chapmen although resident in one town worked a periodic market system. Third, there were many other retailers of cheap books, most notably specialist booksellers but also some shopkeepers. The map is therefore indicative at best.
73. Spufford (1981) p. 126.
74. See Lough (1971); Darnton (1979).
75. Darnton (1979) p. 9.
76. Ibid, p. 7. In fact, much of the *Encyclopédie* represented not much more than a codification of practical knowledge. Ginzburg (1980) p. 22, talks of 'a massive process of culture invasion... the symbol and crucial instrument of this offensive was the French *Encyclopédie*'.
77. There are also problems in mapping the distribution of books sold. First, salesmen were unevenly effective in selling in *Encyclopédies*. Second, the density of booksellers varied. Third, the density of primary and secondary schools varied. However:

    In general, it seems clear that the quarto reached every corner of the country, including the remote areas of the *Pays Basque* and the *Massif Central*. Its diffusion corresponded fairly well to the density of population on a national scale, despite important discrepancies from city to city. (Darnton, 1979, p. 281)
78. This account follows that of Darnton (1979) pp. 287–94.

79. Ibid, p. 299.
80. See especially, Abler, Janelle, Philbrick and Sommer (1975).
81. I know of no research which has considered systematically the common funds of knowledge learnt from the various media or at school, or what the differences are, although these can of course be inferred from the many studies on the media and schooling.
82. See Bourdieu and Passeron (1977; 1980) and Garnham and Williams (1980). Cultural capital does not come just from the knowledge engendered and protected by professions of course, but also from the investment of time in and exercise of various cultural practices which legitimise class and other divisions (see Bourdieu, 1979). The acquisition of this kind of knowledge can be seen in a life-path perspective as a continuous process of the acquisition of various cultural competences at home, in school and elsewhere.
83. On sequestration see Foucault (1977) and Giddens (1981b).
84. See Thrift (1983).
85. The information on Clegg and Kay comes from their diaries edited by Doe (1978) and Brockbank and Kenworthy (1968) respectively.
86. For example, the Reverend John Bent, Dr Samuel Kay and James Day.
87. The exact size of their libraries remains in doubt. Friends of Clegg's whose books he valued on their death had libraries of at least 1500 books, however.
88. See the account of seventeenth-century medical knowledge in Thomas (1971). 'Germs' were not known!
89. I am taking 'political' knowledge here to mean information about political events *and* ways of organising this information of the kind to be found in pamphlets, newspapers, journals and books. I am not including the political messages to be found in literature like the popular novel, however potent these may sometimes be.
90. See Thompson (1968) pp. 711–34, and Calhoun (1982) for further details.
91. See Capp (1979).
92. A phrase originally used by Richard Cobb.
93. However, the carriers and coachmen were mainly restricted to major highways: see Charlesworth (1979).
94. Thompson (1968) pp. 789–90. For details of the press and, in particular, the Radical Press at this time see, for example, Hollis (1970); Koss (1981). For details of radical books available see Vincent (1981); Altick (1957); Webb (1950; 1955). See also the set of maps in Lee (1976) which show the diffusion of newspapers in England and their political affiliation.
95. Charlesworth (1979) p. 46. Thus, in the nineteenth century in particular, different social organisations were effective at different scales, at different 'levels of integration' (see Smith, N. 1982).
96. Stone (1969); Schofield (1973).
97. Further, literacy does not guarantee the habit of reading. See Vincent (1981) p. 110.
98. Burn (1978) p. 94. See also Vincent (1981).
99. The first of these opened in 1811. By 1849 there were some 2000 in London alone.

100. Other libraries and other sources of political knowledge also grew up at the time, of course, although usually of a non-radical nature; for example, those of the Mechanics Institutes, the Society for the Diffusion of Useful Knowledge, chapel libraries, even a few school libraries.
101. Vincent (1981) p. 118.
102. Thompson (1968) p. 783.
103. Calhoun (1982) ch. 8.
104. Foster (1974) p. 147.
105. See reviews in Barnett, Corrigan, Kuhn and Wolff (1979); Swingewood (1977); Corrigan and Willis (1980).
106. Dennis, Lindberg and McCrone (1971).
107. For books, see Mann (1970); Mann and Burgoyne (1969).
108. Abercrombie (1980) p. 176.
109. Barnes (1982) p. 93.
110. One seeming gap in this essay is the work of Foucault, but this is a result of his lack of emphasis on practices.
111. Thrift (1979). See Bhaskar's (1979, 1980) comments on the activity–, concept– and space–time dependence of theories.

Bibliography

(Place of publication of books is London unless otherwise stated.)

Abercrombie, N. (1980) *Class, Structure and Knowledge* (Oxford).
Abercrombie, N. and Urry, J. (1983) *Capital, Labour and the Middle Classes*.
Åberg, A. (1953) *När Byarna Sprängdes* (Stockholm).
Abler, R., Janelle, D., Philbrick, A. and Sommer, J. (1975) *Human geography in a shrinking world* (North Scituate, Massachusetts).
Abrams, P. (1982) *Historical Sociology* (Shepton Mallet).
Abrams, P., Deem, R., Finch, J. and Rock, P. (eds) (1981) *Practice and Progress: British sociology, 1950–1980*
Aglietta, M. (1979) *A Theory of Capitalist Regulation.*
Agnew, J. A. (1981) 'Homeownership and the Capitalist Social Order' in Dear and Scott (eds) (1981) pp. 457–80.
Agnew, J. S. (1979) 'Instrumentalism, Realism and Research on Diffusion of Innovation', *Professional Geographer*, vol. 31, pp. 364–70.
Agulhon, M. (1982) *The Republic in the Village. The people of the Var from the French Revolution to the Second Republic* (Cambridge).
Åkerman, S., Johansen, H. C. and Gaunt, D. (eds) (1978) *Chance and Change: social and economic studies in historical demography in the Baltic area* (Odense).
Albrow, M. (1974) 'Dialectical and Categorical Paradigms of a Science of Society', *Sociological Review*, vol. 22, pp. 183–201.
Alden, J. (1977) 'The Extent and Nature of Double Job-holding in Great Britain', *Industrial Relations Journal*, vol. 8, pp. 14–31.
Alden, J. (1981) in Henry (ed.) (1981).
Alihan, M. (1938) *Social Ecology: a Critical Analysis* (New York).
Althusser, L. and Balibar, E. (1970) *Reading Capital.*
Altick, R. D. (1957) *The English Common Reader: a Social History of the Mass Reading Public 1800–1900* (Chicago).
Åmark, K. (1915) *Spannmålshandel och Spannmålspolitik i Sverige 1719–1830* (Stockholm).
Amedeo, D. and Golledge, R. (1975) *An Introduction to Scientific Reasoning in Geography* (New York).
Anckarsvärd, C. H. (1910–13) 'En Resa i Blekinge och Skåne [document from 1817]', *Historisk Tidskrift för Skåneland*, vol. 4, pp. 68–83.
Anderson, J., Duncan, S. and Hudson, R. (eds) (1983) *Redundant Spaces in Cities and Regions?*
Anderson, M. (1976) 'Sociological History and the Working-class Family: Smelser Revisited', *Social History*, vol. 1 (3) pp. 317–34.
Anderson, P. (1980) *Arguments within English Marxism.*

Areskoug, H. (1949) 'On Språk och Språkgränser på Österlen' *Tumathorps Sanct Knuts Gille Tänkebok*, pp. 69–92.
Ariès, P. (1973) *Centuries of Childhood* (Harmondsworth).
Aronowitz, S. (1978) 'Marx, Braverman and the Logic of Capital', *Insurgent Sociologist*, vol. 8 (2–3), pp. 126–46.
Aronson, R. (1980) *Sartre: Philosophy in the World*.
Ashton, P. (1978) 'The Political Economy of Surburban Development' in Tabb and Sawers (eds) (1978) pp. 64–89.
Asplund, J. (1983) *Tid, Rum, Individ och Kollektiv* (Stockholm).
Aumeeruddy, A. T., Lautier, B. and Tortajada, R. (1978) 'Labour Power and the State', *Capital and Class*, vol. 6, pp. 52–66.
Aydalot, P. (1976) *Dynamique Spatiale et Développement Inégal* (Paris).

Bagnasco, A. (1977) *Tre Italia* (Bologna).
Bagnasco, A. (1981) 'La Questione dell'economia informale', *Stato e Mercato*, vol. 1, pp. 173–96.
Ball, R. M. (1980) 'The Use and Definition of Travel-to-work Areas in Great Britain: Some Problems', *Regional Studies*, vol. 14, pp. 125–39.
Barck, J. (1904–8) 'En Berättelse om Jordbruket i Malmöhus Län [Document from 1759]', *Historisk Tidskrift för Skåneland*, vol. 2, pp. 372–80.
Barnes, B. (1982) *T. S. Kuhn and Social Science*.
Barnett, M., Corrigan, P., Kuhn, A. and Wolff, J. (eds) (1979) *Ideology and Cultural Production*.
Beechey, V. (1977) 'Some Notes on Female Wage Labour in Capitalist Production', *Capital and Class*, vol. 3, pp. 45–66.
Beechey, V. (1978) 'Women and Production: a Critical Analysis of Some Sociological Theories of Women's Work' in Kuhn and Wolpe (eds) (1978).
Bell, C. and Newby, H. (1976) 'Community, Communication, Class and Community Action: the Social Sources of the New Urban Politics' in Herbert and Johnston (eds) (1976).
Berg, G. and Svensson, S. (1934) *Svensk Bondekultur* (Stockholm).
Berger, J. (1971) *The Look of Things* (New York).
Berger, J. and Mohr, J. (1975) *A Seventh Man* (Harmondsworth).
Berger, P. L. and Luckmann, T. (1967) *The Social Construction of Reality: a Treatise in the Sociology of Knowledge* (Garden City).
Berger, S. and Piore, M. (1980) *Dualism and Discontinuity in Industrial Societies* (Cambridge).
Bernal, J. D. (1965) *Science in History*.
Berry, B. J. L. (1968) 'A Synthesis of Formal and Functional Regions using a General Field Theory of Spatial Behaviour' in Berry and Marble (eds) (1968) pp. 419–28.
Berry, B. J. L. and Marble, D. F. (eds) (1968) *Spatial Analysis* (Englewood Cliffs, New Jersey).
Beynon, H. (1973) *Working for Ford*.
Bhagwati, J. N. (ed.) (1972) *Economics and World Order*.
Bhaskar, R. (1975) *A Realist Theory of Science* (Leeds).
Bhaskar, R. (1978a) *A Realist Theory of Science* (Brighton and Atlantic Highlands).
Bhaskar, R. (1978b) 'On the Possibility of Social Scientific Knowledge and

the Limits of Naturalism', *Journal for the Theory of Social Behavior*, vol. 8, pp. 1–28.

Bhaskar, R. (1979) *The Possibility of Naturalism: a Philosophical Critique of the Contemporary Human Sciences* (Brighton).

Bhaskar, R. (1980) 'Scientific Explanation and Human Emancipation', *Radical Philosophy*, vol. 26, pp. 16–28.

Blackburn, P., Green, K. and Liff, S. (1982) 'Science and Technology in Restructuring', *Capital and Class*, vol. 18, pp. 15–37.

Blackburn, R. and Mann, M. (1979) *The Working Class and the Labour Market* (Cambridge).

Blaikie, P. (1978) 'The Theory of the Spatial Diffusion of Innovations: a Spacious Cul-de-sac', *Progress in Human Geography*, vol. 2, pp. 268–95.

Blanch, M. (1979) 'Imperialism, Nationalism and Organised youth' in Clarke, Critcher and Johnson (eds) (1979) pp. 103–20.

Blaut, J. (1961) 'Space and Process', *Professional Geographer*, vol. 13, pp. 1–7.

Blaut, J. (1977) 'Two Views of Diffusion', *Annals of the Association of American Geographers*, vol. 67, pp. 343–9.

Blaut, J. (1980) 'A Radical Critique of Cultural Geography', *Antipode*, vol. 12, pp. 25–9.

Bleitrach, D. and Chenu, A. (1979) *L'usine et la Vie: Luttes Régionales* (Paris).

Bleitrach, D. and Chenu, A. (1981) 'Modes of Domination and Everyday Life: Some Notes on Recent Research' in Harloe and Lebas (eds) (1981) pp. 105–15.

Bluestone, B. and Harrison, B. (1982) *The Deindustrialization of America* (New York).

Boddy, M. and Fudge, C. (1984) *Local Socialism: Labour councils and New Left alternatives*.

Bollème, G. (ed.) (1971) *La Bibliothèque Bleue: la Littérature Populaire en France du XVIe au XIXe siècle* (Paris).

Boudon, R. (1981) *The Logic of Social Action: an Introduction to Sociological Analysis*.

Bourdieu, P. (1977) *Outline of a Theory of Practice* (Cambridge).

Bourdieu, P. (1979) *La Distinction* (Paris).

Bourdieu, P. and Passeron, J. (1977) *Reproduction in Education, Society and Culture*.

Bourdieu, P. and Passeron, J. (1980) *The Inheritors: French Students and their Relation to Culture* (Chicago).

Bradley, T. and Lowe, P. (eds) (1984) *Rurality and Locality* (Norwich).

Braudel, F. (1972) *The Mediterranean and the Mediterranean World in the Age of Philip II* (2nd edn) (2 vols).

Braudel, F. (1980) *On History*.

Braverman, H. (1974) *Labor and Monopoly Capital* (New York).

Briggs, A. and Saville, J. (eds) (1960) *Essays in Labour History*.

Bringéus N.-A. (1964) 'Tradition och Förändring i 1800-Talets Skånska Lanthushållning' in Björklund, C. and Lindbom, G. (eds) (1964) *Kristianstads Läns Hushållnings Sällskap 1814–1964* (Kristianstad) pp. 9–98.

Bringéus, N.-A. (1971) 'Mat och Måltid i Skånska Bondehem: en Oversikt', *Skånes Hembygdsförbund Årsbok*, pp. 9–84.

Broadbent, T. A. (1977) *Planning and Profit in the Urban Economy*.
Brockbank, W. and Kenworthy, F. (eds) (1968) *The Diary of Richard Kay, 1716–51* (Manchester).
Brokensha, D. W., Warren, D. M. and Werner, O. (eds) (1980) *Indigenous Knowledge Systems and Development* (Lanham, Maryland).
Bromley, R. (1978) 'The Urban Informal Sector: Why is it Worth Discussing?', *World Development*, vol. 6 (9–10), pp. 1033–39.
Brown, L. A. and Cox, K. R. (1971) 'Empirical Regularities in the Diffusion of Innovation', *Annals of the Association of American Geographers*, vol. 61, pp. 551–9.
Bruzelius, N. G. (1978 [1876]) *Allmogelivet i Ingelstads Härad i Skåne under Slutet av Förra och Början av Detta Arhundrade* (Lund).
Burawoy, M. (1979) *Manufacturing Consent* (Chicago).
Burke, P. (1978) *Popular Culture in Early Modern Europe*.
Burn, J. D. (1978) *The Autobiography of a Beggar Boy*.
Burokev, J. V. (1981) *Space and Incongruence: the Origins of Kant's Idealism* (Dordrecht, Boston and London).
Buttimer, A. (1974) *Values in Geography* (Association of American Geographers, Commission on College Geography, Resource Paper 24).
Buttimer, A. (1976) 'Grasping the Dynamism of the Life World', *Annals of the Association of American Geographers*, vol. 66, pp. 277–92.
Buttimer, A. (ed) (1983) *The Practice of Geography*.
Bylund, E., Linderholm, H. and Rune, O. (eds) (1974) *Ecological Problems of the Circumpolar North* (Luleå).
Byrne, D. (1982) 'Class and the Local State', *International Journal of Urban and Regional Research*, vol. 6, pp. 61–82.

Calhoun, C. (1982) *The Question of Class Struggle: Social Foundations of Popular Radicalism during the Industrial Revolution* (Oxford).
Cameron, G. (1980) *The Future of the British Conurbations*.
Campbell, Å. (1928) *Skånska Bygder under Förra Hälften av 1700-Talet* (Uppsala).
Caplovitz, D. (1981) 'Making Ends Meet: How Families Cope with Inflation and Recession', *Annals of the American Academy of Political and Social Science*, vol. 456, pp. 88–98.
Capp, B. (1979) *Astrology and the Popular Press: English Almanacs 1500–1800*.
Carchedi, G. (1977) *On the Economic Identification of Social Classes*.
Carchedi, G. (1983) *Problems in Class Analysis: Production, Knowledge and the Function of Capital*.
Carlstein, T. (1978) 'Innovation, Time-allocation and Space–time Packing' in Carlstein, Parkes and Thrift (eds) (1978) vol. 1, pp. 146–61.
Carlstein, T. (1978a) 'Packing Activities in a Settlement Space–time Budget', mimeo.
Carlstein, T. (1980) *Time Resources, Society and Ecology* (Lund).
Carlstein, T. (1981) 'The Sociology of Structuration in Time and Space: a Time-geographic Assessment of Giddens's Theory', *Swedish Geographical Yearbook*.
Carlstein, T. (1982) *Time Resources, Society and Ecology*, vol. 1, *Pre-indus-*

trial Societies.
Carlstein, T., Parkes, D. and Thrift, N. (eds) (1978) *Timing Space and Spacing Time* (3 vols).
Carney, J., Hudson, R. and Lewis, J. (eds) (1980) *Regions in Crisis.*
Carter, H. (1981) *The Study of Urban Geography.*
Castells, M. (1971) *La Question Urbaine* (Paris).
Castells, M. (1976a) 'Is There an Urban Sociology?' in Pickvance (ed.) (1976).
Castells, M. (1976b) 'Theory and Ideology in Urban Sociology' in Pickvance (ed.) (1976).
Castells, M. (1977) *The Urban Question.*
Castells, M. (1978) *City, Class and Power.*
Castells, M. (1983) 'Crisis, Planning and the Quality of Life: Managing the New Historical Relationships between Space and Society' *Environment and Planning D: Society and Space,* vol. 1, pp. 3–21.
Castoriadis, C. (1971) *History and Revolution.*
Cawson, A. and Saunders, P. (1983) 'Corporatism, Competitive Politics and Class Struggle' in King (ed.) (1983) pp. 1–27.
Chapman, G. P. (1983) 'The Folklore of the Perceived Environment in Bihar', *mimeo.*
Charlesworth, A. (1979) *Social Protest in a Rural Society* (Norwich).
Chaytor, H. J. (1945) *From Script to Print* (Cambridge).
Chisholm, M. and Oeppen, J. (1973) *The Changing Pattern of Employment: Regional Specialisation and Industrial Localisation in Britain.*
Chorley, R. J. (ed.) (1973) *Directions in Geography.*
Christaller, W. (1966) *Central Places in Southern Germany* (Englewood Cliffs, New Jersey).
Clanchy, M. T. (1979) *From Memory to Written Record: England 1066–1307.*
Clark, G. and Dear, M. (1984) *State Apparatus: Structures and Language of Legitimacy.*
Clark, G. and Gertler, M. (1983) 'Migration and Capital', *Annals of the Association of American Geographers,* vol. 73, pp. 18–34.
Clark, P. A. (1982) 'A Review of Theories of Time and Structure for Organisational Sociology', University of Aston Management Centre, Working Paper 24.
Clarke, J., Critcher, C. and Johnson, R. (eds) (1979) *Working Class Culture: Studies in History and Theory.*
Clarke, S. (1977) 'Marxism, Sociology and Poulantzas' Theory of the State', *Capital and Class,* vol. 2, pp. 1–31.
Claval, P. (1977) 'Le Marxisme et l'espace', *L'Espace Géographique,* vol. 3, pp. 145–64.
Cliff, A. D. (1968) 'The Neighbourhood Effect in the Diffusion of Innovations', *Transactions of the Institute of British Geographers,* vol. 44. pp. 75–84.
Cliff, A. D. (1979) 'Quantitative Methods: Spatial Diffusion', *Progress in Human Geography,* vol. 3, pp. 143–52.
Cliff, A. D., Haggett, P. and Versey, G. R. (1981) *Spatial Diffusion: an Historical Geography of Epidemics in an Island Community* (Cambridge).
Cohen, G. A. (1978) *Karl Marx's Theory of History: a Defence* (Oxford and Princeton).

Coing, H. (1981) 'Review of *L'usine et la vie: luttes régionales*', *International Journal of Urban and Regional Research*, vol. 5, pp. 433–36.

Collins, R. (1981a) 'On the Micro-foundations of Macro-sociology', *American Journal of Sociology*, Vol. 86, pp. 984–1014.

Collins, R. (1981b) 'Micro-translation as a Theory-building Strategy' in Knorr-Cetina and Cicourel (eds) (1981).

Colson, F. H. (1926) *The Week* (Cambridge),

Connell, R. W. (1979) 'A Critique of the Althusserian Approach to Class' *Theory and Society*, vol. 8, pp. 321–45.

Cooke, P. (1981) 'Inter-regional Class Relations and the Redevelopment Process', *Papers in Planning Research*, UWIST, no. 36.

Cooke, P. (1982a) 'Class Interests, Regional Restructuring and State Formation in Wales' *International Journal of Urban and Regional Research*, vol. 6, pp. 187–204.

Cooke, P. (1982b) 'Class Relations and Uneven Development in Wales' in Day (ed.) (1982).

Cooke, P. (1983a) 'Labour Market Discontinuity and Spatial Development', *Progress in Human Geography*, vol. 7, pp. 543–65.

Cooke, P. (1983b) *Theories of Planning and Spatial Development*.

Corrigan, P. and Willis, P. (1980) 'Cultural Forms and Class Mediations', *Media, Culture and Society*, vol. 2, pp. 297–312.

Cosgrove, D. (1978) 'Place, Landscape and the Dialectics of Cultural Geography' *Canadian Geographer*, vol. 22, pp. 66–72.

Coward, R. and Ellis, J. (1977) *Language and Materialism*.

Cox, K. (ed.) (1978) *Urbanization and Conflict in Market Societies*.

Cox, K. (1981a) 'Bourgeois Thought and the Behavioral Geography Debate' in Cox and Golledge (eds) (1981) pp. 256–279.

Cox, K. (1981b) 'Capitalism and Conflict around the Communal Living Space' in Dear and Scott (eds) (1981) pp. 431–56.

Cox, K., and Golledge, R. (eds) (1981) *Behavioral Problems in Geography Revisited*.

Cressy, D. (1980) *Literacy and the Social Order: Reading and Writing in Tudor and Stuart England* (Cambridge).

Cronin, J. and Schneer, J. (eds) (1982) *Social Conflict and the Political Order in Modern Britain*.

Cutler, A., Hindess, B., Hirst, P. and Husain, A. (1977) *Marx's Capital and Capitalism Today*, vol. 1.

Dahl, S. (1941) 'Storskiftets och enskiftets Genomförande i Skåne', *Skania*, vol. 14, pp. 86–97.

Dahl, S. (1942) *Torna och Bara-Studier i Skånes Bebyggelse – och Näringsgeografi Före 1860* (Meddelanden från Lunds Universitets Geografiska Institution, Avhandlingar 4).

Dahrendorf, I. (1959) *Class and Class Conflict in Industrial Society* (Stanford).

Darnton, R. (1979) *The Business of Enlightenment: a Publishing History of the Encyclopédie 1775–1800* (Cambridge, Massachusetts).

Daunton, M. (1980) 'Miners' houses: South Wales and the Great Northern Coalfield, 1880–1914', *International Review of Social History*, vol. 25, pp. 143–75.

Daunton, M. (1981) 'Down the Pit: Work in the Great Northern and South Wales Coalfields, 1870–1914', *Economic History Review*, vol. 34, pp. 578–97.

Davis, M. (1980) 'Why the US Working Class is Different', *New Left Review*, vol. 123, pp. 3–46.

Dawley, A. (1976) *Class and Community: the Industrial Revolution in Lynn* (Cambridge, Massachusetts).

Day, G. *et al.* (eds) (1982) *Diversity and Decomposition in the Labour Market* (Farnborough).

Dear, M. and Scott, A. J. (eds) (1981) *Urbanisation and Urban Planning in Capitalist Society.*

Dennis, J., Lindberg, L. and McCrone, D. (1971) 'Support for Nation and Government among English Children', *British Journal of Political Science*, vol. 1, pp. 25–48.

de Schlippe, P. (1956) *Shifting Cultivation in Africa: the Zande System of Agriculture.*

Doe, V. S. (ed.) (1978) *The diary of James Clegg of Chapel-en-le-Frith 1708–1755* (2 vols) (Matlock).

Doeringer, P. B. and Piore, M. F. (1971) *Internal Labour Markets and Manpower Analysis* (Lexington, Massachusetts).

Duncan, J. (1980) 'The Superorganic in American Cultural Geography', *Annals of the Association of American Geographers*, vol. 70, pp. 181–98.

Duncan, S. (1974) 'The Isolation of Scientific Discovery: Indifference and Resistance to a New Idea', *Science Studies*, vol. 4, pp. 109–34.

Duncan, S. and Goodwin, M. (1982) 'The Local State and Restructuring Social Relations', *International Journal of Urban and Regional Research*, vol. 6, pp. 157–86.

Durkheim, E. (1964) *The Division of Labour in Society* (London and New York) (first published 1893).

Earman, J. (1970) 'Who's Afraid of Absolute Space?' *Australasian Journal of Philosophy*, vol. 48, pp. 287–319.

Edwards, R. (1979) *Contested Terrain: the Transformation of the Work-place in the Twentieth Century* (London and New York).

Egan, D. (1978) 'The Unofficial Reform Committee and the Miners' Next Step', *Llafur*, vol. 2, pp. 64–80.

Eisenstein, E. L. (1979) *The Printing Press as an Agent of Change: Communications and cultural transformations in early modern Europe* (Cambridge).

Ejder, B. (1969) *Dagens Tider och Måltider* (Lund).

Elias, N. (1978a) *What is sociology?*

Elias, N. (1978b) *The Civilizing Process* (Oxford).

Elias, N. (1982) *State Formation and Civilization* (Oxford).

Elias, N. and Scotson, J. (1965) *The Established and the Outsiders.*

Eliot Hurst, M. (1980) 'Geography, Social Science and Society: towards a de-definition', *Australian Geographical Studies*, vol. 18, pp. 3–21.

Elson, D. and Pearson, R. (1981) 'Nimble Fingers make Cheap Work: an Analysis of Women's Employment in Third World Export Manufacturing' *Feminist Review*, vol. 7, pp. 87–107

Elster, J. (1978) *Logic and Society* (Chichester).

Engels, F (1969a) *The Condition of the Working Class in England* (St Albans).
Engels, F. (1969b) 'The Housing Question' in Marx and Engels (1969) vol. II.
Engström, B. (1928) 'Åldermansskifte och Bystämma i Skänska och Danska Byar', *Fataburen*, pp. 18–39.
Engström, B. (1928) *Byalagen i Bara härad* (Lund).
Ericksen, E. G. (1980) *The Territorial Experience* (Austin).
Erixon, S. (1934) 'Svenskt Byliv', *Självstyrelsen i svenskt samhällsliv*, pp. 35–45.
Erixon, S. (1956) 'Bebyggelsestruktur och Bysamfällighet i Sverige', *Nordisk Kultur*, vol. 13, pp. 275–294.
Erixon, S. (1978) *Byalag och Byaliv* (Stockholm).
Eyles, J. (1981) 'Why Geography Cannot be Marxist: Towards an Understanding of Lived Experience', *Environment and Planning A*, vol. 13, pp. 1371–88.

Favret-Saada, J. (1980) *Deadly Words: Witchcraft in the Bocage* (Cambridge).
Febvre, L. and Martin, H. J. (1976) *The Coming of the Book: the Impact of Printing 1450–1800*.
Foladare, I. (1968) 'The Effect of Neighbourhood on Voting Behaviour', *Political Science Quarterly*, vol. 83, pp. 516–29.
Foot, M. (1962) *Aneurin Bevan, vol. 1, 1897–1945*.
Forer, P. (1978) 'Time–space and Area in the City of the Plains' in Carlstein, Parkes and Thrift (eds) (1978) vol. 1, pp. 99–118.
Forrest, R., Henderson, J. and Williams, P. (eds) (1983) *Urban Political Economy and Social Theory: critical essays in urban studies* (Aldershot).
Foster, J. (1974) *Class Struggle and the Industrial Revolution: Early Industrial Capitalism in Three English Towns*.
Fothergill, S. and Gudgin, G. (1980) 'Regional Employment Change: a Subregional Explanation', *Progress in Planning*, vol. 12.
Fothergill, S. and Gudgin, G. (1982) *Unequal Growth: Urban and Regional Employment Change in the UK*.
Foucault, M. (1970) *The Order of Things*.
Foucault, M. (1977) *Discipline and Punish: the Birth of the Prison*.
Foucault, M. (1980) *Power/Knowledge: Selected Interviews and Other Writings* (Brighton).
Francis, H. and Smith, D. (1980) *The Fed: a History of the South Wales Miners in the Twentieth Century*.
French, P. J. (1972) *John Dee: the World of an Elizabethan Magus*.
Fridlizius, G. (1957) *Swedish Corn Export in the Free Trade Era: Patterns in the Oats Trade 1850–1880* (Lund).
Fröbel, F., Heinrichs, J. and Kreye, O. (1980) *The New International Division of Labour* (Cambridge).
Frödin, J. (1946) 'Skiftesväsende och Jordbrukskrisett Tillägg' *Ekonomisk Tidskrift*, vol. 48, pp. 197–204.
Fromm, E. (1981) *The Greatness and Limitations of Freud's Thought*.
Frostin, E. (1932) 'Byalag i Färs härad', *Skånes Hembygdsförbund-Årsbok*, pp. 1–22.

Frykman, J. (1977) *Horan i Bondesamhället* (Lund).

Frykman, J. and Löfgren, O. (1979) *Den Kultiverade Människa* (Lund).

Gaile, G. (1979) 'Spatial Models of Spread-Backwash Processes', *Geographical Analysis*, vol. 11, pp. 173–88.

Gans, H. (1968) 'Urbanism and Suburbanism as Ways of Life' in Pahl (ed.) (1968) pp. 95–118.

Garnett, C. (1939) *The Kantian Philosophy of Space* (Port Washington).

Garnham, N. and Williams, R. (1980) 'Pierre Bourdieu and the Sociology of Culture: an introduction', *Media, Culture and Society*, vol. 2, pp. 209–23.

Garnsey, E. (1981) 'The Division of Labour', *Theory and Society*, vol. 10, pp. 337–58.

Gaspar, J. and Gould, P. (1981) 'The Cova da Beira: an Applied Structural Analysis of Agriculture and Communication' in Pred (ed.) (1981) pp. 183–214.

Gershuny, J. I. (1978) *After Industrial Society? The Emerging Self-service Economy*.

Gershuny, J. I. (1979) 'The Informal Economy: Its Role in Post-industrial Society', *Futures*, vol. II, pp. 3–15.

Gershuny, J. I. (1982) 'Social Innovation: Change in the Mode of Provision of Services', University of Sussex, Science Policy Research Unit.

Gershuny, J. I. (1983) *Social Innovation and the Division of Labour* (Oxford).

Gershuny, J. I. and Pahl, R. E. (1979) 'Work Outside Employment: Some Preliminary Speculations', *New Universities Quarterly*, vol. 34, pp. 120–35.

Gershuny, J. I. and Thomas, G. S. (1980) 'Changing Patterns of Time-use Data Preparation and Some Preliminary Results, UK 1961–1974/5', University of Sussex, Science Policy Research Unit, Occasional Paper no. 13.

Gershuny, J. I. and Thomas, G. S. (1983) 'Changing Times: Activity Patterns in the UK 1937–1974/5'.

Giddens, A. (1976) *New Rules of Sociological Method*.

Giddens, A. (1979) *Central Problems in Social Theory: Action, Structure and Contradiction in Social Analysis* (London and Berkeley).

Giddens, A. (1981a) *The Class Structure of the Advanced Societies* (2nd edn).

Giddens, A. (1981b) *A Contemporary Critique of Historical Materialism, vol. 1: Power, Property and the State* (London and Berkeley).

Giddens, A. and Mackenzie, G. (eds) (1982) *Social Class and the Division of Labour* (Cambridge).

Ginzburg, C. (1980a) *The Cheese and the Worms: the Cosmos of a Sixteenth-century Miller*.

Ginzburg, C. (1980b) 'Morelli, Freud and Sherlock Holmes: Clues and Scientific Method', *History Workshop Journal*, vol. 9, pp. 5–36.

Gittins, D. (1982) *Fair Sex: Family Size and Structure 1900–39*.

Goffman, E. (1959) *The Presentation of Self in Everyday Life* (New York).

Golledge, R. G., Brown, L. A. and Williamson, H. (1972) 'Behavioural Approaches in Geography: An Overview', *Australian Geographer*, vol. 12, pp. 59–79.

Goody, J. (ed.) (1968a) *Literacy in Traditional Societies* (Cambridge).

Goody, J. (1968b) 'Restricted Literacy in Northern Ghana' in Goody (ed.) (1968a) pp. 198–264.

Goody, J. (1977) *The Domestication of the Savage Mind* (Cambridge).

Goody, J. and Watt, I. (1963) 'The Consequences of Literacy', *Comparative Studies in History and Sociology*, vol. 5, pp. 304–45.

Gordon, D. (1972) *Theories of Poverty and Underemployment: Orthodox, Radical and Dual Labour Market Perspectives* (New York).

Gordon, D. (1978a) 'Class Struggle and the Stages of Urban Development' in Perry and Watkins (eds) (1978) pp. 55–82.

Gordon, D. (1978b) 'Capitalist Development and the History of American Cities' in Tabb and Sawers (eds) (1978) pp. 25–63.

Gordon, D., Edwards, R. and Reich, M. (1982) *Segmented Work, Divided Workers: the Historical Transformation of Labor in the United States* (Cambridge).

Gould, P. (1974) 'Response to S. Duncan', *mimeo.*

Gould, P. (1981) 'Space and *rum*: an English Note on Espacien and Rumian meaning', *Geografiska Annaler B*, vol. 63, pp. 1–3.

Gould, P. (1982) 'Is it Necessary to Choose? Some Technical, Hermeneutic and Emancipatory Thoughts on Inquiry' in Gould and Olsson (eds) (1982) pp. 71–104,

Gould, P. and Olsson, G. (eds) (1982) *A Search for Common Ground.*

Gouldner, A. (1976) *The Dialectic of Ideology and Technology: the Origins, Grammar and Future of Ideology.*

Gramsci, A. (1971) *Selections from Prison Notebooks.*

Gramsci, A. (1977) *Selections from Political Writings 1910–1920.*

Gramsci, A. (1978) *Selections from Political Writings 1981–1926.*

Granovetter, M. S. (1973) 'The Strength of Weak Ties', *American Journal of Sociology*, vol. 78, pp. 1360–80.

Gregory, D. (1978a) 'Social Change and Spatial Structures' in Carlstein, Parkes and Thrift (eds) (1978) vol. 1, pp. 38–46.

Gregory, D. (1978b) *Ideology, Science and Human Geography.*

Gregory, D. (1981) 'Human Agency and Human Geography', *Transactions of the Institute of British Geographers*, vol. 6, pp. 1–18.

Gregory, D. (1982a) 'Solid Geometry: Notes on the Recovery of Spatial Structure' in Gould and Olsson (eds) (1982) pp. 187–219.

Gregory, D. (1982b) *Regional Transformation and Industrial Revolution: A Geography of the Yorkshire Woollen Industry* (London and Minneapolis).

Gregory, D. (forthcoming a) 'Presences and Absences: Time–Space Relations and Structuration Theory' in Held and Thompson (eds).

Gregory, D. (forthcoming b) *Social Theory and Human Geography.*

Gross, D. (1982) 'Time–space Relations in Giddens's Social Theory', *Theory, Culture and Society*, vol. 2, pp. 83–8.

Gustafsson, B. (1956) *Manligt-kvinnligt-kyrkligt in 1800 Talets Svenska Folkliv* (Stockholm).

Habermas, J. (1982a) 'Reply to My Critics' in Thompson and Held (eds) (1982) pp. 219–83.

Habermas, J. (1982b) *Theorie des Kommunikativen Handelns* (Frankfurt).

Hadjimichalis, C. (1980) *The Geographical Transfer of Value: A Comparative Analysis of Regional Development of Southern Europe* (unpublished Ph.D thesis, University of California, Los Angeles: School of Architecture and Urban Planning).

Hägerstrand, T. (1952) 'The Propagation of Innovation Waves', Lund Studies in Geography: Series B: Human Geography, no. 4.

Hägerstrand, T. (1953) *Innovationsförloppet ur Korologisksynpunkt* (Lund).

Hägerstrand, T. (1957) 'Migration and Area' in Hannerberg, Hägerstrand and Odeving (eds) (1957) pp. 27–158.

Hägerstrand, T. (1965) 'A Monte Carlo Approach to Diffusion', *Archives Européenes de Sociologie*, vol. 6, pp. 43–67.

Hägerstrand, T. (1966) 'Aspects of the Spatial Structure of Social Communication and the Diffusion of Information' *Papers and Proceedings of the Regional Science Association*, vol. 16, pp. 27–42.

Hägerstrand, T. (1967) *Innovation Diffusion as a Spatial Process* (Chicago).

Hägerstrand, T. (1969) 'On the Definition of Migration', *Scandinavian Population Studies*, vol. 1, pp. 63–72.

Hägerstrand, T. (1970) 'What about People in Regional Science?', *Papers and Proceedings of the Regional Science Association*, vol 24, pp. 7–21.

Hägerstrand, T. (1973) 'The Domain of Human Geography' in Chorley (ed.) (1973) pp. 67–87.

Hägerstrand, T. (1974) 'On Socio-technical Ecology and the Study of Innovations' *Ethnologica Europaea*, vol 7, pp. 17–34.

Hägerstrand, T. (1974a) 'Commentary' in Buttimer (1974).

Hägerstrand, T. (1974b) 'Ecology under One Perspective' in Bylund, Linderholm and Rune (eds) (1974) pp. 271–76.

Hägerstrand, T. (1975) 'Space, Time and Human Conditions' in Karlqvist, Lundqvist and Snickars (eds) (1975) pp. 3–14.

Hägerstrand, T. (1976) 'Geography and the Study of Interaction between Nature and Society', *Geoforum*, vol. 7, pp. 329–34.

Hägerstrand, T. (1977) 'On the Survival of the Cultural Heritage', *Ethnologica Scandinavica*, vol. 1, pp. 7–12.

Hägerstrand, T. (1978) 'Survival and Arena: On the Life-history of Individuals in Relation to their Geographical Environment' in Carlstein, Parkes and Thrift (eds) (1978) vol. 2, pp. 122–45.

Hägerstrand, T. (1982) 'Diorama, Path and Project' *Tijdschrift voor Economische en Sociale Geografie*, vol. 73, pp. 323–39.

Hägerstrand, T. (1983) 'In Search for the Sources of Concepts' in Buttimer (ed.) (1983) pp. 238–56.

Haggett, P., Cliff, A.D. and Frey, A. (1977) *Locational Analysis in Human Geography*.

Haining, R. (1983) 'Spatial and Spatial–temporal Interaction Models and the Analysis of Patterns of Diffusion', *Transactions of the Institute of British Geographers*, vol. 8, pp.;158–86.

Hall, E. (1966) *The Hidden Dimension*.

Hall, S. (1977) 'The "Political" and the "Economic" in Marx's Theory of Classes' in Hunt (ed.) (1977) pp. 15–60.

Hall, S. (1980) 'Popular Democratic versus Authoritarian Populism: Two Ways of "Taking Democracy Seriously"' in Hunt (ed.) (1980) pp. 157–85.

Hallenborg, C. (1910–13) 'Anmärkningar till Carl von Linnes Skanska resa [document from 1752–175?]' *Historisk Tidskirft för Skåneland*, vol. 4, pp. 291–373.

Hamilton, F. E. I. and Linge, G. J. R. (eds) (1979) *Spatial Analysis, Industry and the Industrial Environment: vol 1: Industrial Systems* (New York).

Hannerberg, D., Hägerstrand, T. and Odeving, B. (eds) (1957) 'Migration in Sweden: a Symposium', Lund Studies in Geography: Series B: Human Geography, no. 13.

Hanson, N. (1969) 'Retroduction and the Logic of Scientific Discovery' in Krimerman (ed.) (1969).

Hanssen, B. (1952) *Österlen-Allmoge, köpstafolk & Kultursammanhang vid Slutet av 1700-Talet i sydöstra Skåne* (Ystad).

Hanssen, B. (1976) 'Hushallens Sammansättning i Österlenska Byar under 300 ar – En Studie i Historisk Strukturalism', *RIG*, vol. 59, pp. 33–61.

Hareven, T. (1982) *Family Time and Industrial Time. The Relationship between the Family and Work in a New England Industrial Community* (Cambridge).

Harloe, M. (ed.) (1977) *Captive Cities* (Chichester).

Harloe, M. (ed.) (1981) *New Perspectives in Urban Change and Conflict*.

Harloe, M. and Lebas, E. (eds) (1981) *City, Class and Capital*.

Harré, R. (1970) *The Principles of Scientific Thinking*.

Harré, R. and Madden, E. H. (1975) *Causal Powers* (Oxford).

Harvey, D. (1969) *Explanation in Geography*.

Harvey, D. (1973) *Social Justice and the City*.

Harvey, D. (1975) 'The Geography of Capitalist Accumulation: A Reconstruction of the Marxian Theory', *Antipode*, vol. 7(2), pp. 9–21.

Harvey, D. (1978) 'The Urban Process under Capitalism', *International Journal of Urban and Regional Research*, vol. 2, pp. 101–31.

Harvey, D. (1981) 'The Spatial Fix: Hegel, von Thünen and Marx', *Antipode*, vol. 13(3), pp. 1–12.

Harvey, D. (1982) *The Limits to Capital* (Oxford).

Hawley, A. (1950) *Human Ecology: a Theory of Community Structure* (New York).

Hechter, M. (1973) 'The Persistence of Regionalism in the British Isles 1885–1966', *American Journal of Sociology*, vol. 79, pp. 319–43.

Hechter, M. (1975) *Internal Colonialism: The Celtic Fringe in British National Development 1536–1966*.

Heckscher, E. F. (1946) 'Skiftesreformen under 1700-talet än en Gång', *Ekonomisk Tidskrift*, vol. 48, pp. 45–51.

Heidegger, M. (1962) *Being and Time*.

Held, D. and Thompson, J. (eds) (forthcoming) *The Critical Theory of the Advanced Societies* (Cambridge).

Hellspong, M. and Löfgren, O. (1974) *Land och stad* (Lund).

Helmfrid, S. (1961) 'The *Storskifte, Enskifte* and *Lagaskifte* in Sweden: General Features', *Geografiska Annaler B*, vol. 43, pp. 114–29.

Henry, S. (ed.) (1981) *Can I Have It in Cash?*.

Herbert, D. T. and Johnston, R. J. (eds) (1976) *Social Areas in Cities* vol. 2 *Spatial perspectives on problems and policies*.

Hill, C. (1982) 'Science and Magic in Seventeenth-century England' in

Samuel and Stedman Jones (eds) (1982) pp. 176–93.
Hindess, B. (1977) *Philosophy and Methodology in the Social Sciences* (Brighton).
Himmelweit, S. and Mohun, S. (1977) 'Domestic Labour and Capital', *Cambridge Journal of Economics*, vol. 1, pp. 15–31.
Hinkfuss, I. (1975) *The Existence of Space and Time* (Oxford).
Hirsch, A. (1981) *The French New Left: An Intellectual History from Sartre to Gorz* (Boston).
Hirst, P. (1982) 'Witchcraft Today and Yesterday', *Economy and Society*, vol. 11, pp. 428–48.
Hirst, P. and Woolley, P., (1982) *Social Relations and Human Attributes*.
Hobsbawm, E. (1981) 'The Forward March of Labour Halted?' in Jacques and Mulhern (eds) (1981) pp. 1–19.
Hollis, P. (1970) *The Pauper Press* (Oxford).
Holloway, J. and Picciotto, S. (1977) 'Capital, Crisis and the State' *Capital and Class*, vol. 2, pp. 76–101.
Holmes, G. (1976) 'The South Wales Coal Industry 1850–1914' *Transactions of the Honourable Society of Cymmrodorion*, pp. 162–207.
Homans, G. C. (1969) 'The Explanation of English Regional Differences' *Past and Present*, vol. 42, pp. 19–34.
Hoppe, G. (1981) 'Enclosure in Sweden: Background and Consequences', Kulturgeografiskt Seminarium (Department of Human Geography, University of Stockholm) no. 9/79.
Hudson, J. C. (1972) *Geographical Diffusion Theory* (Evenston, Illinois).
Hudson, R. (1979) 'Space, Place and Placelessness: Some Questions Concerning Methodology', *Progress in Human Geography*, vol. 3, pp. 169–73.
Hunt, A. (ed.) (1977) *Class and Class Structure*.
Hunt, A. (ed.) (1980) *Marxism and Democracy*.
Hymer, S. (1972) 'The Multinational Corporation and the Law of Uneven Development' in Bhagwati (ed.) (1972) pp. 133–40.

IDS Bulletin (1979) 'Rural Development: Whose Knowledge Counts?', Institute of Development Studies.

Jackson, M. (1982) 'Thinking Through the Body: An Essay on Understanding Metaphor', *mimeo.*
Jacobson, D., Wickham, A. and Wickham, J. (1979) 'Review of *The New International Division of Labour*', *Capital and Class*, vol. 7, pp. 125–30.
Jacques, E. (1982) *The Form of Time.*
Jacques, M. and Mulhern, F. (eds) (1981) *The Forward March of Labour Halted?*.
Janelle, D. G. (1969) 'Spatial Reorganisation: A Model and a Concept', *Annals of the Association of American Geographers*, vol. 59, pp. 348–64.
Jenkins, D. (1980) 'Rural Society Outside' in Smith (ed.) (1980) pp. 114–26.
Jensen-Butler, C. (1981) 'A Critique of Behavioural Geography: An Epistemological Analysis of Cognitive Mapping and of Hägerstrand's Time–space Model', Geografiska Institut, Aarhus Universitet, Arbejdsrapport 12.
Johnson, R. (1979) 'Culture and the Historians' in Clarke, Critcher and

Johnson (eds) (1979) pp. 41-71.
Jones, I. (1980) 'Language and Community in Nineteenth-century Wales' in Smith (ed.) (1980) pp. 47-71.
Joyce, P. (1980) *Work, Society and Politics: The Culture of the Factory in Later Victorian England* (Brighton).
Judt, T. (1979) *Socialism in Provence, 1871-1914* (Cambridge).
Kaldor, M. (1978) *The Disintegrating West* (Harmondsworth).
Kant, I. (1961) *The Critique of Pure Reason.*
Kant, I. (1968) *Kant: Selected Pre-critical Writings* (Manchester).
Karlqvist, A., Lundqvist, L. and Snickars, F. (eds) (1975) *Dynamic Allocation of Urban Space.*
Keat, R. and Urry, J. (1982) *Social Theory as Science* (2nd edn).
Keeble, D. (1977) 'Spatial Policy in Britain: Regional or Urban?' *Area*, vol. 9, pp. 3-8.
Kelly, M. (1982) *Modern French Marxism* (Baltimore).
Kenrick, J. (1981) 'Politics and the Construction of Women as Second-class Workers' in Wilkinson (ed.) (1981) pp. 167-92.
King, R. (ed.) (1983) *Capital and Politics.*
Knorr-Celina, K. and Cicourel, A. V. (eds) (1981) *Advances in Social Theory and Methodology.*
Körner, S. (1955) *Kant* (Harmondsworth).
Kosík, K. (1976) *Dialectics of the Concrete* (Boston Studies in the Philosophy of Science, no. 52).
Koss, S. (1981) *The Rise and Fall of the Political Press in Britain: vol. 1: The Nineteenth Century.*
Kreckel, M. (1982) 'Communicative Acts and Extralinguistic Knowledge' in von Cranach and Harré (eds) (1982) pp. 267-308.
Kreckel, R. (1980) 'Unequal Opportunity Structure and Labour Market Segmentation', *Sociology*, vol. 14, pp. 525-50.
Krimerman, L. (ed.) (1969) *The Nature and Scope of Social Science* (New York).
Kristofferson, A. (1924) *Landskapsbildens Förändringar i Norra och Östra Delen av Fars Härad under de Senaste Två Hundra Åren* (Lund).
Kuhn, A. and Wolpe, A. (eds) (1978) *Feminism and Materialism.*
Kuhn, T. S. (1970) *The Structure of Scientific Revolutions* (2nd edn) (Chicago).

Labour Party Parliamentary Spokesmans Working Group (1980) *Alternative Regional Strategy: A Framework for Discussion.*
Lägnert, F. (1955) *Syd - och mellansvenska växtföljder - I De Äldre Brukningssystemens Upplösning under 1800-talet* (Meddelanden från Lunds Universitets Geografiska Institutions, Avhandlingar 24).
Lakatos, I. (1974) 'The Role of Crucial Experiments in Science', *Studies in History and Philosophy of Science*, vol. 4, pp. 309-25.
Lakoff, G. and Johnson, M. (1980) *Metaphors We Live By* (Chicago).
Lane, R. A. (1966) 'The Decline of Politics and Ideology in a Knowledgeable Society', *American Sociological Review* vol. 31, pp. 649-62.
Lanegran, D. and Palm, R. (1978) *An Invitation to Geography* (New York).

Layder, D. (1981) *Structure, Interaction and Social Theory.*
Lazarsfeld, P. and Rosenberg, M. (eds) (1955) *The Language of Social Research* (New York).
Lazonick, W. (1978) 'The Subjection of Labour to Capital: The Rise of the Capitalist System' *Review of Radical Political Economics*, vol. 10, pp. 1–31.
Lebas, E. (1981) 'The New School of Urban and Regional Research: Into the Second Decade' in Harloe and Lebas (eds) (1981) pp. ix–xxxii.
Lebas, E. (1982) 'Urban and Regional Sociology in Advanced Industrial Societies: A Decade of Marxist and Critical Perspectives' *Current Sociology*, vol. 30(1), pp. 1–107.
Lebowitz, M. (1980) 'Capital as Finite', *Marx Conference*, University of Victoria, Canada.
Ledrut, R. (1977) *L'espace en Question* (Paris).
Lee, A. J. (1976) *The Origins of the Popular Press in England, 1855–1914.*
Lee, C. H. (1971) *Regional Economic Growth in the UK Since the 1880s* (Maidenhead).
Lees, L. H. (1982) 'Strikes and the Urban Hierarchy in English Industrial Towns, 1842–1901' in Cronin and Schneer (eds) (1982) pp. 52–71.
Lefebvre, H. (1946a) *L'existentialisme* (Paris).
Lefebvre, H. (1946b) *Critique de la Vie Quotidienne* (Paris) (reissued 1958).
Lefebvre, H. (1961) *Fondements d'une Sociologie de la Quotidienneté* (Paris).
Lefebvre, H. (1968a) *La Vie Quotidienne dans le Monde Moderne* (Paris).
Lefebvre, H. (1968b) *Le Droit à la Ville* (Paris).
Lefebvre, H. (1968c) *Dialectical materialism.*
Lefebvre, H. (1970) *De Rural à l'Urbaine* (Paris).
Lefebvre, H. (1971) *Au-delà du Structuralisme* (Paris).
Lefebvre, H. (1971a) *Le Manifeste Différentialiste* (Paris).
Lefebvre, H. (1971b) *La Révolution Urbaine* (Paris).
Lefebvre, H. (1972) *La Pensée Marxiste et la Ville* (Paris).
Lefebvre, H. (1973) *La Survie du Capitalisme* (Paris).
Lefebvre, H. (1974) *La Production de l'Espace* (Paris).
Lefebvre, H. (1975) *Le Temps des Méprises* (Paris).
Lefebvre, H. (1976a) 'Reflections on the Politics of Space', *Antipode* vol. 8(2), pp. 30–7.
Lefebvre, H. (1976b) *The Survival of Capitalism* (London).
Lefebvre, H. (1976–8) *De l'Etat* (4 vols) (Paris).
Lefebvre, H. (1980) *Une Pensée Devenue Monde: Faut-il Abandonner Marx?* (Paris).
Lefebvre, H. and Guterman, N. (1936) *La Conscience Mystifiée* (Paris).
Lefebvre, H. and Guterman, N. (1964) *Morceaux Choisis de Karl Marx* (2 vols) Paris).
Lefebvre, H. and Guterman, N. (1967) *Cahiers de Lenine sur la Dialectique de Hegel* (2 vols) (Paris).
Lefebvre, H. and Guterman, N. (1969) *Morceaux Choisis de Hegel* (2 vols) (Paris).
Leibniz, G. W. (1898) *The Monadology and other Philosophical Writings* (Oxford).
Lenntorp, B. (1976) *Paths in Space–time Environments: A Time-geographic*

Study of Movement Possibilities of Individuals, Lund Studies in Geography, Series B, no. 44.

Lever, W. F. (1979) 'Industry and Labour Markets in Great Britain' in Hamilton and Linge (eds) (1979) pp. 89–114.

Lévi-Strauss, C. (1969) *The Elementary Structures of Kinship*.

Ley, D. (1981) 'Cultural/humanistic Geography', *Progress in Human Geography*, vol. 5, pp. 249–57.

Liddington, J. and Norris, J. (1978) *One Hand Tied Behind Us: The Rise of the Women's Suffrage Movement*.

Lipietz, A. (1980a) 'The Structuration of Space, the Problem of Land and Spatial Policy' in Carney, Hudson and Lewis (eds) (1980) pp. 60–75.

Lipietz, A. (1980b) 'International Regional Polarisation and Tertiarisation of Society' *Papers of the Regional Science Association*, vol. 44, pp. 3–17.

Littler, C. (1982) 'Deskilling and Changing Structures of Control' in Wood (ed.) (1982) pp. 122–45.

Littler, C. (1982) *The Development of the Labour Process in Capitalist Societies: A Comparative Study of the Transformation of Work Organization in Britain, Japan and USA*.

Lockwood, D. (1966) 'Sources of Variation in Working Class Images of Society', *Sociological Review*, vol. 14, pp. 249–67.

Löfgren, O. (1974) 'Family and Household among Scandinavian Peasants: An Exploratory Essay', *Ethnologica Scandinavica*, vol. 1, pp.;17–52.

Löfgren, O. (1975) *Arbetsfördelning och Könsroller i Bondesamhället Kontinuitet och Förändring* (Lund).

Löfgren, O. (1978) 'The Potato People: Household Economy and Family Patterns among the Rural Proletariat in Nineteenth-century Sweden' in Åkerman, Johansen and Gaunt (eds) (1978) pp. 95–106.

Löfgren, O. (1980) 'Historical Perspectives on Scandinavian Peasantries' *Annual Review of Anthropology*, vol. 9, pp. 187–215.

Lojkine, J. (1976) 'Contribution to a Marxist Theory of Capitalist Urbanisation' in Pickvance (ed.) (1976) pp. 119–46.

Lojkine, J. (1977) *Le Marxisme, l'Etat et la Question Urbaine* (Paris).

Lojkine, J. (1981) 'Urban Policy and Local Power: Some Aspects of Recent Research in Lille' in Harloe and Lebas (eds) (1981) pp. 89–104.

Lönqvist, N. (1924[1775]) *Berättelse om Bara härad 1775*.

Lösch, A. (1954) *The Economics of Location* (New Haven).

Loubère, L. (1974) *Radicalism in Mediterranean France* (Albany, New York).

Lough, J. (1971) *The 'Encyclopédie'* (New York).

Lovering, J. (1978) 'The Theory of the Internal Colony versus Political Economy of Wales', *Review of Radical Political Economics*, vol. 10, pp. 55–67.

Lucas, J. R. (1973) *A Treatise on Time and Space*.

Luckmann, T. (1982) 'Individual Action and Social Knowledge' in von Cranach and Harré (eds) (1982) pp. 247–65.

Lukács, G. (1971) *History and Class Consciousness* (Cambridge, Massachussetts).

Macfarlane, A. (1970) *The Family Life of Ralph Josselin, a Seventeenth-century Clergyman: An essay in Historical Anthropology* (Cambridge).

420   Bibliography

Macfarlane, A. (ed.) (1976) *The Diary of Ralph Josselin 1616–1683*.
Mackenzie, G. (1982) 'Class Boundaries and the Labour Process' in Giddens and Mackenzie (eds) (1982) pp. 63–87.
Macintyre, S. (1980) *Little Moscows. Communism and Working-class Militancy in Inter-war Britain*.
MacLaren, A. A. (ed.) (1976) *Social Class in Scotland: Past and Present* (Edinburgh).
Marglin, S. (1974) 'What do Bosses Do?' *Review of Radical Political Economics*, vol. 6, pp. 60–92.
Mandrou, R. (1964) *De la Culture Populaire aux 17e et 18e siècles* (Paris).
Mann, P. H. (1970) *Books, Borrowers and Buyers*.
Mann, P. H. and Burgoyne, J. L. (1969) *Books and Reading*.
Mårtensson, S. (1979) *On the Formation of Biographies in Space–time Environments*, Lund Studies in Geography, Series B, no. 47.
Martin, H.-J. (1978) 'The Bibliothèque Bleue: Literature for the masses in the *Ancien Régime*', *Publishing History*, vol. 3, pp. 70–102.
Martins, M. (1983) 'The Theory of Social Space in the Work of Henri Lefebvre' in Forrest, Henderson and Williams (eds) (1983) pp. 160–85.
Marx, K. (1967) *Capital* (first published 1867).
Marx, K. (1973) *Grundrisse* (Harmondsworth) (completed1857–8; first published 1939–41).
Marx, K. and Engels, F. (1969) *Selected Works*, vol. II (Moscow).
Marx, K. and Engels, F. (1970a) *The German Ideology* (completed 1845–6; first published 1932).
Marx, K. and Engels, F. (1970b) *Selected Works*.
Massey, D. (1973) 'Towards a Critique of Industrial Location Theory', *Antipode*, vol. 5(3), pp. 33–9.
Massey, D. (1978a) 'Regionalism: Some Current Issues', *Capital and class*, vol. 6, pp. 106–25.
Massey, D. (1978b) 'Capital and Locational Change: The UK Electrical Engineering and Electronics Industry', *Review of Radical Political Ecoomics*, vol. 10, pp. 39–54.
Massey, D. (1979) 'In What Sense a Regional Problem?', *Regional Studies*, vol. 13, pp. 233–43.
Massey, D. (1980) 'Industrial Restructuring as Class Restructuring', Centre for Environmental Studies, Working Paper 604.
Massey, D. (1981) 'The UK Electrical Engineering and Electronics Industries: The Implications of the Crisis for the Restructuring of Capital and Locational Change' in Dear and Scott (eds) (1981) pp. 199–230.
Massey, D. (1982) 'Industrial Restructuring as Class Restructuring: Some Implications of Industrial Change for Social Structure', Department of Geography, London School of Economics.
Massey, D. (1984) *Spatial Divisions of Labour: Social Structures and the Geography of Production*.
Massey, D. and Meegan, R. (1978) 'Industrial Restructuring Versus the Cities' *Urban Studies*, vol. 15, pp. 273–88.
Massey, D. and Meegan, R. (1979) 'The Geography of Industrial Reorganisation' *Progress in Planning*, vol. 10, pp. 159–237.
Massey, D. and Meegan, R. (1979a) 'Capital and Locational Change: The

UK Electrical Engineering and Electronics Industry', *Review of Radical Political Economics*, vol. 10, pp. 39–51.

Massey, D. and Meegan, R. (1982) *The Anatomy of Job Loss: The How, Why and Where of Employment Decline.*

McDowell, L. (1983) 'Towards an Understanding of the Gender Division of Urban Space', *Environment and Planning D: Society and Space*, vol. 1, pp. 59–72.

Meissner, M. (1975) 'No Exit for Wives: Sexual Division of Labour and the Cumulation of Household Demands', *Canadian Review of Sociology and Anthropology*, vol. 12, pp. 424–39.

Melbin, M. (1978) 'The Colonisation of Time' in Carlstein, Parkes and Thrift (eds) (1978) vol. 2, pp. 100–13.

Metzgar, J. (1980) 'Plant Shutdowns and Worker Response: The Case of Johnstown, Pa.', *Socialist Review*, vol. 43, pp. 9–50.

Middlemass, K. (1979) *Politics in Industrial Society. The Experience of the British System since 1911.*

Minchinton, W. (ed.) (1969) *Industrial South Wales 1750–1914.*

Mingione, E. (1981) *Social Conflict and the City* (Oxford).

Minsky, H. (1983) 'The Crisis of 1983 and the Prospects for Advanced Capitalist Economies', *Centennial Symposium on Marx, Schumpeter and Keynes*, University of Colorado at Denver.

Mollison, D. (1977) 'Spatial Contact Models for Ecological and Epidemiological Spread', *Journal of the Royal Statistical Society*, series B, vol. 39, pp. 283–326.

Molyneux, M. (1979) 'Beyond the Housework Debate', *New Left Review*, vol. 116, pp. 3–28.

Morgan, K. J. (1984) *The Politics of Regional Development* (Cambridge).

Morgan, K. O. (1982) *Rebirth of a Nation: Wales 1880–1980* (Oxford).

Morrill, R. and Pitts, F. (1967) 'Marriage, Migration and the Mean Information Field: a study in uniqueness and generality' *Annals of the Association of American Geographers*, vol. 57, pp. 401–22.

Moser, C. (1978) 'Informal Sector or Petty Commodity Production: Dualism or Dependence in Urban Development?', *World Development*, vol. 6, pp. 1041–64.

Müller, W. and Neusüss, C. (1970) 'The Illusion of State Socialism and the Contradictions Between Wage-labour and Capital', *Telos*, vol. 25, pp. 13–90.

Murgatroyd, L. and Urry, J. (1983) 'The Restructuring of a Local Economy: The Case of Lancaster' in Anderson, Duncan and Hudson (eds) (1983) pp. 67–98.

Murgatroyd, L., Savage, M., Shapiro, D., Urry, J., Walby, S. and Warde, A. (1984) *Localities, class and gender.*

Nagel, E. (1955) 'On the Statement "The Whole is Greater than the Sum of its Parts"' in Lazarsfeld and Rosenberg (eds) (1955) pp. 519–27.

Needleman, L. (ed.) (1968) *Regional Analysis* (Harmondsworth).

Neisser, H. (1965) *On the Sociology of Knowledge* (New York).

Nerlich, G. (1976) *The Shape of Space* (Cambridge).

Neuberg, V. E. (1977) *Popular Literature: A History and Guide* (Harmondsworth).

Newby, H. (1979) *Green and Pleasant Land? Social Change in Rural England.*

Nichols, T. and Beynon, H. (1977) *Living with Capitalism. Class Relations and the Modern Factory.*

Nicolovius (1957 [1847]) *Folklivet i Skytts härad i Skåne vid Början av 1800 Talet* (Stockholm).

Nilsson, A. (1938) 'Ur ett Skånskt Byarkiv' *Svenska Kulturbilder*, vol. 12, pp. 269–88.

Nissell, M. and Bonnerjea, L. (1982) 'Family Care of the Handicapped Elderly: Who Pays?', Policy Studies Institute, London.

Nordholm, G. (1967) *Skånes Äldre Ekonomiska Geografi* (Meddelanden från Lunds Universitets Geografiska Institution, Avhandlingar 51).

Norris, R. (1980) 'Towards a Sociology of Labour Markets', *mimeo*.

Offe, C. and Wiesenthal, H. (1979) 'Two Logics of Collective Action: Theoretical Notes on Social Class and Organisational Form' in Zeitlin (ed.) (1979) pp. 67–115.

Office of Population Census and Surveys (1982) *Monitor*.

Olson, M. (1965) *The Logic of Collective Action* (Cambridge, Massachusetts).

Olsson, G. (1980) *Birds in Egg/Eggs in Bird*.

Østerud, O. (1978) *Agrarian Structure and Peasant Politics in Scandinavia: A Comparative Study of Rural Response to Economic Change* (Oslo).

Paci, M. (1981a) 'Class Structure in Italian Society' in Pinto (ed.) pp. 206–22.

Paci, M. (1981b) 'Internal Migrations and the Capitalist Labour Market' in Pinto (ed.) pp. 33–46.

Pahl, R. (1968) 'The Rural–urban Continuum' in Pahl (ed.) (1968) pp. 263–97.

Pahl, R. (ed.) (1968) *Readings in Urban Sociology*.

Pahl, R. (1975) *Whose City?* (2nd edn).

Pahl, R. (1980) 'Employment, Work and the Domestic Division of Labour', *International Journal of Urban and Regional Research*, vol. 4, pp. 1–20.

Pahl, R. (1981) 'Employment, Work and the Domestic Division of Labour' in Harloe and Lebas (eds) pp. 143–63.

Pahl, R. and Dennett, J. (1981) 'Industry and Employment on the Isle of Sheppey', HWS Project Report, University of Kent at Canterbury.

Pahl, R. and Gershuny, J. I. (1979) 'Work Outside Employment: Some Preliminary Speculations', *New Universities Quarterly*, vol. 34, pp. 120–35.

Pahl, R. and Wallace, C. (1983) 'Household Work Strategies and the Polarisations and Divisions of Work Practices' in Redclift and Mingione (eds) (1983).

Palm, R. and Pred, A. (1978) 'The status of American Women: a Timegeographic view' in Lanegran and Palm (eds) (1978) pp. 99–109.

Park, R. (1952) *Human Communities* (New York).

Parkes, D. and Thrift, N. (1980) *Times, Spaces and Places: A Chronogeographic Perspective* (New York).

Parsons, T., Bales, R. and Shils, E. (1953) *Working Papers in the Theory of Action.*
Pelling, Ha. (1967) *The Social Geography of British Elections.*
Penn, R. (1982) 'The Contested Terrain: A Critique of R. C. Edwards' Theory of Working Class Fractions and Politics' in Day (ed.) (1982) pp. 93–106.
Perry, D. and Watkins, A. (eds) (1978) *The Rise of the Sunbelt Cities* (Beverley Hills).
Pickvance, C. (ed.) (1976) *Urban Sociology: Critical Essays.*
Pickvance, C., (1981) 'Policies as Chameleons: An Interpretation of Regional Policy and Office Policy in Britain' in Dear and Scott (eds) (1981) pp. 231–65.
Pinto, D. (ed.) (1981) *Contemporary Italian Sociology* (Cambridge).
Piore, M. (1979) *Birds of Passage* (Cambridge).
Pollard, A. (1980) 'Teacher Interests and Changing Situations of Survival Threat in Primary School Classrooms' in Woods (ed.) (1980) pp. 34–60.
Popper, K. (1972) *Conjectures and Refutations: The Growth of Scientific Knowledge.*
Poster, M. (1975) *Existential Marxism in Postwar France* (Princeton).
Poster, M. (1979) *Sartre's Marxism.*
Poulantzas, N. (1975) *Classes in Contemporary Capitalism.*
Poulantzas, N. (1978) *State, Power, Socialism.*
Pred, A. (1973) 'Urbanisation, Domestic Planning Problems and Swedish Geographic Research', *Progress in Geography*, vol. 5, pp. 1–76.
Pred, A. (1977) 'The Choreography of Existence: Comments on Hägerstrand's Time-geography and its Usefulness', *Economic Geography*, vol. 53, pp. 207–21.
Pred, A. (1978) 'The Impact of Technological and Institutional Innovations on Life Content: Some Time-geographic Observations', *Geographical Analysis*, vol. 10, pp. 345–72.
Pred, A. (1981a) 'Social Reproduction and the Time-geography of Everyday Life', *Geografiska Annaler B*, vol. 63, pp. 5–22.
Pred, A. (1981b) 'Power, Everyday Practice and the Discipline of Human Geography' in Pred (ed.) (1981) pp. 30–55.
Pred, A. (ed.) (1981c) *Space and Time in Geography: Essays Dedicated to Torsten Hägerstrand*, Lund Studies in Geography, Series B, No. 48.
Pred, A. (1983) 'Structuration and Place: On the Becoming of Sense of Place and Structure of Feeling' *Journal for the Theory of Social Behavior*, vol. 13, pp. 45–68.
Pred, A. (1984) 'Place as Historically Contingent Process: Structuration and the Time-geography of Becoming Places', *Annals of the Association of American Geographers*, vol. 74, pp. 279–97.
Pred, A. (forthcoming) *Becoming Places, Practice and Structure: the Emergence and Aftermath of Enclosures in the Plains Villages of Southwestern Skåne 1750–1850* (Cambridge).
Price, R. (1983) 'The Labour Process and Labour History', *Social History*, vol. 8, pp. 57–75.
Przeworksi, A. (1977) 'Proletariat into a Class: The Process of Class Formation from Karl Kautsky's *The Class Struggle* to Recent Controversies', *Politics and Society*, vol. 7, pp. 343–401.

Rattansi, P. M. (1973) 'Some Evaluations of Reason in Sixteenth- and Seventeenth-century Natural Philosophy' in Young and Teich (eds) (1973) pp. 146–166.

Redclift, N. (1983) 'Relations of Gender in the New International Division of Labour' in Redclift and Mingione (eds) (1983).

Redclift, N. and Mingione, E. (eds) (1983) *Beyond Employment* (Oxford).

Rees, J., Hewings, G. J. D. and Stafford, H. A. (eds) *Industrial Location and Regional Systems* (New York).

Rees, G. and Lambert, J. (1981) 'Nationalism as Legitimation? Notes Towards a Political Economy of Regional Development in South Wales' in Harloe (ed.) (1981) pp. 122–37.

Reissman, L. (1964) *The Urban Process*.

Rex, J. (1968) 'The Sociology of a Zone of Transition' in Pahl (ed.) (1968) pp. 211–231.

Rex, J. (1982) 'The 1981 Urban Riots in Britain', *International Journal of Urban and Regional Research*, vol. 6, pp. 99–113.

Rex, J. and Moore, R. (1967) *Race, Community and Conflict*.

Rex, J. and Tomlinson, S. (1979) *Colonial Immigrants in a British City*.

Righini Bonelli, R. M. and Shea, W. R. (eds) (1975) *Reason, Experiment and Mysticism in the Scientific Revolution*.

Roberts, R. (1971) *The Classic Slum* (Manchester).

Roemer, J. (1982) 'New Directions in the Marxian Theory of Exploitation and Class', *Politics and Society*, vol. 11, pp. 253–87.

Rose, C. (1977) 'Reflections in the Notion of Time Incorporated in Hägerstrand's Time-geographic Model of Society', *Tijdschrift voor Economische en Sociale Geografie*, vol. 68, pp. 43–50.

Rose, R. and Unwin, D. (1975) *Regional Differentiation and Political Unity in Western Nations* (Beverley Hills).

Rosenberg, N. (1976) *Perspectives on Technology* (Cambridge).

Rykwert, J. (1976) *The Idea of a Town*.

Sack, R. D. (1972) 'Geography, Geometry and Explanation', *Annals of the Association of American Geographers*, vol. 62, pp. 61–78.

Sack, R. D. (1973) 'A Concept of Physical Space', *Geographical Analysis*, vol. 5, pp. 16–34.

Sack, R. D. (1974) 'The Spatial Separatist Theme in Geography' *Economic Geography*, vol. 50, pp. 1–19.

Sack, R. D. (1980) *Conceptions of Space in Social Thought* (London and Minneapolis).

Samuel, R. and Stedman Jones, G. (eds) (1982) *Culture, Ideology and Politics: Essays for Eric Hobsbawm*.

Sartre, J.-P, (1976) *Critique of Dialectical Reason*.

Saunders, P. (1979) *Urban Politics* (Harmondsworth).

Saunders, P. (1981) *Social Theory and the Urban Question*.

Saunders, P. (1982) 'Beyond Housing Classes: The Sociological Significance of Private Property Rights in Means of Consumption', University of Sussex, Urban and Regional Studies Working Papers, no. 33.

Saunders, P. (1984) 'Central–local Government Relations and the Politics of Consumption' in Boddy and Fudge (eds) (1984) pp. 22–48.

Saville, J. (1960) 'Trade Unions and Free Labour: The Background to the Taff Vale Decision' in Briggs and Saville (eds) (1960) pp. 317–50.

Sawers, L. and Tabb, W. K. (eds) (1984) *Sunbelt/Frostbelt: Urban Development and Regional Restructuring* (New York).

Sayer, A. (1979a) 'Epistemology and Conceptions of People and Nature in Geography', *Geoforum*, vol. 10, pp. 19–44.

Sayer, A. (1979b) 'Theory and Empirical Research in Urban and Regional Political Economy: A Sympathetic Critique', University of Sussex, Urban and Regional Studies Working Papers, no. 14.

Sayer, A. (1981) 'Abstraction: A Realist Interpretation', *Radical Philosophy*, vol. 28, pp. 6–15.

Sayer, A. (1982) 'Explanation in Economic Geography: Abstraction versus Generalisation', *Progress in Human Geography*, vol. 6, pp. 68–88.

Sayer, A. (1984) *Method in Social Science: A Realist Approach*.

Sayer, D. (1979) *Marx's Method. Ideology, Science and Critique in 'Capital'* (Brighton).

Schofield R. S. (1968) 'The Measurement of Literacy in pre-industrial England' in Goody (ed.) (1968a) pp. 318–25.

Schofield, R. S. (1973) 'Dimensions of Illiteracy 1750–1850', *Explorations in Economic History*, vol. 10, pp. 437–54.

Schutz, A. (1962) *Collected Papers: vol. 1: The Problems of Social Reality* (The Hague).

Schutz, A. and Luckmann, T. (1973) *The Structures of the Life-world* (Evanston, Illinois).

Scott, A. (1980) *The Urban Land Nexus and the State*.

Seabrook, J. (1978) *What Went Wrong?*.

Sekscenski, E. S. (1980) 'Women's Share of Moonlighting Nearly Doubles 1969–1979', *Monthly Labour Review*, vol. 103(5), pp. 57–8.

Shaw, M. (1979) 'Wolverhampton 1871 and 1971', *Population Trends*, vol. 18, pp. 17–23.

Shotter, J. (1983) ' "Duality of Structure" and "Intentionality" in an Ecological Psychology: Towards a Science of Individuality', *Journal for the Theory of Social Behaviour*, vol. 13, pp. 19–43.

Simmel, G. (1950) 'The Metropolis and Mental Life' in Wolff (ed.) (1950) pp. 409–24.

Smart, J. J. C. (1963) *Philosophy and Scientific Realism*.

Smith, D. (1980) 'Tonypandy 1910: Definitions of Community', *Past and Present*, vol. 87, pp. 158–84.

Smith, D. (ed.) (1980) *A People and a Proletariat: Essays in the History of Wales 1780–1980*.

Smith, D. (1982) *Conflict and Compromise: Class Formation in English Society 1830–1914*.

Smith, N. (1979) 'Geography, Science and Post-positivist Modes of Explanation' *Progress in Human Geography*, vol. 3, pp. 356–83.

Smith, N. (1982) *Uneven Development: The Production of Nature under Capitalism* (unpublished Ph.D thesis, The Johns Hopkins University, Baltimore: Department of Geography).

Smith, S. L. (1983) 'From Capitalist Domination to Urban Planning: Three Stages in the Urban Politics of Dartford 1814–1980', *mimeo*.

Smout, T. (1976) 'Apects of Sexual Behaviour in Nineteenth-century Scotland' in MacLaren (ed.) pp. 55–85.

Söderberg, J. (1978) *Agrar Fattigdom i Sydsverige under 1800-talet* (Stockholm).

Sohn-Rethel, A. (1978) *Intellectual and Manual Labour: A Critique of Epistemology*.

Soja, E. (1980) 'The Socio-spatial Dialectic', *Annals of the Association of American Geographers*, vol. 70, pp. 207–25.

Soja, E. (1981) 'A Materialist Interpretation of Spatiality', Workshop on the Geographical Transfer of Value, Department of Human Geography, Australian National University.

Soja, E. (1983) 'Redoubling the Helix: Space–time and the Critical Social Theory of Anthony Giddens' *Environment and Planning A*, vol. 15, pp. 1267–72.

Soja, E. and Hadjimichalis, C. (1979) 'Between Geographical Materialism and Spatial Fetishism: Some Observations on the Development of Marxist Spatial Analysis', *Antipode*, vol. 11(2) pp. 3–11.

Sokoloff, M. J. (1980) *Between Money and Love: The Dialectics of Women's Home and Market Work* (New York).

Solberg, M. (1915–16) 'Folklivet på Söderslätt under Senare Hälften av 1700-talet (document from 176?)' *Historisk Tidskrift för Skåneland*, vol. 6, pp. 384–411.

Sporrong, U. (1970) *Jordbruk och Landskapsbild* (Lund).

Spufford, M. (1979) 'First Steps in Literacy: The Reading and Writing Experiences of the Humblest Seventeenth-century Autobiographers' *Social History*, vol. 4, pp. 407–35.

Spufford, M. (1981) *Small Books and Pleasant Histories: Popular Fiction and its Readership in Seventeenth-century England*.

Stacey, M. (1969) 'The Myth of Community Studies', *British Journal of Sociology*, vol. 20, pp. 134–45.

Stacey, M. (1981) 'The Division of Labour Revisited, or Overcoming the Two Adams' in Abrams, Deem, Finch and Rock (eds) pp. 172–90.

Stafford, F. P. (1980) 'Women's Use of Time Converging with Men's' *Monthly Labour Review*, vol. 104(2), pp. 57–9.

Stark, D. (1980) 'Class Struggle and the Transformation of the Labour Process' *Theory and Society*, vol. 9, pp. 89–130.

Steiner, G. (1978) *On Difficulty and Other Essays* (Oxford).

Stone, L. (1969) 'Literacy and Education in England 1640–1900', *Past and Present*, vol. 42, pp. 69–139.

Storper, M. (1981) 'Towards a Structural Theory of Industrial Location' in Rees, Hewings and Stafford (eds) pp. 17–40.

Storper, M. (1982) *The Spatial Division of Labor: Technology, the Labor Process and the Location of Industries* (unpublished Ph.D. thesis, University of California, Berkeley: Department of Geography).

Storper, M. and Walker, R. (1983) 'The Theory of Labour and the Theory of Location', *International Journal of Urban and Regional Research*, vol. 7, pp. 1–44.

Storper, M. and Walker, R. (1984) 'The Spatial Division of Labor: Labor and the Location of Industry' in Sawers (eds) (1984) pp. 19–47.

Swanander, J. F. (1958 [1796]) *Bara Härad i Slutet av 1700-talet* (Lund).
Swingewood, A. (1977) *The Myth of Mass Culture.*
Szelenyi, I. (1981) 'Structural Change and Alternatives to Capitalist Development in the Contemporary Urban and Regional System', *International Journal of Urban and Regional Reserach.* vol. 5, pp. 1–14.

Tabb, W. K. and Sawers, L. (eds) (1978) *Marxism and the Metropolis: New Perspectives in Urban Political Economy* (New York).
Tambiah, S. J. (1968) 'Literacy in a Buddhist Village in N.E. Thailand' in Goody (ed.) (1968a) pp. 85–131.
Taylor, M. and Thrift, M. (forthcoming) *Capital, Location and Organisation.*
Taylor, P. (1971) 'Distance Transformation and Distance Decay Functions' *Geographical Analysis*, vol. 3, pp. 221–38.
Taylor, P. and Johnston, R. J. (1979) *The Geography of Elections* (Harmondsworth).
Thomas, B. (1969) 'The Migration of Labour into the Glamorganshire Coalfield, 1861–1911' in Minchinton (ed.) (1969) pp. 37–56.
Thomas, G. and Shannon, C. Z. (1982) 'Technology and Household Labour: Are the Times A'Changing?' *mimeo.*
Thomas, K. (1971) *Religion and the Decline of Magic: Studies in Popular Beliefs in Sixteenth- and Seventeenth-century England.*
Thompson, E. P. (1961) 'The Long Revolution', *New Left Review*, vol. 9, pp. 24–33 and vol. 10, pp. 34–9.
Thompson, E. P. (1968) *The Making of the English Working Class* (Harmondsworth).
Thompson, E. P. (1978) *The Poverty of Theory and Other Essays.*
Thompson, J. B. and Held, D. (eds) (1982) *Habermas: Critical Debates.*
Thrift, N. (1979) 'Limits to Knowledge in Social Theory: Towards a Theory of Practice', Department of Human Geography, Australian National University, seminar paper.
Thrift, N. (1983) 'On the Determination of Social Action in Space and Time' *Environment and Planning D: Society and Space*, vol. 1, pp. 23–57.
Thrift, N. J. and Forbes, D. K. (1983) 'A Landscape with Figures: Political Geography with Human Conflict', *Political Geography Quarterly*, vol. 2, pp. 247–63.
Thrift, N. and Pred, A. (1981) 'Time–geography: A New Beginning', *Progress in Human Geography*, vol. 5, pp. 277–86.
Thunell, E. (1952) *Livet på Kabbarp 1 & 6: 1814–1864* (Lund).
Touraine, A. (1977) *The Self-production of Society* (Chicago).
Townsend, P. (1979) *Poverty in the United Kingdom* (Harmondsworth).

Ungerson, C. (1981) 'Women, Work and the "Caring Capacity of the Community"', *mimeo.*
Union of Radical Political Economics (1978) *Review of Radical Political Economics*, vol. 10.
Urry, J. (1981a) *The Anatomy of Capitalist Societies: The Economy, Civil Society and the State.*
Urry, J. (1981b) 'De-industrialization, Households and Forms of Social Conflict', Lancaster Regionalism Group, Working Paper, no. 3.

Urry, J. (1981c) 'Localities, Regions and Social Class', *International Journal of Urban and Regional Research*, vol. 5, pp. 455–74.

Urry, J. (1982) 'Some Themes in the Analysis of the Anatomy of Contemporary Capitalist Societies', *Acta Sociologica*, vol. 25, pp. 405–18.

Urry, J. (1983a) 'De-industrialisation, Classes and Politics' in King (ed.) (1983) pp. 28–48.

Urry, J. (1983b) 'Realism and the Analysis of Space', *International Journal of Urban and Regional Research*, vol. 7, pp. 122–7.

Urry, J. (1984) 'Capitalist Restructuring and Recomposition' in Bradley and Lowe (eds) in press.

Utterström, G. (1957) *Jordbrukets Arbetare: Levnadsvillkor och Arbetsliv på Landsbygden från Frihetstiden till Miten av 1800-talet* (2 vols) (Stockholm).

van Juijn, J. J. (1983) *The Long Wave in Economic Life*.

van Paassen, C. (1976) 'Human Geography in Terms of Existential Anthropology' *Tijdschrift voor Economische en Sociale Geografie*, vol. 67, pp. 324–41.

Vincent, D. (1981) *Bread, Knowledge and Freedoms: A Study of Nineteenth-century Working-class Autobiography*.

von Cranach, M. and Harré, R. (eds) (1982) *The Analysis of Action: Recent Theoretical and Empirical Advances*.

von Linné, C. (1959 [1751]) *Skånska Resa på Höga Överhetens Befallning Förättad ar 1749* (Stockholm).

von Rosen, G. (1908–9) '... till Kungl. Kammarskollegium [document from 1805]' *Historisk Tidskrift för Skåneland*, vol. 3, pp. 297–305.

Walby, S. (1984) 'Women's unemployment: Some Spatial and Historical Variations', in Murgatroyd, Savage, Shapiro, Urry, Walby and Warde (1984) in press

Walker, P. (ed.) (1979) *Between Capital and Labour* (Boston, Massachusetts).

Walker, R. (1978) 'Two Sources of Uneven Development under Advanced Capitalism: Spatial Differentiation and Capital Mobility', *Review of Radical Political Economics*, vol. 10, pp. 28–37.

Walker, R. (1981) 'A Theory of Suburbanisation: Capitalism and the Construction of Urban Space in the United States' in Dear and Scott (eds) (1981) p. 383–430.

Walker, R. and Greenberg, D. (1982) 'Post-industrialism and Political Reform in the City: A Critique', *Antipode*, vol 14(1) pp. 17–32.

Walker, R. and Storper, M. (1981) 'Capital and Industrial Location', *Progress in Human Geography*, vol. 5, pp. 473–509.

Walkowitz, D. (1978) *Worker City, Company Town* (Champaign, Illinois).

Walters, R. (1980) 'Capital Formation in the South Wales Coal Industry', *Welsh Historical Review*, vol. 10, pp. 69–92.

Ward, D. (1980) 'Environs and Neighbours in the "Two Nations": Residential Differentiation in Mid-nineteenth-century Leeds', *Journal of Historical Geography*, vol. 6, pp.133–62.

Warde, A. (1982) 'Comparability in Local Studies: The Case of the De-industrialisation of Lancaster', Lancaster Regionalism Group, Working Paper, no. 4.

Webb, R. K. (1950) 'Working-class Readers in Early Victorian England', *Economic History Review*, vol. 65, pp. 333–57.
Webb, R. K. (1955) *The British Working-class Reader 1790–1848*.
Webber, M. M. (1964) 'Culture, Territoriality and the Elastic Mile', *Papers and Proceedings of the Regional Science Association*, vol. 13, pp. 59–69.
Weber, M. (1958) *The City* (New York).
Weber, M. (1978) *Economy and Society* (Berkeley).
Webster, C. (1982) *From Paracelsus to Newton: Magic and the Making of Modern Science* (Cambridge).
Weibull, C. G. (1923) *Skånska Jordbrukets Historia intill 1800-talets Början* (Lund).
Westaway, J. (1974) 'The Spatial Hierarchy of Business Organisations and its Implications for the British Urban System', *Regional Studies*, vol. 8, pp. 145–55.
Whitehead, A. N. (1930) *The Concept of Nature* (Cambridge).
Wigström, E. (1891) *Allmogeseder i Rönnebärgs Härad i Skane pa 1840-talet* (Stockholm).
Wilkinson, F. (ed.) (1981) *The Dynamics of Labour Market Segmentation*.
Willer, D. and Willer, J. (1973) *Systematic Empiricism: Critique of a Pseudoscience* (Englewood Cliffs, New Jersey).
Williams, G. (1978) *The Merthyr Rising*.
Williams, G. (1980) 'Locating a Welsh Working Class: The Frontier Years' in Smith (ed.) (1980) pp. 16–46.
Williams, G. (1982) *The Welsh in their History*.
Williams, J. (1973) 'The Road to Tonypandy' *Llafur*, vol. 1, pp. 3–14.
Williams, R. (1973) *The Country and the City*.
Williams, R. (1977) *Marxism and Literature* (Oxford).
Williams, R. (1979) *Politics and Letters*.
Williams, R. (1981) *Culture*.
Williams, R. (1982) 'Democracy and Parliament', *Marxism Today*, vol. 26(6) pp. 14–21.
Williams, S. (1981) 'Realism, Marxism and Human Geography', *Antipode* 13(2) pp. 31–8.
Williamson, J. G. (1968) 'Regional Inequality and the Process of National Development: A Description of Patterns' in Needleman (ed.) (1968) pp. 99–159.
Winberg, C. (1978) 'Population Growth and Proletarianization: The Transformation of Social Structures in Rural Sweden During the Agrarian Revolution' in Åkerman, Johansen and Gaunt (eds) (1978) pp. 170–84.
Wirth, L. (1938) 'Urbanism as a Way of Life', *American Journal of Sociology*, vol. 44, pp. 1–24.
Wirth, L. (1945) 'Human Ecology', *American Journey of Sociology*, vol. 50, pp. 483–8.
Wolff, K. (1950) *The Sociology of Georg Simmel* (New York).
Wolpert, J. (1966) 'A Regional Simulation Model of Information Diffusion', *Public Opinion Quarterly*, vol. 30, pp. 597–608.
Wood, S. (ed.) (1982) *The Degradation of Work?*.
Woods, P. (ed.) (1980) *Teacher Strategies*.
Wright, E. O. (1976) 'Class Boundaries in Advanced Capitalist Societies',

New Left Review, vol. 98, pp. 3–41.

Wright, E. O. (1978) *Class, Crisis and the State*.

Wright, E. O. (1980) 'Varieties of Marxist Conceptions of Class Structure', *Politics and Society*, vol. 9, pp. 299–322.

Wright, E. O. (1982) 'The Status of the Political in the Concept of Class Structure', *Politics and Society*, vol. 11, pp. 321–41.

Wright, E. O. (1983) 'Giddens's Critique of Marxism', *New Left Review*, vol. 138, pp. 11–36.

Wright, E. O. and Perrone, L. (1977) 'Marxist Class Categories and Income Inequality', *American Sociological Review*, vol. 42, pp. 32–56.

Yapa, L. S. (1977) 'The Green Revolution: A Diffusion Model', *Annals of the Association of American Geographers*, vol. 67, pp. 350–9.

Yates, F. A. (1964) *Giordano Bruno and the Hermetic Tradition*.

Yates, F. A. (1972) *The Rosicrucian Enlightenment*.

Yates, F. A. (1979) *The Occult Philosophy in the Elizabethan Age*.

Young, R. M. and Teich, M. (eds) (1973) *Changing Perspectives in the Historiography of Science*.

Zeitlin, M. (ed.) (1979) *Political Power and Social Theory* (Greenwich).

Zeleny, J. (1980) *The Logic of Marx* (Oxford).

Zerubavel, E. (1979) *Patterns of Time in Hospital Life* (Chicago).

Zerubavel, E. (1981) *Hidden Rhythms* (Chicago).

Zilsel, E. and de Santillana, G. (1941) *The Development of Rationalism and Empiricism* (Chicago).

Author Index

Subject Index